The A–Z of Social Research

The A–Z of Social Research

A Dictionary of Key Social Science Research Concepts

Edited by Robert L. Miller
and John D. Brewer

SAGE Publications
London • Thousand Oaks • New Delhi

SAGE Publications Ltd
6 Bonhill Street
London EC2A 4PU

SAGE Publications Inc
2455 Teller Road
Thousand Oaks, California 91320

SAGE Publications India Pvt Ltd
B-42, Panchsheel Enclave
Post Box 4109
New Delhi – 100 017

British Library Cataloguing in Publication data

A catalogue record for this book is available
from the British Library

ISBN 0 7619 7132 7
ISBN 0 7619 7133 5 (pbk)

Library of Congress Control Number: applied for

Typeset by Mayhew Typesetting, Rhayader, Powys
Printed and bound in Great Britain by TJ International, Padstow, Cornwall

Contents

Acknowledgements

Even more than the usual edited book, *The A–Z of Social Research* is a joint product. Over 47 individuals contributed directly to the book by authoring or co-authoring at least one entry. Many of the contributors provided the text for more than a single entry, in some cases providing a considerably larger number. The book began as a joint project of the School of Sociology & Social Policy at Queen's University, Belfast and largely remained so through to its end. The majority of my colleagues generously gave of their time and expertise and the backbone of the text was the result. Special acknowledgement must go to Professor John Brewer, who was Head of School throughout the period when the entries were being compiled. John gave vital support from the outset. He saw the *A–Z* as a concrete expression of the collegial atmosphere in the School and was largely responsible for the inclusion of many of our postgraduates among the contributors. He also gave vital encouragement to colleagues that ensured the completion of their entries. In this respect, John very much 'led from the front', contributing more entries than any other contributor.

Outside the School, other colleagues in Queen's University significantly added to the scope of the text. Here, the contributions from the School of Psychology at Queen's deserve special mention. Further afield, Professor Nigel Gilbert of the Department of Sociology at the University of Surrey and editor of *Social Research Update (SRU)* gave permission for a selection of numbers from *Social Research Update* [http://www.soc.surrey.ac.uk/sru/] to be adapted and reproduced as entries in the *A–Z*. These again added significantly to the scope of the text. *The A–Z of Social Research* has benefited immeasurably from the internationally recognised expertise of these authors. I am grateful both for their unanimous agreement with Nigel's decision to cooperate with the production of the *A–Z* and for the extensive rewriting that many of the *SRU* contributors undertook.

Finally, I would like to take this opportunity as co-editor, to thank personally all of the contributors. Collating an edited book where there are so many contributions coming from so many authors is a daunting task. This task was made immeasurably less difficult by the high quality of the submissions received and the serious way that each person strove to conform to the editorial conventions that I had imposed. When reading the entries, I found the editing task often to be a learning experience and much more of a pleasure than I had anticipated. Any plaudits for the quality and incisiveness of the *A–Z* entries belong to their excellent contributors. Responsibility for oversights and inconsistencies must rest solely with me.

Robert L. Miller

Contributors

Ciaran Acton is a Research Fellow in the School of Sociology and Social Policy at Queen's University, Belfast. His research interests are in conversations analysis, speech dysfluencies and research methodology.

Rowland Atkinson and **John Flint** are Researchers at the Department of Urban Studies, University of Glasgow. Both have an interest in the spatial distribution and experience of social exclusion and have been commissioned to devise a methodology for tracing residents who leave regeneration areas in Scotland.

Sandra Baillie is a former postgraduate in the School of Sociology and Social Policy at Queen's University, Belfast and works as a freelance researcher.

Marcus Banks is a Lecturer in social anthropology at the University of Oxford. After a doctorate at the University of Cambridge he trained as a documentary filmmaker on a one-year Royal Anthropological Institute/Leverhulme Fellowship at the National Film and Television School, Beaconsfield. He is the author of *Organizing Jainism in India and England* (Clarendon, 1992), *Ethnicity: Anthropological constructions* (Routledge, 1996), and co-editor of *Rethinking Visual Anthropology* (Yale, 1997).

John Brewer is Professor of Sociology and until recently Head of School in the School of Sociology and Social Policy at Queen's University, Belfast. He specialises in the sociology, criminology and politics of divided societies, ethno-religious conflict, the Scottish Enlightenment, qualitative research methods, interpretative social theory and ethnography and oral history.

Leslie Clarkson is an Emeritus Professor at Queen's University, Belfast.

Colin Cooper is a Senior Lecturer in the School of Psychology, Queen's University, Belfast.

Louise Corti formed part of the team of staff who set up Qualidata, the ESRC Qualitative Data Archival Resource Centre. In 1996 she became Deputy Director and Manager of Qualidata and continues to have key responsibility for qualitative data archives at Essex. In 2001 she joined the UK Data Archive as Director of User Services and Head of Qualitative Data Archives. She has carried out research in the fields of health, education and survey methodology, taught sociology, and recently authored a virtual tutorial for social research methods and has co-edited a specialist issue of the on-line journal, FQS, devoted to qualitative data archives. She sees herself as a methodologist and is interested in both quantitative and qualitative aspects of social research.

Mary Daly is Professor of Sociology in the School of Sociology and Social Policy at Queen's University, Belfast. She specialises in comparative sociology, European welfare states, gender and social policy, sociology of the family, gender and stratification, and poverty and inequality.

Ciara Davey is a Teaching Assistant and a postgraduate student in the School of Sociology and Social Policy at Queen's University, Belfast.

Martin Dempster is a Lecturer in Research Design, Statistics and Health Psychology in the School of Psychology, Queen's University, Belfast.

Paula Devine is a Senior Survey Officer in the Institute of Governance, Queen's University, Belfast and a Research Director of ARK, the Northern Ireland Social and Political Archive.

John Ditch is Assistant Director of the Social Policy Research Unit (SPRU) at the University of York and is responsible for the social security programme.

Lizanne Dowds is a Senior Research Fellow at the University of Ulster and a Deputy Director of ARK, the Northern Ireland Social and Political Archive.

Janet Foster is a self-employed professionally qualified archivist with considerable experience in medical and social policy archives.

Barry Gibson is a Lecturer in Sociology as Applied to Dentistry at Guy's, King's and St Thomas' Dental Institute.

Nigel Gilbert is Professor of Sociology and Pro Vice-Chancellor at the University of Surrey. He became interested in the potential of computer simulation from involvement with several inter-disciplinary projects involving computer scientists and social scientists. He began a series of international workshops on 'Simulating Societies' in 1992 and has published a textbook, *Simulation for the Social Scientist*, with Klaus G. Troitzsch (Open University Press, 1999). He has also edited books on research methods (for example, *Researching Social Life*, second edition, Sage, 2001) and authored works on the sociology of science, science policy, the environment and statistics.

Philip Graham is IPR Manager at Queen's University Belfast and Executive Director of the Association for University Research and Industry Links (AURIL).

Myrtle Hill is Senior Lecturer in Women's Studies and Director of the Centre for Women's Studies at Queen's University, Belfast. She specialises in nineteenth-century women's history (particularly Irish religious history), nineteenth-century social and religious history, women's studies and local studies.

Myra Hird is Lecturer in Sociology in the School of Sociology and Social Policy at Queen's University, Belfast. She specialises in constructions of femininity and masculinity, sexuality, methodology, method, queer theory, feminist theory, theories of family and the sociology of science.

Sandra Hutton is a Research Fellow at the Social Policy Research Unit (SPRU) at the University of York. She has worked on a number of projects about social security using large-scale surveys, secondary data analysis, and qualitative techniques.

John Kremer is a Reader in Psychology at Queen's University, Belfast.

Sean L'Estrange is a Teaching Assistant and a postgraduate student in the School of Sociology and Social Policy, Queen's University, Belfast.

Madeleine Leonard is a Senior Lecturer in Sociology at Queen's University, Belfast. Her research interests are in work, employment and unemployment, informal economic activity and mature students in higher education.

Caroline McAuley is a Research Associate on the Poverty and Social Exclusion in Northern Ireland Survey in the School of Sociology and Social Policy, Queen's University, Belfast.

Carol McGuinness is a Professor of Psychology in the School of Psychology, Queen's University, Belfast.

Eithne McLaughlin is Professor and Head of Social Policy at Queen's University, Belfast.

Norma Menabney is Social Science Librarian at Queen's University, Belfast.

Robert L. Miller is Senior Lecturer in Sociology in the School of Sociology and Social Policy at Queen's University, Belfast and Deputy Director of ARK, the Northern Ireland Social and Political Archive. His research interests are in social stratification and mobility, gender and political activity, life histories and academic freedom.

Gary Nicolaas is Deputy Director of the survey methods centre at the United Kingdom National Centre for Social Research.

Liam O'Dowd is Professor of Sociology at Queen's University, Belfast. His research interests lie in border regions in a comparative perspective, intellectuals and social ideology in twentieth-century Ireland, economic restructuring and localities.

Richard O'Leary is a Lecturer in Sociology at Queen's University, Belfast. He specialises in the sociology of religion, religious, ethnic and linguistic minorities, the comparative study of minority-majority relations and intermarriage.

Roger O'Sullivan is a Teaching Assistant and former postgraduate student in the School of Sociology and Social Policy, Queen's University, Belfast.

Ian Plewis is a Senior Lecturer in Statistics and Social Research Officer at the Institute of Education, University of London and a member of the Centre for Multilevel Modelling. His research interests lie in the design and analysis of longitudinal studies, multilevel modelling of categorical data, evaluation studies and in the determinants of young children's educational progress.

Sam Porter is a Professor of Nursing at Queen's University, Belfast.

Susan Purdon is a Senior Researcher at the Survey Methods Centre at Social and Community Planning Research.

Valinda Ross is a postgraduate student in the School of Psychology, Queen's University, Belfast.

Roy Sainsbury is a Research Fellow at the Social Policy Research Unit (SPRU) at the University of York. He has worked on a number of projects about social security using large-scale surveys, secondary data analysis, and qualitative techniques.

Sally Shortall is a Reader in Sociology at Queen's University, Belfast. Her research interests are in rural sociology, rural development, farm women, women in rural areas and educational inequalities.

James P. Smyth is a Lecturer in Sociology at Queen's University, Belfast. His research interests are the social structure of modern Ireland, nineteenth-century social thought, ideology and social change and the sociology of culture.

Brian J. Taylor is a Research Fellow in the School of Medicine, Queen's University, Belfast.

Roger Thomas is Director of the Survey Methods Centre at Social and Community Planning Research.

Linda Thompson is a former postgraduate student in the School of Sociology and Social Policy at Queen's University, Belfast.

Paul Thompson is Research Professor in the Department of Sociology and founding Director of Qualidata at the University of Essex. He is a founding member of the Department of Sociology at Essex and is the Director of the National Life Story Collection at the British Library National Sound Archive.

Colin Todhunter is a freelance social researcher based in Liverpool, specialising in health, drug misuse and community development.

Nicola Yeates is a Lecturer in Social Policy at Queen's University, Belfast. Her research interests are poverty and social exclusion, gender and welfare, comparative social policy and curriculum development in social policy.

Marysia Zalewski is a Reader in Women's Studies at Queen's University, Belfast. She specialises in feminist theory, women and politics, gender and international relations and science and reproductive technologies.

Introduction

The A–Z of Social Research is a 'research methods' textbook with a difference. Rather than a normal text, this book can be thought of as an encyclopaedia of social research. The *A–Z* is a collection of entries covering the whole expanse of social science research methods and issues, from qualitative research techniques to statistical testing and from the practicalities of using the Internet to the philosophy of social research. Their style and content varies widely but what they all have in common is that the intention of each entry is to provide the student with a quick reference source that summarises and explains the essential points of its topic in a concise and accessible manner. The entries are in alphabetical order and are of various lengths, from just under 800 words for the most brief to a few of about 3,000 words, with the typical entry being approximately 1,500 words in length. This encyclopaedic format is unique among research methods textbooks and has been adopted deliberately in order to meet the needs of social science students at the beginning of the twenty-first century.

In the past, higher education was an ivory tower option available in the main to those from elite origins. Within universities, the study of the social sciences was largely a preoccupation with arcane conceptual debates. Empirical research and the procedures and issues around the collection of 'real data' was most decidedly a poor cousin for the majority of the social sciences. All this has now changed. There has been an exponential expansion of institutions of higher education, both in terms of their sheer numbers and the number and range of students enrolled in them and in terms of the variety of types of higher education on offer. One of the central goals of these expansions has been to increase access to further and higher education for the general population. This goal has been realised, albeit perhaps imperfectly, and a clear result is that the typical student of today is likely to be at least partially self-funding or working part-time, under pressure, and very interested in maximising their investment in education as quickly and efficiently as possible.

Much of the expansion in the higher education sector has taken place in the social sciences. Accompanying its growth in numbers, there has been a shift in emphasis in the social sciences in the direction of a raised profile for empirical research, both towards a product that practitioners and students of the social sciences want to use and also (crucially) towards imparting the skills and techniques needed to carry out, analyse and report social research. Students, particularly those who are practitioners who have returned to education, seek out training in research skills that they can subsequently employ in their work (or use to obtain employment). Modern society demands more and more reliable social information for its functioning. Sponsors of higher education, particularly government funders, perceive a general shortfall in the professional skills required to carry out social research and take active steps to encourage or force students to undergo practical training in research.

A result is that the nature of typical social science students today and the type of research training they seek and are being offered has changed. Research training today, rather than a contemplative 'grand tour' course that stretches across an academic year or the whole of a degree programme, instead is delivered in short distinct modules centred around specific topics that last for the duration of a few weeks, a month or, at most, a semester. Students themselves are under pressure, both financial pressure, as debts incurred through student loans or bank advances mount up, and in terms of pressure of time, as they try to juggle the demands of course attendance and assignment preparation with those of part-time employment. The result of these changes is that the style of instruction and the way that students approach their academic work has changed.

Research methods textbooks have lagged behind these changes. Most still are thick single-authored tomes designed to service the year-long course that adopt a 'jack of all trades' approach and attempt to cover the whole gambit of research issues and techniques, from conceptual perspectives on research through qualitative techniques to statistical analysis procedures. The main alternative is an edited book of readings with each chapter written by a specialist author. These provide in-depth coverage of the chosen subjects, but at the cost of missing out everything else. Neither style really fits with the short topic modules that make up most current research methods courses.

Using *The A–Z of Social Research*

In contrast to more traditional textbook formats, *The A–Z of Social Research* will fit into the structure of present-day research methods training. The wide topic spread of the entries means that the main issues of virtually any research methods module are covered. The *A–Z* is intended as a resource that provides support on a topic immediately after it has been introduced by a course instructor. After having received their basic orientation from an introductory reading or a lecture that surveys the area, students use the *A–Z* to access succinct information written by experts on key concepts and core topics. There are many viewpoints on research in the social sciences and competing perspectives often are diametrically opposed to each other. As well as giving the arguments in favour of 'their' research technique, each contributor has endeavoured to present a balanced account of their topic that, where relevant, alerts the reader to controversies and the 'con' as well as the 'pro' arguments.

The entries are arranged in alphabetical order by title. Where a topic could be labelled by more than one title, the student is directed to the heading used by the textbook (for instance, students who look for an entry on the 'World Wide Web' will be referred to the topic **Internet**). Similarly, a topic that is covered in the textbook under the entry for a larger more general topic will be cross-referenced in a similar manner (so, students won't find an entry for the topic 'Theoretical sampling' but will be directed to the more general entry **Grounded theory**).

By their nature, the separate entries in the *A–Z* each are designed to provide essential information on a tightly circumscribed topic. However, sometimes broader or more comprehensive information is needed. The text can answer these needs as well. Where appropriate, students are directed to other entries on closely related or complementary topics (for example, the entries on **Induction** and **Deduction** each refer to the other). To cater for those who need to delve deeper, many entries make up to three informed suggestions for further, more in-depth, reading.[1]

The contributors hope that *The A–Z of Social Research* succeeds in fulfilling its intent as a resource that can convey essential information about research issues, practices and procedures across the whole gamut of the social sciences.

Note

[1] While *The A–Z of Social Research* is designed to be used as a text on research methods training courses, it also can be seen as a general reference source.

A

Abduction and retroduction

'Any social scientist who cannot think of at least three equally valid separate theoretical explanations for any single empirical fact should consider changing career.' – Paraphrase of a remark attributed to Friedrich Tönnies.

The role of empirical testing or research in the development or refinement of conceptual ideas or theories is usually discussed in terms of deduction and induction. In deduction, a pre-existing body of abstract concepts or general ideas, a theory, is used to make predictions about (to deduce) what will be observed in the real world. The researcher moves from the general to the particular. In induction, empirical observations, the findings of research, are generalised to more abstract concepts. To the extent that these abstract concepts can be linked into a coherent whole, a theory can be said to result. This process is often depicted in research methods textbooks as a 'wheel' with the starting point of the research process either being:

(1) *Theory*. Research is a process of generating/deducing research propositions (hypotheses) from abstract theory and concepts which are then tested by empirical observations (research). If the proposition/hypothesis is confirmed

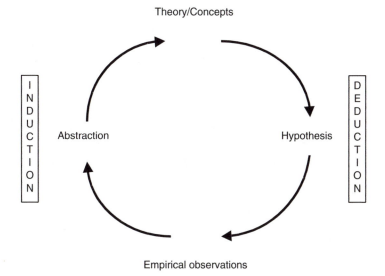

Figure 1   *Traditional depiction of the processes of logical inference in research*

by research, the researcher induces that his/her theory has been confirmed. If the findings do not confirm the hypothesis, the researcher induces that his/her theory may be in error or need of modification.

(2) *Observations*. Research is a process of concept generation by abstracting from observations. The concepts are then refined and linked into a coherent body, a 'theory'.

Abduction

In effect, both induction and deduction refer to ways of generating research hypotheses, either from observations or theory respectively. *Abduction*, proposed by the American philosopher Charles Sanders Pierce, is a related process that also refers to the generation of hypotheses. Abduction refers to the moment of creative inspiration during which the researcher conceives of a hypothetical explanation for some empirical fact.

A researcher can hypothetically explain any single set of empirical observations by a number of alternate explanations. As more evidence becomes available, some of these potential explanations will be ruled out, simplifying the range of choices for a single correct explanation – the remaining explanations will have gained credibility due to their survival. At the same time, however, the additional information also may generate *new* hypothetical explanations – complicating the search for a single correct explanation that fits all the available information. If the abductive process is working correctly, however, eventually each additional bit of information eliminates more hypothetical explanations than it generates so that, in the end, only a single hypothesis remains that fits all available information.

Figure 2 attempts a simplified diagram of this process. At 'Fact 1', the researcher generates five potential explanations, H1 to H5. 'Fact 2' allows the researcher to eliminate two of the explanations (H2 and H4) but also causes the generation of additional versions of H1 and H5. 'Fact 3' rules out hypotheses H1a and H5b, but generates three new versions of H3 plus two new versions of H1b (H1b^1 and H1b^2). 'Fact 4' eliminates some hypotheses (H1b^1, H3a, H3c^2 and H5b) while also generating more complex versions of others (H1b^{2a}, H1b^{2b}, H3c^{2a} and H3c^{2b}). Finally, 'Fact 5' rules out all surviving explanations except one, H1b^{2b}.

Retroduction

Retroduction can be seen as a 'real world' combination of the various 'ductions'. In reality, the logical processes of the generation and elimination of hypothetical explanations never goes as smoothly as the diagrams and research texts depict. The positivist cycle of a hypothesis being deduced solely from pre-existing theory, being tested against empirical observation and then, depending on whether it has been accepted or rejected by the data, used to confirm or disconfirm theory, is a sanitised version of events. Similarly, the model of pure grounded theorists inducing their conceptual abstractions solely from observations without any prior expectations is also an idealised after-the-fact account.[1]

Processes of logical inference in real research are in fact quite messy. Ideas for research will come partially from the researcher's conceptual knowledge, partially

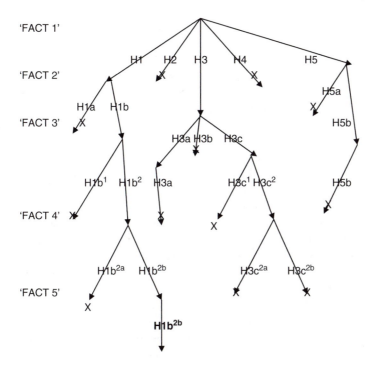

Figure 2   *The process of abduction*

from their personal experiences and perhaps partially from intuition. There will be false starts and backtracking. Proposed hypothetical explanations will be modified in the light of preliminary results or discussion, perhaps leading to the collection of further data. The writing-up of the research for presentation or publication, rather than a true depiction of the process of logical inference that took place during the research, can be seen more accurately as a specialised account: the employing of a set of literary conventions in order to communicate the research findings in a recognised manner to an expert audience. Research is not pure with distinct stages of deduction, induction or abduction, but a combination of all three, often going on simultaneously. Retroduction is a term applied to this process that recognises its 'retro' or constant backtracking, nature.

Abduction applied

In qualitative research in recent years, the process of abduction has been applied consciously to the intense analysis of small segments of interview text; a so-called 'micro-analysis'. The researchers select a short passage of text from a longer interview. The criteria for selection being that the passage relates to a crucial point of the interview in which the subject matter is likely to be a complex multi-layered combination of meanings which the respondent may have had difficulty expressing consciously (for example, the point in an interview where the respondent first begins to relate their experience of sexual abuse as a child). The analysis ideally is carried out by a team of individuals from different backgrounds.

The team is given an initial segment of text; typically a single sentence or perhaps even only part of a sentence. The team 'brainstorms' over the possible meanings of this single text segment – in effect 'abducting' a set of proto-hypotheses.[2] Once the team appears to have reached their limit for possible explanations of the first text segment, abduction continues with the next text segment being revealed. Many of the potential proto-hypotheses will be dismissed as a result of this second text segment. At the same time, however, the second segment also will cause some first stage explanations to be refined (as well as generating entirely new explanations). This painstaking process will continue with each new segment from the block of selected text being revealed in turn. Ideally, the eventual result of the analysis should be that the revealing of additional text segments do not lead to the generation of new hypotheses and that all of the competing hypothetical explanations except one have been eliminated.[3]

The logistics of the approach, having to assemble a diverse team of professional and semi-professionals with the necessary commitment and time, are such that pure examples of 'micro-text analysis' are rare. (For an example of a pure application of the method, see Jones, 2003.) Properly employed, this method of text analysis is remarkably effective at validly reaching a deep structure of meaning that respondents may be capable of alluding to consciously in only a vague manner.

In fact, the method can be so effective that its use raises ethical issues. An effectively working 'micro-analysis' team is capable of delving so deep into the meanings in an interview that the analysis almost can be seen as an after-the-fact interrogation.[4] Whether an interviewee would knowingly consent to such an intense examination of their inner psyche is a moot point.

Notes

1 No trained social science researcher can turn off their training in order to become a complete cultural and sociological 'dope'.
2 The advantages of having a team drawn from diverse backgrounds rather than a single analyst is that the team will generate a much wider range of potential explanations for a text passage.
3 Text blocks are rarely more than ten sentences in length. Even so, the analysis of a single block can take hours and often the team will not reach the end of the block in a single session.

    Also, arriving at a single explanation is the ideal goal. It is entirely possible that several competing hypotheses may survive.
4 There are reports of police and internal security forces using abductive techniques in order to extract information from interviews with suspects and other textual material.

Reference

See also entries on: **Deduction** and **Induction**.

Jones, Kip (2003) 'The Turn to a Narrative Knowing of Persons: One Method Explored', *NT Research*. 8 (1): 60–71.

ROBERT MILLER

Action research: a case study

Introduction

In a period of officially endorsed consumerism within social policy which stresses the role of community participation, user-led provision and user involvement, the potential for the collective expression of discontented voices has (unwittingly) been thrown open (Pilgrim et al., 1997). Within this context, action research can be a powerful vehicle for such voices, and research commissioners must be fully aware of its potential. That potential involves action research becoming a tool for wider citizen complaints resulting in 'action' with which agencies may find themselves uncomfortable. Just because organisations now stress the importance of the view 'from below' does not mean that their interests or purposes are the same as those who participate in the research.

The role of action research

Action research may be regarded as part of interactive social science research – a pragmatic, utilitarian, or user-oriented approach to research (Bee Tin, 1989) and incorporates a value-base that is committed to promoting change through research. It has been used as a tool for bringing about change, emancipation and social justice based on the desires and direct involvement of ordinary people (Fisher, 1994). The process of action research involves people reflecting on issues and processes during the research, participants as co-researchers, and entails an element of risk given that the process and outcomes are in a state of on-going change (Winter, 1989). It is transformed by emergent findings which, in turn, impact upon the process itself and subsequent outcomes (Bell et al., 1990). As the process becomes redirected, outcomes may not be readily predicted and, for this reason alone, power holders may not be fully at ease with what they are not in control of – in terms of the 'knowledge' it produces, the thinking it stimulates, or the action it promotes (Fals-Borda and Rahman, 1991).

An important element of action research is participation by 'informants' in the process. The researcher may eventually disappear from sight as other participants mobilise to enact social change. Participatory action research can be defined as 'collective, self-reflective enquiry undertaken by participants in social situations in order [to] improve the rationality and justice of their own social . . . practices' (Kemmis and McTaggart, 1988: 5). Key features are empowerment through participation (Tandon, 1981), interaction between residents and researcher, and an emphasis on processes and outcomes, making it a means to an end rather than an end in itself (Rappert, 1997).

Commissioning agencies tend to use research to further their stated goals and explicit agendas. When commissioning research, an organisation may perceive that subsequent outcomes will take place within specified parameters that will help to further its overall aims, including the need to develop or maintain working relations with other bodies. What they may not realise, however, is that action research has the potential to instigate certain forms of action which undermine the 'collaborative' framework that they seek. Unlike more professionally directed models of research, action research can be difficult to 'manage' once underway.

Action research in practice: a case study in drugs prevention

In the area of drugs prevention, action research has been used in tandem with an approach that stresses the role of community development and community involvement. As a philosophy, 'community drugs prevention' entails residents gaining access to a range of social, political and economic resources (Henderson, 1995). In this respect, drugs prevention may be more concerned with wider quality of life issues that residents define as important and will serve to reduce the demand for drug use. Action research has been used to mobilise communities in order to achieve these objectives (Henderson, 1996).

The research used as a case study for the purpose of this entry took place in a locality exhibiting the usual indices of long-term social and economic decline, including widespread drugs-related difficulties. Initially, the commissioning agency (administered by the United Kingdom Home Office) was committed to devising a community-led drugs prevention strategy. Its original intention was that through operationalising its concept of 'action research', community concerns about drug misuse would be elicited alongside residents' perceptions of what 'drugs prevention' should involve, and residents would be encouraged to get involved in setting up projects and lobbying policy makers for relevant change. Residents' views and their subsequent commitment to the project would in essence shape the nature of the research process. In effect, it was envisaged that it would be 'resident-led'.

Initially, in-depth individual and group interviews were central to the research process. Later, a series of small-scale public meetings occurred, and community newsletters were produced. At the meetings the earlier findings were fed back to residents who, in turn, commented on them and suggested future directions that the project should take. The newsletters served a similar purpose of dissemination and feedback. Initially, the project had been researcher-led but more direct community involvement occurred as time progressed through the formation of a regular and on-going forum that provided a degree of momentum which was more independent from 'professionals'.

An implicit assumption underpinning the research was that all (potential) partners – the commissioning agency, the residents and other local organisations – possessed common interests and a universal goal and that through this general consensus the research could progress. As the research developed, however, it was apparent that although they had a universal goal, to reduce drug misuse, a commonality of interest was lacking. The research was highly successful in eliciting residents' views about drugs and drugs prevention and in stimulating awareness. The research, however, also highlighted deep-seated tensions between sections of the community and the local urban regeneration agency, which was having a major impact in the area at the time of the study. (Furthermore, the agency was potentially a key player as a fund provider for initiatives and projects that might emerge as a result of the research.) Residents perceived that drug misuse was symptomatic of social and economic decline. Drugs prevention was synonymous with community development and economic regeneration as, according to certain residents, a range of drugs-specific programmes (for example, education, awareness campaigns) had been tried and had failed over a period of 20 years. At the same time, however, residents were highly critical of the approaches adopted by the regeneration organisation towards community participation, development and economic regeneration. The research became a vehicle for challenging the hegemony of the market- and business-led approach to regeneration that existed in the locality.

The research had stimulated community awareness around 'drugs prevention' issues, had succeeded in producing an action plan for prevention, and a drugs prevention forum had emerged comprising local residents and representatives from some key agencies. At this stage, however, the regeneration agency (which had not been involved in the research process) became critical of the agency that had commissioned the research, the researcher, and the 'biased' outlooks of residents. According to its view, the research was merely serving to stir up and magnify unjustified hostility toward its role in the area. The consequence was that other key agencies in the area were reluctant to support the activities of the drugs prevention forum out of fear of producing tensions between themselves and the powerful regeneration agency. Consequently, as the forum lacked backing from key voluntary and statutory sector agencies, the regeneration agency felt justified in not providing funding for projects outlined in the action plan. Funding for the action research and for the researcher expired after a six month period and residents were either unable or unwilling to continue with their activities through the forum.

Lessons to be learnt

In some ways the action research ignited a powder keg that had been waiting to go off. Simmering tensions between sections of the community and the regeneration agency had frequently boiled over during a long period of time prior to the research. The locality traditionally had a strong and vocal community sector, and was predominantly staunchly left-wing in political outlook. They possessed little faith in the overall aims and objectives of the regeneration agency dating from shortly after its inception – perceiving it to be an imposition from central government whose outlook was regarded as having changed little from those of previous Conservative administrations. The action research had become part of the local politicised culture.

At the outset, the commissioning body expressed a commitment toward 'community involvement' in drugs prevention, but it is doubtful whether or not it had appreciated fully the potential implications of the action research. Based on a model used elsewhere, the agency had perceived that the research would primarily involve a consultation exercise culminating in an integrated approach to prevention with greater levels of community representation in existing and potential new projects.

Residents expressed a strong commitment to action research, given the emancipatory and participatory background of the paradigm, and viewed it as a welcome change from previous professionally controlled research that they regarded as having been an end in itself: a mechanism for integrating residents and community groups into government and prevailing structures thereby giving programmes a degree of credibility and legitimacy, but not bringing about the changes for communities and residents that they desired (Todhunter, 2001). However, although action research may appear to offer a potential for change, just how much change may be expected given the wider interests of agencies and organisations that may be juxtaposed to proposed change?

Agencies may (unconsciously) seek to define residents' needs according to their specific remit, and attempt to set a research agenda accordingly – even though they may label it as 'action' research. In the case outlined here, the commissioning body appeared to put into operation their own limited notion of 'action research'. However, through the research residents emphasised a desire for exerting more direct power alongside their identity and rights as citizens. In effect, they challenged the prevailing power structures by questioning the legitimacy of key agencies, including that of the research commissioner. Subsequently, the latter was not able to respond fully to the needs or views of residents once unpacked.

In the shorter term, action research may produce a 'feel good' factor among participants – consciousness raising, 'participation' and mobilisation may instil a self-belief in ordinary people's capacity to bring about change. In the longer term, real and radical change may indeed come about. In order to do this, however, commitment to change must be forthcoming among all local agencies and interest groups. Otherwise, action research may leave a bitter taste in the mouths of lay people, whose expectations are raised, and subsequent programmes for change may have to cope with the damage done by previous projects that failed to deliver. Any good faith which may have been present among the public may have drained away leaving an embittered community that is hostile or cynical toward future programmes.

Commissioning bodies need to be fully aware of the potential pitfalls of undertaking action research. They must understand what 'action research' implies, and that it does not sit easily with conventional and easily manageable 'consultation' exercises – thus making it a high risk strategy. By committing to a process of action research, agencies are legitimising residents' voices and actions and their participation in social policy. In some respects they will be embarking upon a programme that bucks a wider cultural and social trend encouraging 'involvement' which seeks to guarantee consensus and integration rather than change (Bauman, 1987).

Agencies must appreciate what imposing a standardised model of action research on a specific place and context entails. They need to decide how feasible action research and change may be, given wider trends and local political situations, and also must prepare the groundwork effectively prior to committing to the research, bringing on board key players and institutions who may find themselves bearing the brunt of residents' frustrations. Subsequently, all players, instead of reacting negatively to particular research outcomes, may feel more inclined to respond positively to, for instance, challenges to their legitimacy.

Failure to do this may lead to the research grinding to a halt, a souring of inter-agency relations, and increased disillusionment in the community – as was the case in the study outlined here.

References

Bauman, Z. (1987) 'The Left as the Counter Culture of Modernity', *Telos*, (Winter): 83–93.

Bee Tin, Tan (1999) 'Interactive Social Science Research, User Groups and Thesis Students', *TESOL Matters*, Oct/Nov.

Bell, B., Gaventa, J. and Peters, J. (1990) *We Make the Road by Walking: Conversations on Education and Social Change*. Philadelphia: Temple University Press.

Fals-Borda, O. and Rahman, M. (1991) *Action and Knowledge: Breaking the Monopoly with Participatory Action-Research*. New York: Apex Press.

Fisher, R. (1994) *Let the People Decide: Neighborhood Organizing in America*. New York: Twayne Publishers.

Henderson, P. (1995) *Drugs Prevention and Community Development – Principles of Good Practice*. London: Home Office Central Drugs Prevention Unit.

Henderson, P. (1996) *Merseyside Drugs Prevention Team Action Research Development Project: An Evaluation*. London: Home Office Drugs Prevention Initiative.

Kemmis, S. and R. McTaggart (1988) *The Action Research Planner*. Geelong: Deakin University.

Pilgrim, P., Todhunter, C. and Pearson, M. (1997) 'Accounting for Disability: Customer Feedback or Citizen Complaints?', *Disability and Society*, 12 (1): 3–15.

Rappert, B. (1997) 'Irreconcilable Differences? The Business of Social Science Research and Users', *Higher Education Quarterly*, 51: 239–50.

Tandon, R. (1981) 'Participatory Research in the Empowerment of People', *Convergence*, 24 (3): 20–9.

Todhunter, C. (2001) 'Subversion, Domination and Good Faith: Drugs Prevention and Urban Regeneration Partnerships', *Qualitative European Drugs Research Network Journal*, www.qed.org.uk

Winter, R. (1989) *Action Research and the Nature of Social Inquiry: Professional Innovation and Educational Work*. Aldershot: Gower.

See also
Participatory Action Research and **Policy Research**.

COLIN TODHUNTER

Analysis of variance (ANOVA)

Several tests have been developed to test for the statistical significance between two or more groups of the mean values of some characteristic. Analysis of variance (ANOVA) is by far the most powerful, because it is not limited to comparing the means of only two groups. For example, a researcher might wish to compare the ages of death of randomly drawn samples of people in 10 different countries in order to determine whether there are real differences in lifespan between the countries (that is, that the differences between mean ages of death in the various countries are so substantial that it is improbable that such large differences would have been observed if people lived to the same age in all of the countries surveyed). It would be highly misleading to test the average longevity of each country against the average longevity of every other country because this would require a total of 45 statistical tests. Furthermore, if the tests were performed at the 0.05 level of significance there is literally a one-in-twenty chance of making an incorrect inference from each test. Thus, if 45 different tests are performed, one would expect to make about 45 × 0.05 or 2 incorrect inferences, erroneously concluding that the mean ages of death in two countries are different when in reality they are not.

In analysis of variance, the variable being measured (age at death in this example) is known as the *dependent* variable because its values are assumed to be affected by (or to depend upon) another variable. It is assumed to follow a bell-shaped ('normal') distribution: that is, most values are close to the mean. The variable which is hypothesised to influence the dependent variable (in this example, country of residence) is known as the *independent* variable because it is assumed to affect (or cause). As the survey compares the longevity of samples from ten countries, this independent variable is said to have ten levels.

A major benefit of analysis of variance is that it is possible to test for the influence of more than one variable: that is, to carry out analyses where there is more than one independent variable. If there are two independent variables, the ANOVA is described as a 'two-way' design, three independent variables, a 'three-way' design and so on. For example, to convert the above example into a two-way design, the researcher may choose to test whether country of residence *and gender* influence longevity: the independent variables will be country of residence (10 levels) and gender (2 levels).

Furthermore, a great advantage of 'n-way' analysis of variance is that as well as the main effects (nationality, gender, etc.) an 'n-way' ANOVA can reveal complex patterns of interaction between two, three or more independent variables which are often of far more interest than are the main effects. For instance, in our example here, ANOVA can show us whether the gender difference in longevity is the same for each country. It might be the case that females outlive males by a substantial margin in seven of the countries, but that the difference is much smaller or even the reverse in the other three countries. These instances, where the effect of one independent variable varies when considered in combination with the effect of another independent variable is known as an *interaction*.

The result of calculating an analysis of variance is conventionally shown in a single table:

Example of output from a two-way ANOVA

Source	df	SS	MS	F	p
Country	9	90	10	1.0	0.49
Gender	1	40	40	4.0	0.04
Country x Gender	9	630	70	7	0.005
Error	1000	10000	10		

The first two rows of the table show the two independent variables, country and gender. The next row (Country x Gender) is known as the 'country by gender interaction'. It shows whether the sex-difference in longevity is the same in all countries. The final row of the table, is known as the 'error term', and is used in computing the F-statistic. The column headed df ('degrees of freedom') shows the number of levels of each independent variable minus one. (The degrees of freedom for the 'sex by country interaction' is the number of degrees of freedom for the gender effect (1) multiplied by the degrees of freedom for Country (9).) The degrees of freedom for the error term is related to the total number of people who took part in the study.

The column headed F shows the statistic (F) which is used to determine whether an independent variable is significant – that is, whether one should conclude that the differences between the various levels of the independent variable are so substantial that they are unlikely to have arisen if there is really no difference between the levels in the population. The value in the final column (p) gives the probability of obtaining such a large value of F from the sample if, in the population, there is really no difference between the groups. From this one can decide whether or not to reject the null hypothesis, which in analysis of variance is always that 'there is no difference between the means of the various groups'. In this example one would not conclude that there are real differences in longevity between countries, since there is a 49% chance of getting a value of F as large as 1.0 even if, in reality, there are no differences in longevity. On the other hand, the chances that gender does have a significant effect are quite high ($p < 0.04$ means that the odds are only 4 in 100 that a one would obtain a value of F which is 4.0 or more if there is in reality no difference between the longevity of males and females in the population). In addition, there is a very significant interaction between gender and country ($p < 0.005$, odds of less than 5 in 1,000). To tease out the form of combined effect of country and gender that this significant interaction implies, it would be necessary to perform further analyses (the analysis of simple effects).

Analysis of variance becomes unwieldy when there are more than three or four independent variables; in this case large samples are required to ensure that there are a reasonable number of people in every condition. For example, suppose that month of birth (12 levels) was included in the above design. It would be necessary to check that each country included a reasonable-sized sample (say at least 20) of men born in January, women born in January etc., requiring a minimum overall sample size of at least $12 \times 10 \times 2 \times 20 = 4800$ people.

It is possible to carry out analysis of variance where individuals provide more than one score: for example, where patients complete a mood questionnaire just after diagnosis of cancer, then after six months and again twelve months later. It is necessary to distinguish between the types of independent variable which divide the sample into groups (for example, country of residence) and those which indicate repeated measures over time. The former are known as 'between subject factors', and the latter as 'within subject factors'. Here the independent variable for the three times (at diagnosis, six months later, twelve months later) ('occasion') is referred to as a 'within subjects factor with three levels', as each participant provides a score on three occasions.

Analysis of variance has long been used in experiments where it is reasonably easy to develop designs which produce data at every combination of levels of all the independent variables. Applying the technique to social surveys based on random sampling can be more problematic, as it can happen that cells for rare combinations of variables (for example, divorced men under the age of 25) are seriously underrepresented in the sample.

A related (but statistically rather more complex) technique known as multi-variate analysis of variance studies how several independent variables influence not one but several dependent variables. For example, one could assemble half a dozen indices of health (of which longevity would be one) and use multivariate ANOVA to determine whether country of residence and gender influence all of these variables taken together. It is also possible to perform analysis of covariance, where the effect of some variable on the dependent variable is controlled. For example, it might be hypothesised that a person's socio-economic status may affect their longevity: incorporating socio-economic status as a covariate shows whether it does indeed have an effect, and also what effect gender and country of residence would have if all members of the sample were brought to the same level of socio-economic status.

Suggested further reading

Howell, D.C. (1996) *Statistical Methods for Psychology*, 3rd edn. New York: Wadsworth.

Roberts, M.J. and Russo, R. (1999) *A Student's Guide to Analysis of Variance.* London: Routledge.

COLIN COOPER

Attitudes

An attitude is a tendency to respond in a consistently favourable or unfavourable manner towards a specific topic, concept or object. It does not necessarily predict a specific behaviour, but does indicate a certain amount of affect towards the object in question. Louis Thurstone was the social psychologist who first established an attitude-measurement methodology. He defined attitude as 'the sum total of a man's [sic] inclinations and feelings, prejudice and bias, preconceived notions, ideas, fears, threats, and convictions about any specified topic' (Thurstone, 1928). Attitude measurement involves locating someone's position on an affective continuum ranging from very positive to very negative towards an attitudinal object.

Attitudes and behaviour

The extent to which attitudes genuinely exist and can predict behaviour is contested by theorists. Nonetheless the use of attitude surveys for decision-making by businesses, market research companies and political pollsters continues unabated. By and large it is assumed by those commissioning such surveys that attitudes will influence behaviour; for example, indicating how people will vote in elections, whether a new product will be a market success, whether new working practices are likely to be resisted by employees and so forth. In social research, the effect of attitudes towards another ethnic or religious group may not be so extreme as to predict violence by one group against members of another but it may predict the degree of contact and the type of social interaction between the two.

The relationship between attitudes, beliefs and values

Values are more abstract, higher order constructs than attitudes and represent an enduring belief that one way of behaving (or being) is personally or socially preferable to the reverse mode of conduct. Values are more permanent and resistant to change and may have a direct or indirect influence on attitudes and behaviours. Thus values are determinants of attitudes, but a single attitude can be 'caused' by many values.

Our beliefs about things affect the attitudes we hold towards them. Our beliefs in turn are influenced by our attitudes. Attitude measurement often involves asking respondents not just what they feel about a particular object, but what they believe about it. We might have largely positive attitudes towards a particular political leader, influenced both by a belief in the many good qualities of that person and the liberal values expressed by him/her that correspond to our own liberal values. Similarly, what we feel about a new brand of washing powder may be influenced by whether we believe the advertising claims and whether our values suggest to us that the damage it will potentially do to the environment precludes our buying it.

A positive attitude towards an object may result from beliefs that the person or thing is positively associated with the fulfilment of important values. A negative attitude may result from beliefs that the attitudinal object is inconsistent with highly revered values or linked with negatively valued objects and concepts.

Measuring attitudes

Likert scales

One of the most commonly used methodologies for measuring attitudes (certainly in survey research) is that of Likert scaling. This involves the summing of respondents' answers to a series of positive or negative statements about the attitudinal object. For example, the British Social Attitudes Survey includes a 'Welfarism' scale consisting of a balanced pool of clearly positive or clearly negative statements about the welfare state. Examples of the statements used to create the scale include:

The creation of the welfare state is one of Britain's proudest achievements.
Many people who get social security don't really deserve any help.

For each item, respondents are asked whether they: *Strongly agree/Agree/Neither agree nor disagree/Disagree/Strongly disagree/Don't know.*

The index for the scale is formed by scoring the most pro-welfare position as '1' and the most anti-welfare position as '5' on each item. The 'neither agree nor disagree' option is scored as '3'.

For Likert scaling (as well as other types of scaling) items where there is almost universal consensus and little discrimination between respondents (e.g., 'All children deserve the best possible education') are to be avoided. An 'Alpha coefficient' can be calculated to measure the reliability of an item battery. In practice, Likert scaling is by far the most commonly used form of attitude measurement.

Guttman scales

Guttman scales are strictly unidimensional and list items in order of favour-ableness. The attitudes they measure tend to be more tightly focused than those measured using Likert or other methods. An often cited example of a Guttman scale measuring attitudes to abortion is the following:

Abortion is acceptable under any circumstances
Abortion is an acceptable mechanism for family planning
Abortion is acceptable in cases of rape
Abortion is acceptable if the foetus is found to be seriously malformed
Abortion is acceptable if the mother's life is in danger.

A respondent who agrees with the first statement is assumed to agree with all subsequent statements. In fact based upon any respondent's score, it should be possible to reproduce his or her responses to all the scale items. This feature is called 'reproducibility' and, when constructing Guttman scales, a coefficient of reproducibility is calculated to determine the extent to which the scale conforms to this requirement.

Thurstone scales

Thurstone scaling also involves generating a pool of statements about the atti-tudinal object. Unlike Likert scaling – neutral statements *must* be included as well as statements ranging from highly favourable to highly unfavourable. A large pool of about 50 items might be generated at the outset. Judges are used to rate the relative favourableness of each item and the judges' ratings are then averaged to determine actual scale values for all the items. Items upon which judges tend not to agree are eliminated. Respondents then are asked to agree or disagree with the statements on the final list and their average scale score calculated to determine an attitude score for each respondent.

Suggested further reading

Schuman, H. and Presser, S. (1996) *Questions and Answers in Attitude Surveys*. California: Sage.

Reference

Thurstone, L.L. (1928) 'Attitudes can be Measured', *American Journal of Sociology*, 33: 529–54.

LIZANNE DOWDS

Autobiography

See **Biographical method**.

B

Biographical method

The biographical method is the collection and analysis of an intensive account of a whole life or portion of a life, usually by an in-depth, unstructured interview. The account may be reinforced by semi-structured interviewing or personal documents. Rather than concentrating upon a 'snapshot' of an individual's present situation, the biographical approach emphasises the placement of the individual within a nexus of social connections, historical events and life experiences (the life history). An important sub-stream of the method focuses upon the manner in which the respondent actively constructs a narrative of their life in response to the social context at the time of interview (the life story).

'The biographical perspective' and the use of life histories as a method of social research has a long pedigree, stretching back to Thomas and Znanicki's highly influential *The Polish Peasant in Europe and America* (1918–20), which devoted a whole volume to the life history of a Polish immigrant, and the collection of life histories by the influential Chicago School of the 1920s. The rise of quantitative social science in the United States caused the method to go into a precipitate decline in the 1940s which was only reversed as part of the general blooming of qualitative methods of research in the 1970s. Plummer (2001) provides an excellent overview of the early stages of life history research and places the method in the context of the broad spectrum of qualitative research techniques, in particular those that use personal documents as a primary source.

Credit for the current revival of the biographical perspective and the use of life histories should go largely to Daniel Bertaux, a French sociologist who set up an international working group on life histories in the late 1970s which quickly developed into the 'Biography and Society' Research Committee 38 of the International Sociological Association (ISA). This ISA Research Committee acts as the main international contact point for sociologists carrying out biographical research. Within Europe the 'Biographical Perspectives on European Societies' Research Network of the European Sociological Association is also important.

Current methodological debate in the area centres upon two differing viewpoints of the central task of biographical research. One perspective sees the analysis of biographies and life histories as a technique for the development of theory through using biographical information as data for the evaluation of concepts. This perspective can be subdivided further between 'realists', who emphasise the development of social concepts through the use of grounded theory techniques and others who emphasise the neo-positivist testing of existing theory.

A second perspective, influenced by post-modernist viewpoints and ethnomethodology, can be termed 'the narrative'. 'Narrativists' emphasise the essentially fluid nature of the interplay that takes place during the social context of an interview when a narrator constructs their life story for a listener. Much of the current development of this perspective is taking place outside anglophone sociology, particularly among German-speaking sociologists – major proponents of this view have included Fritz Schütze, Wolfram Fischer-Rosenthal, Gabriele Rosenthal, and Gerhard Riemann. While this perspective is characterised by intense internal debate among its proponents, the general approach can be seen in an elaborated form in the 'Biographical Narrative Interpretive Method' (BNIM). This style of biographical method elicits an interview through a single question designed to provoke the telling of a life story (the 'Single Question aimed at Inducing Narrative (SQUIN)'), that is backed up by the collection of a 'life history' of the substantive events in an interviewee's lifetime. More direct questioning takes place in a subsequent semi-structured interview that is led by a conceptually-driven questioning strategy based upon information provided in the initial contact. Analysis takes two forms:

(a) 'Thematic Field Analysis (TFA)'. A procedure of *abduction* (the generation of all possible hypotheses and then their gradual elimination by contrary evidence) in order to produce a 'Biographical Data Chronology (BDC)' (a life history of lived events)

(b) 'Text Structure Sequentialisation (TSS)'. The construction of the thematic structure of the life as a story told to the interviewer.

Finally, the two parts, the BDC and the TSS, are cross-referenced together (that is, combining the event-based 'factual' account and the narrative in order to produce a 'case history' that is the unification of an objective 'life history' and a subjective 'life story'). Wengraf (2001) provides a definitive English-language introduction to the 'German school' of intense narrative interviewing.

A 'biographical turn' in social science research has been a feature across many disciplines in recent decades as a recognition of the utility of the perspective for investigating the placement of the individual within a nexus of social networks and an evolving historical context has become more widespread. Interesting recent developments have been the application of qualitative life history data to the study of social policy issues (for examples, see Bourdieu et al., 1999) and, relatedly, a recognition of the relevance of the method for professional case workers in the social services (see the publications from the 'Social Strategies in Risk Society' (SOSTRIS) project, especially Chamberlayne et al., 2001).

Suggested further reading

Miller, Robert L. (2000) *Researching Life Stories and Family Histories*. London: Sage.

This text is an entry-point to the biographical perspective and contrasts the so-called 'Realist' approach to life history research with the 'Narrative' approach to collecting life stories. Linkages are made to closely aligned methods for collecting family histories and the interplay between historical events and time periods, aging and life course, and generations and cohorts are discussed. Practical advice is given on interviewing and analysis within different methodological approaches to biographical research.

Chamberlayne, Prue, Bornat, Joanna and Wengraf, Tom (eds) (2000) *The Turn to Biographical Methods in Social Science: Comparative Issues and Examples*. London: Routledge.

An edited text of readings on 'the turn to biographical methods in social science'. Methodological issues feature prominently in this volume, including discussion of: 'biographical work' (structuring narrative accounts of lives); hermeneutics and subjectivity; comparison across cultures; the interplay between structure and agency; generalising or theorising in biographical analysis. Strong points of this text are the participation of prominent German and English practitioners and the illustration of methodological issues through social policy relevant case studies.

Roberts, Brian (2002) *Biographial Research*. Buckingham: Open University Press.

This book is a thorough review of all aspects of the area and the practicalities of carrying out biographical fieldwork. There is a particular emphasis on oral history.

References

Bourdieu, Pierre et al. (1999) *The Weight of the World: Social Suffering in Contemporary Society*. Oxford: Polity Press.

Plummer, Ken (2001) *Documents of Life 2*. London: Sage.

Wengraf, Tom (2001) *Qualitative Research Interviewing*. London: Sage.

ROBERT MILLER

C

CAPI (Computer Assisted Personal Interviewing)

CAPI, or Computer Assisted Personal Interviewing, is a simple idea. Instead of collecting data on paper questionnaires, interviewers use portable computers to enter data directly via a keyboard. Computer assisted interviewing has been used in the past for, for example, telephone surveys but it is only in the last 15 years or so that it has been used for face-to-face interviews.

Most of the early applications of CAPI in this country were limited to large scale, continuous surveys for government and the commercial sector. In contrast, the number of one-off social surveys using CAPI were small. The reasons for this mostly derive from the relatively high start-up costs such as the purchase of lap-top computers and the training of programmers and fieldwork staff. It is not surprising therefore, that companies able to provide CAPI initially sought large ongoing contracts. However, the number of large continuous surveys is limited and now more companies are seeking contracts for one-off surveys.

In this entry we examine the advantages and disadvantages of CAPI in prin-ciple and compare these with our own experiences at the Social Policy Research Unit at the University of York of using CAPI in a survey of over 1,100 income support recipients. This survey sought to quantify, over a six-month period, changes in claimants' circumstances and the resulting impact on their lives and on their social security benefits. The survey was part of a project commissioned by the United Kingdom Department of Social Security to investigate the effects of changing circumstances on benefit recipients and on the administration of income support.

The main part of this entry looks at aspects of CAPI which anyone considering using it will need to weigh against traditional paper and pencil techniques, including the quality of the data, speed of delivery and cost.

Quality of data

CAPI claims to enhance the quality of survey data in a number of ways:

- routing problems within the questionnaire are eliminated
- interviewers cannot miss questions or ask the wrong questions
- questions are 'customised' correctly
- mathematical calculations can be carried out within the program
- the computer checks for inadmissible or inconsistent responses
- errors from separate data entry are eliminated.

The way CAPI handles routing is one of its most impressive features. Rather than having to decipher routing instructions during an interview, the computer program takes interviewers automatically to the next appropriate question. This is particularly important when the questionnaire includes complex routing (as ours did). Similarly, if a set of questions has to be asked a number of times (for example, for everyone in a household), the computer will automatically repeat the questions (go round the 'loop') the correct number of times and then move on. CAPI's routing capabilities have two main advantages over paper and pencil techniques. First, the possibility of error from interviewers failing to follow routing instructions is eliminated; they cannot follow a wrong route and ask inappropriate questions nor can they inadvertently skip over questions. All the appropriate questions are asked of each respondent and no questions are over-looked. Secondly, the interview flows much more smoothly since the interviewer does not have to keep referring to earlier answers to establish the correct route through the questions.

Interviewing is also made easier by the 'customising' of questions. The computer program can recall a piece of data from its memory, such as a name or a date and insert it in the appropriate place in a question. For example, it is common for a paper questionnaire to include questions such as: 'How often do/does (you/ NAME) use (TYPE OF TRANSPORT)?'. Using CAPI, interviewers would not have to keep a check on which member of the household and which type of transport they are asking about. Instead they would be faced with a series of questions like 'How often does Bill use the train?'. In this way the accuracy of the question and the smoothness of the interview are both improved. The data retrieved can not only be text but also be the result of a calculation based on several earlier pieces of data, for example computing a single figure for disposable income from a number of sources.

Another of the major advantages of CAPI is its ability to spot inadmissible or inconsistent responses that could be the result of either interviewer or respondent error. For example, 'range checks' can be carried out to ensure that an answer falls within an acceptable range. In our questionnaire we asked respondents for the dates of changes happening to them in a six-month period beginning 1 August 1992. If they gave a date before then or an earlier date was keyed in the computer would display an error message allowing the interviewer to identify the source of the error and enter the correct answer. CAPI also allows 'logic checks' that can identify inconsistent or contradictory responses. For example, it is inconsistent for the date of an increase in child benefit payments to precede the date given for the birth of a child. The computer can raise an error message allowing the interviewer to investigate the inconsistency. Range and logic checks are powerful features of CAPI which improve the quality of the data at source.

Because CAPI interviewers enter data directly into a computer, the separate process of data entry, familiar in paper and pencil surveys, is unnecessary. This eliminates one source of error and saves time and money. Responses to open-ended questions can also be typed in directly. There is no need for separate transcription later.

Before leaving the topic of data quality we should put the claims and promises of CAPI in perspective. Paper and pencil surveys can, and do, produce high quality data. The claim of CAPI to produce higher quality data clearly should be tested empirically in a way that allows us to measure the magnitude of any improvement.

Time

The effect of CAPI on the timing of a survey is twofold. First, the process of converting a paper questionnaire into a CAPI computer program is time-consuming. The timetable for a survey using CAPI therefore should allow ample time between the design of a questionnaire and the start of fieldwork. This is particularly important if the fieldwork has to be carried out between specified dates. In our survey we needed the fieldwork to be completed before the annual uprating of benefits at the beginning of April. Allowing eight weeks for fieldwork meant that we had to have a finished CAPI version of the questionnaire at the beginning of February 1993. Our timetable, we thought, allowed sufficient time to achieve this but problems identified during piloting in December 1992 resulted in a rush of last minute changes, one or two of which led to some minor problems with the data later.

As mentioned earlier, CAPI eliminates a separate process of data entry. As a result, the time between the end of fieldwork and the supply of a clean data set is reduced. However, there may still be a need for some data cleaning, albeit on a smaller scale than for a paper and pencil survey. For example, despite the best intentions of the program designers, some of the possible range or logic checks can be overlooked. Hence, some inconsistent or invalid data may result and these will need checking in the normal time-consuming way.

Costs

CAPI, compared with paper surveys, generates both extra costs and savings. If we contrast set-up costs only, CAPI will always be more expensive due to the time needed to convert paper questionnaires to a computer version. This time, and therefore the cost, will be greater for complex questionnaires than for more simple designs. Because each paper questionnaire has an associated data entry cost, the savings generated by CAPI (which has no separate data entry) increase as the size of the survey population increases. The costs of cleaning data are also higher for paper surveys since, in a CAPI interview, respondent and interviewer errors are rectified during the interview itself. Administration costs for paper surveys, which include the printing and distribution of questionnaires, also tend to be higher than for CAPI surveys.

Clearly the costs of any survey will depend, among other things, on the length and complexity of the questionnaire and the size of the target population. Though we cannot state definitively that CAPI is cheaper or more expensive than paper surveys it does seem that, in general, the extra set-up costs required for CAPI are more likely to be offset when the survey population is large and the questionnaire design is complex. This is certainly our experience. When we invited tenders for our survey three companies offered traditional paper and pencil methods and one offered CAPI. To our surprise the CAPI quote was not the most expensive.

Other advantages and disadvantages

During the ongoing process of amendment and refinement when creating a CAPI interview schedule there is a danger of researchers losing control of the questionnaire. To avoid this it is important that they keep in close touch with the CAPI program writers and that regular up-to-date paper versions of the CAPI questionnaire are supplied.

Face-to-face interviews rarely follow the course intended by researchers or interviewers. Respondents change their minds about earlier answers, or suddenly remember something relevant later in the interview. In addition, range or logic checks reveal inconsistencies in previous answers that require changing. Interviewers, therefore, need to be able to move back and forth easily within the questionnaire. At present this is not one of the strengths of CAPI although it is likely that we can expect improvements in the future.

No matter how careful the preparation of a questionnaire there always will be occasions when interviewers struggle to fit a respondent's answer into its structure. In paper and pencil surveys the interviewers can make notes on the questionnaire and the researchers then decide how to deal with them. In contrast, the facilities for CAPI interviewers to make notes are not yet well-developed though again we can expect improvements as CAPI is refined.

An early concern of ours was the possibility that respondents might be put off or intimidated by an interviewer armed with a lap-top computer, although earlier applications of CAPI had suggested that such a fear was groundless. We were reassured to learn from the pilot exercise (in which we participated) that respondents generally have no problems when faced with this new technology. Indeed, for some it was of interest in itself and contributed to the rapport between them and the interviewer. CAPI was also popular with the interviewers. Among other things, they liked the ease with which they could progress through the questionnaire and the air of professionalism that using computers bestowed upon them.

Conclusion

In the past researchers planning large surveys requiring a face-to-face interview could only use paper and pencil techniques. With the introduction of CAPI there is now a choice. We have tried to elaborate some of the factors which researchers might want to consider in making that choice. Our own experience has shown us that there need not be any sacrifice of time or money in using CAPI and that the promises of better quality data are probably justified (a judgement admittedly made in the absence of any comparative evidence). In our view, CAPI has a great deal to offer as an alternative to traditional paper and pencil techniques, particularly where the length or complexity of a questionnaire suggests that there is a possible risk to the quality of data. CAPI is largely used as a straight replacement for paper questionnaires but the computer's existing potential for using graphics and sound (let alone the possibilities created by artificial intelligence) could lead to new forms of questionnaire that could transform the nature and potential of the research interview.

Note

An earlier version of this entry appeared as *Social Research Update* 3 (Department of Sociology, University of Surrey).

Suggested further reading

Bateson, N. and Hunter, P. (1991) 'The Use of Computer Assisted Personal Interviewing for Official British Surveys', OPCS, *Survey Methodology Bulletin*, 28: 26–33.

Costigan, P. and Thomson, K. (1992) 'Issues in the Design of CAPI Questionnaires for Complex Surveys' in Westlake et al. (eds) *Survey and Statistical Computing*. London: North Holland. pp. 147–56.

Manners, T. (1990) 'The Development of Computer Assisted Interviewing for Household Surveys: The Case of the British Labour Force Survey', OPCS, *Survey Methodology Bulletin*, 27: 1–5.

Martin J. and Matheson, J. (1992) 'Further Developments in Computer Assisted Personal Interviewing for Household Income Surveys', OPCS, *Survey Methodology Bulletin*, 31: 33–6.

Saris, W.E. (1991) *Computer-Assisted Interviewing*. Newbury Park: Sage.

ROY SAINSBURY, JOHN DITCH AND SANDRA HUTTON

Cartographic techniques

See **Geographic information systems**.

Case study

The case study, as a social scientific method of research, has a long and controversial history. A case study may be defined as 'an empirical inquiry that investigates a contemporary phenomenon within its real-life context when the boundaries between phenomenon and context are not clearly evident, and in which multiple sources of evidence are used' (Yin, 1989: 23). Let us examine how case studies are employed in social science research, and then consider the various criticisms of this method.

Case studies are used extensively across a range of social sciences such as sociology, political science, psychology, history, economics, planning, administration, public policy, education and management studies. The case study approach arose out of the desire to comprehend social phenomena in both their complexity and 'natural' context (see the entry on **Ethnography** for a critique of the 'real'). In order to emphasise the 'real-life' character of social relations, a holistic approach is sought that will allow for the maximum number of contexts of each case to be taken into account. In this sense, the case study is the opposite of an experiment, in which the researcher attempts to control the context of the interaction completely. Indeed, the case study method evolved through the recognition that the contexts and variables of some phenomena we wish to study cannot be controlled.

We may gain some purchase on the case study emphasis upon the limitation of control by considering what counts as a case. A case refers to an individual, several individuals (as in multiple-case study), an event or an entity. For example, Sigmund Freud famously used the case study method with a series of individuals who he treated in a clinical setting. From these famous cases (which included 'Little Dora', 'The Rat Man', 'The Wolf Man' and other intriguingly sub-titled cases) Freud constructed a powerful and controversial theory of human unconsciousness and its relation to conscious behaviour. In another famous example, William Whyte used the case study method to explore the lives of Italian-American men in a poor urban neighbourhood that he published as *Street Corner Society* (1943). This book has become a classic example of a multiple-case study involving several individuals and their interpersonal relations in a specific subculture. In yet another example, Bernstein and Woodward's famous account of the Watergate scandal in *All the President's Men* (1974) took Watergate as an event for study.

Thus, a 'case' may involve the study of one individual or several, or a particular event. Researchers tend to use multiple sources of evidence, including archival records, interviews, direct observation, participant-observation, and/or physical artefacts. Whilst most case study findings are written, the results of some case studies appear as films, videos or audiotapes.

It is at the point of determining the criteria for judging the success of the case study analysis that the case study method encounters most criticism. The 'poor relation' status of case study research results largely from the charge that case studies lack objectivity and are non-generalisable (these criticisms are often levelled at qualitative research in general). It is certainly true that case studies lack a sufficient sample size for statistical testing. However, it is not the case that generalisation of findings must be limited to large-scale, statistically tested, surveys or experiments. Here, the distinction between analytical and statistical generalisation is useful. Surveys rely on statistical generalisation, whereas case studies and experiments rely on analytical generalisation – that is, generalisation to theory. Generalisation is based on repeated observation and, like a single experiment, one case study provides an observation that can be generalised to a general theory, particularly when considered in concert with the results from other studies. For instance, in the sociological classic *Tally's Corner* (1967), Elliot Liebow provided a case study analysis of one group of black men living in a poor, inner city American neighbourhood. Liebow used the data from this analysis to build upon a theory of subculture existence, which was in turn utilised by other researchers interested in the character of subcultures. Thus, the results of Liebow's analysis were generalised to issues such as group structure and dynamics, as well as the structural relations between subcultures and their dominant society.

It is also difficult to sustain the argument that case studies lack rigour, any more than it is possible to argue that all experiments and surveys (for example) are necessarily rigorous. *All* research methods depend upon the skill of the researcher, the context of the research and the subject of analysis. What distinguishes case studies here is that the subject of study cannot be manipulated in the way that experiments that rely upon subject and environment can. Despite criticisms, case studies continue to provide some of the most interesting and inspiring research in the social sciences.

Suggested further reading

Freud, S. (1999[1899]) *The Interpretation of Dreams*. Oxford: Oxford University Press.

References

Whyte, W. (1943) *Street Corner Society: The Social Construction of an Italian Slum*. Chicago: Chicago University Press.

Yin, R. (1989) *Case Study Research: Design and Methods*. Newbury Park and London: Sage.

MYRA J. HIRD

Causation

Causation has had a chequered history in social research. Closely tied to quantitative analysis, its star has waxed and waned as social scientists have experimented with and developed different ways of understanding society and social phenomena. Very strong in the late nineteenth century, it was rejected for a time in the early twentieth century but from about the middle of the century on, causation has had a firm, but not uncontested, place in social research.

Causation is part of the territory of explanation (rather than description). The case for causation has been advanced by and through empirical, variable-orientated research. In understanding causation it is helpful to distinguish between two types: *deterministic* and *probabilistic*. A deterministic approach to causality holds to the view that causes necessitate certain effects; it speaks in terms of absolutes and general laws. Less certain about the linear nature of social life, probabilistic causation operates to the logic whereby certain events raise the chance of occurrence of other events rather than actually causing them. Social scientists tend now to subscribe to probabilistic causation since it is the form of causation that is demonstrable through statistics.

Dependence and independence

Not only are there particular procedures for establishing causality but there is a language of causation as well. The 'dependent' or outcome variable is that which is to be explained. In a causal analysis it is posited to be the result or effect of other factors. The 'independent variables' are those which are deemed to be the most likely explanatory factors. These are sometimes divided into two sets of factors: on the one hand the 'cause' or the 'treatment' variables and on the other the control variables. The causal sets of relationships involved are verified through hypothesis testing. Hypotheses posit a relationship between variables so that, if the independent variables take on a particular set of values, specified values are also predicted for the dependent variable. Control variables are used to test the possibility that an empirical relationship between the independent and dependent variables is spurious, that is, caused by some other set of factors. They act to reduce the risk of attributing explanatory power to independent variables which are not responsible for the occurrence of the variation or the effect found between the independent and dependent variables.

Conditions

Causation has to be demonstrated and for this purpose there are particular conditions that have to be met. The following are the main building blocks of causal argumentation or rules of causal evidence in the social sciences (Lewins, 1992):

(1) *Covariation.* For a causal relation to be able to be established there must be at least two values of the independent variable and at least two values of the dependent variable and the relationship must be in the same direction. Association (although not causation) is established in this way: for example, high unemployment associating with high poverty and low unemployment associating with low poverty. The classical statistical technique here is correlation.

(2) *Constancy of association.* This is a requirement that covariation or association must remain constant over time. An inconsistency undermines any assumption of a causal relationship. For example, if the relationship between high unemployment and high poverty were to be observed only in the months of March, June, August and September, then it would be dangerous to posit causality between these two variables. The idea of regularity is central – something can only be explained if it is (part of) a regular occurrence.

(3) *Cause must take place prior to effect.* This criterion is a qualification of covariation, ordaining that it is not sufficient to know that an association exists – a particular temporal relationship must also be observed. While it is to some extent obvious that cause must come before effect, it is not always easy in the social sciences to establish that this is the case.

(4) *Independent and dependent variables must be discrete.* The researcher must ensure that they are not dimensions or aspects of the same phenomenon.

(5) *Non-spuriousness.* The researcher must establish that the relationship between two factors is not the result of a third, independent factor. Guarding against rival explanations is a very large part of all research. So in designing research and in deciding on the kind and volume of information which is collected, researchers should always be conscious of the possibility of counter explanations. This is another reason why controlling for the existence and effects of other factors is so important.

Strengthening the contribution of causation

Causation is the source of considerable debate and disagreement in the social sciences. Dispute has been occasioned not *per se* by the fact that the origins of much causal thinking lie in science but rather in questions about how and whether this kind of thinking can be transferred to the analysis of society. Social action and social phenomena are by their very nature infinite and multi-dimensional. The extent to which it is possible to apply the degree of control and manipulation necessary to establish causation has therefore been questioned. The second source of discontent is with the role and place of knowledge of the subject matter which is being studied. In the more strongly science biased approaches to causation, explanation is taken to follow from the empirical relationships found. Sometimes explanation is treated as a technical outcome – if it is demonstrated by the statistics then it exists. The respective contributions of statistics and theory are at issue here, the underlying concern being the extent to which causation is treated as a function of empirical data and techniques of data manipulation alone.

Mindful of these critiques, some recent work identifies practices which I believe can serve to strengthen the contribution of causation to sociology.

In the first instance the search after causation has to be closely oriented to theoretical development – otherwise it runs the risk of being fragmented and not building up a body of knowledge. Likewise theories, especially if they are designed to show the causes of a phenomenon or set of phenomena, must include an interrelated set of causal propositions. King et al. (1994: 100–14) suggest five sets of 'good practices' for the purpose of formulating theories. These I believe have quite wide application.

(1) *Theories or propositions must be falsifiable.* Emphasising the tentative nature of any theory, this means that theories or propositions should be designed in such a way that they can be shown to be wrong as easily and quickly as possible. The question to be asked all the time is: What evidence would falsify the relationship?

(2) *We should build theories that are internally consistent.* Hence they should be reasoned and no part, or hypothesis deriving therefrom, should be in contra-diction with other parts. One method of producing internally consistent theories is that of formal modelling. Examples include rational choice models or those based in game theory.

(3) *Dependent variables should be selected very carefully.* It is especially important that dependent variables represent the variation which the researcher wishes to explain.

(4) *Concreteness should be maximised* in that all variables should be observable. This means that we must take care when using abstract concepts, like culture or identity for example, to try and define them in such a way that they or their implications can be observed and measured. In this kind of decision the researcher has to focus on finding empirical evidence pertaining to the concept and for this purpose one or a number of indicators of the concept are chosen.

(5) *Theories are stated in as encompassing a manner as possible.* Hence a theory or proposition should explain as much of the field as possible.

Another emphasis in recent work makes a strong case for causal analysis as *process* (see especially Goldthorpe, 2001). Process has two meanings in this regard. The first pertains to how we understand the way that social effects are brought about. These always occur through a process. For example, to say that unemployment causes poverty has little meaning without an analysis and understanding of the process whereby this occurs. The second meaning of process pertains to the sequence in which the researcher undertakes causal analysis. Goldthorpe suggests that there should be three steps in this. Firstly, the researcher should establish 'what is happening'. That is, s/he should ensure that the phenomena which are to be explained actually exist and that they have sufficient regularity to require and allow explanation. For this purpose descriptive statistics (distribution, patterns of association) are very important. The second step is to construct hypotheses about how these social regularities are to be explained. This is where processes relating to social action must be brought in. The final stage brings statistics in again as it consists of testing hypotheses. Proceeding in this way allows the respective roles of theory and statistics to be clarified and is, according to Goldthorpe, appropriate to sociology as a discipline in which the concept of social action is central.

Before we leave the subject, it is important to put causation in context. First, let us remember that it is one of a number of modes of explanation used in the social sciences. Other forms of reasoning include functionalist, historical and structural explanations. Secondly it is also important to point out that many branches of social science disciplines consider the search for causation something of a dead end. In this 'interpretive' view, the appropriate task is to identify meaning in all its diversity and complexity.

Suggested further reading

Lewins, F. (1994) *Social Science Methodology: A Brief but Critical Introduction.* Sydney: Macmillan.

References

Goldthorpe, J.H. (2001) 'Causation, Statistics and Sociology', *European Sociological Review*, 17 (1): 1–20.
King, G., Keohane, R.O. and Verba, S. (1994) *Designing Social Enquiry: Scientific Inference in Qualitative Research*, Princeton NJ: Princeton University Press.

Lewins, F. (1992) *Social Science Methodology: A brief but critical introduction.* Melbourne: Macmillan.

MARY DALY

Central tendency

The concept of central tendency refers to the 'average' or 'most typical' value of a distribution. While the overall aim is to produce a single number that best represents the 'centre' or 'level' of a batch of data there are a number of different ways of doing this. The three most common measures of central tendency are: the mean; the median; and the mode. Which of these we choose will depend primarily on the level of measurement of the data.

The arithmetic *mean* is the most familiar of all the measures of central tendency and corresponds with most people's notion of what an average is. The mean possesses a number of important mathematical properties and should be calculated for interval or ratio data only.

To calculate the mean, add together all the values in a batch and divide the total by the number of values. For example, if a tutorial group consisted of eleven students with the following ages: 18 + 19 + 19 + 20 + 20 + 20 + 20 + 20 + 21 + 21 + 22 (= 220); the mean age would be 20 (220 divided by 11).

One of the attractions of the mean over other measures of central tendency is the fact that it makes use of all the values in a distribution. This, however, is a double-edged sword because the mean may be disproportionately affected by extreme values. So, if we replace the 22-year-old in the tutorial group with a 66-year-old mature student the mean age rises to 24 (264 divided by 11). We can see, then, that one student can drag up the average age of the class considerably, even though the other ten students are 21 or under. Hence, if there are extreme values in your batch the mean could be misleading. In such circumstances it may be preferable to use an alternative measure of central tendency such as the median.

The *median* is the most suitable measure of central tendency for ordinal data although it is also widely used with interval/ratio variables. It is simply the middle value in a distribution when the scores are ranked in order of size. To return to the tutorial example used above, the median age of our original eleven students (18, 19, 19, 20, 20, **20**, 20, 20, 21, 21, 22) would be 20. This is the value that splits the batch in two with five scores ranked above it and five scores ranked below it. Unlike the mean, the median is *resistant* to extreme values and the introduction of our mature student in place of the 22-year-old would not have any effect on the result; 20 still remains the middle value (18, 19, 19, 20, 20, **20**, 20, 20, 21, 21, 66) in the batch. (Note that if there is an even number of scores (for example, eight students: 17, 18, 18, **19**, **20**, 20, 56, 60) we will have two middle values (19 and 20). In this case to get the median we simply calculate the average of these two values (19 + 20 divided by 2 = 19.5)).

The *mode* is the simplest measure of central tendency to calculate and is the only measure that is appropriate for nominal/categorical data. The mode is simply the value that occurs most often in a distribution. Although the mode is very easy to calculate, it has a number of disadvantages. For a start, it is not particularly informative. The mode will tell us which category of a variable occurs most frequently, but nothing about the number of cases that fall into that category or about any of the other values in the batch. Another drawback in using this as a measure of central tendency is that a variable may have two or more modal values (these are referred to as bimodal and multimodal distributions respectively). It is even possible for a variable to have no mode at all (if each of the categories had the same frequency).

Suggested further reading

Clegg, Francis (1990) *Simple Statistics: A Course Book for the Social Sciences*. Cambridge: Cambridge University Press.

Hinton, Perry (1990) *Statistics Explained: A Guide for Social Science Students*. London: Routledge.

Weisberg, H.F. (1992) *Central Tendency and Variability*. Newbury Park: Sage.

See also
Dispersion and
the normal
distribution.

CIARAN ACTON

Child research

There exists a dearth of literature reflexively giving accounts of undertaking social research with children, not least when compared with the voluminous amount of literature produced on doing research with adults (Morrow and Richards, 1996). This is perhaps understandable given that the social sciences traditionally disregarded the views and opinions of children, but certainly not excusable given the right of children to be recognised as active participants in society and decision-making processes. Children were traditionally regarded in the social science literature as immature and incompetent. Whilst their immaturity is an undeniable biological fact, the meaning attached to their immaturity is a cultural construction (James and Prout, 1997). Thus rather than conducting research *on* children, priority should be given to conducting research *with* children, respecting them as subjects who can tell adults a great deal about who they are. The 1989 United Nations Convention on the Rights of the Child marked a watershed in its axiom that children not only have the right to articulate their opinions on issues which affect them but they have the right to have their views listened to. Until relatively recently, however, children have been largely ignored as a potential source of data despite the fact that it is children who are most likely to experience the brunt of political, educational, legal and administrative processes on their lives in relation to issues such as poverty, health, education and work. How do we ensure that children's voices are heard so that their views can be incorporated into policy decisions that affect their lives?

Ethical issues

Answering this question requires the researcher to consider carefully which research methods will fully maximise children's input into the research whilst recognising children's vulnerability and the inherent power relationship that exists within the adult–child relationship. These issues make child centred research markedly different to research with adults on three main counts. Firstly, because children's competencies differ from those of adults, consideration must be given to finding appropriate data collection methods that are respectful and fair to children and allow them full participation in the research. Secondly, obtaining informed consent from children to participate in research ultimately is subject to the amount of access adult gatekeepers are willing to grant researchers. In most cases, permission is sought from a range of adults responsible for the well-being of children (that is, parents, teachers, school principals, local education authorities). Consequently, children's consent to participate in research is often considered to be of secondary importance to adult consent, which may take precedence over children's right to choose whether or not they want to participate in the research. The duty of the researcher to protect the well-being of their subjects is also complicated by the fact that children are relatively powerless and therefore vulnerable to abuse or exploitation. This leads to a third issue which concerns confidentiality and whether/how this should be tackled/breached if a child discloses information which raises cause for concern or if the research draws attention to an issue the child did not perceive to be problematic in the first place (Morrow and Richards, 1996).

The latter ethical dilemmas infiltrate all stages of the research process. However some practical advice has been offered to deal with these issues. In the first instance, researchers need to supply children with clear and unambiguous information regarding why the research is needed, what methods they intend to use and how the results will be disseminated. This information needs to be couched in language appropriate to the age group of the children participating in the study and should be delivered in a manner so that the children (as well as their parents) understand that participation is voluntary and that they have the right to terminate involvement at any stage they feel appropriate. In addition, children have the same right to confidentiality as adults and any final report should be written in such a way so that no individual child can be identified.

The conduct of research

When actually carrying out research, consideration must also be given to the age of the children participating, their cultural background and the social context in which the research will take place (Hood et al., 1996). For example, if conducting research with young children the researcher may consider using pictures, photographs, role play or toys to tell a story or to end a story or sentence started by an adult. Asking children to draw a picture about a particular issue/event can also reveal a great deal about how children view themselves and their social worlds not least because of children's familiarity with these mediums in school. Whilst some children may find it easier to communicate their thoughts visually rather than verbally other children may prefer to express themselves through a story. Writing can provide an invaluable insight into children's private thoughts since it allows children to express their experiences in their own words free from the researcher's preconceived issues of interest. Alternatively, focus group techniques could be used to elicit children's views and opinions in a peer supportive environment. This may prove particularly advantageous when conducting research with children familiar with oral traditions. To reduce the physical difference in status in the adult–child relationship, it is recommended that researchers communicate with children at eye level (for example, by sitting with them on the floor rather than at desks or tables) or that they give children full control of the tape recorder by allowing them to turn it on and off if they so wish. The latter techniques can be combined either during the data collection process or before the research actually begins. In so doing, children are empowered to guide and control the research in accordance with their way of seeing the world, as opposed to squeezing the data derived from children into a preconceived adult-centred interpretative framework. Note that, as well as empowering child subjects of research, these techniques enhance the reliability and validity of the data, making it more representative of the issues children consider meaningful and important to them.

Of course, using child friendly techniques will not necessarily negate the unequal power relationship between the researcher and the child. Special consideration must be given to the impact this will have on the data. In particular, the issue of adult control over the research process raises a fundamental question over the ability of researchers (as adults) to interpret and understand accurately what children say. Ideally, researchers should check their interpretations with children or at the very least inform them of the main research findings in a report written specifically for them. Alternatively they may consider enlisting older children as research assistants and data collectors. (However, this strategy is complicated by the issue of payment and the potential exploitation of children in relation to the degree of responsibility required to elicit information and interpret data.) Readers should also be aware that the manner in which the research is conducted and written up depends ultimately on the researcher's view of children. For example, James 1990 (cited in Morrow and Richards, 1996: 99) usefully identifies four 'ideal type' models of the child: the 'tribal child'; the 'developing child'; the 'adult child'; and the 'social child'. Each paradigm distinctly affects how researchers choose to investigate the live worlds of children and how they present their findings.

Conclusion

As the above discussion illustrates, empowering children through research does raise many grey areas not least in relation to the power adult researchers hold over which issues will be investigated, which tools will be used to collect data and how the information supplied by children will be interpreted and presented. These ethical and methodological issues and the need to both protect and promote the rights of children have made child research one of the most innovative and challenging epicentres in current social research.

Suggested further reading

James, A. and Prout, A. (1997) *Constructing and Reconstructing Childhood: Contemporary Issues in the Sociological Study of Childhood* detail the latest developments in the main paradigmatic frameworks in research with children across the social sciences. This work is of great seminal importance because it problematises the extent to which children are treated as actors in their own right and the massive implications this has for the data collection and interpretative process.

References

Hood, S., Kelley, P. and Mayall, B. (1996) 'Children as Research Subjects: A Risky Enterprise', *Children and Society*, 10 (2): 117–28.

James, A. and Prout, A. (1997) *Constructing and Reconstructing Childhood: Contemporary Issues in the Sociological Study of Childhood*. London: Falmer Press.

Morrow, V. and Richards, M. (1996) 'The Ethics of Social Research with Children: An Overview', *Children and Society*, 10 (2): 90–105.

CIARA DAVEY

Comparative analysis

The comparative method is one of the oldest in the social sciences. In the eighteenth century, John Hume and Adam Smith both outlined what they called the constant comparative method; nineteenth century sociology was premised on comparisons of social processes across nations, an approach fundamental to such divergent people as Karl Marx, Herbert Spencer, Emile Durkheim and Max Weber. Durkheim even wrote in his famous *Rules of Sociological Method* (1895) that the comparative method was not a branch of sociological method but was sociology itself. That is, all sociology is comparative in that social phenomena are affected by the location and setting of their production and reproduction and thus to understand social life is to make comparisons across settings and locations. Modern day social science considers comparative analysis essential to most types of research. However, it is used in two ways. The first is *internal comparison*. A particular phenomenon is compared across time, culture and space in order to identify its variations. These variations will disclose patterns of difference and similarity. A good example might be marriage, the forms, rites and rituals of which can be compared across cultures, space and time in order to exemplify better the internal features of marriage as a social institution. Another kind is *external comparison*. Two or more different phenomena are compared against each other, now or in the past, in one society or several, in order to identify variations. These variations will again disclose the patterns of difference and similarity between the phenomena. A good example might be a comparison of marriage and cohabitation across time, space or culture in order to exemplify better the patterns of convergence or divergence between the phenomena now or in the past, in one place and culture or another.

Internal and external comparisons are not mutually exclusive, nor do they suggest any limit on what can be compared. They should have a definite purpose however. To compare for comparison's sake just because the variations are there and real is possible but not necessarily desirable. Comparisons are more useful when the variations discovered contribute useful knowledge to the betterment of society. The differences between chalk and cheese are real but the comparative method is more useful when put to understanding the variations in socially worthwhile practices, policies, processes and institutions. There have been two sorts of comparative approach in social science to the study of these things. The comparative method is normally associated with cross-national research in a quantitative manner using deduction as its general approach, whereby hypotheses are drawn from a general theory and tested in several societies. Patterns of convergence and divergence can then be documented and fed back into the general model or theory. Patterns of social stratification, social mobility and crime trends are aspects of social life frequently studied in this way, relying on official social statistics or social survey data from each society. At the other end of the continuum of the comparative method are studies within the general approach of induction, done on different cultures, groups and settings in order to show the specificity of social life. Weber's use of the comparative method is an excellent example, for much of his sociological work was devoted to demonstrating the specificity of social arrangements in what he called the Occident (Europe and North America) to explain its different patterns of social development. This example shows that it is not the unit of analysis that distinguishes these two approaches to comparative analysis, for both can focus on the nation state or states; it is the search for variance or similarity that separates them. Deductive comparative studies tend to seek patterns of convergence between nation states to support the validity of the general theory that is applied to understand and explain the social process under study. Inductive comparative studies tend to focus on patterns of variance to support the contention that social life is historically specific and culturally bound.

The contrast between quantitative and qualitative comparative analysis is not the same antinomy as deductive and inductive comparative analysis. The former is a contrast in the methods used in the comparative analysis, the latter the general purpose to which the comparison is put. Quantitative and qualitative analyses do not necessarily differ in the unit of analysis in the comparison, in that quantitative studies do not have to focus on nation states, although they often do. Neither are qualitative studies always focused on the local, as Weber's specification of the Occident showed. Qualitative studies can also end up with the formulation of general statements developed inductively, as Durkheim's 1912 theorisation of the elementary rules of religious life illustrated, based as it was on secondary material from qualitative anthropological studies of pre-industrial cultures and groups. Qualitative comparative analysis therefore describes the methods used to undertake the comparison and not the unit of analysis, the purpose of the comparison or the level of general abstraction that is achieved. Comparisons are a vital part of the development of inductive generalisations and were central to the procedures in grounded theory; all these comparisons can be made by means of qualitative research and its associated methods and data collection techniques. Indeed, one of the ways in which empirical generalisations and theoretical inferences can be made by means of ethnography is to design the research comparatively. This can be achieved by studying the same process in different fields or different processes in the same field, in order better to understand their local specificity or generality. Miller's (1997) ethnography of modernisation in Trinidad was based on comparisons between four field sites on the island in order to understand the way in which modernisation was experienced by Trinidadians. This is a good example of what Ragin called case oriented comparisons. Charles Ragin usefully contrasted what he called variable and case oriented comparisons. He challenged the association of the comparative method with multivariate statistical techniques to study social processes across nation states. This type of comparative analysis is perforce quantitative but is only one kind of comparison. The other he called case oriented, and involves the holistic comparison of cases. It is perforce qualitative and inductive. Most qualitative comparative analysis is of no more than a few cases with localised units of analysis, but Ragin's formulation involved the development of a new technique that used Boolean algebra to permit qualitative study of macrosocial phenomena. As outlined in *The Comparative Method* (1987), Ragin described a procedure that he felt made it possible to bring the logic and empirical intensity of qualitative approaches to studies that embrace more than a handful of cases. Boolean methods of logical comparison represent each case as a combination of causal and outcome conditions. These combinations can be compared with each other and then logically simplified through a bottom-up process of paired comparison using computer algorithms for simplifying the data. A computer package, *Qualitative Comparative Analysis*, has been developed by Charles Ragin to assist in the process. It is a considerable extension of qualitative comparative analysis as this is normally understood and practised.

Suggested further reading

Ragin, C. (1991) *Issues and Alternatives in Comparative Social Research*. Leiden: E.J. Brill.

Oyen, E. (1990) *Comparative Methodology*. London: Sage.

The computer package, *Qualitative Comparative Analysis*, is accessible at: http://www.northwestern.edu/ sociology/tools/qca/fsqca.zip

References

Miller, D. (1997) *Modernity: An Ethnographic Approach*. Oxford: Berg.

Ragin, C. (1987) *The Comparative Method*. Berkeley: University of California Press.

JOHN BREWER

Computer simulation of social processes

Most social research either develops or uses some kind of theory or model: for instance, a theory of deviance or a model of the class system. Generally, such theories are stated in discursive English. Sometimes the theory is represented as a structural equation (for example, when doing regression). During the last decade, researchers have begun to explore the possibilities of expressing theories as computer programs. The great advantage is one can then simulate the social processes of interest in the computer and in some circumstances even carry out 'experiments' that would otherwise be quite impossible.

This entry introduces the computer simulation of social processes and phenomena and suggests further reading for additional detail and advice. Although it helps to have some knowledge of computer programming to develop simulations, no such experience is needed to understand what simulations aim to do or to follow this entry. In practice, many researchers involved closely with simulations have colleagues with computer science backgrounds who do the actual programming.

The logic underlying the methodology of simulation is not very different from the logic underlying statistical modelling. In statistical modelling, a specification of a model is constructed (for example, in the form of a regression equation) through a process of abstraction from what are theorised to be the social processes that exist in the 'real world' (Gilbert, 1993). By means of some statistical technique, the model is used to generate some expected values that are compared with actual data. The main difference between statistical modelling and simulation is that a simulation model can be 'run' to produce output, while a statistical model requires a statistical analysis program to generate expected values.

The development of social simulation

Although the simulation of social dynamics has a long history in the social sciences (Inbar and Stoll, 1972), the advent of much more powerful computers, more powerful computer languages and the greater availability of data have led to increased interest in simulation as a method for developing and testing social theories (see Chapter 3 of Whicker and Sigelman (1991) for a historical review).

Simulation comes into its own when the phenomenon to be studied is either not directly accessible or difficult to observe directly. For example, simulation has been used to investigate the emergence of increased social complexity amongst hunter-gatherers in Upper Palaeolithic France, 20,000 years ago (more about this study below). Instead of studying the society (the target) itself, it is often useful to study a model of the target. The model will be more accessible and smaller scale, but sufficiently similar to the target to allow conclusions drawn from the model to be (tentatively) generalised to the target. The model might be statistical, mathematical or symbolic (based on logic or a computer program). The important point about a model is that it must be designed to be similar to the target in structure and behaviour.

Generally, a model is defined in terms of a mathematical or logical specification (Doran and Gilbert, 1993). Sometimes it is possible to derive conclusions about the model analytically, by reasoning about the specification (for example, with mathematical proof procedures). Often, however, this is either difficult or impossible, and one performs a simulation. The simulation consists of 'animating' the model. For example, if the model is expressed as a computer program, the simulation consists of running the program with some specified inputs and observing the outputs that result.

Simulation as a method

Paradoxically, one of the main advantages of simulation is that it is hard to do. To create a simulation model, its theoretical presuppositions need to have been thought through with great clarity. Every relationship to be modelled has to be specified exactly, for otherwise it will be impossible to construct the simulation. Every parameter has to be given a value. These strictures mean that it is impossible to be vague about what is being assumed. It also means that the model is potentially open to inspection by other researchers in all its detail. These benefits of clarity and precision also have disadvantages, however. Simulations of complex social processes involve the estimation of many parameters and adequate data for making the estimates can be difficult to come by.

Another, quite different benefit of simulation is that it can in some circumstances give insights into the 'emergence' of macro level phenomena from micro level action (Conte and Gilbert, 1995). Thus, a simulation of interacting individuals may reveal clear patterns of influence when examined on a societal scale. A simulation by Nowak and Latané (1993), for example, shows how simple rules about the way in which one individual influences another's attitudes can yield results about attitude change at the level of a society, and one by Axelrod (1995) demonstrates how patterns of political domination can arise from a few rules followed by simulated nation states.

A problem which has to be faced in all simulation work is the difficulty of validating the model. Ideally, a simulation should produce outputs which match those of the target for all possible inputs which can be envisaged to occur in reality, and should fail to produce output in all other circumstances. In practice, it is neither feasible to examine all input combinations, nor is it possible to assess whether the outputs from a wide range of inputs do indeed match those of the target, because the target may only be observable for some rather limited range of conditions. Sometimes a statistical solution to these problems is advocated (for example, Bratley et al., 1983), but in practice it is hard to abide by the kinds of assumptions which conventional statistical tests require. Nevertheless, simulation always has a valuable role in helping to clarify ideas and theories, even if complete validation cannot be carried out.

An example: dynamic micro-simulation

The above advantages and disadvantages will be illustrated with some examples taken from recent work. The first uses an approach which has come to be called *dynamic micro-simulation*. Dynamic micro-simulation is used to simulate the effect of the passing of time on individuals and, often, on households (Harding, 1990). Data from a large, usually random sample from some population (the 'base data set') is used to characterise the initial features of the simulated individuals. For example, there may be data on the age, sex, income, employment status and health of several thousand people. A set of transition probabilities is used to simulate how the characteristics of these individuals will change over a time period such as one year. For instance, there will be a probability that someone who is employed at the start becomes unemployed during a simulated year. These transition probabilities are applied to the data set for each individual in turn, and repeatedly re-applied for a number of simulated time periods (years). In some simulations, it is also important to model births, that is, the addition of new members to the data set, and marriage, death and the formation and dissolution of households, in order that the data set remains representative of the target population.

The adequacy and value of such simulation depends on the availability of two kinds of data: a representative sample of the target population to form the base data set, and a sufficiently complete and valid set of transition probabilities. In the simplest simulations, these probabilities consist of an array of constant values, each indicating the chance of some specific change occurring given the current state of an individual. In more complex models, the coefficients can be made to vary according to the situation of other members of the individual's household or wider social context.

The model can then be used to simulate developments in the future, for example to predict the number of those retired compared with those in work, and to explore the long term effect of social policy options. Of course, the accuracy of such predictions depends on the adequacy of the model and the validity of the implied assumption that there will not be major social changes at the macro level.

Artificial intelligence based simulations

In conventional micro-simulations, the behaviour of each simulated individual is regarded as a 'black box'; that is, behaviour is modelled by probabilities and no attempt is made to justify these in terms of individual preferences, decisions or plans. Moreover, each simulated person is considered individually without regard to their interaction with others. The remaining examples of simulation to be described focus specifically on the simulation of individual cognitive processes and on communication between people, using techniques drawn from artificial intelligence (AI). AI is a discipline devoted to the design and construction of computer software that has some of the characteristics commonly ascribed to human intelligence. Simulation based on distributed artificial intelligence uses many AI programs, each representing an 'agent', which interact with each other and with a simulated environment (Bond and Gasser, 1988).

A computer 'agent' typically has three components: a memory; a set of goals; and a set of rules. The memory is required so that the agent can remember past experience and plan ahead on this basis. The agent's objectives are defined by its goals, which may be as simple as to survive in a hostile environment in the face of depleting food or energy reserves, or may be more complex involving conflicts between alternative goals. The rule set defines the agent's behaviour and consists of condition-action rules. The condition part of each rule is matched against the contents of memory and input from environmental 'sensors'. If there is a match, the corresponding action is taken: this may be 'internal', affecting only the state of the agent's memory, or 'external', affecting the environment, for example, the sending of a message through the environment to another agent. The simulation works by cycling through each agent in turn, collecting messages sent from other agents, updating the agent's internal state by checking for any applicable rules, deciding on an action for the agent to take and finally communicating messages and the effects of the action to the environment, which then responds appropriately. This is repeated for every agent and these cycles continue indefinitely until the simulation is stopped or all the agents have 'died'.

An example of a simulation in this style is work Jim Doran, Mike Palmer, Paul Mellars and I have done studying the 'Emergence of Social Complexity' amongst hunter-gatherers in Upper Palaeolithic South-west France (Doran et al., 1993). Many archaeologists believe that at that time there was a change from an egalitarian, low density society in which people lived in small, migratory groups and there was little political organisation and a simple division of labour by gender, to a somewhat more complex society, involving larger concentrations of people, some status differentials, role differentiation and more centralised decision-making. Associated with these changes were changes in burial patterns and the emergence of cave art and various symbolic artefacts.

The question which the simulation explored is what caused this change. One theory centres on the effect of glaciation in concentrating food resources in particular locations (for example, the migratory routes of reindeer) in a predictable annual cycle (Mellars, 1985). As people gathered in these locations, there was 'crowding', causing logistical problems (Cohen, 1985). The growth of social complexity was a solution to this, as means were found to schedule activities so that there were not too many people attempting to secure the same resources at the same time; so that there was an appropriate division of labour; and so that people could relate to other people through stereotypical roles rather than on an individual basis.

We simulated this theory using agents that have the ability to plan their actions depending on the situation they find themselves in, to recruit 'followers' into groups and to communicate with other agents. The simulation was used to investigate issues such as whether the formation of groups increases the chances of survival of the agents.

The steps involved in simulation

The basic method of simulation involves a number of steps:

- Since no social phenomenon can be examined in its entirety, the first step is to select those aspects which are of interest. The selection must be influenced by theoretical preconceptions about which features are significant.

- The modelling approach to be adopted is chosen. As well as the micro-simulation and AI based approaches mentioned above, there are simulations based on techniques drawn from operational research (for example, Bulgren, 1982; Gottfried, 1984; Pooch and Wall, 1993) and on the construction of differential equations relating the rate of change of quantities to other parameters (for example, Spriet and Vansteenkiste, 1982). A further approach uses symbolic logic or symbol manipulation as the basis of the model (Widman et al., 1989; Zeigler, 1990; Gilbert and Doran, 1993).
- Whichever approach is adopted, a further decision has to be made about the appropriate level of abstraction for the model. An important aspect of this is the level of aggregation selected for the units. For example, one might model the world economy using the major power blocks, individual countries, or (less practically) individual people as the units.
- It is then necessary to select the form in which the model is to be represented. If the model is to be a computer program, the decision mainly concerns the choice of computer language, although there will also be choices about how the program should be structured. Languages commonly used are BASIC, C, Java, Prolog and Smalltalk (the latter two are languages developed by Artificial Intelligence researchers). In addition, there are specially developed toolkits being developed to assist in building simulations (search for Repast, Ascape, SDML or Swarm on the World Wide Web).
- Once all these preliminaries have been decided, the model can be constructed, the simulation run and the output examined.
- In practice, there is likely to be a period of modifying and testing gradually improving models. The simulation will be run a number of times, each time with a slightly 'better' model.
- Once the model is considered to be satisfactory, it is important to carry out sensitivity analyses. These examine the effect of small changes in the parameters of the model on its output. If small changes make large differences, one needs to be concerned about the accuracy with which the parameters have been measured; it is possible that the output is an artefact of the particular values chosen for the parameters.

Note

Based on an article published under the same name in *Social Research Update*, 6 (1993) Department of Sociology, University of Surrey.

Suggested further reading

There is an electronic journal that publishes papers using social simulation and reports on the latest developments: the *Journal of Artificial Societies and Social Simulation* (http://www.soc.surrey.ac.uk/JASSS/).

A site that contains links to social simulation resources on web is http://www.soc.surrey.ac.uk/research/simsoc/.

Recent papers are also to be found in the edited collections below:

Gilbert, N. (ed.) (1999) *Computer Simulation in the Social Sciences, American Behavioral Scientist.* Thousand Oaks, CA: Sage.

Kohler, T. and Gumerman, G. (eds) (2000) *Dynamics in Human and Primate Societies: Agent-Based Modeling of Social and Spatial Processes.* Oxford: Oxford University Press.

Troitzsch, K.G., Mueller, U., Gilbert, G.N. and Doran, J.E. (eds) (1996) *Social Science Microsimulation.* Berlin: Springer.

References

Axelrod, R. (1995) 'A Model of the Emergence of New Political Actors', in G.N. Gilbert and R. Conte (eds), *Artificial Societies: The Computer Simulation of Social Life.* London: UCL Press.

Bond, A.H. and Gasser, L. (1988) *Readings in Distributed Artificial Intelligence.* San Francisco: Morgan Kaufmann.

Bratley, P., Fox, L. and Schrage, L.E. (1983) *A Guide to Simulation.* New York: Springer-Verlag.

Bulgren, W.G. (1982) *Discrete System Simulation.* Englewood Cliffs, N.J.: Prentice-Hall.

Cohen, M.N. (1985) 'Prehistoric Hunter-Gatherers: The Meaning of Social Complexity', in T. Douglas-Price and J.A. Brown (eds) *Prehistoric Hunter-Gatherers: The Emergence of Cultural Complexity.* New York: Academic Press. pp. 99–119.

Conte, R. and Gilbert, G.N. (1995) 'Introduction', in G.N. Gilbert and R. Conte (eds), *Artificial Societies.* London: UCL Press.

Doran, J. and Gilbert, G.N. (1993) 'Simulating Societies: an Introduction', in G.N. Gilbert and R. Conte (eds), *Artificial Societies.* London: UCL Press.

Doran, J., Palmer, M., Gilbert, N. and Mellars, P. (1993) 'The EOS Project: Modelling Upper Palaeolithic Change', in G.N. Gilbert and J. Doran (eds), *Simulating Societies: The Computer Simulation of Social Processes.* London: UCL Press.

Gilbert, G.N. (1993) *Analyzing Tabular Data: Loglinear and Logistic Models for Social Researchers.* London: UCL Press.

Gilbert, G.N. and Doran, J. (eds) (1993) *Simulating Societies: The Computer Simulation of Social Processes.* London: UCL Press.

Gilbert, N. and Troitzsch, K.G. (1999) *Simulation for the Social Scientist.* Milton Keynes: Open University Press.

Gottfried, B.S. (1984) *Elements of Stochastic Process Simulation.* Englewood Cliffs, N.J.: Prentice-Hall.

Harding, A. (ed) (1996) *Microsimulation and Public Policy.* Amsterdam: Elsevier Science B.V.

Inbar, M. and Stoll, C.S. (1972) *Simulation and Gaming in Social Science.* New York: Free Press.

Mellars, P. (1985) 'The Ecological Basis of Social Complexity in the Upper Palaeolithic of Southwestern France', in T. Douglas-Price and J.A. Brown (eds), *Prehistoric Hunter-Gatherers: The Emergence of Cultural Complexity.* New York: Academic Press. pp. 271–97.

Nowak, A. and Latané, B. (1993) 'Simulating the Emergence of Social Order from Individual Behaviour', in N. Gilbert and J. Doran (eds), *Simulating Societies: The Computer Simulation of Social Phenomena.* London: UCL Press.

Pooch, U.W. and Wall, J.A. (1993) *Discrete Event Simulation: A Practical Approach.* New York: CRC Press.

Spriet, J.A. and Vansteenkiste, G.C. (1982) *Computer-Aided Modelling and Simulation.* New York: Academic Press.

Whicker, M.L. and Sigelman, L. (1991) *Computer Simulation Applications.* Applied Social Research Methods Series. Newbury Park: Sage.

Widman, L.E., Loparo, K.A. and Nielson, N.R. (1989) *Artificial Intelligence, Simulation and Modelling.* New York: Wiley.

Zeigler, B.P. (1990) *Object Oriented Simulation with Hierarchical, Modular Models.* New York: Academic Press.

NIGEL GILBERT

Confirmatory statistics

See **Hypothesis testing**.

Constructionism, social

The social constructionist perspective within the social sciences is part of a much wider tradition which has been labelled constructionist or constructivist. Constructionism argues that knowledge arises from social processes and interaction – in principle social scientific knowledge is no different from everyday knowledge. Constructionists believe that people make their own reality and that there are no universal laws external to human interaction waiting to be discovered.

Constructionist assumptions have methodological implications in that social researchers are not distinct from their subject matter – they cannot study social life as scientists might do in a laboratory. Instead their interaction with their subjects is itself a key part of the sociological enterprise. Thus there is no sharp distinction between sociological knowledge and social reality. In the views of some constructionists drawing on the work of Weber and others, this does not make the social sciences any less scientific than science that deals with non-human subjects or inanimate objects. Rather sociologists as human beings use the common capacities they share with their subjects to provide a deeper understanding and interpretation of social life.

Categories such as gender, sexual orientation, ethnicity, class, nationality are social constructs which may vary across time and culture depending on the specific circumstances, processes and forms of interaction. Constructionists are sceptical that there are natural, essential or unchanging human traits which are rooted in biology, psychology or other natural characteristics. They argue, for example, that ideas of masculinity and femininity vary considerably across societies and historical periods. Definitions of womanhood current in middle class Victorian society involved exclusion from paid work, physical delicacy and muted sexual feeling. Women in many contemporary African societies, the other hand, may be breadwinners, physically robust and sexually confident. In other words, constructionists would argue that there is no necessary connection between male or female bodies and particular gender characteristics.

Origins and development

The origins of social constructionism are deeply rooted in the history of the social science disciplines. While Marx, Weber and Durkheim are not constructionists in a modern sense, there are constructionist dimensions to their thought. Marx, for example, in some of his earlier writings, emphasises the way in which people shape their own circumstances and produce the ideas, ideologies or conventional wisdom which pervade their societies at particular historical junctures. Weber's actor-oriented sociology focuses on the way in which social meaning is created through interaction. Even Durkheim, often deemed to lean towards naturalism and positivism, sees a social fact like religion as a product of human activity.

The more immediate foundations of constructionism are to be found in the phenomenology of Alfred Schutz and the Chicago School of the early twentieth century including the work of W. I. Thomas. The latter's oft-quoted statement 'when people define situations as real, they become real in their consequences' is an early example of social constructionism. Symbolic interactionism with its roots in the work of G.H. Mead, Herbert Blumer and Erving Goffman is constructionist in that it emphasises how meaning, identity and culture are created in the process of interaction. It emphasises the context-bound, fluid and open-ended nature of social relationships. Symbolic interactionism underwent a revival with a rejection of the dominant paradigm of structural functionalism and the influence of Goffman's dramaturgical sociology and labelling theory in the study of crime, deviance and sexuality. The most formal statement of sociological constructionism in the 1960s was Berger and Luckmann's (1967) *Social Construction of Reality*.

Constructionism was further developed through the influence of Michel Foucault and other post-structuralists. Here 'discourse' was moved to the centre of analysis drawing attention to the way in which the 'expert' discourses of professionals and power-holders of all kinds privilege certain ways of seeing and doing while repressing others. There is an emphasis here on the task of 'decon-structing' or 'decoding' dominant discourses. The development of postmodernism questioned the existence of a dominant ideology or way of seeing the world. It rejected the notion of grand societal or theoretical narratives and underlined the existence of a plurality of narratives or 'ways of seeing' in all societies. Con-structionism has been a powerful influence on recent developments in cultural studies, communication theory and theories of identity. It fuses with post-modernism in underlining the existence of plural narratives, identities and cultures in any given society.

In its contemporary manifestations, constructionism encourages reflexivity – the truth claims of social scientific investigation are not privileged with respect to other existing truth claims advanced by other groups. The social scientist is very much part of the life-world being studied and acts as an interpreter, mediator or communicator in this world. This form of sociological engagement is quite different from that of the positivist who gathers 'objective' facts, looks for general explanations and seeks to inform public policy from an 'external' position based on specialist expertise. Critics of contemporary constructionism have questioned whether its relativism is intellectually coherent and whether it is equipped to analyse the more enduring power structures in society. Authors such as Bhaskar

(1989) and Layder (1998) have sought to develop a critical or reflexive realism which accommodates the analysis of both structure and discourse.

Suggested further reading

Berger, P. and Luckmann, T. (1967) *The Social Construction of Reality: a Treatise in the Sociology of Knowledge*. Garden City, NY: Anchor Books.

References

Bhaskar, R. (1989) *Reclaiming Reality: a Critical Introduction to Contemporary Philosophy*. London: Verso.

Layder, D. (1998) *Sociological Practice: Linking Theory and Social Research*. London: Sage.

LIAM O'DOWD

Content analysis

Content analysis involves the description and analysis of text in order to represent its content. This takes the form of enumeration, such as counting the frequency of words and the number of column inches, and more qualitative assessment of the words and terms used, as undertaken in certain forms of discourse analysis. It is different from hermeneutics, which analyses texts in order to establish their essential truth and meaning; in content analysis the focus is on description of the contents of the text. Content analysis establishes 'meaning' only in the sense of what is explicit in the words used in the text and what is implied by their use from the range of alternatives that could have been employed. There is no suggestion that the text has an *essential* meaning. Moreover, hermeneutics accesses this meaning through what is called the 'double hermeneutic', in which the reader's interpretations of the essential meaning of the text are refracted through an interpretation of what the author's intentions were as embodied in the text and the context that led to its production. In contrast, content analysis is a simple affair of describing the actual content of a text.

Content analysis can be undertaken quantitatively and qualitatively or both. The text can be written forms, such as newspaper articles, official and personal documents, books, pamphlets, tracts and the like, or the accounts people proffer in interview and later transcribed in written form.

The first main use of content analysis in social research was in the immediate period after the Second World War when American sociologists used it to quantitatively and systematically describe and analyse the content of communications containing propaganda. In the context of understanding the growth of Nazism and the immediate post-war fear about Communism, content analysis was put to serve wider questions in politics about who says what to whom, how and to what effect. One of the leading proponents was the US-based sociologist Harold Lasswell (*Propaganda, Communication and Public Opinion*, 1946 and *Language and Politics*, 1949) who sought to enquire into techniques of propaganda and political persuasion. Some of the early textbooks on research methods which addressed content analysis as a 'new field' illustrated its potential by reference to its ability to substantiate people's impressions that some newspaper or other had Nazi or Communist sympathies (see Goode and Hatt, *Methods in Social Research*, 1952). Since then it has been applied to describe and analyse the contents of a wider range of communications, and particularly those that access popular culture, such as magazines, cinema, radio, television, advertisements and newspapers. In the process it has become a part of the repertoire of qualitative research and discourse analysis.

Used quantitatively, the important point about content analysis is the application to texts of predetermined or indigenous categories that enumerate the contents and thus yield a description and analysis of it. The frequency of particular words can be counted, as well as the number of times one descriptive term is used rather than another, the column inches devoted to one topic over another, the variants of particular words and the conceptual categories used in the text, amongst other things. In itself this enumeration may not seem to be revealing, but it has limitless potential in social research. It is possible, for example, to test hypotheses about the attention particular newspapers give to one topic rather than another, the use of various terms and conceptual categories in advertisements aimed at one section of the population rather than another, the status of various categories of people and social groups as depicted in popular fiction, or the way in which official reports on an incident structure a 'reading' of it by use of the words used and the frequency of certain conceptual terms and images over others. Sociological variables like class, race and ethnicity, social status, gender and age can be imposed on the resulting data as codes in order to analyse its contents to establish what is being said to whom. The gender content of various messages in advertisements is one example of how sociological variables can structure the analysis as codes.

It is the enumeration of the contents that distinguishes the quantitative application of content analysis, but much the same focus is used in qualitative studies minus the quantification. In qualitative studies much more stress is laid on the social meaning explicit and implicit in the categorisations used in the text. The gendered nature of much advertising is an example, enabling the social researcher to study competing notions of, say, masculinity as they are communicated in different magazines and in different advertisements. One particular qualitative usage is associated with ethnomethodology and the work of Harvey Sacks, where texts are analysed for the various 'membership categorisation devices' used. A membership categorisation device is a term that categorises a person's membership of society, such as 'mother', father', 'terrorist', 'freedom fighter' and so on, and several can be applied to the same person – 'father', 'husband', 'lover', 'teacher', 'son' and so on. Activities and social behaviours are associated with these categories. Without it being made explicit, because of mutual and shared common-sense knowledge, readers of a text know the membership activities connected with 'mothers', 'terrorists' and so on, and the related categorisations associated with one device, such as 'mother' and 'carer' or 'terrorist' and 'criminal'. Thus implications for understanding the text follow from use of one membership categorisation device rather than another. Discourse analysis expands the conceptual apparatus by which content analysis is done qualitatively but the principle remains the same: texts and accounts are analysed in terms of the composition of their contents. It is clear that in both its quantitative and qualitative modes, coding is an indispensable part of content analysis. In quantitative applications of content analysis these codes tend to be pre-existing conceptual categories having to do with the language, grammar and semantics, or part of a discipline's conceptual apparatus, like class, racism, gender or whatever. The codes can also be indigenous ones based on the data themselves, as they tend to be in qualitative research based on induction. By means of these codes, the contents of the text or account are classified in terms of its structure as embodied in the words used and the ideas, categories and concepts employed.

This association with coding suggests a second meaning for content analysis. Rather than solely a data collection technique, content analysis can become a stage in data analysis itself. Content analysis can be a routine part of coding in qualitative data analysis, in which the data are analysed in the same terms as if they were texts. Content analysis in this sense is part of the coding exercise in qualitative research and is a critical stage in qualitative data analysis. The data are read as if a text and codes developed to structure the description and analysis of their content. Qualitative data analysis by computer furnishes software packages that facilitate content analysis of data 'at the press of buttons' by means of the codes developed from reading it.

Suggested further reading

Brewer, J.D. (2000) *Ethnography*. Buckingham: Open University Press.
Jayyusi, L. (1984) *Categorization and the Moral Order*. London: Routledge.

Potter, J. and Wetherell, M. (1994) 'Analyzing Discourse', in A. Bryman and R. Burgess (eds), *Analyzing Qualitative Data*. London: Routledge.

See also
Discourse analysis,
Hermeneutics.

JOHN BREWER

Contingency tables

A contingency table is a table of counts from data that displays the relationship between two or more variables. It is also known as a crosstabulation. The table is presented in two dimensions, corresponding to rows and columns. One variable, the *row variable*, goes across the horizontal axis and the other variable, the *column variable*, goes down the vertical axis (illustration below). It is called a contingency table because what is found in one axis is contingent on the other.

Two key terms which are used to describe the structure of a contingency table are *cells* and *marginals*. Each cell (a box in the contingency table) is formed by the intersection of a category of the row variable and a category of the column variable. The different cells in the table contain all possible combinations of categories of the row and column variables. The information in the cells is usually given not only as counts of the number of cases that fall into that cell but also as percentages in terms of the row or column totals. The totals of each row and column are termed respectively the row and column marginals.

Contingency tables are used when one wants to display the combination, or association, of two variables that are at the nominal or ordinal level of measurement.[1]

Reading contingency tables

When you encounter a contingency table in a text, the first question to ask yourself is why it was produced. Hopefully the person who constructed the table had a clear rationale for producing that table out of all the possible tables which could have been produced, and tells us what that rationale is.

The main purpose of the contingency table is to highlight the possible existence of a relationship between variables which have categories. The relationship is described as an *association* or *dependence* between the variables. Two variables are said to be associated when the distribution of values on one variable, varies for values of the other variable. For example, consider the two variables of 'gender' and 'whether one voted' in Table 1. If responses on whether one voted differ according to the categories of gender (which they do, more women than men voted), then this is evidence that 'whether one voted' and gender are associated. If they do not differ then they are not associated, a situation which can also be described as independence between the variables.

We next may ask ourselves whether dependent and independent variables have been specified. In so far as the relationship can be understood in terms of causality, we designate one variable as the *dependent* variable and the other the *independent* variable. The convention in presenting a contingency table is that the independent variable is placed along the top as the column variable and that the dependent variable becomes the row variable. In Table 1, we are investigating whether gender 'causes' whether or not one voted (that is, that the values of 'whether voted' will depend upon gender), so gender goes across the top as the independent variable. (Note that it will not always be clear which of the two variables should be designated as dependent and independent.)

The table here is an example of a contingency table. It is the simplest example in that the two variables each have only two categories. This is called a 2 × 2 (two by two) contingency table. In this table a decision was made to display not just the counts in the four cells but also to present that data in terms of column

Table 1   *Whether one voted by gender*

		GENDER		
		Male	Female	TOTAL
WHETHER ONE VOTED	Yes	258	298	556
		57.3%	64.5%	61.0%
	No	192	164	356
		42.7%	35.5%	39.0%
TOTAL		450	462	912
		100.0%	100.0%	100.0%

percentages, which total to 100% down each column. This has an advantage in reading and interpreting the table since the number of cases in each column of the table are not the same. Given that column percentages are used, we read/compare across the categories of the column variable. The percentage allows us to see if the responses on 'whether one voted' vary according to gender; that is, if they appear to be dependent on gender. This is in fact the case; a greater percentage of women (64.5%) than men (57.3%) voted. We can conclude that in this particular example there is an association between gender and 'whether one voted'. When the data come from a sample we can test for the statistical significance of any association we find; that is, whether the association is also likely to be found in the whole population. (There are a large number of tests of statistical significance that can be used with contingency tables; the Chi-square (χ^2) test is the best known of these.)

Producing your own contingency tables

While contingency tables produced by others may not always be straightforward to read, when we produce our own tables we can enhance the clarity. The first thing to do is to decide the purpose of the table. Think about why you want to produce this table, with these particular variables, rather than a table with some other variables. It may be possible to think of a potentially causal relationship between two variables and this may be a reason for choosing them. With computer statistical packages it is all too easy to churn out endless contingency tables only to be overwhelmed by a mass of confusing printout.

After deciding on the particular variables consideration needs to be given to the choice of categories. We wish to avoid having too many categories as this may make the table difficult to read and may result in some cells that are empty or have low counts, which can cause problems for statistical analyses. Combining categories (through recoding) should be done in a thoughtful manner. Similar categories may be grouped together if in doing so we do not hide some interesting patterns. Where categories are combined the reader should be informed of this.

Having decided which variables and which categories to examine in a bivariate analysis, we must decide the format of the table. It is preferable to examine percentages rather than the cell counts. However, given that each cell count can be expressed in terms of a percentage of the row total, a column total or the overall total, a choice on percentaging needs to be made. Where the independent variable is the column variable, and we are interested in investigating association, we run the column percentages to 100%. In this case additional row and total percentages are superfluous and their inclusion will only make the table unnecessarily detailed and hard to read. The counts in the column marginals may be preserved so that we can see the totals upon which the percentages are based and can later recreate cell percentages in terms of the row marginals or the overall total if required.

Further interpretation of contingency tables

Having established that there is an association between the variables, we can proceed to examine the strength of that relationship. A comparison of the percentages found in different categories may reveal large differences which can provide an indication of a strong relationship. However care must be taken in doing this as it is affected by the way the table is percentaged. We can measure the strength precisely with an appropriate statistic of correlation or association.

With data at the ordinal level of measurement we can also specify the direction of the relationship, in terms of whether it is positive or negative. If low values on one variable tend to go with low values on the other and high values with high values, the relationship is described as *positive*. Conversely, if low values on one variable tend to go with high values on the other, the relationship is described as *negative*.

Contingency tables are usually more complex than the 2 × 2 example. They often have more than two variables and contain multiple categories of each. When there are more than two variables the variables are presented in layer format. This can make the options for percentaging quite complex and so we need to remain clear as to what our purpose is.

When there are more than two variables, say three, our purpose usually is to try to establish whether the bivariate relationship between the independent variable and the dependent variable holds for different categories of another variable. Essentially we are reproducing the bivariate contingency tables for the different categories of the third variable. If the pattern in each of these bivariate tables is *not* the same for the different categories of the third variable then this suggests that the third variable is having some effect of its own. The introduction of this control variable also allows us to investigate whether the association between the independent and dependent variable is spurious. Where there are complex relationships between three or more variables, it may be appropriate to move to more advanced techniques such as loglinear analysis.

Note

1 It is possible to display in a contingency table the association of variables at the interval or ratio level of measurement by combining the large number of individual values of those variables into a small number of categories, which then make up the rows and columns of the contingency table.

Suggested further reading

See also
Loglinear analysis.

De Vaus, D.A. (1996) *Surveys in Social Research*, 4th edn. London: UCL Press.

Frankfort-Nachmias, C. and Nachmias, D. (1996) *Research Methods in the Social Sciences*, 5th edn. London: St. Martin's Press.

RICHARD O'LEARY

Conversation Analysis

The discipline of conversation analysis first emerged in the early 1960s as result of a fusion of the traditions of interactionism and ethnomethodology and as such drew heavily on the observations of Harold Garfinkel and Erving Goffman. While conceptually ethnomethodological it developed its own distinctive approach, methodology and topics of interest, based largely on the pioneering work of Harvey Sacks and his associates, Gail Jefferson and Emanuel Schegloff.[1] Sacks believed that sociology could be a 'natural observational science', one that would be able to handle the details of actual events, 'formally and informatively' (Sacks, 1984). This is the context in which he began to work with tape-recorded conversations. The following extract helps to clarify his position:

> Such materials had a single virtue, that I could replay them. I could transcribe them somewhat and study them extendedly – however long it might take. It was not from any large interest in language or from some theoretical formulation of what should be studied that I started with tape-recorded conversations, but simply because I could get my hands on it and I could study it again and again, and also, consequentially, because others could look at what I had studied and make of it what they could, if, for example, they wanted to be able to disagree with me. (1984: 21–7)

The central goal of conversation analytic research, which is to describe and explicate 'the competences that ordinary speakers use and rely on in participating in intelligible, socially organised interaction' (Heritage and Atkinson, 1984: 1), clearly conforms to the ethnomethodological principles of locating and describing the methods and techniques that people use to produce and interpret social interaction. This represents a clear shift away from traditional sociological concerns. In fact it is somewhat paradoxical that while talk is fundamental to social interaction the focus of conventional sociology has been on the content of talk rather than the analysis of talk as a subject in itself. Conversation analysis redresses this imbalance to some extent, and by treating talk as a topic of inquiry in its own right, seeks to examine the structure and organisation underlying it.

Clearly conversation analysis represents a radical departure from the methods of social research traditionally adopted by social scientists. However this entails not just a rejection of the quantitative techniques associated with survey and experimental research but also those methods typically favoured by ethnographers. Although conversation analysis involves the qualitative analysis of naturally occurring data it differs from conventional field research in that it does not rely on the observer's notes and recall. The problem with traditional ethnography according to Psathas (1990: 9) is that because field notes are 'subject to all the vagaries of attention, memory, and recall' we cannot recover and re-examine the interactional phenomena themselves. By contrast, the employment of audio and video technology enables conversation analysts to examine systematically and repeatedly the raw data of conversational interaction in its original form. This also allows other researchers to have direct access to the data, making the analysis subject to more detailed public scrutiny (Atkinson and Heritage, 1984: 238).

Those working within the conversation analytic tradition insist upon the use of 'naturally occurring' conversations as it is only through the systematic examination of actual talk that we can uncover the fine-grained minute details of conversational interaction. If we wish to illuminate the methods and procedures which conversationalists employ then we need to have access to their 'language-in-use'. Hence, there is a strong emphasis within conversation analysis on what actually takes place during ordinary talk rather than analysts' interpretations or reconstructions of what goes on. In direct contrast to 'official' linguists, who often create artificial material in order to overcome the problems associated with the apparently disorderly nature of real-life talk, those working within the conversation analytic tradition have demonstrated clearly that conversation is extremely orderly and rule-governed. Moreover, this orderliness is produced by the participants themselves, 'making sense of what one another said or did, and fitting their utterances appropriately to their understandings' (Drew, 1990: 29). Heritage and Atkinson (1984: 5), in their critique of speech act theory in linguistics, go to the very heart of conversation analysis when they state that 'it is sequences and turns within sequences, rather than isolated sentences or utterances, that have become the primary unit of analysis'.

This interest in the sequential organisation of interaction has produced a substantial and cumulative body of work which has helped to uncover the fundamental structures of talk-in-interaction. The initial concern was to describe and explicate the basic organisational features of ordinary conversation, such as the 'turn-taking system', 'adjacency pairs', 'preference organisation' and 'repair'. Subsequent research has steadily built upon these foundational studies and one area where this approach has made a particularly significant contribution is that of 'institutional interaction'.[2]

While the study of social interaction in the workplace is not new to the discipline of sociology there has been a recent burgeoning of research which sets out to examine the structures of interaction in institutional and work settings explicitly from a conversation analytic perspective. Many of these studies have contributed to the comparative and cumulative nature of conversation analysis by examining institutional discourse in relation to ordinary conversation and describing the specific patterns of interaction that take place within institutions. In effect, the findings regarding the organisation of mundane conversation have been used as 'a kind of benchmark against which other more formal or "institutional" types of interaction are recognised and experienced' (Drew and Heritage, 1992: 19). For example, some of the early studies, using Sacks et al.'s (1978) study as a point of departure, focused on such features as the specialised forms of turn-taking that operate within particular institutions and occupations (for schools see Mehan, 1979, 1985, McHoul, 1978; for courts see Atkinson and Drew, 1979, Maynard, 1984; for news interviews see Greatbatch, 1988, Clayman, 1988).

More recently, however, 'institutional' research within conversation analysis has seen this narrow focus on the formal mechanisms of alternative speech exchange systems replaced by a much broader and more diverse range of interests. While some of the data has been collected in designated physical settings, such as schools and courtrooms, other interaction has taken place within the home, emphasising the point that the institutionality of an interaction is not determined by its setting. For example, whereas the institutional activities of doctors, health visitors or market researchers may take place within the home environment, participants based in the workplace may switch between ordinary conversation and task-related institutional talk. As Drew and Heritage (1992: 3–4) point out 'interaction is institutional insofar as participants' institutional or professional identities are somehow made relevant to the work activities in which they are engaged'.

The last decade has witnessed an enormous upsurge in conversation analytic research and rather than attempt to summarise this diverse body of work it may be more profitable to turn our attention to the more practical aspect, data transcription.

Data transcription

As the emphasis in CA is on the structure rather than the content of talk, the transcription system used by researchers in this field is fundamentally different from that associated with other forms of data analysis. Like all transcription systems it is inevitably selective, and the main concern has been to capture the sequential features of talk-in-interaction. The development of such a system has emerged progressively over the last three decades, primarily through the efforts of Gail Jefferson.

Transcription not only makes the data more amenable for analysis, but also represents an important stage in the analytic process itself. Indeed it is through the process of transcribing the data that the analyst begins to apprehend the under-lying structural and organisational characteristics of the interaction. Fundamental as this process may be, it is nevertheless important to remember that it is the original recordings that constitute the data. The transcripts merely facilitate the process of analysis and serve to make the findings available to a wider audience. Moreover, as Paul ten Have (1999: 77) points out, they are 'selective "theory-laden" renderings of certain aspects of what the tape has preserved of the original interaction, produced with a particular purpose in mind, by this particular transcriptionist, with his or her special abilities and limitations'. In practice, therefore, most analysts tend to work with the recordings and the transcriptions alongside one another.

Many studies, particularly in the early years, focused on telephone conversations as this type of interaction has a number of inbuilt benefits for the analyst. Not only do telephone recordings provide complete conversational episodes, but they also allow the analyst to control out the various nonverbal behaviours that are an integral part of face-to-face interaction. As telephone communication is limited to sounds, analysts are able to focus exclusively on the most basic elements of talk-in-interaction. Moreover, since telephone talk usually involves only two speakers, attention is focused on what is 'specifically dialogic in conversation: how speech action emerges across speaker turns' (Hopper, 1992: 9).

For the uninitiated, the Jeffersonian transcription system can appear opaque and disconcerting. Pauses, silences, overlaps, laughter applause, tone and volume are just some of the features that are transcribed in an attempt to capture not only the content of the talk, but also the way in which it is produced. The key features of a recording are rarely apparent on the first hearing and the analytic process therefore involves repeated listening to the original tape recordings in order to become familiar with the complexities of the interaction.

The emergence of relatively cheap video-recording technology has enabled researchers to incorporate non-verbal behaviours into their analysis. While this form of CA is growing, visual data generally has been used to supplement audio analysis. A nonverbal notation system has been developed and the strategy usually adopted involves adding the relevant non-verbal information (direction of gaze, posture, pointing and so on) to the audio transcriptions.

While CA emerged as the result of an attempt by Sacks and his colleagues to create an alternative to traditional forms of sociological enquiry, it has since developed into a truly interdisciplinary endeavour. This is evidenced not merely by the diversity of topics currently examined using a CA framework, but also by the extent to which the concepts and ideas developed by Harvey Sacks have permeated a variety of other subject areas.

Notes

1 Psathas (1995: 3–8) provides an interesting and succinct account of some of the key influences and developments that paved the way for the emergence of conversation analysis as a distinct theoretical and methodological approach.
2 See Drew and Heritage (1990: 21–5; 59) for clarification on how the term 'institutional interaction' is employed within conversation analysis.

Suggested further reading

Hutchby, I. and Wooffitt R. (1998) *Conversation Analysis*. Cambridge: Polity.

References

Atkinson, J.M. and Drew, P. (1979) *Order in Court: The Organisation of Verbal Interaction in Judicial Settings*. London, UK: Macmillan Press and Atlantic Highlands, NJ: Humanities Press.

Atkinson, J.M. and Heritage, J.C. (eds) (1984) *Structures of Social Action: Studies in Conversation Analysis*. Cambridge: University of Cambridge.

Clayman, S. (1988) 'Displaying Neutrality in Television News Interviews', *Social Problems*, 35: 474–92.

Drew, P. (1990) 'Conversation Analysis: Who Needs It?', *Text*, 10 (1/2): 27–35.

Drew, P. and Heritage, J.C. (1992) *Talk at Work*. Cambridge: Cambridge University Press.

Greatbatch, D. (1988) 'A Turn-taking System for British News Interviews', *Language in Society*, 17, 401–30.

Have, P. ten (1999) *Doing Conversation Analysis: a Practical Guide*. London: Sage.

Heritage, J.C. and Atkinson, J.M. (1984) 'Introduction', in J.M. Atkinson and J.C. Heritage (eds), *Order in Court: The Organisation of Verbal Interaction in Judicial Settings*. London, UK: Macmillan Press and Atlantic Highlands, NJ: Humanities Press. (1984). pp. 1–15.

Maynard, D.W. (1984) *Inside Plea Bargaining: The Language of Negotiation*. New York, NY: Plenum.

McHoul, A.W. (1978) 'The Organization of Turns at Formal Talk in the Classroom', *Language in Society*, 7: 183–213.

Mehan, H. (1979) *Learning Lessons: Social Organization in the Classroom*. Cambridge, MA: Harvard University Press.

Mehan, H. (1985) 'The Structure of Classroom Discourse', in T. Van Dijk (ed.), *Handbook of Discourse Analysis, Vol. 3: Discourse and Dialogue*. London, UK: Academic Press. pp. 120–31.

Psathas, G. (ed.) (1990) *Interaction Competence*. Washington, DC: University Press of America.

Psathas, G. (1995) *Conversation Analysis*. Thousand Oaks, CA: Sage.

Sacks, H. (1984) 'Notes on Methodology', in J.M. Atkinson and J.C. Heritage (eds), *Order in Court: The Organisation of Verbal Interaction in Judicial Settings*. London, UK: Macmillan Press and Atlantic Highlands, NJ: Humanities Press. pp. 21–7.

Sacks, H., Schegloff, E.A. and Jefferson, G. (1978) 'A Simplest Systematics for the Organization of Turn-taking in Conversation', in J. Schenkein (ed.), *Studies in the Organization of Conversational Interaction*. New York: Academic Press. pp. 7–55.

> **See also**
> **Ethnomethodo-**
> **logy**.

CIARAN ACTON

Correlation and regression

Correlation

Correlation is concerned with the association between variables. The general term is most commonly applied to investigations where the variables are at the interval or ratio level of measurement, and it is this application which is discussed here.

When investigating the association between two variables at the interval/ratio level of measurement, we should begin by plotting the values of one variable against the other. This graph is known as a *scattergram* or *scatterplot*. It is helpful to do this before we proceed to examine correlation. From the scattergram we can get some indication of the type of relationship. If the data points of one variable plotted against the other tend to gather around what could be imagined as approximately a straight line, then we can say that there is an indication of a linear relationship between the variables. Other types of relationship, such as a curvilinear relationship where the relationship can be depicted by a curved rather than straight line, may be seen. Of course, it may be that there is no relationship between the variables; in which case no clear pattern will be visible.

Where we can observe a linear relationship we use a measure of correlation which is suitable for that situation; the best known being Pearson's Product-Moment Correlation Coefficient, also known as Pearson's r. Visually, Pearson's r can be thought of as the straight line that, if it were drawn onto the scattergram, would come closest to representing all the data points of one variable plotted against another variable.

With Pearson's r statistic we can determine whether the apparent linear association visible in the scattergram is likely to exist in the population from which the sample of data points is drawn. Pearson's r can give us a precise measurement of the strength of the association and it reports the direction of that relationship.

The strength of the correlation is captured by the size of the correlation coefficient on a scale from −1.00 through 0.00 to +1.00. If the data points in the scattergram tend to be close to the envisaged straight line, this suggests a higher correlation and will produce a larger correlation coefficient. (However, a low correlation score does not in itself indicate that there is no relationship between the two variables as they could have a non-linear relationship or a weak, but genuine, relationship.) In the social sciences we do not often find correlation scores which are close to the top of the scale.

A positive or negative sign is reported with the correlation coefficient to show the direction of the relationship. By this is meant the direction of the plotted data points. If low values on one variable tend to go with low values on the other and high values with high values, the relationship is described as *positive*. In the scattergram this will appear as a clustered line of data points from bottom left to top right. Where an increase in one variable goes with a decrease in the other variable, a negative relationship is implied. Note that a strong relationship between two variables can be either positive or negative; for instance, a correlation of –0.675 is just as strong as a correlation of +0.675.

Correlation matrix

In correlation we are reporting on bivariate relationships, that is, relationships between two variables. We can report in a single table the results of many correlations between multiple pairs of variables. This square table is known as a correlation matrix and is illustrated below:

A correlation matrix

	Variable 1	Variable 2	Variable 3
Variable 1	1.00	0.65	0.22
Variable 2	0.65	1.00	-0.09
Variable 3	0.22	-0.09	1.00

While this is a convenient form of presentation, there are some potentially confusing features. Given the format, the central diagonal is redundant as it simply reports each variable correlated with itself (showing a perfect correlation of 1.00). Furthermore, the top right triangle will be a mirror image of the bottom left.

Regression

If there is a high correlation between two variables, then knowing the values of one variable is useful as it can help us to estimate values of the other. However, this does not imply that there is necessarily a causal relationship between them. Where we think there is causation we may proceed to use *regression*. The elementary type of regression, known as linear regression, is a clear development of correlation. We are still looking at the relationship between two variables, both of which are at the interval/ratio level of measurement. Again, regression depends on there being a linear relationship between the two variables. Our focus is on calculating the straight line which 'best fits' the data points in the scattergram and provides a summary of the relationship between the two variables. It envisages a relationship of causation so it is necessary to describe one variable as the independent (causal) variable and the other as the dependent ('caused') variable. Causation requires that the independent variable precedes in time the dependent variable. For causation we should also try to rule out the possibility that the association can be attributed to some third variable.

A main application of regression is prediction. Once we have calculated our 'best fitting' line and the equation which summarises the relationship between the independent and dependent variable, we may use values of the independent variable to predict values of the dependent variable. For example, we might try to predict the annual income of managers by their age.

The relationship between the two variables can be presented visually in a scattergram showing the 'best fitting' line and mathematically with the equation which describes that line. First, lets look at the visual representation.

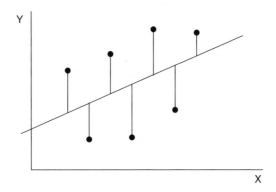

The spread of observations or data points in the scattergram indicates that the values of Y vary in a straight line with the values of X. The 'best fitted' line is the one which minimises the vertical distances from all the data points to that line. The differences between the actual observed data points and the predicted points that would fall on the regression line also are referred to as the *residuals* or errors of the cases. The best fitting line will have the smallest sum of squared residuals.[1] The method is sometimes referred to as Ordinary Least Squares Regression.

Graphically the line has a slope (called b), and an intercept (a point called a) where the line intercepts the vertical or Y axis. The slope will be steeper if the dependent variable increases (or decreases) sharply with the independent variable. Once we have fitted a regression line, then that line predicts the values of the dependent variable (Y) for values of the independent variable (X). The line is described by the following mathematical equation:

$$Y = a + bX + e$$

Y is the dependent variable and X is the independent variable. Mathematically, 'a' (the 'Y intercept') is the value of Y when X is zero (substantively, this may not be meaningful). The slope of the line is represented by the regression coefficient 'b'. It will be preceded by a positive sign if the direction of the relationship is positive (visually the line will run from bottom left to top right) and by a negative sign if the direction of the relationship is negative (visually the line will run from top left to bottom right). A steeper slope will mean a larger value of the coefficient, b, and represents the rate at which changes in X produce changes in Y. The letter e refers to what we call an 'error term'. This reflects the fact that even the 'best fitted' line will not be a perfect fit to the data and that our independent variable does not explain all the variance in the dependent variable.

This equation is also what we use for prediction. This is one of the major attractions of regression. Once we have calculated 'b' and 'a' we can insert new values of the independent variable X (for which we do not have data) into the equation in order to predict values of the dependent variable Y.

For example, if we had data on the years of education and the income of a sample of managers, a regression of income (Y) on years of education (X) might produce the following result:

$$Y = 10,498 + 2,044X$$

The equation would tell us that there is a positive relationship between education and income so that, on average, for each extra year of schooling, managers' income would be predicted to rise by 2,044. If a manager hypothetically had no education, the equation would predict an income of 10,498. (This of course is nonsensical since all managers would be expected to have at least some schooling. Here, the 'a' of 10,498 can be better thought of as an indication of the general level of managers' incomes.) Finally, regarding prediction, if a manager was newly appointed who had, for instance, 14 years of education, the equation would predict his/her income to be 39,114 ($Y = 10,498 + 2,044(14)$).

Regression output

When we use a computer statistical package to do regression, we get a considerable amount of output, some of which is in the form of an ANOVA table. It will include some tests of statistical significance. The main parts of the output to inspect are those we have already discussed. The output will show a value for the intercept, 'a', also known as the constant. It will show a value for the regression coefficient 'b'. We need these to write our regression equation. The regression coefficient 'b' is also presented in a standardised form (see Z-scores in **Dispersion** and **Standardisation**). Standardised coefficients range between −1.00 to +1.00 in a similar way to a correlation cofficient. They are needed when you are trying to compare two different independent X variables that are on radically different scales (for instance, an X variable like years of education where the values range from about 6 up to no more than 24 years with another X variable like 'days out of work' which could range from 0 up to hundreds or even thousands of days). The output will include a correlation coefficient (called R here) measuring how closely the data points fit the regression line. The output also will display a summary measure (R squared) giving the proportion of variance in the dependent variable that can be accounted for by the independent variable. This provides some indication of how well the equation works.

Some statistical assumptions are made when applying linear regression that are similar to those for correlation and the user needs to be satisfied that these assumptions are met. There must be an underlying linear relationship between the two variables. It is also assumed that the spread of data points about the regression line is fairly regular (that is, the residuals should be normally distributed).

It is possible to use two or more independent variables in a regression equation; this is called *multiple regression*. The formula and results follow the same format, only each independent X variable will have its own 'b' coefficient which is a measure of its unique effect upon the dependent variable Y. (For instance, our 'income of managers' analysis could be expanded to include the effect of 'years employed by the firm' as well as 'years of education' – managers who had worked longer for the firm could be expected to earn more without regard to their years of education.)

With two or more independent variables high correlations may occur among them. This is referred to as multicollinearity and can cause problems in a regression analysis because it may be difficult to establish how much of the effect on the dependent variable should be attributed to each of the independent variables. There is debate about how high the correlations between the independent variables need to be before their occurrence should give rise to concern. When multiple regression is being used and multicollinearity exists between two or more of the independent variables, the results of the regression need to be interpreted with some caution.

Note

1 Since some of the residuals are above the line and others below, they have plus and minus signs, and they would cancel each other out when added up unless we first square them.

Suggested further reading

Agresti, A. and Finlay, B. (1997) *Statistical Methods for the Social Science.* London: Prentice Hall.

Clegg, F. (1982) *Simple Statistics.* Cambridge: Cambridge University Press.

RICHARD O'LEARY

Critical theory

The essence of critical theory lies in its interest in the ways people think and act and how social circumstances influence those thoughts and actions. The way these problems are approached owes much to the long tradition of German philosophy in which the main critical theorists were and are deeply immersed.

The epithet 'critical' is taken from the work of Immanuel Kant (1724–1804) who argued that, rather than taking our reason and knowledge for granted, we can only gain understanding through critical engagement with the conditions that make such reason and knowledge possible. From G.W.F. Hegel (1770–1831), critical theorists took the notion that critical analysis, by eradicating superstitions and distortions in knowledge, can enable us to move towards an authentic knowledge of reality. From Karl Marx (1818–83) were taken two main ideas. First, an acceptance of the crucial influence of socio-economic relations over the way people think about and approach the world in any given society. Thus, those socio-economic relations became the focus of critical thought. Second, his critique of capitalism that saw it as an unequal and exploitative form of social relations. Those exploitative social relations in turn have alienating consequences upon the thoughts and actions of those subjected to them. To pull all this together, the aim of critical theory is to look beneath the surface of knowledge and reason (Kant), in order to see how they are distorted in an exploitative society (Marx), and thus show the possibility of less distorted forms (Hegel).

This core approach of critical theory can be seen clearly in Horkheimer and Adorno's seminal work, *The Dialectic of the Enlightenment* (1978 [1947]), which involved a sustained critique of the cultural ideology of modernity. The narrow focus of their book involved an attempt to explain why, contrary to traditional Marxist prognostications, proletarian revolution had failed to materialise in advanced capitalist societies. They argued that this was because the working class to a large extent had been integrated into the culture of capitalism by means of a powerful 'cultural industry': 'The flood of detailed information and candy-floss entertainment simultaneously instructs and stultifies mankind' (Horkheimer and Adorno, 1978: xv). Here we can see how critical theory moves beyond the economism of vulgar Marxism in order to assert the importance of culture and ideology in the maintenance of social relations. The broader focus of *The Dialectic of the Enlightenment* involved a critique of the entire Enlightenment project, and its paradigmatic tool, science. Rather than being used to understand the world as fully as possible, Horkheimer and Adorno argued that science had been reduced to a tool of technology, the purpose of which was to manipulate and control both nature and society.

Critical theory reached the apotheosis of its popular appeal in the 1960s, primarily through the work of Herbert Marcuse (1898–1879). Marcuse argued that in capitalism, social relations, rather than involving human expressions of love and friendship, simply become part of the capitalist commodity market. As a result, the human condition becomes that of *One Dimensional Man* (Marcuse, 1964). While Marcuse accepted the Marxist theory that the alienation of the human spirit was caused by capitalism, he argued that it would not be possible to overcome that alienation without the development of a critical free consciousness amongst those who were oppressed by capitalism. Thus, he argued that an adequate understanding of society should be based on a synthesis of Marxism and *phenomenology*. Marxism could be used as a basis for examining wider social and historical forces, and how those forces affected the human condition, while phenomenology could provide a method for understanding lived experience and how that experience could transcend the constraints imposed by an alienating culture.

The most influential contemporary critical theorist is Jürgen Habermas (1929–). Once again, Habermas' critical focus is on the type of consciousness generated by modern social relations. Here, a major influence is the work of Max Weber (1864–1920), who argued that capitalism had bequeathed upon us a certain type of thinking and acting, which he termed 'purposive-rational action' (1968). This involves simply working out the most efficient way of attaining a certain end. What that end is, is of no moral concern. In other words, purposive-rational action is based upon technical rather than ethical considerations. To take an extreme example, the gas chambers of the Holocaust could be seen as instances of purposive rationality, in that they were technically efficient means of exterminating those that the Nazis believed should be exterminated. This of course has nothing to do with the value rationality that we may apply to doctrines of genocide. For Weber, the 'pure utilitarianism' of purposive rationality was the 'iron cage' within which capitalism had imprisoned us. In modernity, the powerful technical means that have been developed have blinded us to any sort of worthwhile end that we might consider.

Habermas accepts Weber's notion of the iron cage, arguing that with the subsequent development of capitalism since the time of Weber's writings, the grip of what he calls 'technocratic consciousness' (Habermas, 1971) has become ever tighter. However, Habermas is less fatalistic that Weber and, in large part, his aim is to develop an escape route from the iron cage. For Habermas, the key to this escape route is the manner in which we communicate to each other. Through the structure of communication 'autonomy and responsibility are posited for us' (1972: 314). Thus, he comes to see human freedom as the ability to communicate with each other using the power of the argument rather than the power of the person, as the tool of persuasion. This, he asserts, should be the value rationality that we use to govern our actions. Habermas does not dismiss purposive rationality, but argues that, rather than governing our decision making, it should only be the means to ends developed through 'communicative action', where 'the actions of the agents involved are coordinated not through egocentric calculations of success but through acts of reaching understanding' (1984: 285).

As can be seen from the brief synopses above, critical theory tends to involve high theorising about society and how it impinges upon the ways we think and act. What pertinence, one might ask, does all this have for the practical social researcher? There are at least two approaches that may be taken here, one formal and one substantive.

In terms of formal issues, critical theorists had harsh things to say about the practices of 'traditional' social scientists who adhered to *positivism*. They attacked the assumption that society could be studied in ways similar to the ways nature can be studied. For critical theorists, this involved giving structures too great a causal power and hence denying the possibility that things could be changed by means of social action: 'Social study was to be a science seeking social laws, the validity of which was to be analogous to that of physical laws. Social practice, especially the matter of changing the social system, was herewith throttled by the inexorable' (Marcuse, 1964: 343). Thus, despite its pretensions to value-neutral social science, positivism was in fact an inherently reactionary position. While positivism may now be a straw person, the wider, and still pertinent, issue here is critical theory's assertion that social research will always be animated by values – that it is impossible to conduct value-free social research. It is therefore incumbent upon social researchers to clarify and explicate the values under which they are labouring. Not to do so leads to the danger of the social researcher being complicit in technocratic manipulation, and worse still, hiding that manipulation under the cloak of scientific neutrality.

Related to this is the critique of 'fact gathering' social research. For critical theorists, it is not enough to simply discover and record social behaviour. For social research to be useful, the further stage of explaining that behaviour in terms of socio-economic and cultural context is essential. This is not to say that this context will determine behaviour, the promise of critical theory is that people are not mindless dupes and are capable, given the right circumstances, of developing strategies of resistance when faced with exploitative circumstances. Once again, we can see the central theme of critical theory that research is a political activity, working either for or against the status quo.

In relation to substantive research, there is an increasing volume of work that uses the ideas of Habermas as its foundation. An early and influential example of this was a study by Eliot Mishler (1984) of interaction between physicians and patients. Mishler noted that communication between them was distorted by considerable power differentials, which were embedded in different views of the world. The 'voice of medicine' was one of purposive rationality, which regarded events in patients' lives as technical issues, decontextualised from particular personal or social troubles. In interactions, physicians sought to impose this technocentric interpretation upon patients. They did this by dominating communication, and undermining patients' self-understanding of the problems that they were experiencing. Mishler concluded from his evidence that the achievement of human care depends upon the empowerment of the voice of the patient.

It can be seen from this example how it is possible for empirical social researchers to use critical theory as a basis for uncovering social inequality at the micro-level of one-to-one interaction. This sort of operationalisation of critical theory, which allows for the uncovering of power at the point at which it is exercised, has the benefit of bringing critical theory down from the rarefied atmosphere of high theory to a point where it can help explain the dynamics of day-to-day life.

References

Habermas, J. (1971) *Towards a Rational Society*. London: Heinemann.

Habermas, J. (1972) *Knowledge and Human Interests*. London: Heinemann.

Habermas, J. (1984) *The Theory of Communicative Action, Vol. I: The Critique of Functionalist Reason*. London: Heinemann.

Horkheimer, M. and Adorno, T. (1978 [1947]) *The Dialectic of the Enlightenment*. London: Allen Lane.

Marcuse, H. (1964) *One Dimensional Man*. London: Routledge and Kegan Paul.

Mishler, E. (1984) *The Discourse of Medicine: Dialectics of Medical Interviews*. Norwood, NJ: Ablex.

SAM PORTER

Crosstabulation

See **Contingency tables**.

Cultural analysis

The adoption of a cultural analysis paradigm or perspective presupposes a belief in the explanatory power of culture and cultural activity. That is, it places considerable importance on the meaningfulness of the production and reproduction of culture and cultural artefacts in the course of everyday human social life.

In 1965 Mark Abrahms characterised the social scientific research process as involving three interlinked levels:

(1) the definition and conceptualisation of 'the problem'
(2) the design of research strategies for 'attacking' that particular problem
(3) the pursuit of these strategies in the most efficient ways (Abrahm's evidence to the Heyworth Committee cited in King (1987: 14)).

The term cultural analysis may be used to designate a conceptual perspective which influences both the definition and conceptualisation of the research problem (Abrahm's level 1) and the design of strategies for 'attacking' the problem (level 2) but does not predetermine choice of the most efficient or effective techniques for pursuing that strategy (level 3).

In the 1950s, Kluckholn and Parsons agreed that the term culture should be restricted to transmitted and created content and patterns of values, ideas and other symbolic-meaningful systems, and that its study was the preserve of social anthropologists (Kuper, 2000: 14–15). On the other hand, they proposed that 'society and social system' should be used to designate the specifically relational system of interaction among individuals and collectivities. Parsons later introduced further distinctions between expressive culture, cognitive culture and values and norms. Schneider subsequently and influentially argued that culture excluded norms. Culture being a system of symbols whereas norms are prescriptions for action.

Adam Kuper concludes his position on cultural analysis as follows:

> Believing, with Max Weber, that 'man' is an animal suspended in webs of significance he himself has spun, I take culture [to be] those webs, and the analysis of it is therefore not an experimental science in search of [universal laws] but an interpretative one in search of meaning. It is explication I am after, construing social expressions on their surface [as] enigmatical. (Kuper, 2000: 98)

While such a perspective is logically compatible with a considerable range of research methods and techniques, the focus on culture and on the production and attribution of meaning and processes of signification almost inevitably pulls practitioners towards that group of methods and techniques loosely known as qualitative. In the early twentieth century, culture was regarded by some in the social scientific community as a concept of enormous, almost limitless, scientific promise. 'In explanatory importance and in generality of application it is comparable to such categories as gravity in physics, disease in medicine, evolution in biology' (Kuper, 2000). In contemporary times, however, such enthusiasm for the explanatory power of culture has become more muted and the scholarly consensus is much more that,

> appeals to culture can offer only a partial explanation of why people think and behave as they do, and of what causes them to alter their ways. Political and economic forces, social institutions, and biological processes cannot be wished away, or assimilated to systems of knowledge and belief. And that . . . is the ultimate stumbling block in the way of cultural theory, certainly given its current pretensions. (Kuper, 2000: xi)

While cultural analysis is no longer antithetical to the study of social structures and institutions, cultural analysts are drawn towards analysis of the ways in which humans socially, consciously and unconsciously, construct and understand their lived experiences of social structures (that is, a Kluckhonian approach to social structure).

The key role of language in both expressing and creating culture and meaning, including deep levels of grammar and syntax and modes of thinking, means that many cultural analyses employ research techniques developed specifically to study language and its use, for example, discourse and content analysis (see their entries in this volume).

However, important as language is, it is by no means the only expression, still less the only creator, of human culture. A cultural analysis may involve use of a wide range of research techniques in order to study such diverse expressions of culture as human dress, body decoration and clothing, and the form and content of other types of material culture from packaging, to consciously 'artistic' products, to technologies such as modes of transportation.

This is because, once created and used by humans, all material objects in a given social and historical context, 'carry' culture and are liable to use in the further production and recreation of culture. Cultural analysis places at the foreground of social research issues of signification in social life, whether such signification occurs through the use of language or the use of material objects.

Two principle post 1950 approaches to cultural analysis can be identified.

Interpretivism

> The first recommended the sympathetic exploration of a native worldview, its translation and interpretation. Weber's name was evoked, the word *Verstehen* pronounced reverently, if not always accurately. Geertz chose this course, which he identified initially as Parsonian, then as Weberian, and later as a form of hermeneutics. (Kuper, 2000: 1)

The Geertzians were consistently dismissive of any suggestion that there could be a science of culture. Culture was indeed rather like language, but their preferred model of, or analogy for, culture was the text. Accordingly they drew upon literary theory rather than linguistics. It was this approach that prospered, and interpretivism became the orthodoxy in mainstream American cultural anthropology. Culture may be a text, but it is a fabricated text, a fiction written by the ethnographer. The clear message of deconstruction is that texts do not yield unequivocal messages. Postmodern anthropologists prefer to imagine the realm of culture as something more like an unruly democracy than a theocratic state or absolutist monarchy. Uneasy about the totalitarian overtones of the term *culture*, some even prefer to write about habitus, ideology or discourse. Whichever term is used, the assumption remains that people live in a world of symbols dominated by processes of signification. Actors are driven and history is shaped by . . . ideas (Kuper, 2000: 19).

Universalism

The alternative, now little used, approach was, in contrast, scientific, reductionist, generalising. It began with the premise that culture – a symbolic discourse – was very like language, and accordingly the study of culture should follow the path that was being blazed by modern linguistics, and like it seek to discover universal laws (Kuper, 2000: 17).

The Geerztian deconstructivist approach to cultural analysis prefigured the development of postmodernism in the social sciences by some three decades and effectively stamped out the universalist approaches to cultural analysis.

Suggested further reading

Collins, C. (1999) 'Applying Bakhtin in Urban Studies: the Failure of Community Participation in the Fergushie Park Partnership', *Urban Studies*, 36 (1): 73–90. An unusual example of cultural analysis in the field of Urban and Policy Studies, although the example is restricted to examination of signification through the use of language.

Hebdige, D. (1979) *Subculture: the Meaning of Style*. London: Methuen. A good British example of a deconstructivist approach to cultural analysis, focusing on culture as a way of forming collective identities through an analysis of the social life, and cultural forms of punk.

References

King, D. (1987) 'Creating a Funding Regime for Social Research in Britain'. The Heyworth Committee on Social Studies and the Founding of the Social Science Research Council, *Minerva*, 35: 1–26.

Kuper, A. (2000) *Culture: the Anthropologists' Account*. London: Harvard University Press.

EITHNE MCLAUGHLIN

D

Data archives

At its simplest level, a data archive is a 'library' of datasets, which makes previously-collected data available for use by other researchers – secondary analysis. For most secondary analysts, their first port of call is a data archive.

Hakim (1982) outlines three main functions of a data archive:

- The preservation and storage of data
- The dissemination of data
- The development of methods and procedures to stimulate the widest use of data.

The type of data lodged in different archives can vary in many ways, although all are computer-readable. Archives can specialise in a specific topic area, such as the National Data Archive on Child Abuse and Neglect, at Cornell University (http://www.ndacan.cornell.edu/). Archives can operate at different geographic levels and so can be at regional, state or national centres. Some operate at international level, for example, the Council for European Social Science Data Archives (CESSDA) (www.nsd.uib.no/Cessda) facilitates access to the catalogues of ten national archives across the world via their Integrated Data Catalogue.

Some of the datasets lodged in archives were collected specifically for a one-off research project. Other datasets are collected regularly and routinely by government departments, mostly to inform social policy; for example, the General Household Survey conducted by the Office for National Statistics in Britain. This survey is carried out for a number of government departments for planning and policy purposes, as well as to monitor progress towards achieving targets. Data are collected annually on housing, employment, education, health, and family information for approximately 9,000 British households.

The main advantage of archiving data is that datasets, which have been extremely costly and time consuming to create, are conserved and available to other users. In the United Kingdom, the Economic and Social Research Council (ESRC) requires all their award holders to deposit all machine readable datasets with the UK Data Archive. In this way, other researchers have access to this raw data, and can undertake analysis themselves, adding use value to the dataset.

When lodging a dataset, the depositor needs to provide full documentation for the archive. This generally includes questionnaires, an account of fieldwork and research design, information on sampling methodology and sampling errors, plus a list of any publications that have arisen from analysis of the data. Such information constitutes *metadata*, which is basically data about data. Complete metadata is necessary to allow the accurate archiving and dissemination of datasets. The significance of data archives for social research can be demonstrated by the following descriptions of just a few of the many archives throughout the world.

UK Data Archive

The United Kingdom Data Archive is based at the University of Essex, and is a national archive for social science and humanities data. Data is acquired from the academic, commercial and public sectors. However, the most widely requested datasets originate from UK government departments and are regular, multi-faceted, national surveys such as the annual General Household Survey and the quarterly Labour Force Survey. The Archive does not own the data, but holds and distributes them using licences signed by data owners. The UK Data Archive website (http://www.data-archive.ac.uk) provides various methods of searching for information, such as the BIRON catalogue search facility, as well as full descriptions and documentation of datasets, and facilities for ordering data and documentation.

As well as archiving quantitative datasets, the UK Data Archive is involved in a series of other intiatives. The Flexible Access to Statistics, Tables and Electronic Resources project (FASTER) is developing a flexible tool to allow access to official and other statistical data, and takes advantage of recent developments in metadata, and web security. The Archive is also involved in improving access to the Collection of Historical and Contemporary Census (CHCC) Data and Related Materials, as well as developing learning and teaching resources. Qualidata is an archive of qualitative data, especially those related to oral history, in-depth interview studies in sociology and anthropology. Qualidata has preserved a range of important qualitative studies which were in danger of being lost and promotes the importance of qualitative data more generally.

Central Archive for Empirical Social Research

The Central Archive for Empirical Social Research is located at the University of Cologne, and is the German data archive for survey data. This archive also holds data from international studies and on twelve specific topic areas. The Central Archive is the official archive for the International Social Survey Programme (ISSP). Within this programme, the same module of questions on an important social science topic is fielded annually in over thirty countries worldwide. The Central Archive provides access to the data from individual countries, as well as to a merged datafile, which combines data from all participating countries for each year. The English language version of the website can be found at http://www.gesis.org/en/za/index.htm.

Inter-University Consortium for Political and Social Research

The Inter-University Consortium for Political and Social Research (ICPSR), at the University of Michigan, was established in 1962. ICPSR (http://www.icpsr.umich.

edu/) provides access to a large archive of social science data. At present, the ICPSR catalogue contains nearly 5,000 titles and over 45,000 individual files. ICPSR consists of over 400 member colleges and universities around the world, and is also involved in special topic archives that focus on specific subject areas. These include the Health and Medical Care Archive, the International Archive of Education Data and the National Archive of Criminal Justice Data.

Accessing data

Traditionally, users interested in acquiring a dataset applied to the relevant archive, who then sent them the dataset on magnetic tape, floppy disk or CD, or via File Transfer Protocol (FTP). However more recent developments, especially those in web technology, have added new methods of data access. In particular, users can now use an archive's website to access particular tables, or to download the data directly onto their personal computer.

NESSTAR is one such resource for disseminating via the Internet. This project was funded by the European Union's Information Engineering Programme, and is a partnership between the UK Data Archive, the Norwegian Social Science Data Serve and the Danish Data Archive. NESSTAR allows archives to provide on-line services, such as the facility to browse information about the data sources, undertake simple data analysis and visualisation over the web, or download the data.

NESSTAR makes use of developments from the Data Documentation Initiative (DDI). This initiative aims to establish international standards and methodology for the content, presentation, transport and preservation of metadata about datasets. Using developments from DDI, metadata can now be created with a uniform structure that is easily and precisely searched. Multiple datasets can also be searched. In fact, NESSTAR server software is likely to become the replacement for the CESSDA Integrated Data Catalogue referred to above.

As well as archiving and disseminating data, archives are involved in other activities promoting the use of new initiatives, such as the application of DDI to archiving quantitative and qualitative data. Many archives hold workshops on quantitative methods, thus facilitating secondary analysis of their data holdings.

Suggested further reading

See also
Secondary data analysis and **Secondary analysis of qualitative data**.

Hakim, Catherine (1982) *Secondary Analysis in Social Research: a Guide to Data Sources and Methods with Examples.* (Contemporary Social Research: 5.) London: George Allen & Unwin.

Kiecolt, K. Jill and Nathan, Laura E. (1985) *Secondary Analysis of Survey Data.* (Quantitative applications in the Social Sciences, Paper 53.) Beverley Hills, CA: Sage.

PAULA DEVINE

Deduction

To deduce means to draw logical conclusions by a process of reasoning; deduction is the process of reasoning by which logical conclusions are drawn from a set of general premises. In the methodological literature, deduction is an approach to data analysis, explanation and theory that sees empirical social research as conducted on the basis of a hypothesis derived from social theory which is then tested against empirical observation and then subsequently used to confirm or refute the original theoretical proposition. This approach is called deduction because research hypotheses are deduced from theory by a process of logical reasoning. It is associated with positivism and natural science models of social research and is the inverse of induction. Deduction has a long pedigree in the philosophy of science, where it is more properly termed the 'hypothetico-deductive method', and was seen as one way to establish natural laws in science.

Generalisations are drawn from the theorisation of the natural law, from which hypotheses are deduced, which are then tested in empirical observation by research which looks for confirming or falsifying cases or for cases that could be predicted should the law operate. The notion in the philosophy of science that hypotheses are better tested by means of refutation rather than confirmation is associated with the work of Sir Karl Popper (1963) and was part of Popper's own critique of analytical positivism. According to Popper no amount of empirical observations could confirm the law that all 'As' are 'Bs' since research can never be comprehensive enough to eliminate all possibility of negative cases. One counter instance of an 'A' not being a 'B' would disconfirm the generalisation and thus lead to certainty in knowledge. Thus, where confirmation of generalisations is the model of research, knowledge remains fallible and conditional and refutation should be the principle of scientific method.

In this way, Popper revised the orthodox positivist understanding of science. The goal of science is not to deduce generalisations and undertake research to confirm them, but to deduce 'conjectural hypotheses' and engage in research to *reject* them. Theories are best when they lend themselves to predictions that can be tested in research but for which no negative cases then are found. It has to be possible to deduce a generalisation from the general theory or law that is falsifiable by empirical observation or prediction for it to be scientific. Theories that cannot be rendered into hypotheses tested by empirical research or prediction and thus which are in effect unfalsifiable are poor and unscientific.

Irrespective of whether in its verificationist or falsificationist version, the hypothetico-deductive method has been a powerful model for natural science research and thus to those positivists who seek to apply the methods and approach of the natural sciences to the study of society. This is despite the fact that the implication of Popper's argument is that most sociological theories are unscientific because they do not lend themselves either to predictions or to hypotheses capable of falsification by means of empirical research. With terms like prediction, law and deduction however, the method has an obvious attraction for those social scientists that aspire to be like natural scientists. Irrespective of the difficulties in translation to the social world, this method remains very much part of the aspiration of social researchers within the natural science model of social research.

Deduction is not only an approach to research method and methodology, it is also an approach to explanation. In the philosophy of science this mode of explanation is more properly called 'nomological-deductive explanation'. This approach to explanation takes data and applies a general theory to them in order to deduce from that theory an explanation for empirical findings. This approach to explanation is an inherent part of the hypothetico-deductive method and sees explanations of data taking a sequential form. The general theory comes first, then the explanation derived from it; and the capacity to deduce an explanation of the data from that theory can itself form part of either the refutation or confirmation of the original law or general theory. This model of explanation and scientific method has been heavily criticised by proponents of qualitative research, who advocate the methodological position of naturalism which sees the goal of social research to be understanding (*Verstehen*) and interpretation (hermeneutics) of the meaning of social actors as understood in their own terms, where there is a preference for induction as an approach to data analysis and theory generation.

The contrast between deduction and induction is not as stark as it is often suggested. It has been known since the work of John Stuart Mill in the philosophy of science that deductive approaches to science require an initial act of induction. That is, the formulation of the general law, from which deduction determines all subsequent procedures within the scientific method, requires an initial imaginative act based on the inductive analysis of one empirical or predicted case. Theories are often induced from the commonalities of a set of cases before the deduction of generalisations and hypotheses intended to verify or refute them. Inductive approaches, such as those recommended in grounded theory, also involve an element of deduction in that hypotheses which are formulated from the emerging theory are then tested (by means of what is called theoretical sampling) and used to refine the finesse of the emerging theory. However, this process is not understood by inductive analysts as a form of deduction but is referred to instead as 'iterative'. Researchers go between data and theory constantly, revising the theory by means of more data and onwards to the refinement of the theory, an approach that, while called iterative, is in effect an oscillation between induction and deduction.

Suggested further reading

Hindess, B. (1977) *Philosophy and Methodology in the Social Sciences*. Hassocks: Harvester Press.

Hughes, J.A. (1990) *The Philosophy of the Social Sciences*. London: Longman.

Ryan, A. (1970) *The Philosophy of the Social Sciences*. London: Macmillan.

See also
Abduction and retroduction, **Hypothesis testing**, **Induction**, **Positivism** and **Theory**.

Reference

Popper, K. (1963) *Conjectures and Refutations*. London: Routledge.

JOHN BREWER

Diaries, self-completion

Biographers, historians and literary scholars have long considered diary documents to be of major importance for telling history. More recently sociologists have taken seriously the idea of using personal documents to construct pictures of social reality from the actors' perspective. In contrast to these 'journal' type of accounts, self-completion diaries are used as research instruments to collect detailed information about behaviour, events and other aspects of individuals' daily lives.

Self-completion diaries have a number of advantages over other data collection methods. First, diaries can provide a reliable alternative to the traditional interview method for events that are difficult to recall accurately or that are easily forgotten. Second, like other self-completion methods, diaries can help to overcome the problems associated with collecting sensitive information by personal interview. Finally, they can be used to supplement interview data to provide a rich source of information on respondents' behaviour and experiences on a daily basis. The 'diary interview method' where the diary keeping period is followed by an interview asking detailed questions about the diary entries is one of the most reliable methods of obtaining information.

The following discussion is largely concerned with fairly 'structured' diaries, as opposed to free text diaries, and with those where events or behaviour are recorded as they occur ('tomorrow diaries', rather than 'yesterday' or retrospective diaries).

The subject matter of diary surveys

A popular topic of investigation for economists, market researchers, and more recently sociologists, has been the way in which people spend their time. Accounts of time use can tell us much about quality of life, social and economic well-being and patterns of leisure and work. The 'time-budget' schedule, pioneered by Sorokin in the 1930s involved respondents keeping a detailed log about how they allocated their time during the day. More qualitative studies have used a 'standard day' diary which focuses on a typical day in the life of an individual from a particular group or community.

One of the most fruitful time-budget endeavours, initiated in the mid-1960s, has been the Multinational Time Budget Time Use Project. Its aim was to provide a set of procedures and guidance on how to collect and analyse time-use data so that valid cross-national comparisons could be made. This group has contributed much to our knowledge of time budget methodology, and for researchers wishing to conduct their own survey into time use, writings published by this group should be their first port of call (Harvey, 1990).

Two other major areas where diaries are often used are consumer expenditure and transport planning research. For example, the UK Family Expenditure Survey

(OPCS) uses diaries to collect data for the National Accounts and to provide weights for the Retail Price Index. In the National Travel Survey (OPCS) respondents record information about all journeys made over a specified time period in a diary. Other topics covered using diary methods are social networks, health, illness and associated behaviour, diet and nutrition, social work and other areas of social policy, clinical psychology and family therapy, crime behaviour, alcohol consumption and drug usage, and sexual behaviour. Diaries are also increasingly being used in market research.

Using diaries in surveys

Diary surveys often use a personal interview to collect additional background information about the household and sometimes about behaviour or events of interest that the diary will not capture (such as large items of expenditure for consumer expenditure surveys). A placing interview is important for explaining the diary keeping procedures to the respondent and a concluding interview may be used to check on the completeness of the recorded entries. Often retrospective estimates of the behaviour occurring over the diary period are collected at the final interview.

Diary design and format

Diaries may be open format, allowing respondents to record activities and events in their own words, or they can be highly structured where all activities are pre-categorised. An obvious advantage of the free format is that it allows for greater opportunity to recode and analyse the data. However, the labour intensive work required to prepare and make sense of the data may render it unrealistic for projects lacking time and resources, or where the sample is large.

Although the design of a diary will depend on the detailed requirement of the topic under study, there are certain design aspects which are common to most. Below are a set of guidelines recommended for anyone thinking about designing a diary. They are by no means definitive and readers should consult existing examples of protocols (see References). Furthermore, the amount of piloting required to perfect the diary format should not be under-estimated.

(1) An A4 booklet of about 5 to 20 pages is desirable, depending on the nature of the diary. Disappointing as it might seem, most respondents do not carry their diaries around with them.

(2) The inside cover page should contain a clear set of instructions on how to complete the diary. This should stress the importance of recording events as soon as possible after they occur and how the respondent should try not to let the diary keeping influence their behaviour.

(3) A model example of a correctly completed diary should feature on the second page.

(4) Depending on how long a period the diary will cover, each page should denote either a week, a day of the week or a 24-hour period or less. Pages should be clearly ruled up as a calendar with prominent headings and enough

space to enter all the desired information (such as what the respondent was doing, at what time, where, with whom and how they felt at the time, and so on).

(5) Checklists of items, events or behaviour to help jog the diary keeper's memory should be printed somewhere fairly prominent. Very long lists should be avoided since they may be off-putting and confusing to respondents. For a structured time budget diary, an exhaustive list of all possible relevant activities should be listed together with the appropriate codes. Where more than one type of activity is to be entered, that is, primary and secondary (or background) activities, guidance should be given on how to deal with 'competing' or multiple activities.

(6) There should be an explanation of what is meant by the unit of observation, such as a 'session', an 'event' or a 'fixed time block'. Where respondents are given more freedom in naming their activities and the activities are to be coded later, it is important to give strict guidelines on what type of behaviour to include, what definitely to exclude and the level of detail required. Time budget diaries without fixed time blocks should include columns for start and finish times for activities.

(7) Appropriate terminology or lists of activities should be designed to meet the needs of the sample under study, and if necessary, different versions of the diary should be used for different groups.

(8) Following the diary pages it is useful to include a simple set of questions for the respondent to complete, asking, among other things, whether the diary-keeping period was atypical in any way compared to usual daily life. It is also good practice to include a page at the end asking for the respondents' own comments and clarifications of any peculiarities relating to their entries. Even if these remarks will not be systematically analysed, they may prove helpful at the editing or coding stage.

Data quality and response rates

In addition to the types of errors encountered in all survey methods, diaries are especially prone to errors arising from respondent conditioning, incomplete recording of information and under-reporting, inadequate recall, insufficient cooperation and sample selection bias.

Diary keeping period

The period over which a diary is to be kept needs to be long enough to capture the behaviour or events of interest without jeopardising successful completion by imposing an overly burdensome task. The OPCS National Travel Survey and the Adult Dietary Survey use seven-day diaries, while the UK Family Expenditure Survey uses a 14-day recording period. For collecting time-use data, anything from one- to three-day diaries may be used. Household expenditure surveys usually place diaries on specific days to ensure an even coverage across the week and distribute their field work over the year to ensure seasonal variation in earnings and spending is captured.

Reporting errors

In household expenditure surveys it is routinely found that the first day and first week of diary keeping shows higher reporting of expenditure than the following days. This is also observed for other types of behaviour and the effects are generally termed 'first day effects'. They may be due to respondents changing their behaviour as a result of keeping the diary (conditioning), or becoming less conscientious than when they started the diary. Recall errors may even extend to 'tomorrow' diaries. Respondents often write down their entries at the end of a day and only a small minority are diligent (and perhaps obsessive!) diary keepers who carry their diary with them at all times. Expenditure surveys find that an intermediate visit from an interviewer during the diary keeping period helps preserve 'good' diary keeping to the end of the period.

Literacy

All methods that involve self-completion of information demand that the respondent has a reasonable standard of literacy. Thus the diary sample and the data may be biased towards the population of competent diary keepers.

Participation

The best response rates for diary surveys are achieved when diary keepers are recruited on a face-to-face basis, rather than by post. Personal collection of diaries also allows any problems in the completed diary to be sorted out on the spot. Success may depend on the quality of interviewing staff who should be highly motivated, competent and well-briefed. Appealing to the respondent's altruistic nature, reassuring them of confidentiality and offering incentives are thought to influence co-operation in diary surveys. Some surveys offer small fees or promotional items.

Coding, editing and processing

The amount of work required to process a diary depends largely on how structured it is. For many large-scale diary surveys, part of the editing and coding process is done by the interviewer while still in the field. Following this is an intensive editing procedure which includes checking entries against information collected in the personal interview. For unstructured diaries involving coding of verbatim entries, the processing can be very labour intensive, in much the same way as it is for processing qualitative interview transcripts. Using highly trained coders and a rigorous unambiguous coding scheme is very important particularly where there is no clear demarcation of events or behaviour in the diary entries. Clearly, a well-designed diary with a coherent pre-coding system should cut down on the degree of editing and coding.

Relative cost of diary surveys

The diary method is generally more expensive than the personal interview, and personal placement and pick-up visits are more costly than postal administration. If the diary is unstructured, intensive editing and coding will push up the costs. However, these costs must be balanced against the superiority of the diary method in obtaining more accurate data, particularly where the recall method gives poor results. The ratio of costs for diaries compared with recall time budgets are of the order of three or four to one (Juster and Stafford, 1985).

Computer software for processing and analysis

Probably the least developed area relating to the diary method is the computer storage and analysis of diary data. One of the problems of developing software for processing and manipulating diary data is the complexity and bulk of the information collected. Although computer assisted methods may help to reduce the amount of manual preparatory work, there are few packages and most of them are custom built to suit the specifics of a particular project. Time-budget researchers are probably the most advanced group of users of machine readable diary data and the structure of these data allows them to use traditional statistical packages for analysis. More recently, methods of analysis based on algorithms for searching for patterns of behaviour in diary data are being used (Coxon, 1991). Software development is certainly an area which merits future attention. For textual diaries, qualitative software packages such as The ETHNOGRAPH can be used to code diaries in the same way as interview transcripts.

Archiving diary data

In spite of the abundance of data derived from diary surveys across a wide range of disciplines, little is available to other researchers for secondary analysis (further analysis of data already collected). This is perhaps not surprising given that the budget for many diary surveys does not extend to systematic processing of the data. Many diary surveys are small-scale investigative studies that have been carried out with very specific aims in mind. For these less structured diaries, for which a common coding scheme is neither feasible, nor possibly desirable, an answer to public access is to deposit the original survey documents in an archive. This kind of data bank gives the researcher access to original diary documents allowing them to make use of the data in ways to suit their own research strategy. However, the ethics of making personal documents public (even if in the limited academic sense) have to be considered.

Note

An earlier version of this entry appeared as 'Using Diaries in Social Research' in *Social Research Update* 2.

Suggested further reading

Plummer, K. (2000) *Documents of Life 2.* London: Sage.

Szalai, A. et al. (eds) (1972) *The Use of Time.* The Hague: Mouton.

References

Coxon, A.P.M. (1991) 'The structure of sexual behaviour', Research paper, ESRC Research Centre, University of Essex.

Harvey, A.S. (1990) *Guidelines for Time Use Data Collection,* Working paper No. 5, General Social Survey, Statistics Canada.

Juster, T. and Stafford, F.P. (eds) (1985) *Time, Goods and Well-being.* Ann Arbor: Institute for Social Research, University of Michigan.

LOUISE CORTI

Discourse analysis

Discourse analysis or 'pragmatics' is the social study of language as used in talk, text and other forms of communication. Think for a moment: what is it that people do compulsively and enjoy, which is done everywhere and under all conditions, something that can be done alone – although it is considered abnormal to do so – is often done in pairs but can be done in groups with careful organisation, and something so universal and ubiquitous that even animals do it, although differently from humans? The answer is the use of language. Something so ubiquitous is seen as ordinary and everyday and thus as simple and unworthy of serious attention. Language, however, is complex and intricate and has been the topic of considerable study. But mostly the attention has been on the content of the talk – it is what the talk is about that has interested social researchers in the past, the structure of the talk itself was not the focus.

Outside the social sciences, there has been a long-standing philosophical interest in language (Wittgenstein, Austin). Disciplines like phonetics and semantics have studied pronunciation and grammar, and socio-linguistics has focused on how language correlates with social variables like class, sex, age, region and ethnicity. But what is characteristic about these approaches is that they focus on isolated sentences or grammar divorced from their context, and often study idealised, hypothetical or contrived language. The language is neither natural or real nor related to the social setting in which it is produced; it is decontextualised and idealised and thus of little interest to the social researcher. In contrast, pragmatics or discourse analysis studies language as a social phenomenon. It focuses on actual language used by real people in naturally occurring social settings, either spoken in talk or written in text. A preferred term for this approach is the study of natural language (Brewer, 2000).

Sometimes language is studied in this way because the organisation of talk is itself the topic, but often because it reveals something about the social situation in which the language is used. In this latter regard, studies of natural language are a data collection technique. There are at least three reasons why this is so: language is a form of social interaction; it presupposes shared knowledge; and it is inseparable from its social setting. Data can be collected on all these things as part of a social research design. For example, language is vital to the interactions that make up society and texts of many kinds adorn social life. We initiate and conduct relationships by means of language, among other things; there are some actions that can only be performed by means of language. Language could not achieve these interactive purposes without the shared knowledge it presupposes. An array of taken-for-granted mutual knowledge is implicit in language, such as the meaning of words and techniques for organising turns to speak. The context of an utterance, for example, can help in interpreting its meaning since its meaning can be over and above the literal words used, and shared assumptions are necessary for ambiguous words to be interpreted the same way between hearer and speaker. This shows how language is inseparable from its social context. The language of the rugby changing room is not used in church on Sunday; priests do not deliver sermons in the language of lawyers or footballers. Part of social development is the skill to match language and setting and people develop a 'verbal repertoire' that enables them to connect discourse with appropriate social settings: people know how to talk when meeting their future in-laws and at a job interview compared to a night out with friends in a pub. Language and setting are so closely tied, for example, that it is sometimes possible to reconstruct from a fragment of conversation the whole social world that produced it. The single word 'nagging', for example, conjures a whole universe of gender relations and social stereotypes. So closely tied are language and setting that we are able to identify quickly whether we are listening to a sermon, sports commentary or news broadcast, and to feel embarrassment, confusion or hilarity when the language of one setting is used inappropriately in another (a vicar saying orgasm instead of organism in the sermon, or the *faux pas* of a radio announcer).

Five types of discourse analysis are relevant to the study of social behaviour. The first is the analysis of the discrete discourse styles that relate to particular social settings, or what Goffman (1981) calls 'forms of talk', such as the types of discourse associated with, say, teaching, the court room or radio announcing. An interesting feature of this type is the analysis of errors, such as slips of the tongue or words and phrases with double meanings that illustrate the inappropriate match of discourse style and setting, most of which end up being funny or rude. In a crossover of setting and style, words and phrases in one setting have their meaning altered when used in another, which is again sometimes funny ('Bill posters will be prosecuted' the sign reads, underneath which some wag has written, 'Bill Posters is innocent'). The second direction for discourse analysis is what Hymes calls the 'ethnography of communication', where the analysis is devoted to the functions of language as it is used in particular natural settings and the 'communicative competences' needed to realise this communicative purpose. These competences are linguistic, such as rules for language structure and use, as well as cultural, such as knowledge about social statuses, settings and the like as they impinge on language. Good examples of research of this type are the function of humour in drawing moral boundaries, doctor-patient communication in establishing professional distance, or what Emmison calls 'defeat talk' amongst sports people by which in their language use, such as during media interviews after a loss, they adjust to defeat without losing faith in their ability. The third is known as conversation analysis, associated with Harvey Sacks and ethnomethodology, which explores how conversations are organised and structured into the turn-taking format. The fourth is the analysis of accounts, textual or verbal. In this respect, accounts are analysed for the descriptions and social representations they contain, the practical reasoning that seems to lie behind the choice of words used and their order from the range of alternatives that could have been used, and the design features of the talk or text. This approach has been used to study a range of social phenomena, such as the accounts people give of the paranormal (Wooffitt, 1992), scientists' accounts of their work (Gilbert and Mulkay, 1984) and the analysis of many official reports and reports of public inquiries.

The final type is what can be called 'critical discourse analysis'. This draws on two closely aligned traditions. The first is the work of Michel Foucault, the second that of critical linguists. Foucault denied that there is such a state as absolute truth and objective knowledge and instead addressed the processes by which claims about truth are established. He drew attention to 'discursive formations', which are like cultural codes or systems of language that contain, among other things, practices for producing and encoding knowledge by certifying some claims as authoritative and truthful and others not. This directs attention to the rules and practices speakers and writers use to give legitimacy to their claims and thus to the analysis of the origins, nature and structure of the discursive themes by which the discourse or text is produced. It encourages a critical view of truth and authority claims since discourse and texts should not be treated as accurate representations of the external world but as artefacts to be explained by the discursive rules, themes and practices that constitute the discursive formation in which they are produced. Critical linguists often seek to distance themselves from Foucault, in part because they themselves wish to accord their accounts with authority. The key idea of these authors is that language, power and ideology are inseparable so that analysis of discourse and text should focus on the ways in which the language benefits economic, political and social elites, and is structured and deployed in ways that disguise or conceal this. They look for texts and discourse – interviews with politicians, government reports, party manifestos and advertisements, management consultant reports – for the 'real' message underlying the language used and which is revealed nonetheless in the words, metaphors, schema and sentence structure of the discourse or text. Good examples of work of this kind are Fairclough's (2000) study of the language of New Labour and the Conservative government of Mrs Thatcher (Fairclough, 1989).

Suggested further reading

Fairclough, N. (1994) *Discourse and Social Change*. Cambridge: Polity.

Have, P. ten (1999) *Doing Conversational Analysis*. London: Sage.

Nofsinger, R. (1991) *Everyday Conversation*. London: Sage.

Potter, J. and Wetherell, M. (1987) *Discourse and Social Psychology*. London: Sage.

Stubbs, M. (1983) *Discourse Analysis*. Oxford: Blackwell.

References

Brewer, J. (2000) *Ethnography*. Buckingham: Open University Press.
Fairclough, N. (1989) *Language and Power*. London: Longman.
Fairclough, N. (2000) *New Labour, New Language*. London: Routledge.

Gilbert, N. and Mulkay, M. (1984) *Opening Pandora's Box*. Cambridge: Cambridge University Press.
Goffman, E. (1981) *Forms of Talk*.
Wooffitt (1999) *Telling Tales of the Unexpected*. Brighton: Harvester Wheatsheaf.

> **See also**
> **Conversation analysis** and **Ethnomethodology**.

JOHN BREWER

Dispersion and the normal distribution

Measures of dispersion are used with measures of central tendency to describe how data are distributed. The term dispersion indicates the variation or spread in the values of a variable. When the values are widely spread the dispersion is large and when they are narrowly spread the dispersion is small.

Measures of dispersion differ from measures of central tendency, such as the median or mean, in the following way. Central tendency reports an average or typical value of a distribution. Measures of dispersion indicate the extent to which scores in the distribution deviate from this typical value. It is important to have this information when examining distributions because data which have very different spreads could still have the same average. For example, two districts in cities could have the same average price for residential property. Yet, in one district there could be some very expensive houses and also some very cheap houses while in the other district nearly all the houses could cost close to the average price. Therefore, we cannot rely on measures of central tendency alone to describe distributions.

We make our description of distributions more comprehensive by looking at measures of dispersion such as the range, the variance and the standard deviation. The appropriateness of particular measures of dispersion will partly depend on the level of measurement of the variable. Let us take a batch of 12 family members aged 1, 8, 10, 12, 20, 22, 24, 25, 26, 30, 38 and 75 and use their ages in examples of how to calculate various measures of dispersion.

The range

The range is a suitable measure of dispersion for data at the ordinal level of measurement. The range is the most straightforward measure of dispersion and is calculated simply by subtracting the highest value from the lowest value in a distribution; in our example the range will be 74 (75 − 1).

The interquartile range

However, the range can be affected profoundly by the presence of outliers or extreme values (note that the ages of the youngest and oldest people in our family added 44 years to the range!). We need to treat the range with caution if either of the end values differ substantially from the rest of the values in a batch, being unusually lower or higher than the rest. In such cases, we may use the *interquartile range*, which is designed to overcome the main flaw of the range by eliminating the extreme scores in the distribution. It is obtained by ordering the batch from lowest to highest, then dividing the batch into four equal parts (quartiles) and concentrating on the middle 50% of the distribution. The interquartile range therefore is the range of the middle half of the observations, the difference between the *first quartile* and the *third quartile* (when all the values in the data are ordered, the first quartile is the point one quarter of the values from the bottom (the 25% point) and the third quartile is the point three-quarters of the values from the bottom (the 75% point)). In our example the lower quartile is 10 (3 values from the bottom) and the upper quartile is 30 (3 values from the top), so the interquartile range is 20 (30 − 10). If you are using the median as the measure of central tendency, the interquartile range is the most appropriate measure of dispersion to accompany it.

Variance (s²)

The variance and the standard deviation are suitable measures of dispersion for data at the interval or ratio level of measurement. Both tell us how widely dispersed the values in an interval/ratio distribution are from the mean. If the cases are far from the mean, the variance will be larger than if the cases are concentrated close to the mean. To compute the variance we subtract each individual score from the mean. These differences from the mean we call deviations. To avoid positive and negative deviations from the mean cancelling each other out in our calculation, we square these deviations and add them all up, and divide by the number of cases. So, in general terms, the variance represents the average squared deviation from the mean. It is usually symbolized by s squared: s^2

$$\text{Variance} = \frac{\text{Sum of (individual score minus the mean) squared}}{\text{Number of cases}}$$

In our family, the variance will be 344 (the squared sum of 4,129 divided by 12).

Standard deviation (s or sd)

The variance is hard to interpret intuitively because it is not measured in the same units as the original variable (since the individual deviations from the mean have been squared). In order to understand the dispersion in terms of the same units as the variable, we take the square root of the variance in order to obtain the most commonly used measure of dispersion, the standard deviation. The standard deviation is usually indicated by the letter s or letters sd (for our family the square root of 344 is 18.5 years). As with the variance, the more dispersed the values in the distribution, the larger the standard deviation will be. When the standard deviation of a particular distribution is small rather than large then the dispersion is low and so the mean can be viewed as a relatively good summary measure of central tendency. Therefore, when the mean is reported, the standard deviation is often reported as well.

Sometimes when the data comes from a sample, the standard deviation is calculated using the total minus one case (N – 1) rather than the total number of cases. This increases the standard deviation slightly and is done to compensate for the fact that the dispersion captured by a sample is likely to be slightly less than that which is to be found in the population as a whole.

It is important to remember that the variance and standard deviation are calculated using all the observations in a batch of data. Hence, like the range, they easily can be distorted by a few extreme values (that is, they are not *resistant* to extreme values). As a general rule, it is advisable to check your data for any unusually high or low values before employing these statistics. If you do find extreme values at either end of the distribution, you may want to consider using the median and the interquartile range instead. (While we are restricted to the range and the interquartile range when using ordinal data, all measures of dispersion can be employed with interval/ratio data. There are no appropriate measures of dispersion for nominal variables.)

The standard deviation and the normal distribution

The standard deviation can be particularly useful when the data has what is called a normal distribution. An easy way to see whether our data form a normal distribution is to graph it, say with a stem and leaf graph. Data which are normally distributed have a recognizable shape when graphed. The graph will have a bell shaped curve, with most of the data values clustered in the middle of the graph around the mean, with a symmetrical tailing off to the right and to the left. A perfect normal distribution will be perfectly symmetrical, as illustrated here. Many distributions are approximately normally distributed, such as weights and heights in a population and also, the distribution of marks in many standard tests such as in university exams. When data have an approximately normal distribution the mean, median and mode will be very similar.

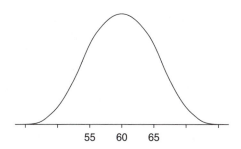

In the example above, the mean score of the distribution is 60. We can see from the normal distribution curve that most scores are close to the mean with some tapering off higher and some tapering off lower. The standard deviation is 5. This information is particularly meaningful when the data is normally distributed.

This is because a remarkable feature of the normal distribution is that a fixed percentage of the data values will be found between the mean and X number of standard deviations. So, when a distribution is normal:

- 68% of cases will lie within the range of 1 sd above or below the mean
- 95% of cases will lie within 2 sd above or below the mean
- 99% of cases will lie within 3 sd above or below the mean.

With a mean of 60 and a standard deviation of 5, this means we can report that 68% of the cases are to be found between the scores of 55 (1 sd below the mean) and 65 (1 sd above the mean). Where data is normally distributed we can calculate the percentage of cases which lie within any two points on the distribution.

We can also work out the percentage of cases to be found above or below any particular data point. In doing this we convert the raw values into what we call standardised or Z scores.

Suggested further reading

Agresti A. and Finlay B. (1997) *Statistical Methods for the Social Science*. London: Prentice Hall.

Clegg, Francis (1990) *Simple Statistics: a Course Book for the Social Sciences*. Cambridge: Cambridge University Press.

Hinton, Perry (1992) *Statistics Explained: a Guide for Social Science Students*. London: Routledge.

See also Central tendency.

RICHARD O'LEARY AND CIARAN ACTON

Documentary sources

Documentary sources may be defined loosely as records relating to individuals or groups of individuals that have been generated in the course of their daily lives. As such, they are bread and butter to social historians and to scholars whose approach to social investigation is more inclined to empiricism than to over-arching theory. This is not to say that documentary sources do not require a structured approach; on the contrary, the use of letters, diaries and the like need a careful methodology in order to extract their relevance for the understanding of society.

Documentary sources are sometimes described as life stories because they are the accounts of the lives of individuals, families, or other social groups. They include diaries, letters, memoirs, photographs, even shopping lists and random jottings. Cinema has been a source for a century and, more recently, video and similar technologies have become available. Oral histories are also life stories, although they are rarely spontaneous (but neither are diaries or memoirs). Newspapers and works of fiction are other sources that can throw light on human behaviour and the workings of society. A social historian might also include in the *genre* documents *about* people generated in the past such as published censuses, taxation lists, and legal records.

Censuses are particularly valuable to students of societies in former times. It may be queried whether these are really life stories since they are responses to officialdom and not tales told by individuals. But the inhabitants of Britain and Ireland – and many other countries – have become accustomed to filling in census forms every 10 years or so, thus committing some aspects of their lives to an official record. In Britain the process started in 1801, in Ireland effectively in 1821. In most case the enumerators' forms (the pieces of paper filled in on the doorstep or on the kitchen table) have not survived or are barred to researchers under the 100-year rule. But published censuses are a rich source of information about (nameless) individuals, household and family groups, age cohorts, religion and ethnic origins, educational standards, occupations, living conditions and much else. The material is not consistent from place to place and decade to decade, but censuses are an important starting point for many social investigations.

Censuses conducted by the state do not extend back much before 1800, but for earlier periods there are population listings for towns and regions compiled by persons in authority – a landlord, perhaps, or a tax collector – for their own purposes. These can be quite simple, consisting merely of a list of names, or they can be highly detailed, combining individuals into families and households, describing the relationships between individuals, and giving information about ages and occupations. Irish historians have long used hearth money returns (the hearth tax was a form of property tax) from the late seventeenth century to calculate the number of houses in Ireland in the pre-census period as a first step in estimating the rate of growth of population before the Great Famine. In England Peter Laslett used household lists from 409 English communities to demonstrate that the nuclear family household was common long before the industrial revolution (Laslett, 1972). This finding challenges the widely held belief that the nuclear family was the product of industrialisation. The study was later extended by Laslett and his colleagues to embrace much of Europe and has added greatly to our understanding of the structure and functions of this fundamental social unit (Wall et al., 1983).

Diaries and memoirs, biographies and autobiographies fall more obviously into the category of life histories than do population lists. Diaries are particularly useful for the study of the behaviour and beliefs of individuals and the relationships between individuals. Diaries are sometimes written specifically for social investigators. For example, these may be work diaries, that is records of the proportion of the working day that employees spent carrying out particular tasks. Or they may be daily or weekly diaries recording expenditure on food; such studies became common from the late nineteenth century as part of investigations into nutritional standards and household consumption patterns. For a discussion of diaries requested by social scientists see Plummer (2001).

Diaries used by historians were by definition not kept for the benefit of investigators. One of the best known English examples is Samuel Pepys' dairy, written during the 1660s, but there are many others. In 1983 Linda Pollock published a study of parent–child relations between 1500 and 1900 based on 144

American diaries, 236 British diaries, and 36 autobiographies (Pollock, 1983). Her book questions three deeply entrenched beliefs about childhood held by sociologists and historians: that there was no concept of childhood before the seventeenth century; that relationships between parents and children in the past were distant; and that up to the eighteenth and early nineteenth centuries children were often brutally exploited.

Letters, according to one authority, 'remain a relatively rare document of life in the social sciences' (Plummer, 2001: 52). But social and business historians have used them extensively. They are a rich source of information for historians of migration. For countries such as Ireland and the United States where society has been shaped by sustained emigration or immigration, the surviving letters of migrants tell us much about both the sending and the receiving countries and – more importantly – the motives of the migrants themselves. A major example is Kerby Miller's 1985 study of emigration from Ireland to North America (Miller, 1985).

Documentary sources supply the empirical evidence that can support sociological theories. But documents are tricky; they tell us what the author wants us to know, which is not necessarily what the researcher is really interested in. They offer a version of events from the perspective of the narrator. This is the case even of documents generated officially, but the opportunities for putting a gloss on reality are all the greater in diaries, letters and memoirs.

The golden rule when using such sources is to search out the context and to understand why the document was created. Take diaries as an example. Researchers who use diaries must ask two questions: why was the diary written? And who was the intended audience? Diaries may be no more than ephemeral records of daily appointments, but they are often much more. Those that have endured may be slanted in some way, depending on why they were written in the first place. Harold Nicholson, the English politician and essayist, kept a diary 'out of habit'. He claimed he had no thoughts of publication. Field Marshal Lord Alanbrooke, Britain's Commander-in-Chief during the Second World War wrote a diary every night as a way of 'talking' to his wife. It was prefaced by the injunction, 'ON NO ACCOUNT MUST THE CONTENTS OF THIS BOOK BE PUBLISHED'. Yet Nicholson's and Alanbrooke's diaries have both been published. Did both authors actually believe that their handiwork would eventually see the light of day?

Motive colours content. This does not mean that diaries are valueless as life stories, but users must approach them with care. Investigators must also be aware that the questions they themselves pose of the sources and the assumptions behind the questions will affect their interpretations. There are, for example, some people who believe that generals are congenitally out of touch with their troops. One reading of the Alanbrooke diaries can be made to show that he spent a lot of the war dining in London clubs. But he spent many thousand hours more planning strategy and visiting the battlefronts. It is easy to misread documents.

Memoirs written later in life are likely to be even more distanced from reality than diaries. Memoirs reflect a past mediated through time and memory. In the early nineteenth century the daughter of a Church of Ireland rector, then in her early forties, recalled her life back to the 1770s. She was an unhappy woman when she took up her pen, mourning the death of her father, believing her mother and brothers were ill-treating her, and lamenting an unrequited love. She was an acute observer of social behaviour but her interpretations of the past were disturbed by the turmoil of her mind (Cullen, 1988).

All documentary sources – diaries, letters, memoirs, fiction, film – relate the life stories as remembered and interpreted by individuals. That is their strength. Communities are composed of hundreds and thousands of men, women and children and the stories they tell are the stuff of human experience. The problem for social scientists is how to make sense of the infinite variety of life stories. They have three paths open to them. The first – and this must be followed in all cases – is to test the veracity of the document. It is not unknown for such documents to be fakes (the *Hitler Diaries* are a famous example). More likely, though, the narrator has a particular tale to tell and tells it in a particular way. We must have an ear for the accent of the story-teller. The second approach is to read as many life stories as possible in the hope of establishing general patterns of behaviour. The difficulty with the inductive method is that the researcher becomes over-whelmed by a mass of empirical evidence. And so the third approach is to turn to theory to explain the data. It may of course happen that the available theories are inadequate to explain the evidence, in which case new theories may have to be developed.

Documentary sources contain stories told by men and women about men and women. Plummer (2001: 7–15) has argued that they restore humanism to the social sciences. They put flesh and blood into the models that have been developed to explain human behaviour.

References

Cullen, Louis (1988) *Retrospections of Dorothea Herbert 1770–1806, with accompanying commentary by Louis Cullen (1988)*. Dublin: Town House.

Laslett, Peter (1972) *Household and Family in Past Time*. Cambridge: Cambridge University Press.

Miller, Kerby (1985) *Emigrants and Exiles: Ireland and the Irish Exodus to North America*. New York: Oxford University Press.

Plummer, Ken (2001) *Documents of Life 2*. London: Sage Publications.

Pollock, Linda (1983) *Forgotten Children: Parent–Child Relations from 1500 to 1900*. Cambridge: Cambridge University Press.

Wall, Richard, et al. (eds) (1983) *Family Forms in Historic Europe*. Cambridge: Cambridge University Press.

See also
Historical
methods.

LESLIE CLARKSON

E

Ecological fallacy

A fallacy is an error of logic usually based on mistaken assumptions. The ecological fallacy is an error of deduction that involves deriving conclusions about individuals solely on the basis of an analysis of group data. For example, a study of the drinking habits of students in two universities, A and B, might find that students in A consumed far more units of alcohol than in B. On meeting an individual university student from A, the 'heavy drinking' university, however, we should not automatically expect that he or she is a heavy drinker. It may be that many of the students in A are in fact teetotal but that this abstinence is compensated for by extremely high levels of alcohol consumption among other students. Another example is the 'hung' jury. We cannot deduce, because a jury cannot reach a verdict, that each of its individual members is undecided. In fact, the reverse may be the case – it may be that they are too decided but are split on the decision. In sum, we cannot infer individual characteristics from group-level characteristics. Of course, there is also a reverse fallacy – the exception fallacy, which generalises from individual to group-level characteristics, a practice which informs much stereotyping, sexism and racism.

The classic illustration of the ecological fallacy is by Robinson (1950) who demonstrates that there may be inconsistencies between correlations at different levels of aggregation. For example, it is fallacious to infer that the same correlation between income and life-expectancy, for example, will hold at national, regional, city and neighbourhood level. Robinson developed two indices for each of the 48 states in the USA of 1930 – the percentage foreign-born and the percentage who are literate. He confined his calculations in each case to those who were 10 or older. He found a correlation of +0.53 between the 48 pairs of numbers. This was an ecological correlation in that his units were the states rather than the individuals in the states. His ecological correlation suggested a positive relationship between foreign birth and literacy – in other words the foreign-born were more likely to be literate than the native-born. In fact, when data on foreign-born *individuals* were computed the correlation was negative, -0.11. The reason for the discrepancy was that the foreign-born tended to live in states where the literacy rate was high. This demonstrates the fallacy of inferring that relationships between aggregates hold for individuals – the ecological fallacy.

Health data often takes ecological form and also needs to be handled with care. For example, countries that consume large amounts of fatty foods can be shown to have high rates of heart disease. In the absence of data for individuals, however, we must be careful about making inferences from aggregate data about individuals.

Nevertheless, aggregate national health data are socially useful in that they can stimulate policies aimed at improving diet generally which in turn will impact on the diet of individuals. Durkheim's *Suicide* is a classic example of ecological reasoning in sociology. Using aggregate data, he found that countries with more Protestants had higher suicide rates but his data do not link individual suicides to any particular faith. Hence, it is an ecological fallacy to argue on the basis of aggregate data alone that Protestants are more likely to commit suicide than adherents to some other faiths.

It would be wrong to conclude, because of the dangers of the ecological fallacy, that aggregate data are suspect or that they have no implications for individuals. Social researchers typically rely on aggregate data, frequently in the form of official statistics. The latter are more accessible and economical to use than individual level data that can be costly and time-consuming to collect. Moreover, the social whole may be greater than the sum of the parts. For example, 'poor areas' in cities are insufficiently understood simply as an aggregate of the poverty of individuals within them. It may be the case that most poor people do not live in poor areas but the poor areas represent a constellation of inter-related deprivations – such as bad housing, high crime rates, run-down environment, and a stigmatised reputation. To recognise that 'poor areas' may constitute social entities is not to commit an ecological fallacy. These areas are more than the sum of the individually poor people within them – indeed, they may include relatively well off people. But they do exert a variety of influences on the circumstances of poor individuals and families with them. They may act as a magnet for poor people because they are perceived as 'undesirable' areas and therefore are cheaper to live in. Their stigmatised reputation may make it harder for their residents to get jobs or less likely that businesses will invest in these areas. The analysis of urban ecology or spatial processes does not necessarily involve the ecological fallacy unless direct deductions are made about individual behaviour within these areas solely on the basis of aggregate data.

Suggested further reading

Schwartz, S. (1994) 'The Fallacy of the Ecological Fallacy', *American Journal of Public Health*, 84 (5): 819–24.

Spicker, P. (2001) 'Poor Areas and the "Ecological Fallacy"', *Radical Statistics*, 76: 38–49.

Reference

Robinson W.S. (1950) 'Ecological Correlations and the Behavior of Individuals', *American Sociological Review*, 15: 351–7.

See also
Secondary data analysis.

LIAM O'DOWD

e-mail as a research tool

- Using e-mail as a research tool potentially offers researchers many advantages such as easy access to world-wide samples, low administration costs (both financially and temporally) and its unobtrusiveness and 'friendliness' to respondents.
- However, e-mail's application as a research tool is constrained by its, as yet, limited and biased population of users (in terms of age, income, gender and race).
- Response rates to e-mail questionnaires appear favourable as does the ease of distribution and response times. Nevertheless, ensuring respondents' anonymity is virtually impossible.
- Using e-mail as an interview tool eschews the conventional constraints of spatial and temporal proximity between interviewer and respondent and offers the considerable practical advantage of providing 'ready-transcribed' data. However, e-mail interviews suffer from a lack of tacit communication.

The rapid permeation of new telecommunications technologies throughout society has seen the emergence of electronic mail (e-mail) as an increasingly pervasive means of communication. Over the last decades, due to its relative simplicity and effectiveness, e-mail has quickly been integrated into business and commerce as well as being widely adopted by 'private' individuals and, indeed, the academic community. Yet, given its growing importance as a medium of communication, discussion of e-mail as an academic *research* tool has, to date, been scarce.

There is an emerging literature surrounding the use of electronic mail in academe. Applications include the use of e-mail in undergraduate teaching, student teacher mentoring and for scholarly discussion groups (Berge and Collins, 1995; Huff and Sobiloff, 1993; Wild and Winniford, 1993; Pitt, 1996). Following on from trends in market research (Mehta and Sivadas, 1995) there have been tentative moves toward using e-mail as a research tool, primarily in the form of quantitative instruments such as electronic questionnaires and also, to a lesser extent, qualitative methods such as electronic interviews and electronic 'focus' groups. Careful consideration of these new methods is needed if they are to be used effectively in the social sciences.

Methodological considerations

The principal feature of using e-mail as a research tool is the speed and immediacy it offers. An almost instantaneous dialogue between researcher and subject can be arranged if desired. However, this speed also lends e-mail a certain ephemerality that may compromise its effectiveness as a research tool. As Thach (1995) argues, e-mail messages can be deleted as quickly as they were sent and unlike the standard mail questionnaire or interview the respondent can discard e-mail at the touch of a button.

Nevertheless, there are many advantages of using e-mail as a research tool. In particular electronic communication sets up a 'democratisation of exchange' that eludes more conventional research methodologies. As Boshier argues:

> E-mail appears to provide a context for the kind of non-coercive and anti-hierarchical dialogue that Habermas claimed constitutes an 'ideal speech situation', free of internal or external coercion, and characterised by equality of opportunity and reciprocity in roles assumed by participants. (1990: 51)

In this way e-mail goes some way to transcending the traditional biases that beset interviewing techniques. As Spender (1995) notes, the concepts of race, gender, age and sexuality do not necessarily apply when communicating electronically. Furthermore, the potential for asynchronous communication that e-mail offers is an attractive feature when considering its use as a research tool (Thach, 1995). Subjects are not constrained to synchronous communication but can respond when and how they feel comfortable. In short, e-mail's primary advantage is its 'friendliness' to the respondent.

The rise in use and availability of communication technologies has coincided with an increase in the popularity of qualitative research methods which rely on textual data (Foster, 1994). This lends electronic mail an attractiveness to researchers which nevertheless obscures some inherent weaknesses in its validity as a research method. The fundamental failing of using e-mail is the extremely self-selective, limited and therefore biased population that it covers. E-mail is limited to those individuals with access to a computer, a population which is severely constrained along lines of class, race, age, income and gender. Furthermore, although expanding in popularity, use of e-mail remains a minority pastime among many computer users. As Kenway (1996) highlights, a disproportionate number of people 'on-line' are from high income professions or involved in higher education, with the predominant group consisting of 18–24 year old male university students. Indeed, this 'limited coverage' was the main factor cited by Katori (1990) as limiting e-mail as a viable tool in market research.

As e-mail use becomes more widespread the problem of limited coverage may decrease but other difficulties will arise. In particular, as electronic communication becomes more common, there will be *information overload* and research via e-mail runs the risk of becoming marginalised as a form of electronic 'junk mail'. Berge and Collins (1995) argue that, as electronic discourse increases the average individual will be inundated with e-mail; so much so that attending to every mail message will be almost impossible. Unsolicited attempts to gain information via e-mail by researchers (however genuine) may be simply ignored by the deluged recipient at the other end of the line.

With this background we can now examine the strengths and weaknesses of two particular e-mail methodologies: electronic questionnaires and electronic interviewing.

Electronic questionnaires

An obvious application for electronic mail is its use as a replacement for the conventional postal questionnaire. Indeed, early quantitative studies seem to indicate that 'electronic' questionnaires had a very favourable response rate when compared to the typical 20–50% response rates usually achieved by conventional mail surveys (Frankfort-Nachmias and Nachmias, 1996). Aside from seemingly higher response rates, electronic questionnaires have other inherent advantages. E-mail questionnaires cost considerably less to administer, both in terms of money and time. As it is possible to send the same e-mail to multiple addresses in one action, a large 'mail-shot' of subjects is relatively straightforward. Most e-mail software also allows the dispatcher of the message the option of notification when the recipient has received the message and when they have read it. Although this possibility raises questions of confidentiality, e-mail does offer the researcher slightly more 'control' over the questionnaires once they have been sent.

However, there are corresponding features of e-mail which are less compatible with sending e-mail questionnaires. For example it is virtually impossible to guarantee the respondent anonymity as their name (or at least their e-mail address) is automatically included in their reply. Although, as Thach (1995) points out, this lack of anonymity does not preclude the researcher still guaranteeing the respondent confidentiality, the validity of the e-mail questionnaire is compromised in this way.

Electronic interviewing

Whereas using e-mail for electronic surveys directly replaces the role of conventional mail, electronic interviewing makes use of the more interactive and immediate nature of e-mail, either in the form of one-to-one interviewing or the setting up of electronic focus groups. The practical advantages of electronic interviewing are two-fold. First, as Foster (1995) points out, interviewing by electronic mail is not constrained by geographical location or time-zone; the need for proximity between the interviewer and interviewee is no longer an issue. Secondly, electronic interviewing data require no additional transcription – the text from e-mail interviews can easily be tailored for any word processing package or computer-based qualitative analysis package with a minimum of alteration. As well as saving the researcher time and money this also eliminates any errors introduced through incorrect transcription. With e-mail interviewing the data that is eventually analysed is exactly what the interviewee wrote.

Nevertheless, as Boshier (1990) argues, most discussion of the benefits and drawbacks of e-mail ignores the 'human' factors enhanced and impaired by its use.

E-mail interviewing reduces the problem of interviewer effect, whether resulting from visual and non-verbal cues or status differences between interviewee and interviewer. It also can reduce problems caused by dominant and shy participants, particularly in electronic focus groups. As Roberts et al. (1997) discuss, the negative effects of shyness are often overcome when communicating via electronic mail. In this way, electronic interviewing goes a long way to alleviating some of the interpersonal problems commonly associated with conventional interviewing techniques. Nevertheless, the fact remains that e-mail interaction is not comparable to verbal interaction in many ways. 'On-line' discussion requires different skills from both the interviewer and the subject. As Bannon (1986: cited in Boshier, 1990) notes, the content and style of e-mail messages lie somewhere between a telephone call and a memo. Indeed, the language of all computer-mediated communication tends toward a simplified register due to the space and time constraints of the medium, in effect making e-mail messages a hybrid of oral and written language (Murray, 1995). Although often seen as a less accurate reflection of a respondent's thoughts than verbal data, the 'mute evidence' of written data can offer the (sometimes necessary) convenience of both spatial and temporal distance between subject and researcher (Hodder, 1994).

This lack of non-verbal communication can be a problem for both the interviewer and respondent. A great deal of tacit information that would be conveyed in a conventional interview situation is lost. What electronic interviewing can be seen to gain in accuracy it therefore loses in terms of the additional, and often valuable, non-verbal data. As King (1996) reasons, non-verbal communication and active listening are integral elements of the effective interview. Although 'netiquette' makes clumsy attempts to substitute paralinguistic and non-linguistic cues with emoticons (for example, typing :-) after a sentence denotes humour, multiple vowels indicate rising intonation, such as 'sooooo') e-mail's lack of verbal interaction is an obvious limitation to its use as an interviewing tool.

Conclusion

The proliferation of e-mail, along with the increasing ease of carrying out e-mail and internet based research (for example, Schmidt 1997a) suggests that the use of electronic methodologies are likely to increase in popularity in the near future, in both quantitative and qualitative studies. However, there remain significant problems in using e-mail in social science research.

Despite the rapid expansion of e-mail, its use as a research tool will reflect the demographically based biases of current usage patterns of the medium, in much the same way that early telephone surveys were also hindered by the clear social class bias resulting from unequal ownership of the facility (Babbie, 1992). Thus at present, as Schmidt (1997b) suggests, electronic methodologies can only be considered a valid alternative to traditional techniques for research which targets specific and narrowly defined populations with easy access to the World Wide Web and e-mail.

At present the fragmented and disparate character of e-mail and the Internet has blocked the development of widely accepted criteria for its use in academic research (Langford 1995a, 1995b). Yet it is only by use of the medium, taking heed of conventional ethical and methodological criteria as well as the emerging field of 'cyberspace' ethics, that answers to these issues will develop. Although the biases that e-mail usage currently contain must not be overlooked, e-mail should be recognised as an appropriate social research tool whose potential transcends its current restricted use. As Coomber (1997) contends, the demographic disparities that currently restrict on-line research are fast diminishing; 'the relative exclusivity of current internet [and e-mail] use needs to be considered seriously but it does not preclude attempts to do useful and informative sociological research' (para. 1.1). At the present time using e-mail offers the researcher many advantages, temporally, spatially and in terms of easy access to otherwise unreachable samples. Nevertheless, its use should always be offset against the wider considerations of population access to the medium and the limitations of the (admittedly plentiful) data that are generated.

Note

This is a revised and updated version of an article first published in *Social Research Update*, 21 (Department of Sociology, University of Surrey).

Suggested further reading

Gorard, S. and Selwyn, N. (2001) *101 Key Ideas in Information Technology*. London: Hodder Stoughton.
Jones, S. (ed.) (1999) *Doing Internet Research*. London: Sage.

Mann, C. and Stewart, F. (2000) *Internet Communication and Qualitative Research: a Handbook for Researching Online*. London: Sage.

References

Babbie, E. (1992) *The Practice of Social Research*, 6th edn. Belmont, CA: Wadsworth.
Berge, Z.L. and Collins, M. (1995) 'Computer Mediated Scholarly Discussion Groups', *Computers and Education*, 24 (3): 183–9.
Boshier, R. (1990) 'Socio-psychological Factors in Electronic networking', *International Journal of Lifelong Education*, 9 (1): 49–64.
Coomber, R. (1997) 'Using the Internet for Survey Research', *Sociological Research Online*, 2 (2), http://www.socresonline.org.uk/socresonline/2/2/2.
Foster, G. (1994) 'Fishing the Net for Research Data', British *Journal of Educational Technology*, 25 (2): 91–7.
Frankfort-Nachmias, C. and Nachmias, D. (1996) *Research Methods in the Social Sciences*, 5th edn. London: Arnold.
Hodder, I. (1994) 'The Interpretation of Documents and Material Culture', in N.K. Denzin and Y.S. Lincoln (eds), *Handbook of Qualitative Research*. Thousand Oaks, CA: Sage.

Huff, C. and Sobiloff, B. (1993) 'Macpsych: An Electronic Discussion List and Archive for Psychology Concerning the Macintosh Computer', *Behaviour Research Methods, Instruments and Computers*, 25 (1): 60–4.
Katori, K. (1990) 'Recent Developments and Future Trends in Marketing Research in Japan Using New Electronic Media', *Journal of Advertising Research*, 30 (2): 53–7.
Kenway, J. (1996) 'The Information Superhighway and Post-Modernity: the Social Promise and the Social Price', *Comparative Education*, 32 (2): 217–31.
Kerka, S. (1995) *Access to Information: To Have and Have Not*. Colombus, OH: Center on Education and Training for Employment.
King, E. (1996) 'The Use of the Self in Qualitative Research', in J.T.E. Richardson (ed.), *Handbook of Qualitative Research Methods for Psychology and the Social Sciences*. Leicester: BPS Books.

Langford, D. (1995a) 'Law and Disorder in Netville', *New Scientist*, 146: 52–3.

Langford, D. (1995b) *Practical Computer Ethics*. Maidenhead: McGraw Hill.

Mehta, R. and Sivadas, E. (1995) 'Comparing response rates and response contact in mail versus Electronic Mail Surveys', *Journal of the Market Research Society*, 37 (4): 429–39.

Murray, D.E. (1995) *Knowledge Machines: Language and Information in a Technological Society*. London: Longman.

Pitt, M. (1996) 'The Use of Electronic Mail in Undergraduate Teaching', *British Journal of Educational Technology*, 27 (1): 45–50.

Roberts, L.D., Smith, L.M. and Pollock, C. (1997) '"u r a lot bolder on the net": the Social Use of Text-Based Virtual Environments by Shy Individuals', paper presented to First International Conference on Shyness and Self-Consciousness, Cardiff University, July 1997.

Schmidt, W. (1997a) 'World-Wide Web Survey Research Made Easy with WWW Survey Assistant', *Behaviour Research Methods, Instruments and Computers*, 29: 303–4.

Schmidt, W. (1997b) 'World-Wide Web Survey Research: Benefits, Potential Problems and Solutions', *Behaviour Research Methods, Instruments and Computers*, 29: 274–9.

Spender, D. (1995) *Nattering on the Net: Women, Power and Cyberspace*. Melbourne: Spinifex Press.

Sproull, L.S. (1986) 'Using Electronic Mail for Data Collection in Organisational Research', *Academy of Management Journal*, 29: 159–69.

Thach, E. (1995) 'Using Electronic Mail to Conduct Survey Research', *Educational Technology*, March–April: 27–31.

Wild, R.H. and Winniford, M. (1993) 'Remote Collaboration Among Students Using Electronic Mail', *Computers and Education*, 21 (3): 193–203.

See also Internet.

NEIL SELWYN AND KATE ROBSON

Empiricism, abstracted empiricism

Empiricism

Empiricism, at its strongest, is the doctrine that knowledge is based on experience. A slightly weaker version entails the claim that all statements purporting to express knowledge about facts depend upon experience for their justification. In philosophy, this position has been contrasted with that of *rationalism*, which involves the claim that it is possible to obtain knowledge about what exists by reason alone. The form of logic used by rationalists is that of deduction, whereby the conclusion of an argument leads from its premises, such that if all the premises are true, the conclusion must be true. A simple example would be: Premise 1: Sam is a human. Premise 2: All humans are mortal. Conclusion: Sam is mortal.

From the empiricist point of view, there are a number of problems with deduction. First, it is difficult to see how, on its own, it is capable of generating new knowledge, in that the conclusion must be implicit in the original premises. Second, it is based on the tenet that *if* all the premises are true, then the conclusion must be. Empiricists would argue that the only way to find out if all the premises are true is to use our experience. As a result, empiricists adopt inductive reasoning, which involves moving from premises concerning that which has been observed to a conclusion concerning that which has not. Usually this involves making a general claim in the conclusion on the basis of particular observed instances. Thus, if all particular swans observed are seen to be white, one will come to the inductive conclusion that all swans are white. The crucial difference between deduction and induction is that, even if all the premises in an inductive argument are true, there is no guarantee that the conclusion will be true. This 'problem of induction', identified by David Hume (1969 [1739]) *après la lettre*, has dogged empiricism for quarter of a millennium. The problem is that no matter how many specific instances are observed indicating a particular general conclusion, one cannot be sure that that conclusion is true. To return to the example of swans, the conclusion that all swans are white was based on experiences gained in the northern hemisphere. With experience of antipodean black swans, the conclusion was falsified.

While the above may seem a rather esoteric philosophical discussion, it is far from it, because it strikes at the core of claims made by empirical science. The methods of science, and paradigmatically, experimental science, have traditionally been based on the empirical assumptions that (a) the most reliable knowledge is gained through rigorously controlled experience and (b) that the process by which that experience should be analysed is one of induction. The problem is that no matter how rigorously and frequently scientific investigations are made into phenomena, there can be no proof that the general conclusions generated will be true.

The most famous attempt to overcome the problem of induction in science was made by Karl Popper (1959), who argued that the role of science, rather than being to verify previous findings should be to falsify them. While the verity of a general conclusion could never be proved, its falsity could. For Popper, scientific theories can never be afforded more than provisional acceptance. Unfortunately, Popper's hypothetico-deductive method is vulnerable to the same sort of criticisms as inductivism. No matter how sustained scientific efforts are to find negative instances that would falsify a provisional hypothesis, and no matter how often those efforts fail to falsify it, we are no nearer to being sure that the hypothesis is true.

These problems with inductivism and its hypothetico-deductivist alternative have led theorists and researchers to seek alternatives in two different directions. The first direction is that of scepticism. Here, the failure of empirical science to establish the absolute veracity of the knowledge it generates has led to rejection of the privileged position claimed by science. For those who adhere to *postmodernism*, science has lost its dominance as the most effective method of attaining knowledge about the world and takes its place amongst many competing discourses, none of which can claim superiority.

An opposing direction is taken by those who wish to strengthen the epistemological claims of science through rejection of its exclusive dependence on empiricism. The argument here is that science should not merely be about the observation of the world, but should also involve rationalist processes of theory production to explain and contextualise those observations. An important philosophical school here is that of *realism*, which holds the ontological assertion that objects exist independently of our empirical perception of them. The epistemological corollary to this assertion is that non-empirical (that is, theoretical) methods are required in addition to empirical methods to fully understand the world.

Abstracted empiricism

A seminal advocate of the need for social researchers to adopt a judicious balance of theory and empiricism was C. Wright Mills. This balance was, for him, at the core of *The Sociological Imagination* (1970 [1959]). He argued that, unfortunately, many social researchers failed to grasp this point, and erred in favour of relying exclusively on either theory or empiricism.

In relation to the former error, Mills launched what many saw as a devastating attack on the rather lugubrious theoretical efforts of Talcott Parsons and his functionalist colleagues. He accused them of confining their attention to the artificial esoteria of 'grand theory', which he described as 'an arid and elaborate formalism in which the splitting of Concepts and their endless rearrangement becomes the central endeavour' (1970: 30). The role of theory in social science, according to Mills, is to 'fly high for a little while in order to see something in the social world more clearly, to solve some problem that can be stated in terms of the historical reality in which men and institutions have their concrete being' (1970: 58). In their obsession with the creation of sophisticated and unifying theoretical models, grand theorists lose their connection with the real world. Rather then being only part of the process of social research, theory becomes its be all and end all. As a result, it cannot be operationalised and thereby tested through empirical research. For Mills, grand theory was a 'formalist withdrawal [in which] what is properly only a pause seems to have become permanent. As they say in Spain, "many can shuffle cards who can't play"' (1970: 58–9).

Mills was equally critical of the opposing tendency which abandoned theory altogether, coining for it the pejorative term of 'abstracted empiricism'. For Mills, abstracted empiricism involved the almost random gathering of social facts, without any theoretical framework to order those facts or to assess their significance. 'As a style of social science, abstracted empiricism is not characterized by any substantive propositions or theories. It is not based upon any new conception of the nature of society or of man or upon any particular facts about them' (1970: 65). Instead, the intellectual efforts of abstracted empiricists concentrated upon the development of sophisticated methods by which facts were to be collected. This, he argued, entailed 'formal and empty ingenuity' (1970: 86), the results of which 'no matter how numerous, do not convince us of anything worth having convictions about' (1970: 65). In short, abstracted empiricists were accused of fetishising reliability at the cost of relevance.

While Mills' excoriating critique of abstracted empiricism may have been unfair to many of his colleagues, not least to his primary victim, Paul Lazarfeld, the general point he was making has had considerable influence on social research. That point is that if social researchers fail to engage in theoretical examination of the nature and significance of the problems they are addressing, then they will be in grave danger, no matter how sophisticated their data gathering and analytic techniques may be, of producing a finished result that is trite and banal. Empiricism abstracted from theory is not an adequate foundation for good social research.

References

Hume, D. (1969 [1739]) *A Treatise of Human Nature*. Harmondsworth: Penguin.

Mills, C.W. (1970 [1959]) *The Sociological Imagination*. Harmondsworth: Penguin.

Popper, K. (1959) *The Logic of Scientific Discovery*. London: Hutchinson.

SAM PORTER

Epistemology

Epistemology is from the Greek words 'episteme', meaning knowledge, and 'logos', meaning explanation. The term is concerned with the nature of knowledge and justification, how we know what we know. In the philosophy of the social sciences, *epistemology* explores how we know that we know something, *ontology* explores the nature of social reality, what kinds of things can be said to exist, and in what ways, and *ethics* deal with what we ought to do. Mainstream Anglo-American tradition separates epistemology from philosophy of science. These thinkers attempt to link epistemology with nature and ordinary knowledge and link the philosophy of science with natural sciences generally and particular sciences.

In the seventeenth century there were two main opposing philosophical schools concerned with establishing secure foundations for knowledge. These were the *rationalists* or *idealists*, of whom Descartes is one of the most famous members, who appealed to rational and formal reasoning, and the *empiricists*, who appealed to sensory perceptions. Rationalists argued that reality could be reasoned logically by working from established concepts. In contrast, empiricists disputed the idea that a priori knowledge existed before sensory experience. Empiricist philosophers, the logical positivists, believed in genuine scientific knowledge as opposed to religious belief. Their framework included an emphasis on observation. This rules out the study of phenomena that cannot be experienced. They attempted to identify recurring patterns and establish them as scientific laws. Testablity is a key feature of empiricism. Science needs to be objective and factual; it needs to be free of subjective value judgments. The positivist model is committed to value neutral theory choice. The empiricists wanted to find a set of rules which justified the foundation of their knowledge. The standard illustrative example is that of white swans. The sentence 'All swans are white' is a statement which needs to be tested. This assertion has many problems, we cannot prove with certitude and non-inferentially that it is true. Even if we examined all the swans in the world we could not prove the truth claim as we could not be certain we had found them all. The whole hypothesis can be disproved by the observation of one black swan. Many sciences such as physics and chemistry rely on empiricist knowledge claims.

Kuhn, Feyerabend and Polanyi have all challenged the traditionally positivist view of science. All of them believed that for science to make progress it must be revolutionary. Kuhn's most important work was *The Structure of Scientific*

Revolutions (1962) in which he outlined his theory of the paradigm shift. Dis-agreements about the nature of legitimate scientific problems led Kuhn to recognise the role of paradigms. 'These I take to be universally recognized scientific achievements that for a time provide model problems and solutions to a com-munity of practitioners.' Science thus becomes socially situated. Polanyi says 'We must recognize belief once more as the source of all knowledge'. Karl Mannheim developed this idea in the sociology of knowledge. He saw knowledge as his-torically determined, tied to both time and circumstances. He believed that intellectuals had a more detached view due to their training and could therefore make better judgments. The sociology of knowledge is a tool in pointing to social conditions and ideologies that are affecting our judgments.

Suggested further reading

Benton, T. and Craib, I. (2001) *Philosophy of Social Science.* Houndmills, Basingstoke: Palgrave.

Bhaskar, R. (1975) *A Realist Theory of Science.* York: Blackwell.

SANDRA BAILLIE

Ethics

Introduction

The ethics of social research is about creating a mutually respectful, win-win rela-tionship in which participants are pleased to respond candidly, valid results are obtained, and the community considers the conclusions constructive.

Social research is a dynamic process that often involves an intrusion into people's lives and therefore largely depends on the establishment of a successful rela-tionship between the researcher and respondent(s). Central to this relationship is ethical responsibility, integral to the research topic and to research design and planning. Since the scope of social research incorporates many methodological approaches, however, a single set of ethical rules or prescriptions is not possible or helpful. Indeed, consensus is lacking amongst social researchers as to what actually constitutes an ethical issue. This ambiguity has precluded the emergence of a clear typology or set of classifying characteristics by which to describe and contrast particular studies. This is not however to undermine the importance of ethics to the social researcher. Ethical responsibility is essential at all stages of the research process, from the design of a study, including how participants are recruited, to how they are treated through the course of these procedures, and finally to the consequences of their participation. Despite the ambiguities surrounding the application of ethics in the social research context, the literature consistently does highlight a number of key considerations that researchers should adhere to throughout the course of any research venture. As will become apparent in the ensuing discussion, these ethical issues do not take effect in isolation but rather combine and interact to ensure an overall ethically robust framework for effective social research.

Voluntary consent

Voluntary consent is considered by many as the central norm governing the relationship between the researcher and participant. A major tenet of medical research is that participation must be voluntary and this applies to social research also. Simply put, this means that an individual partakes in research according to his/her own freewill and therefore a good researcher should inform participants that the research is voluntary and that they can withdraw at any time. However, sound methodological considerations potentially may conflict with ethical principles. For instance, voluntary consent does not sit easily with the core principle of random sampling, as given the choice, certain types of people are more likely to decline to participate in a survey, thereby creating a biased sample. Although there are ways of statistically adjusting for known sample biases, from the point of view of sampling it is best to maximise the proportion of responses from the population and do everything possible to encourage voluntary participation. The use of consent forms in qualitative research provides another example of the potential for conflict between ethical principles and methodological considerations. The use of consent forms in qualitative interviewing is increasing. Prior to commencing any interviewing the researcher provides the interviewee with a consent form. The form can be in effect a 'contract' in which important considerations such as whether the interviewee can withdraw any information given at any stage in the research, up to and including publication, are laid out explicitly. Ethically this is a sound procedure, clarifying for the research subject the extent of control they will (or will not) retain over any information they may give. However, this can inadvertently formalise what may have seemed to the research subject at the outset to be a casual procedure and inadvertently compromise rapport between the researcher and participant – an effect which will be detrimental to the overall quality and/or extent of data gathered.

Informed consent

Closely aligned to voluntary participation is the principle of informed consent. On ethical, as well as methodological grounds, encouraging individuals to participate in research requires that clear and accurate information about the research is delivered to them. Information given should cover all aspects of the research in question, such as the research aims, methods to be used and intended outcomes. Also, this information should be presented in lay terms that are easily understood, as bombarding potential participants with technical research jargon obviously is more likely to cause confusion than clarification. Furthermore, too much detail about the research may 'overload' the subject or just bore them. Therefore, the researcher needs to follow a balanced approach, presenting adequate and relevant information concisely so as to appraise respondents of their potential role in the research fully. The duty to provide informed consent does not stop after the information sought has been provided. Participants have the right to be kept informed about the uses to which their information is being put; in some cases this should include the right to be debriefed fully as soon as practicable after the completion of data collection. When the research involves working with vulnerable populations such as children or retarded adults, participation must still be voluntary but consent should be obtained from other responsible people as well as the participant.

Some practitioners argue that the principle of informed consent can be compromised if the goals of the research cannot be realised by any means other than the covert collection of information. In this instance, *at a minimum*, it is essential that the research is significant enough to justify covert methods.

Anonymity and confidentiality

One of the most important aspects of social research is the protection of the participants' identity. Participants should not have to share highly personal information with a researcher unless they and the researcher can be certain that their data will be kept from falling into the wrong hands. As part of obtaining informed consent it should be made clear to participants how their responses will be treated. Adhering to the principles of anonymity and confidentiality are therefore imperative ethical considerations when undertaking any social research.

While these terms are used interchangeably, there are important distinctions between them. *Anonymity* means that the researcher will not and cannot identify the respondent; for example, a postal survey in which questionnaires are returned with no identifying labels or codes. *Confidentiality* means that the researcher can match names with responses – for example, a face-to-face interview – but ensures that no one else will have access to the identity of the respondent. Confidentiality should only be assured if it can be genuinely maintained; it is not enough to state that material will be 'confidential' without also taking concrete steps to ensure that this in fact will be the case.

No harm to participants

The danger of potential harm caused by partaking in research may be more obviously evident in medical or psychological experiments; nevertheless, whilst perhaps less evident, dangers in social research can and do exist. Social research should *never* in any instance cause harm, whether physical or mental, to the participants involved. Again, however, there is no absolute means by which to mitigate against potential harm to a research participant. Very often research may ask participants to express deviant and/or unpopular attitudes, or require them to reveal demeaning personal characteristics such as low income or poor educational attainment and this may make many people feel uncomfortable. Social research, particularly that which involves in-depth interviewing or probing lines of questioning, may also force people to face aspects of themselves that they do not normally consider. This can result in personal agony for the participant. The very selection of participants for a particular study may invoke adverse reactions, wherein a particular population, for example, victims of domestic violence, are distressed and/or humiliated as being identified as such.

It is not only at the stage of data collection that the risks of harm are present. If there is a chance of latent misgivings or adverse effects, respondents should be followed up by the researcher later. Relatedly, interviewees or other research subjects, particularly the elderly, can become anxious about their participation at a later time. The researcher should provide information so that participants can contact them later on if necessary. When reading the outcomes of a particular study in which they participated, individuals may locate themselves within the report and find that they have been characterised in a way which they find troubling and at odds with their self-image. The extent to which a researcher gives participants the right to comment on research findings – from no access or right to comment after data has been collected (probably the most typical practice), up to the right to demand that any material involving them be deleted from final write-ups or publications – is an ethical issue.

Ethics and the academic community

Ethics within social research do not solely rest upon the relationship between the researcher and participant. Particularly in view of the increasing commercialisation of research, there is an ethical responsibility upon the researcher to his/her wider research community for many reasons, not least that a piece of research and the way in which it is conducted can bring the profession into disrepute. While the deliberate falsification of results obviously is inexcusable, inappropriate analysis and reportage of findings can be as misleading as deliberate falsification of data. In any rigorous study, the researcher should reveal the technical shortcomings of the research and, moreover, report all results whether positive or negative. Many findings may be arrived at unexpectedly and the researcher should make no attempt to conceal information, even if it lies at odds with the original research hypotheses. Doing so is dishonest and moreover masks the complexities of the particular social aspect under enquiry. Replication of results is one of the key safeguards against falsification of data and enables checks against the veracity and reliability of any set of results. This process has been greatly enhanced by the proliferation of social research findings made available on-line, enabling wider, more extensive secondary analysis.

In so far as maintaining professional ethical conduct in respect of other colleagues, researchers should refrain from criticising other research studies on the basis of polemic, personal bias or collective interests and instead should be honest, sincere and responsible in their critiques in order to justify their views. Following on from this, one final point perhaps more commonly known as a breach of ethical conduct, is plagiarism. Under no circumstances should any researcher use another's work without rightful and/or appropriate acknowledgement.

Conclusions

Researchers undertaking applied social research have an ethical responsibility to themselves, their colleagues and most importantly to the participants in their research. Since social research is a dynamic and unpredictable process however, it relies substantially on mutual trust and co-operation, as well as accepted conventions and expectations between the various parties involved. In this context researchers work in the field of research with few distinct limits. As much as lax or consciously unethical behaviour, it is this relative freedom of scope and genuine ambiguity about what constitutes ethical behaviour that can give rise to breaches of ethical codes. Ethics however are established and utilised to protect the social scientist, his/her work and the subjects of research. The application of ethical principles within the social research framework is imperative, no matter how ambiguous and/or obstructive they may be to a specific research project or agenda.

Suggested further reading

Homan, Roger (1991) *The Ethics of Social Research*. London: Longman.
Kimmel, Alan J. (1988) *Ethics and Values in Applied Social Research*. London: Sage.

May, Tim (2001) *Social Research: Issues, Methods and Process*, 3rd edn. Buckingham: Open University Press.

CAROLINE MCAULEY

Ethnography

Ethnography has a distinguished history in the social sciences. There have been 'travellers' tales' for centuries, going back even to antiquity, which count as a form of ethnographic research in that they purported to represent some aspect of social reality on the basis of close acquaintance with and observation of it. But it begins properly only at the beginning of the twentieth century with two entirely independent intellectual developments: the classical tradition of social anthropology in Britain and the Chicago School of sociology. The former referred to its practices as ethnography and the latter as participant observation. However, its meaning has broadened since then, although the term ethnography is still mistakenly used interchangeably with participant observation. Ethnography is also occasionally misunderstood as synonymous with qualitative research as a whole. More properly, ethnography is understood as 'field research' or 'fieldwork'. In this manner ethnography can be defined as the study of people in naturally occurring settings or 'fields' by means of methods which capture their social *meanings* and ordinary activities, involving the researcher participating directly in the setting (if not always the activities) in order to collect data in a systematic manner but without meaning being imposed on them externally. The capture of these social meanings was called by Clifford Geertz 'thick description' to emphasise the richness and depth of ethnographic data, and is more colloquially called 'telling it like it is' or 'insider knowledge'.

Ethnography is not one particular method of data collection but several which are combined flexibly to achieve the aims and approach that distinguish ethnography as a style of research. Following on from the definition of ethnography above, its objectives are to understand the social meanings and activities of people in a given 'field' or setting, and its approach involves close association with, and often participation in, this setting. Several methods of data collection tend to be used in ethnography, such as unstructured interviewing, participant observation, personal documents, vignettes and discourse analysis. In this way ethnography tends routinely to involve triangulation of methods. While these methods also are used outside ethnographic research what distinguishes their use in ethnography is utilisation towards meeting the characteristic aims and approach of ethnography.

There is a further reason for understanding ethnography as a style of research rather than a single method of data collection. It is umbilically tied to naturalism as a theoretical and philosophical framework so that method and methodology are interpolated in ethnography to the point of being almost indistinguishable. Ethnography is predisposed to naturalism: it concentrates on topics that lend themselves readily to the study of people's views, beliefs and meanings. And while it is the case that most topics can be addressed in various ways, ethnographers are predisposed to ask certain sorts of questions that access people's meanings, beliefs and interpretations. Above all, ethnography focuses on those naturally occurring non-experimental situations that characterise the methodological position of naturalism. However, the interpolation of method and methodology in ethnography has been problematic. Within naturalism ethnography was privileged as the principal method and its weaknesses were overlooked in exaggerated claims for its efficacy, while critics of naturalism as a theory of knowledge rejected ethnography out of hand. This has led to two sorts of criticisms of ethnography.

The natural science critique condemns ethnography for failing to meet the canons of natural science. Some principles it offends have to do with the role of the researcher. The natural science model of research, for example, does not permit the researcher to become a variable in the experiment yet ethnographers are not detached from the research but rather are themselves part of the study or by their obtrusive presence come to influence the field. If participant observation is used in data collection, ethnography can involve introspection, whereby the researcher's own experiences and attitude changes while sharing the field become part of the data. Another principle ethnography offends concerns methods of data collection. Methods that are unstructured, flexible and open-ended can appear to involve unsystematic data collection, in which the absence of structure prevents an assessment of the data because differences that emerge can be attributed to variations in the way they were collected. The rationale behind the highly structured methods of the natural sciences is to minimise extraneous variations in order to isolate 'real' differences in the data. This is why methods within natural science models of social research are designed to eliminate both the effects of the researcher and of the tool used to collect the data. Ethnography also breaches dearly held principles about the nature of data. The natural science model of social research seeks to describe and measure social phenomena by assigning numbers to the phenomena. Ethnography also describes and measures, but it does so by means of extracts of natural language and deals with quality and meanings, which seem shifty, unreliable, elusive and ethereal.

The other set of criticisms constitutes what can be called the postmodern critique. This attacks the exaggerated claims made by some ethnographers who fail to recognise not only its weaknesses but also those of science generally in the light of postmodernism's deconstruction of science as an intellectual enterprise. In this respect, all knowledge is relative, so there are no guarantees as to the worth of the activities of researchers or the truthfulness of their statements. This 'moment' in the development of ethnography is referred to by postmodern critics as the 'double crisis'. The first is the crisis of representation. The claim was challenged that ethnography can produce universally valid knowledge by accurately capturing the nature of the social world 'as it is' – a view described as 'naïve realism'. All accounts are constructions and the whole issue of which account more accurately represents social reality is meaningless. The second is the crisis of legitimation. In as much as ethnographic descriptions are partial, selective, even autobiographical, because they are tied to the particular ethnographer and the contingencies under which the data were collected, the traditional criteria for evaluating ethnography become problematic, as terms like 'validity', 'reliability' and 'generalisability' lose their authority to legitimate the data.

These crises have implications for how we should understand ethnographic accounts, for they do not neutrally represent the social world. There are implications for the claims ethnographers are able to make about their account, for it is no longer a privileged 'thick description' of the social world from the inside. And there are implications for the written text, which attempts to represent in writing the reality of the 'field', for ethnographers should no longer make foolish authoritative claims in order to validate their account as the accurate representation of reality but instead be 'reflexive'.

However, ethnography has not been left completely in a postmodern state of total scepticism and relativism in which 'anything goes'. Some ethnographers have rescued it from the worst excesses of postmodernism while still accepting some of the more valid criticisms of naïve realism. A number of sets of guidelines exist by which the practice of ethnography is codified and can be made rigorous. What one might call 'post postmodern ethnography' advocates the possibility and desirability of systematic ethnography and remains rooted in weaker versions of realism. The best example would be Martyn Hammersley's notion of 'subtle realism'. Post postmodern ethnography contends that while no knowledge is certain, there are phenomena that exist independent of us as researchers and knowledge claims about them can be judged reasonably accurately in terms of their likely truth. This shares with naïve realism the idea that research investigates independently knowable phenomena but breaks with it in denying that we have direct access to these phenomena. It shares with anti-realism the recognition that all knowledge is based on assumptions and human constructions, but rejects that we have to abandon the idea of truth itself.

Theoretical niceties, however, have not infected all modern ethnographers and many ethnographers carry on regardless of the critique proffered by postmodernism. Inspired by realism and hermeneutic methodologies, classic ethnographic studies continue in which it is believed that thick descriptions are possible and that by close familiarity with people in the field an insider's account can accurately capture social reality and unambiguously represent it in textual form.

Methodological disputes notwithstanding, ethnography remains a very useful approach to study those parts of society that quantitative methods cannot access and where the social meanings of the people, families, groups and communities which inhabit this world are unknown or unusual. It has seen applications to most areas of social science, particularly in the past to the study of work, deviance, communities, policing and health and medicine. It can also be applied to the study of social policy and to policy making.

See also
Discourse analysis,
Participant observation
and **Vignette**.

Suggested further reading

Atkinson, P., Coffey, A., Delamont, S., Lofland J. and Lofland, L. (2001) *Handbook of Ethnography*. London: Sage.

Brewer, J.D. (2000) *Ethnography*. Buckingham: Open University Press.
Hammersley, M. (1992) *What's Wrong with Ethnography?* London: Routledge.

JOHN BREWER

Ethnomethodology

Ethnomethodolgy emerged in the 1960s as a critique of mainstream social research and, in particular, the problematic relationship between the research strategies traditionally employed and the nature of the data collected. The term was coined by the American sociologist, Harold Garfinkel and quite literally means the study of ('ology') the methods ('method') that people ('ethno') employ to make sense of the social world. Social life for ethnomethodologists is a constant achievement and is something that we create and recreate continuously. Consequently, the main aim of this programme is to uncover the everyday practices through which people construct social reality and make sense of their own and other's activities.

Garfinkel outlined the main themes and ideas underpinning this approach in his book *Studies in Ethnomethodology* (1967) and this remains one of the most influential texts in the field. Drawing upon the phenomenological writings of Edmund Husserl and Alfred Schutz, Garfinkel declared that one of the key tasks of ethnomethodology was to make the taken-for-granted unnoticed features of everyday life a matter of theoretic interest. As ethnomethodology is based on the assumption that social order is constructed in the minds of society's members through a process of common-sense reasoning, it was necessary to develop ways of making this process subject to analytic scrutiny. To achieve this ethnomethodologists developed a variety of techniques that were designed to disrupt the taken-for-granted nature of everyday life and thereby illuminate the 'rules' and procedures that people used to maintain order and stability. For example, one of Garfinkel's 'breaching' or 'demonstration' experiments involved his undergraduate students behaving as lodgers in their own homes. They were instructed to carry out their activities in a polite and circumspect manner and to speak only when they were spoken to. The reactions of family members to this behaviour, which ranged from bewilderment and embarrassment to shock and outright anger, demonstrated to Garfinkel the fragile and precarious nature of social order and brought into view the interpretive work that people carried out in an attempt to restore orderliness.

Members of society have to accomplish or achieve their social world and, according to Garfinkel, one of the ways in which this is done is through the 'documentary method of interpretation'. This refers to the way in which we select certain aspects of a situation which seem to conform to a pattern and then interpret these on the basis of that pattern. Then once this pattern has been established we use it to interpret other aspects of the situation which may arise. To illustrate the documentary method in action Garfinkel set up an experiment in which 10 student volunteers were invited to attend a 'counselling session' and seek advice on a particular problem they had. The 'counsellor', who was in fact part of the experiment, was only allowed to give 'yes' or 'no' responses and, unknown to the students, these answers were predetermined by a table of random numbers. After each answer the student was asked to evaluate the advice given and record her/his comments. Garfinkel found that although the counsellor's responses were predetermined the students found the advice helpful. Where answers appeared problematic the students were prepared to wait for later ones before deciding on the meaning of previous responses. They were able to detect an underlying pattern in the advice and through their use of the 'documentary method' they imposed meaning and made sense of what were meaningless and senseless responses.

Two of the most important concepts in ethnomethodology are those of *indexicality* and *reflexivity*. Indexicality refers to the inextricable relationship between the meaning of words and actions and the context within which they are situated. For example, the way in which the students interpreted the 'advice' given by the 'counsellor' in the example described above demonstrates that the meaning of an utterance cannot be divorced from the context in which the words are spoken.

Reflexivity refers to the fact that the orderliness of everyday life is a practical accomplishment. Social reality is created through talk and therefore to describe a situation is at the same time to create it. In other words, for ethnomethodologists the features of a particular social setting should be regarded as identical to the way in which members perceive them. Because the sense-making work by which the social order is produced is not itself a topic of members' enquiries it is perceived as a factual order. It is the ethnomethodologists' task to describe these taken-for-granted methods.

These concepts are central to ethnomethodology's critique of traditional social science approaches. For ethnomethodologists the methods of sociology are also practical accomplishments and deserve to be studied as topics in their own right.

While Garfinkel's breaching experiments provided a range of fascinating insights into the nature of intersubjectivity, there has been a move away from these artificially created scenarios and later ethnomethodological studies based their analysis on naturally occurring disruptions of the social order.

Ethnomethodology is now a permanent feature of the sociological landscape and, while less prominent than it once was, continues to exert its influence on the social sciences. This is particularly true of conversation analysis, which has had a profound impact on other disciplines such as psychology, sociology, anthropology and linguistics. Indeed conversation analysis, which adheres to the methodological principles propounded by Garfinkel in its attempt to explicate the rules and regularities underpinning talk-in-interaction, is currently the most productive form of ethnomethodological research.

Suggested further reading

Benson, D. and Hughes, J.A. (1983) *The Perspective of Ethnomethodology*. London: Longman.

Garfinkel, H. (1967) *Studies in Ethnomethodology*. Englewood Cliffs, NJ: Prentice-Hall.

Heritage, J. (1984) *Garfinkel and Ethnomethodology*. Cambridge: Polity Press.

CIARAN ACTON

Exploratory data analysis

Exploratory data analysis (EDA) represents a particular approach to data analysis, which is characterised by informality and flexibility and relies heavily on diagrammatic and pictorial representations of the data. The techniques that fall under the rubric of EDA are designed to highlight the underlying patterns and structure of a set of data. Through the use of graphs, plots and diagrams they bring unusual patterns and irregularities to the surface and help the analyst to investigate the data open-mindedly. John Tukey (1977), the person primarily responsible for developing and popularising this approach, aptly describes it as 'numerical detective work'. This implies that the emphasis is on the search for clues and patterns in the data rather than the evaluation of evidence and the proof or disproof of hypotheses (a process that is reserved for confirmatory data analysis in the form of various statistical tests). It is important to point out that these two approaches are complementary with the flexible and informal EDA procedures often serving as a precursor to the more formal process of hypothesis testing. Indeed it is good practice to examine a data set closely before carrying out statistical tests. One advantage of EDA procedures is that they are generally easier to understand than confirmatory techniques and most can be computed relatively quickly by hand.

EDA techniques generally rely on *resistant* measures (for example, the median rather than the mean) that are relatively unaffected by extreme values or outliers.

Although there is an extensive range of EDA techniques available to the social researcher, we will restrict the current discussion to two of the most popular procedures, the stem and leaf display and the box plot.

Stem and leaf display

The stem and leaf display is one of the most widely used EDA procedures and it is extremely easy to construct and interpret. Although similar in appearance to a histogram, the stem and leaf diagram has an added advantage in that it provides a good visual representation of the distribution while retaining the original information in the data. It draws our attention to some of the most important features of a distribution, including the level, spread and shape, and allows the analyst to easily identify any extreme or unusual values.

The best way to illustrate this technique is to work through an example. Below we have the exam marks for a group of 18 students:

48, 54, 44, 56, 55, 62, 68, 40, 42, 48, 25, 62, 66, 46, 50, 75, 65, 52

To produce a stem and leaf display for this (or any other) set of figures we need to carry out the following steps:

(1) The first step is to split the values into two separate components, one for the 'stem' and one for the 'leaf'. For the current batch of figures this is fairly straightforward, with the tens representing the stem and the units the leaf (see Figure 1). If you have decimals in your data and want to eliminate these before you proceed any further, you can do so either through rounding[1] or truncation.[2]

(2) Construct a column for the stems, allocating a separate line for each possible value in the dataset, and draw a vertical line to the right of this column. As the exam scores above range from 25 to 75 we will need to create a column that begins with 2 and ends with 7.

(3) Finally, we need to take each data value and record the trailing digit (the leaf) next to the appropriate stem, arranging them in ascending order. For example the lowest score in the distribution is 25, which is represented in the diagram as a stem of 2 and a leaf of 5. The next value is 40 which has a stem of 4 and a leaf of 0 and so on.

```
2 |  5
3 |
4 |  0 2 4 6 8 8
5 |  0 2 4 5 6
6 |  2 2 5 6 8
7 |  5
```

Stem: tens
Leaf: units

Figure 1   *Basic stem and leaf diagram*

As alluded to above, one of the main strengths of EDA techniques is their flexibility. There are a wide range of variations on the basic stem and leaf format described above and the type you employ will depend largely on the nature of your data. For example, if you have a large number of values you may end up with too many leaves on each line. To overcome this problem you can sub-divide the stem across a number of different lines. In Figure 2 there are two lines for each stem and we simply record leaves 0 through 4 on the * line and 5 through 9 on the • line.

2*	
2•	5
3*	
3•	
4*	0 2 4
4•	6 8 8
5*	0 2 4
5•	5 6
6*	2 2
6•	5 6 8
7*	
7•	5

Figure 2   *Half stem and leaf diagram*

Another useful variation is the back-to-back stem and leaf diagram which facilitates the comparison of two distributions. For example, Figure 3 uses the same data as the previous graphs but in this instance we are able to compare male and female exam performance. The key differences in the distributions are immediately apparent. The scores for males are concentrated around the 40s and low 50s, while the main concentration of female scores is in the 60s.

Males		Females
	1	
	2	5
	3	
8 8 6 2 0	4	4
6 4 2	5	0 5
2	6	2 5 6 8
	7	5
	8	
	9	

Figure 3   *Back-to-back stem and leaf diagram*

The stem and leaf diagram provides a good illustration of the EDA approach in general. It is an extremely flexible technique which provides a clear visual representation of the data and it allows us to identify key features such as central tendency, spread, skewness and any outlying values.

The box plot

The box plot (sometimes referred to as the box-and-dot or the box-and-whisker plot) was also developed by John Tukey and represents one of the most popular and effective EDA techniques. Its utility derives from the fact that it provides a visual representation of what is known as the 'five-number summary' (the median, the upper quartile, the lower quartile, the highest value and the lowest value). By drawing attention to these and other key features of the data, box plots force the analyst to focus on the most important aspects of the distribution and enable quick comparisons to be made between batches.

Like stem and leaf diagrams, they are relatively easy to construct and interpret. Figure 4 highlights the various elements of a typical box plot. The box itself is one of the most important features of the plot as it represents the middle, and most reliable, portion of the data. The top of the box corresponds to the upper quartile and the bottom of the box the lower quartile (referred to as 'hinges' in Tukey's terminology). Consequently the length of the box represents the midspread or interquartile range (the middle 50% of the data). The median is the line that divides the box, with half the values on either side. The precise location of the median provides an indication of the extent to which the data is skewed (for example, in a symmetrical distribution it will be equidistant from both ends of the box). The lines protruding from the box are sometimes referred to as 'whiskers' and extend as far as the adjacent values. (The 'adjacents' are the most extreme values in a batch that do not qualify as outliers.)

For a value to qualify as an outlier it needs to be a certain distance away from the quartiles. Inner and outer 'fences'[3] are constructed to help us identify these

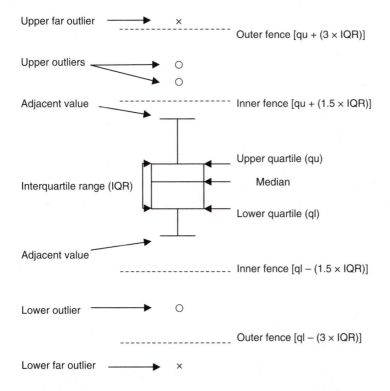

Figure 4   *The structure of a box plot*

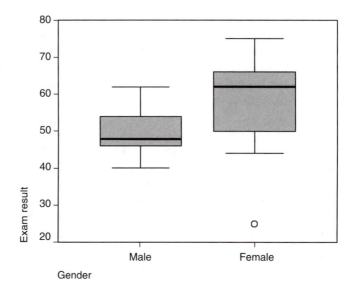

Figure 5 *Box plot for exam score by gender*

extreme values. Outliers are any values that fall outside the inner fences. Any values that fall outside the outer fences are categorised as far outliers.

The exam scores data that were employed in the stem and leaf diagrams above has also been utilised for the box plot[4] in Figure 5. The utility of the EDA approach is clearly demonstrated by this diagram which alerts us to some of the key differences between male and female students.

If we focus first on central tendency we can see immediately that the median for females is higher than that for males. However the female distribution also has a greater spread than the male distribution. In particular you will notice that the box in the male plot is much more compressed, indicating that the middle half of the data falls within a relatively narrow range of scores. The fact that the median for males is closer to the lower quartile than the upper quartile suggests that the data has an upward skew. By contrast the female distribution has a downward skew. Boxplots also draw our attention to unusual or extreme cases. Here, the female who scored an unusually low 25% in the exam is clearly identifiable as an outlier.

Notes

1 Decimals from .5 to .9 are rounded up to the next whole number and values of .4 or below are rounded down. For instance, 6.4 would be rounded down to 6, whereas 6.5 would be rounded up to 7.
2 'Truncation' involves dropping the decimals altogether. Using this method, 6.4 and 6.5 would both become 6. One of the advantages of using truncation as opposed to rounding is that it is easier to return to the original data values.
3 To calculate the inner fences, multiply the interquartile range (IQR) by 1.5. Then add this value to the upper quartile (qu) in order to obtain the inner fence for the top of the box and dot plot and subtract it from the lower quartile (ql) to obtain

the inner fence for the bottom. The same procedure is used to calculate the outer fences for the top and bottom except the IQR is multiplied by 3.

4 This box plot was created using the Explore procedure in SPSS.

Suggested further reading

Erickson, B.H. and Nosanchuk, T.A. (1992) *Understanding Data*. Buckingham: Open University Press.

Hartwig, Frederick with Dearing, Brian E. (1979) *Exploratory Data Analysis*. London: Sage.
Marsh, C. (1988) *Exploring Data*. Oxford: Blackwell.

Reference

Tukey, John W. (1977) *Exploratory Data Analysis*. Reading, MA: Addison-Wesley.

CIARAN ACTON

F

Factor analysis

The term factor analysis refers to two quite different statistical procedures which analyse the correlations between several variables. Both assume that the data are numerical ('interval scales') and are based on the responses of substantial samples of people (at least 200). They both try to explain the correlations between the observed variables in terms of a smaller number of 'latent variables' or 'factors'; the terms are synonymous. For example, an occupational psychologist might have administered 10 personality and ability scales to a large sample of people as part of a firm's selection procedure. Logically speaking these 10 tests may not necessarily assess 10 completely different aspects of the candidates' performance: they may overlap to some extent. That is, the 10 tests may perhaps only measure two or three distinct factors.

Exploratory factor analysis

Exploratory Factor Analysis is the original technique: an author who merely specifies 'factor analysis' will invariably mean exploratory factor analysis. It is purely descriptive and does not require the user to have any preconceived ideas or hypotheses about the structure of the data, and does not involve any form of significance testing. Instead, exploratory factor analysis shows:

- how many different factors are required to represent the data
- which variables are influenced by each factor. A table known as the 'factor matrix' or 'factor pattern matrix' shows the size of the relationship between each variable and each factor: under some circumstances these correspond to the correlations between each item and each factor
- a score for each person on each factor ('factor scores').

Exploratory factor analysis has several important uses in the social sciences. First, it may be useful in reducing a huge mass of data to manageable proportions (data reduction). For example, a researcher may compile a 200-item questionnaire about attitudes to sexual practices and behaviours, and administer this to a large sample of people. To analyse the answers to all 200 questions would be time consuming to perform and it would be difficult to interpret and digest so many results. In any case, it is probable that many of the questions will overlap. For example, it may well be the case that people show similar levels of tolerance towards all sexual minorities, and this will influence how they respond to all the questions involving these minority groups. Thus, it may be that the pattern of responses to all the questions about sexual minorities will be very similar, falling into a distinct group which we can call a *factor*. Hence, rather than analysing the responses to each individual question, it may be useful to perform a preliminary factor analysis, and then analyse the factors which emerge.

The second main use of exploratory factor analysis is in checking whether the items in questionnaires form the scales that they are supposed to. Many psychological tests and questionnaires claim to measure several distinct aspects of personality, ability, etc. If the test is working correctly, then factor analysing the correlations between the test items should produce a solution where the number of factors corresponds to the number of scales in the questionnaire, and the factor matrix shows that all the items which are supposed to measure the same trait correlate substantially with the same factor. For example, if two questions which are supposed to measure two different personality traits both show substantial correlations with the *same* factor (implying that in fact they both measure the same thing) then the test is clearly flawed and should not be used.

The third use of factor analysis is more controversial. Authors such as Raymond Cattell claim that the factors which emerge from factor analysis represent genuine causal influences. Suppose that one assessed several behaviours such as (in)ability to walk in a straight line, volubility of speech and feeling of well-being in a large sample of people, some of whom have been drinking alcohol to various extents. Alcohol will influence all three behaviours. If, when the data are factor analysed, the three items are found to form a common factor, the result of the factor analysis can be interpreted as revealing that these three variables have a common physical cause – alcohol. Several researchers have attempted to construct a personality questionnaire by assembling all of the items which could possibly be used to describe personality ('grumpy', 'anxious', 'self-effacing', etc.). Large samples were asked to rate how well each of these terms described them, and the results were factor analysed: factors which the researchers chose to give labels such as 'Neuroticism' and 'Extroversion' have been reliably identified in several such studies. Does it follow that these factors emerge because of a single (social/biological/genetic/

cognitive) process? That is, should the reliable presence of a factor necessarily be taken to indicate validly a single, causal, influence on behaviour?

Confirmatory Factor Analysis

Confirmatory Factor Analysis requires the experimenter to have clear expectations *before analysing the data* about the underlying structure which is expected. For example, from inspecting the nature of the test items it might seem likely that the candidates' scores on tests 1, 4 and 8 will all be influenced by the same factor (for example, their level of verbal skills), their scores on tests 3, 5, 9 and 10 will all reflect a second factor corresponding to a second aspect of personality or ability (for example, anxiety) and that their scores on tests 2, 6 and 7 will be influenced by a third factor (for example, numerical skill). Specialised computer programs (for example, LISREL, EQS or MX) are used to test this hypothesis. They provide various indices showing how closely the model fits the data, together with a significance test. If the model does not provide a particularly good fit to the data then it is possible to repeatedly refine it (for example, such that scores on test 6 are influenced by both anxiety and verbal ability) in an attempt to find a model which provides a good fit to the data. However this can be dangerous practice, as it is possible to capitalise on chance (sampling) variations in the data. Confirmatory factor analysis is a fairly recent development, and is a special case of the statistical method known as structural equation modelling discussed by Loehlin (1998) amongst others.

If the 10 occupational tests can be shown to only measure three factors, then one would probably not lose much by discarding seven of them, retaining only one test to represent each factor. This may well offer a substantial saving in time and money for the organisation.

Performing factor analysis

The technicalities of exploratory factor analysis are covered extensively in texts such as Comrey and Lee (1992). There are in fact several methods of performing factor analyses, which simulation studies have shown to produce highly similar results most of the time. However, three issues do need to be mentioned. Tests for determining the most appropriate number of factors are problematical, since they frequently produce contradictory results. To make matters worse, several well-known statistical packages use as their default a test which is known to be severely flawed (the Kaiser-Guttman 'eigenvalues-greater-than-1.0' criterion). Second, replicable results can only be obtained from factor analyses if a technique known as 'factor rotation' is performed. Finally, when performing such factor rotation it is necessary to specify whether the factors should be forced to have zero correlations with each other ('orthogonal rotation') or whether the factors are allowed to correlate with each other if the data so dictate ('oblique rotation').

As an example of an exploratory factor analysis. Suppose that 10 tests were administered to a large sample of people, giving the following table of correlations.

Correlations between 10 tests

Variable 1	1.00	.12	−.16	.40	−.01	.11	.11	.60	−.13	−.09
Variable 2	.12	1.00	.04	.17	.23	.56	.49	.16	−.04	−.23
Variable 3	−.16	.04	1.00	−.15	.60	.11	−.22	.07	.70	.50
Variable 4	.40	.17	−.15	1.00	.13	.08	−.16	.55	.07	−.04
Variable 5	−.01	.23	.60	.13	1.00	−.19	.22	.00	.60	.44
Variable 6	.11	.56	.11	.08	−.19	1.00	.63	.00	−.08	.04
Variable 7	.11	.49	−.22	−.16	.22	.63	1.00	.03	.11	.04
Variable 8	.60	.16	.07	.55	.00	.00	.03	1.00	−.11	−.17
Variable 9	−.13	−.04	.70	.07	.60	−.08	.11	−.11	1.00	.55
Variable 10	−.09	−.23	.50	−.04	.44	.04	.04	−.17	.55	1.00

Factor analysis indicated that there are three factors in these data. These three factors together explain about 70% of the variance in the original correlation matrix – so not too much information is lost by thinking in terms of three factors rather than 10 test scores. The result of the factor analysis, a *factor matrix*, is shown below. Entries above 0.4 (or less than −0.4) are, by convention, highlighted to show which variables have substantial correlations with which factors. From the factor matrix it can be seen that tests 3, 5, 9 and 10 form one factor (that is, measure much the same thing), tests 2, 6 and 7 form another factor, and tests 1, 4 and 8 form a third factor.

Thus if the data came from 10 tests administered to job applicants, the employer would be well advised to consider saving costs by dropping all but tests 7, 8 and 9, as these are the tests that show the highest correlations with the factors.

Factor matrix: 10 Variables and 3 Factors

	Factor 1	Factor 2	Factor 3
Variable 1	−.077	.099	**.769**
Variable 2	.036	**.793**	.190
Variable 3	**.851**	−.025	−.004
Variable 4	.082	−.04	**.807**
Variable 5	**.827**	.118	.148
Variable 6	−.039	**.854**	−.022
Variable 7	.042	**.868**	−.087
Variable 8	.009	.007	**.875**
Variable 9	**.879**	.003	−.007
Variable 10	**.725**	−.051	−.114

If the data represent individual items in a survey of sexual attitudes, then it is obvious that the items overlap considerably (otherwise they would have to be represented by 10 factors (one per item) instead of three). So, rather than testing for sex differences by performing t-tests or analyses of variance on the 10 original items, it would be reasonable to combine scores on items 3, 5, 9 and 10 and perform a t-test/analysis of variance on this total, and likewise for items 2, 6 and 7 and 1, 4 and 8.

If the 10 variables represent questions in an established questionnaire, the scoring key should show that questions 3, 5, 9 and 10 form one scale, questions 2, 6 and 7 form another, and questions 1, 4 and 8 form a third scale. The respondents' scores on questions 1, 2, 3 and 4 should not be added together, as it is clear that these four items do not measure the same underlying variable, but instead relate to different scales.

References

Comrey, A.L. and Lee, H.B. (1992) *A First Course in Factor Analysis*, 2nd edn. Hillsdale, NJ: Lawrence Erlbaum.

Loehlin, J.C. (1998) *Latent Variable Models*, 3rd edn. Mahwah, NJ: Lawrence Erlbaum.

COLIN COOPER

Feminist epistemology

Epistemology is concerned with the nature of knowledge and the justification of what we claim to know. With the expansion of feminist scholarship in the 1960s and 1970s, it was inevitable that feminists would investigate the biases of mainstream epistemology as one of feminists' main concerns was to provide true knowledge about women's lives (Harding, 1986; Harding and Hintikka, 1983). They discovered three main problems with 'malestream' epistemology (O'Brien, 1980).[1] The first was that the vast majority of the knowledge that was produced was based on men's lives (empirically speaking) and 'masculine' values, (meaning that standard methodologies reflected masculine values, values whose normative status derives from their association with maleness); second, within this knowledge base, women's lives and traditional activities were largely deemed to be irrelevant and unimportant to the construction of knowledge; and third, women themselves were generally regarded as inadequate and incredible producers of knowledge. As Lorraine Code puts it in her discussion of traditions in epistemology, 'Aristotle is just one of a long line of western thinkers to declare the limitations of women's cognitive capacities' (1991: 9).

Feminist epistemological responses came in three main forms: feminist empiricism; feminist standpoint; and feminist postmodernism (Harding, 1986).

Feminist empiricism

Feminist empiricists argue that sexism and androcentrism (male bias) are social biases, prejudices based on false beliefs and hostile attitudes. These prejudices enter social and political research at the stage of identifying what problems or issues are to be researched as well as in the design of research and collection of evidence and data (Harding, 1986: 161). The feminist empiricist solution is to apply the norms of social scientific enquiry more strictly. There is, however, a contradiction at the heart of feminist empiricism, namely that the empiricist reliance on positivist methodology is incompatible with feminist exposure of these methods as androcentric. In fact, feminist empiricism deeply subverts traditional empiricism; through its revelations that the methods, practices and processes of the norms of scientific enquiry are deeply sexist, it annihilates the latter's claim to

objectivity (Harding, 1986: 25). A further reason that feminist empiricism subverts the project of malestream empiricism is that its proponents believe that
women as a social group are more likely to notice sexist bias than men. This is in
opposition to the traditional positivist, empiricist faith in the irrelevance of the
identity of the 'knower' to the production of knowledge.

Feminist empiricism has been re-worked by scholars such as Lynn Hankinson
Nelson (1990) and Helen Longino (1990). These scholars have attempted to find a
compromise between knowledge as a construction of communities and maintaining a commitment to a measure of communal objective standards against which
to measure claims to the truth. Once the idea has been mooted that what has
masqueraded as objective truth is instead prejudice, however, it becomes difficult
for feminists to remain fully committed to anything approximating mainstream
methods. Hence, the boundary between feminist empiricism and feminist standpoint has been blurred.

Feminist standpoint

In order to combat sexist bias in academic work, feminist scholars inspired by
radical feminism, psychoanalytic feminism and Marxism began developing feminist standpoint theory (Collins, 1989; Haraway, 1988; Rose, 1983; Smith, 1987).

Standpoint feminism is often equated too simply with the experiential
dimension of women's lives. While experience is important for the development
and articulation of standpoint epistemology, it is vital to understand the complexities of the relationship between 'experience', 'knowledge' and 'reality'.
Grounded in a post-Marxist analysis of the effects of gendered divisions of
activity upon intellectual structures (Harding, 1986: 42) and heavily influenced
by Hegel's master/slave dialectic, feminist standpoint theorists argued that
women potentially occupy positions of epistemic privilege. The logic of this
position depends on the understanding that the 'master's position' in any set of
dominating social relations tends to produce distorted visions of the 'real
regularities and underlying causal tendencies in social relations' (Harding, 1986:
191). Additionally, women, from their positions on the margins of society, are
able to understand the 'master's position', but are also able to perceive a different set of stories about reality – stories that value and centralise women's lives
and needs. Crucially, these alternative realities were not just to be understood as
existing at the empirical level but also in the arena of concepts, ideas and beliefs.
This is not surprising given the Marxist notion that daily activity is constitutive of
conceptual frameworks and belief systems.

Feminist standpoint scholars took this idea further by claiming that women's
lives are more heavily imbricated in the disorder and the 'messiness' of the everyday. On the other hand, men's lives are more ordered and removed from these
kinds of realities. The reasons put forward for these gender differences are varied.
One involves the notion that men and women have traditionally (and still do to a
certain extent) led different lives based on sexual difference (whether essential or
constructed difference). This has meant traditionally that women are involved in
child rearing, housework or relatively menial, repetitive paid work (typing for
example). Men, on the other hand, have less involvement with these 'basic' areas

of life and indeed generally have someone (wife, secretary) to carry out these tasks for them. This, arguably, leads men and women to occupy different epistemological terrains. In other words, they know different things and, more importantly, they develop and value certain types of knowledge differently.

The latter explanation is based on the experiential dimension of sexually differentiated lives. However, psychoanalytic theory, specifically object-relations theory, offers another reason for different approaches to and understandings of knowledge. Girls' and boys' different resolutions of the Oedipus Complex, imply that adult males and females have different relationships both with people and to ideas and concepts. Simplistically, this might imply that women are more 'relational' and emotional than men, whereas men are more 'distant' and rational than women.

Whatever the sources of sexually differentiated lives (if indeed we can continue to understand them as differentiated in this way), the more significant feminist standpoint insight is that activities, ideas, belief and values that are *associated* with men, maleness and masculinity (whatever forms these take) are valued more than those associated with women, femaleness and femininity. A classic elucidation of this is Carol Gilligan's work in *In A Different Voice* (1982). She argues that traditionally psychological analyses of the development of children's sense of justice were based on boy's lives and masculinist understandings of appropriate articulations of justice. Gilligan claims that there were different gendered approaches to ideas about justice and it was inappropriate that the forms associated with masculinity were favoured over those associated with femininity.

Other significant uses of feminist standpoint epistemology include Sara Ruddick's, *Maternal Thinking* (1989) and Joan Tronto's, *Moral Boundaries* (1993). Ruddick's work focuses on the possibilities of using 'maternal thinking' in order to pursue policies and practices of peace. Her work does not imply that women or mothers are inherently more peaceful than men, only that the *practice* of good mothering may provide new epistemological frameworks which would facilitate peace rather than its opposite. Joan Tronto similarly argues that epistemological and therefore political use can be made of the traditional association of women with morality, but only if we move towards thinking about a generic 'ethic of care'.

Contradictions and problems

Feminist standpoint is an achieved position – one that can only be reached with struggle (emotional and intellectual) and political commitment. It is not a position that can be articulated through untheorised 'women's experiences'. However, the logic of standpoint is that the knowledge produced is 'more' true and/or objective than that produced by malestream methods. This would be the case because it would use the more complete and less distorting categories available from the standpoint of historically locatable subjugated experiences. This view is somewhat at odds with the idea that all knowledge is socially mediated which suggests that one story about women's lives may be just as 'true' or 'false' as another.

Partly because of this fundamental contradiction along with the emerging contentious debates over the issue of difference within feminist theory in the 1990s and 2000s, feminist standpoint has lost much of its credibility. However, one of its key articulators, Sandra Harding, has persistently refined this position, developing notions of 'strong objectivity' and a 'postmodernist standpoint approach'. Moreover, feminist standpoint has been undergoing something of a recent revival (Allen and Howard, 2000). However, challenges to standpoint (and empiricist) epistemology continue to come from those scholars influenced by postmodern and poststructural thought.

Feminist postmodernism

As Foucault might argue, all knowledge is partial and the vision of the oppressed is itself (only) another discourse. Feminist scholars of this persuasion have given up on the goal of 'telling one true story' about women or gender. In this sense, feminist postmodern epistemology is something of an oxymoron, as postmodernist ideology advocates a profound scepticism towards universalising claims about the existence, nature and powers of reason, scientific and positivist methodologies, progress, language and the subject/self (Flax, 1983). As such, postmodern reflections on epistemology leads onto a fundamental questioning of the feminist epistemological project itself.

Questioning feminist epistemology

Feminist scholars have an ambivalent relationship with epistemological issues. On the one hand, the intellectual and political legitimacy associated with authoritative epistemological positions has been very attractive to feminists wishing to have their claims to knowledge validated. On the other hand, the classic feminist argument that culturally generated gendered beliefs and practices play a part in the production of knowledge makes it difficult to claim that a neutral or objective epistemological position is possible.

As such, there is an on-going debate about the most appropriate future route for feminists to take, epistemologically speaking. Those feminists attached to modernist political commitments insist on a return to 'innocent'[2] knowledge as a necessary pre-condition to increase the general sum of human emancipation. Others, notably postmodern and poststructural feminists, maintain that there can be no feminist epistemology as many of the basic dichotomies of epistemology – the possibility of objective knowledge, the separation between 'subject' and 'object', mind/body, reason/emotion, public/private – have been fundamentally destabilised by feminist work (Code: 1991). This begs the question as to whether feminism itself is a postmodern discourse in its own right. The debate will be sure to continue.

Notes

1 Mary O'Brien (1980) first suggested that mainstream epistemology should be re-named 'malestream' epistemology to reflect the dominance of men, masculine values and ideologies.
2 Jane Flax uses the phrase, 'innocent knowledge' to describe the Enlightenment hope that it is possible to obtain 'better' and 'untainted' knowledge (1993: 142).

References

Allen, Carolyn and Howard, Judith A. (eds) (2000) *Provoking Feminisms*. Chicago: University of Chicago Press.

Code, Lorraine (1991) *What Can She Know?: Feminist Theory and the Construction of Knowledge*. New York: Cornell University Press.

Collins, Patricia Hill (1989) 'The Social Construction of Black Feminist Thought', *Signs: Journal of Women in Culture and Society*, 14 (4): 745–73.

Flax, Jane (1993) *Disputed Subjects: Essays on Psychoanalysis, Politics and Philosophy*. London: Routledge.

Gilligan, Carol (1982) *In a Different Voice*. Cambridge, MA: Harvard University Press.

Haraway, Donna (1988) 'Situated Knowledges: The Science Question in Feminism and the Privilege of Partial Perspective', *Feminist Studies*, 14: 575–99.

Harding, Sandra (1986) *The Science Question in Feminism*. Milton Keynes: Open University Press.

Harding, Sandra and Hintikka, Merrill (eds) (1983) *Discovering Reality: Feminist Perspectives on Epistemology, Metaphysics, Methodology, and the Philosophy of Science*. Dordrecht: Reidel.

Longino, Helen (1990) *Science as Social Knowledge*. Princeton, NJ: Princeton University Press.

Nelson, Lynn Hankinson (1990) *Who Knows: From Quine to a Feminist Empiricism*. Philadelphia: Temple University Press.

O'Brien, Mary (1980) *The Politics of Reproduction*. London: Routledge and Kegan Paul.

Rose, Hilary (1983) 'Hand, Brain and Heart: a Feminist Epistemology for the Natural Sciences', *Signs: Journal of Women in Culture and Society*, 9: 73–90.

Ruddick, Sara (1989) *Maternal Thinking: Toward a Politics of Peace*. Boston: Beacon.

Smith, Dorothy (1987) *The Everyday World as Problematic: a Feminist Sociology*. Boston: Northeastern University Press.

Tronto, Joan (1993) *Moral Boundaries: a Political Argument for an Ethic of Care*. London: Routledge.

See also
Feminist
methodology.

MARYSIA ZALEWSKI

Feminist methodology

Since the emergence of second wave feminism in the late 1960s, feminists have advocated a distinctive approach to research in the social sciences. As with feminist theory itself, however, there is considerable diversity of opinion about what such an approach should entail. Moreover, feminist approaches to research methodologies are not static, but constantly evolving. While early feminist scholarship was particularly concerned to establish a link between academic social science and activism, during the 1990s attention shifted to the need to develop a 'feminist epistemology'. Divisions within and between feminists have ensured that the whole question of 'how to do feminist research' has been the focus of intense scholarly debate.

The feminist challenge

At the core of the feminist challenge to mainstream research methodologies was the contention that, by defining society and science in terms of male values, social research reflected existing power relations in society and thus perpetuated gender inequalities. Feminists argued that claims of scientific objectivity in the social sciences were in fact based on socially constructed assumptions about the nature of the category 'woman', and that the imposition of external criteria inevitably led to the generalisation, marginalisation, distortion or exclusion of actual female experience. The utilisation of gender as a basic theoretical concept, 'an organising category in social life and social science', was seen as critical in overturning these 'built-in' limitations and biases.

Commonalities

Stanley and Wise have pointed out that 'the idea that there is only "one road" to the feminist revolution, and only one type of "truly feminist" research, is as limiting and as offensive as male-biased accounts of research that have gone before' (Stanley and Wise, 1993: 26). But while there is no unified approach, it is possible to identify several defining characteristics of feminist research, which reflect a combination of personal, political, academic and ethical considerations. Firstly, feminist research should be 'on, with and for', rather than just about women. Women, it was argued were better equipped than men to understand and empathise with issues of importance to women, and to interpret their experiences. This privileging of women's 'way of knowing' above others was labeled 'feminist standpoint'. Emphasis on the experiential led to feminist rejection of quantitative research methods, which, it was claimed, silenced women's voices and placed them in pre-determined categories. Qualitative methods, particularly the one-to-one interview situation, were seen as more relevant to the exploration of women's experiences. Arguing that it was neither possible nor desirable for the collection and measurement of data to be objective or value-free, and that research was a two-way process, feminists also considered the relationship between researcher and researched to be critical. They stressed that the relationship should be not be hierarchical or exploitative, but based on consent and collaboration, and that continual reflection on the process take place with the subjectivities of both parties and their interaction taken into account. It was also seen as important that the research was both empowering for the individuals concerned and directed towards social change. As has often been pointed out, none of the concerns or approaches outlined above is limited to or specific to feminism, but taken together, and applied within a feminist theoretical framework, they constitute the substance of feminist research practice.

Debates within feminism

From the 1980s, reflecting developments within theory and practice, different aspects of these orthodoxies became a matter of debate amongst feminists. Some have pointed, for example, to the necessity of sometimes focusing on men and masculinity in order to examine issues relating to women's experience fully. 'Gender', after all, is about relations between the sexes, and to illuminate power dynamics both the oppressed and the powerful need to be studied (Maynard and Purvis, 1994: 15). There has also been some rethinking about the employment of quantitative methods. Some have argued that positivism is not *intrinsic* to quantitative research, and that it is not the data itself which lacks objectivity, but the use to which it is put. It has been pointed out that statistical data can provide a context for research, help develop and test theory and that analysis of such material can be backed up, if necessary, with complex qualitative questions. The usefulness of the experiential account has also come under scrutiny, with Kelly amongst others arguing that the way in which we refer to experience can be dangerously deterministic or essentialist. Some feminists are therefore advocating the use of a mixture of qualitative and quantitative measures. Fonow and Cook (1991) and Kelly are amongst those who have suggested that in some instances carefully designed questionnaires can facilitate rather than damage the 'ease' of disclosure, and prove beneficial to both researcher and researched. Indeed, recognition of the complexity of the power dynamics of this relationship has been the subject of much discussion, with some feminists acknowledging the impossibility of eliminating all objectification in the course of the research process.

A related issue is the question of differences between women, and the possibility of not one, but many standpoints, which may be variously related to each other. Awareness of the ways in which gender intersects with other social categories, such as race, ethnicity, class and disability, problematises the research process. While some regard pluralism as positive, for others it disputes the notion of being able to represent any 'voice'. Feminist postmodernism of course goes further, rejecting not only universalist approaches, but the existence of an authentic self. Focusing instead on 'fragmentation, multiple subjectivities, pluralities and flux', postmodernist deconstruction poses many challenges for traditional feminist methodologies.

While the destabilisation of the category 'woman' (amongst others) raised fears amongst many that it represented a defeatist stance on the political goals of feminism, others have disagreed. Indeed, postmodernist Judith Butler points out that 'to deconstruct the subject of feminism (woman) is not to censure its usage, but, on the contrary, to release the term into a future of multiple significations'. She goes on to suggest that 'paradoxically, it may be that only through releasing the category of women from a fixed referent that something like "agency" becomes possible' (Butler, 1995: 50). It has also been argued that a more focused and intellectually rigorous attention to reflexivity could help resolve some of the issues raised. While Mary Maynard notes the difficulty of reconciling abstract theoretical considerations with the practicalities of research, the modernist/ postmodernist debate will no doubt ensure the continual reworking of how feminist research is carried out.

Concern with the relationship between epistemology and method has proved a fruitful and challenging area of enquiry for feminist research; with the questioning of how we know what we know rendering the debate ever more complex. The diversity of contested feminist epistemologies and continuing intellectual interrogation of the issues also will guarantee the rich and vibrant nature of the process.

References

Butler, Judith (1995) 'Contingent Foundations', in S. Benhabib et al., *Feminist Contentions*. London: Routledge. pp. 35–57.

Fonow, Mary Margaret and Cook, Judith (1991) *Beyond Methodology: Feminist Scholarship as Lived Research*. Indianapolis: Indiana University Press.

Maynard, Mary and Purvis, June (eds) (1994) *Researching Women's Lives from a Feminist Perspective*. London: Taylor & Francis.

Stanley, Liz and Wise, Sue (1993) *Breaking Out Again: Feminist Ontology and Epistemology*. London: Routledge.

See also
Feminist
epistemology.

MYRTLE HILL

Focus groups

Focus groups can be described as a research approach whereby a group of individuals are selected to discuss together, in a focused and moderated manner, the topic under research.

Up until the 1980s focus groups were, in effect, unused within modern social science. Although previously used by Merton and Kendall in the 1940s, since that period they were predominately a market research method. In more recent years the use of focus groups and the esteem in which they are held have increased among social scientists, particularly with the publication of David Morgan's practical guide *Focus Groups as Qualitative Research* in 1988 and again in 1997. However, despite the growing usage of focus groups as a research method, it still occupies only a small corner of qualitative research. The suspicion of using 'new methods' such as focus groups is unfounded. It is in reality no different than other qualitative research techniques in that the researcher aims to discover what people believe and feel by actually asking their opinion, albeit unusually for sociologists, in a group setting.

Focus groups can be used both as a self contained method and a technique which may be used in conjunction with others. Flexibility therefore is one of the greatest benefits of this approach. Focus groups however are often perceived as a quick and easy approach to carrying out research. This is of course a misconception that regularly tarnishes the image of qualitative research as a whole.

The focus group method is often thought of as another form of group interviewing. However, it is important to highlight the differences between both approaches. With group interviewing, the emphasis is placed on the questions and responses between the researcher and participants. Focus groups, on the other hand, rely on the interaction within the focus group itself. Advantageously a real benefit of this interaction is the sharing of views, experiences and stories between participants, and the insightful and rich data which is often produced. Consequently this can often be more intense and valuable than if all the participants were interviewed separately. Observing this interplay and the positions taken within the focus group has direct linkages for the researcher with the technique of participant observation.

Planning is an essential aspect of all research, but it is a fundamental dimension of focus group research. Many of the problems associated with focus groups are usually based on poor preparation and unclear objectives. As in all research, one should be clear when it is most appropriate to use a particular research technique, be it in a self contained, supplementary or multi method approach. The easiest test for whether or not the focus group approach should be used, is to test how easily participants could discuss the topic under investigation in a group manner. If one decides that the issues are too sensitive then this is perhaps a justification for using another technique. Alternatively this sensitivity in itself could form part of the research process but must be borne in mind when thinking through the practical steps.

The practical organisation of focus groups involves issues relating to formu-lating the research questions, which should be open ended and tested so that they are easily understood. The more unstructured the focus group, the less questions should be used, in order to give ample time for wider discussion. Unstructured focus groups usually have between two to three questions for a two-hour session. On the other hand, structured focus groups are more tightly facilitated with the aim being to gain as much data on the particular set of questions – usually four to five distinct issues – as possible.

The recommended number of people per group is usually six to ten although it can work with a few more or less either way. It is common to have only one focus group meeting with a particular group of people. The researcher, however, may on occasion deem it necessary to have more than one meeting with a particular group and therefore delve that much deeper into the subject with that group.

The total number of focus groups within a research project is dependent on issues such as timescale, financial budget, and the issue under investigation. In the main, it is usually between three to five per subject area.

It is essential that the targeted research group is clearly established. The researcher must be clear if there is a specific type or category of people whom they wish to participate in the focus group, for example, rural dwellers. It is also important to establish if participants are to be further refined by social grouping or category such as age, class, marital status, occupation, geographical location. While focus group participants do not have to be considered 'experts' on the subject matter, it is necessary that they have a specific experience or opinion about the issue under discussion. Recruitment to focus groups may require the assistance of *gatekeepers* to legitimise the piece of research that is being undertaken in order to gain a representative sample. A letter of invitation to the participant explaining the background to the research and how they were selected may often be enough to get people to attend. However, a follow up telephone call can usually help to confirm numbers attending and minimise potential 'no-shows'.

Focus group sessions usually last from one to two hours. Anything less than one hour would not allow enough time to get to grips with the subject. Some form of icebreaker at the beginning of the session can help to make participants feel at ease. It is crucial to introduce and explain what is being researched, why the individuals are being asked to participate and why their views are being sought. The time slot of focus groups should be sensitive to the target group to ensure as full an attendance as possible. Likewise, the choice of venue can help avoid either negative or positive associations with a particular location.

One should recognise that the researcher within the focus group setting moves into the role of facilitator/moderator. Therefore you should strive to ensure that participants feel they are in a comfortable, safe environment with everyone being given an equal opportunity to participate. Some form of simple agreed ground rules for discussion can help to eliminate any potential problems. If deemed necessary, the facilitator can stimulate the discussion, draw out key issues and help keep the focus group on course.

As in any situation a range of group dynamics can occur from the type of interplay and interaction of the gathered participants. The most fruitful group dynamics for the gathering of direct data develop when there is a building of rapport which usually evolves out of the sharing of experiences, views and stories by participants on the research topic. The facilitator's role is to open the discussion, ensuring during the duration of the focus group that the specific research issues are addressed and any clarification obtained. Simultaneously the interaction within the focus group can sometimes stimulate new thoughts from respondents, reflection and sharing of information. The energy which can evolve around the topic under research, if facilitated with the aim of the research clearly in mind, can often lead to discussion which is both exciting and insightful and can even on occasion modify the focus of the research. The value of the focus group approach is that a group of people with a particular interest in or knowledge of the research topic are in the one room to discuss the research topic which can in turn be a resource for both the researcher and the participants.

Group dynamics and interaction, the environmental condition of the research and naturalness of the research process clearly form part of the writing up and data analysis process. It is important to understand that while other forms of qualitative research may be carried out in more *naturalistic* surroundings, focus groups do not claim to be more than what they are, the mechanism to gather/collect focused qualitative data and sets of social interaction with a selected group within a set time frame.

Recording the focus group meeting is a matter for the researcher. It could take the form of audio or video tape or notes being taken during the focus group or written afterwards. Each individual researcher will make the decision on the most appropriate technique and consider the various trade-offs. Some researchers find it helpful to also distribute a questionnaire to gather more general details about the background make-up of the focus groups. Both aspects of data collection are of course not separate from ethical considerations which should be borne in mind when reporting the findings.

According to Morgan (1997), the three most common means of coding focus group data are to note each mention of a given issue, each participant's mention of the issue, and each focus group's discussion of the particular issue. Likewise when interpreting the data it is valuable to note how many groups mentioned the topic, how many people within the groups raised the topic and the level of interest generated by the topic.

It is worthwhile when planning and undertaking the focus group that the researcher reflects upon their own involvement within the research process, especially so in the writing up of the data. For example, could the researcher's gender or identity have impacted upon the discussion in any way?

Focus groups deserve more usage within the social sciences, if not for the benefit of producing qualitative data then in order to compare a broader range of research experiences. The process of undertaking focus group research can be one of the most rewarding experiences, offering a challenge for the researcher and often an empowering opportunity for the participants.

Suggested further reading

Merton R.K. and Kendall P.L. (1946) 'The Focused Interview', *American Journal of Sociology*, 51: 541–57.

Morgan D.L. and Spanish, M.T. (1984) 'Focus Groups: a New Tool for Qualitative Research', *Qualitative Sociology*, 7: 253–70.

Kitzinger J. (1995) 'Introducing Focus Groups', *British Medical Journal*, 311: 299–302.

Reference

Morgan D.L. (1997) *Focus Groups as Qualitative Research*, 2nd edn. London: Sage.

See also
Interviews.

ROGER O'SULLIVAN

Frankfurt School

See **Modernity**.

G

Gender Identity Dysphoria Assessment

In the same (1980) edition of the *American Psychiatric Association's Diagnostic and Statistical Manual (DSM-III)*, which removed homosexuality as a classification, transsexualism became an official 'disorder'. Although 'transsexualism' is the most familiar term within public discourse, the American Psychiatric Association Committee replaced transsexualism with Gender Identity Disorder (GID) in the fourth edition of the manual (*DSM-IV*) in 1994. GID now relates to a group of 'disorders', one of which is transsexualism. The *DSM-IV*, refers to GID of Childhood, Adolescence, or Adulthood. In the *DSM-IV*, the characteristics of GID are given as: (1) a consistent and persistent psychological identification with the 'opposite' sex; (2) a persistent discomfort with one's own sex; and, (3) the disturbance causing clinically significant distress or impairment in social, occupational or other important areas of functioning.

The aetiology of GID is usually presented as a complex interaction between biological, familial and psychic factors. Given the focus of both psychology and psychiatry on individual level explanations, concerns with the structural construction of both sex and gender in society tend to be limited to what *gender role behaviours* are socially acceptable. The remainder of this entry will focus on two controversial aspects of GID assessment. The first source of controversy involves the understanding of the concepts of sex and gender. The second controversy surrounds the basis of GID assessment.

For the most part, psychology subscribes to the view that 'sex' refers to biological differences between females and males, whilst 'gender' signifies the practices of femininity and masculinity within social relations. For this reason, both the *International Classification of Diseases –10* and the *DSM-IV* refer to individuals who identify with the 'opposite' sex, where sex is defined by genitals. In stark contrast, a social view explicitly questions the relationship between sex and gender. Given this understanding of *both* sex and gender as outcomes of social interaction rather than human 'nature', the sociological view charges psychology and psychiatry with policing the boundaries of the modern two sex/gender system.

The assumption that gender identity develops from a stable morphological base seems to allow therapists to delineate between a majority 'normally' gendered population, and a minority 'deviant' population suffering from an individual 'pathology'. That clinicians use variation to define normality and then attempt to eliminate the variation that defined normality, is a profound irony not yet acknowledged in GID assessment. Consequently, usually absent from a clinical treatise on GID is any discussion of the structural construction of gender within society. For instance, the assessment criteria used by the clinicians are highly stereotyped and outdated. Behaviours which signal GID in children include identity statements, dress-up play, toy play, role play, peer relations, motoric and speech characteristics, statements about sexual anatomy, involvement in rough-and-tumble play, as well as signs of stress and discomfort about being either a boy or a girl (Zucker and Bradley, 1995: 11). For instance, 'normal' girls are expected to wear skirts and dresses whereas 'normal' boys should prefer trousers. 'Normal' boys urinate in a standing position and like to engage in 'rough-and-tumble' play.

From a sociological perspective, highly stereotyped behavioural cues provide *social* rather than *individual* expectations of gender. In other words, the assessment criteria for GID are signifiers of masculinity and femininity, not maleness and femaleness. The resilience of these out-dated signifiers of femininity and masculinity is curious given the existence of widespread and long-standing feminist and sociological critiques.

According to the *DSM-IV*, GID is considered a disorder if it causes 'distress, disability and disadvantage'. In terms of the distress criterion, clinicians seem most often to refer to the distress of the parents who bring their children to clinical attention. In these cases, it is the parents whose children do not adhere to normative expectations of gender performance who experience 'distress'. A number of researchers have attempted to link GID with 'other' psychopathology. However, no associative link can be found. Indeed, against the repetitive studies which seem to seek the opposite, studies of children who fit the complete GID criteria are more likely to be young, middle class and come from intact, two-heterosexual-parent families. Another limitation of the 'distress' criterion for assessment is that it doesn't address the source of this discomfort. Most clinicians acknowledge that distress results largely from social ostracism, particularly from peers but do not then reflect upon the implications of this source of distress. Put another way, would children who are uncomfortable with their gender experience the same degree of distress if their social context did not adhere to a rigid gender binary? Because clinicians a priori define stable identification as normative, children who express discomfort with this rigidity are necessarily treated as individual 'deviant cases'.

The second criterion, 'disability', is very difficult to assess. This term is defined in narrow terms because GID in not causally associated with any other pathology. Zucker and Bradley write 'children with gender identity disorder were more likely than controls to misclassify their own gender, which, *given the ubiquity of gender as a social category*, surely must lead to confusion in their social interactions' (my emphasis) (1995: 58). 'Disability', then, entirely refers to a child's gender self-classification: the further this classification is from normative expectations, the greater the child's 'disability'.

Finally, the assessment criterion of 'disadvantage' seems to boil down to the clinician's assessment of the individual's impairment to the formation of intimacy. Here the assumed relationship between stable gender identification and gender desire is most transparent. Not only does our society assume that we need to be *either* women or men to form intimate relationships (an assumption that individual intersex experience contests), but also that 'pair-bonds' are a source of 'adaptive functioning'. *Heteronormative* familial ideology propagates this assumption despite consistent evidence to the contrary. Furthermore, seeking recourse in biology (humans as a 'gregarious species') demonstrates a lack of knowledge about the jubilant promiscuity of human sexual evolution (Margulis and Sagan, 1997).

This third criterion most strongly links gender identification and gender desire, thereby illuminating one of the most troubling aspects of therapeutic intervention with GID. Homosexuality may have been removed from the DSM classification of pathology, but it is far from removed from the minds of clinicians. Once again we are reminded that it is not the children themselves who necessarily experience discomfort with their gender or gender desire, but society.

In summary, the current classification emphasises the supposed consequences, rather than aetiology, of GID. Treatment is rationalised in largely pastoral terms (especially when the client is a child) of relieving distress, disability and disadvantage. The onus remains on the individual to adhere to the two-gender, heteronormative system, rather than challenging society in any way. And clinicians have recalled homosexuality into the clinical field by identifying the *prevention* of homosexuality as within their purview.

Suggested further reading

Hird, M.J. (in press) 'For a Sociology of Transsexualism', *Sociology*.

W. Meyer III (Chairperson), Bockting, W., Cohen-Kettenis, P., Coleman, E., DiCeglie, D., Devor, H., Gooren, L., Joris Hage, J., Kirk, S., Kuiper, B., Laub, D., Lawrence, A., Menard, Y., Patton, J., Schaefer, L., Webb, A. and Wheeler, C. (February 2001) 'The Standards of Care for Gender Identity Disorders – Sixth Version', *International Journal of Transgenderism*, 5 (1). http://www.symposion.com/ijt/soc_2001/index.htm.

Wilson, K. 'The Disparate Classification of Gender and Sexual Orientation in American Psychiatry'. http://www.priory.com/psych/disparat.htm.

References

Margulis, L. and Sagan, D. (1997) *What is Sex?* New York: Simon and Schuster.

Zucker, K. and Bradley, S. (1995) *Gender Identity Disorder and Psychosexual Problems in Children and Adolescents.* New York and London: The Guildford Press.

MYRA J. HIRD

Generalisation

Generalisation involves two processes, theoretical inference from data in order to develop concepts and theory, and the empirical application of the data to a wider population. In the first instance we infer a general statement about the data, in the second we apply that statement beyond the data on which it is based. The process by which the general statement is made is the same in both types of generalisation; it is the nature of the statement that differs depending on whether it is empirical or theoretical. To research in this way requires confidence that data reveal and contain the general in the particular. This involves sampling – selecting the case or cases for study from the basic unit of study where it is not feasible to cover all instances of that unit.[1] In these circumstances, a sample is drawn from the universe of units. Empirical generalisations involve the statements based on the sample being applied to the wider universe of units. Theoretical inferences involve the development of theoretical statements that are generalised to all like cases. All this applies irrespective of whether the research is quantitative or qualitative, although the terms and reasoning often mistakenly are associated with the former only. What differs between them are the sampling procedures by which the generalisations are made and the level of confidence and the logical reasoning underlying their application to the wider universe of units.

Quantitative generalisation

The sampling procedures employed in quantitative generalisation rely on the principle of chance. A subset of cases is randomly drawn from the whole universe of the target population. If the number of cases is sufficiently large and the selection is essentially both random and unbiased, the characteristics of the sample will mirror the characteristics of the large universe population from which they are drawn. Hence, any features or relationships found in the sample should reflect genuine features or relationships existing in the whole population.

A great advantage of quantitative analysis based upon large random samples is that it is possible to estimate fairly precisely the potential amounts of error in any figures or relationships observed. For any figure in a sample, the potential range of error, its *confidence interval*, can be given. The most typical example would be the opinion polls that take place in the run-up to an election. The polling agencies typically report their results in the form that 'Party X will receive 46% of the vote, and this estimate is accurate to within 2%'. What this means literally is that the *sample estimate* of 46% is within plus or minus 2% of the *true population parameter* (that is, that the real support for Party X falls somewhere in a range of 44 to 48%). The pollsters cannot discover the 'true' population parameter unless they go out and ask every person in the whole population, so they have to rely on the estimate provided by their sample survey.

Statistical testing for associations or relationships in a sample follow a similar logic. The results of quantitative statistical tests are invariably given in terms of their probability of being correct. For instance, a researcher may report that: 'maths and verbal aptitude scores were found to be positively correlated at a 0.01 level of statistical significance'. What this means, literally, is that the odds that the positive association observed in the sample is only a fluke rather than a genuine feature is only 1 in 100.

Generalisation in quantitative research hence can be seen as a process of first establishing the empirical reliability of facts and then using these facts to assess the validity of theory.

Qualitative generalisation

Generalisation in qualitative research can be viewed as reversing this balance. Because it involves a limited number of cases, or just a single case, in a restricted field or setting, qualitative research is better at making theoretical inferences rather than applying them to a wider population. However, empirical generalisations to a wider population are feasible despite the limited number of cases if the cases permit comparisons and have been selected by a sampling procedure. There are two ways this can be done. First it is possible to design the individual project in the mould of similar ones in different fields so that comparisons can be made across them and a body of cumulative knowledge can be built up that is longitudinal, historical and comparative. The second is to design the project as a series of parallel qualitative studies with different cases or with the same case in different fields, perhaps even using multiple researchers.

The key to making generalisations from qualitative comparisons therefore is the effective sampling of cases. A distinction is made between probability and non-probability sampling. In the former, each instance of the unit has a known probability of being included in the sample, in the latter there is no way of estimating this probability, nor even any certainty that every instance has some chance. This is relevant to sampling in qualitative research in two ways. Probability sampling in qualitative research can be used when surveys of the population are used as a form of triangulation to accompany more qualitative methods, most frequently in community studies where the universe of units (the people who live there) is clearly identifiable and accessible. Usually, however, qualitative researchers use non-probability sampling to select cases from a wider universe. Such sampling can be done of the fields in which to site the research (selecting the location of the case or cases) and of the units of study within them (such as selecting informants from the universe of people in the field who exemplify the case).

Because the prefix 'non' implies that probability sampling is the standard, those qualitative researchers who reject the natural science model of social research and its associated forms of sampling procedure, prefer other terminology with which to describe their sampling practice. For example, Denzin (1970) prefers the nomenclature of 'interactive' and 'non-interactive' sampling, in which the former becomes the standard to analyse 'natural' interaction. In their development of grounded theory, Glaser and Strauss use the term theoretical sampling to describe the inductive approach of the qualitative researcher. These semantics, however, do not alter the basic procedures used to obtain non-statistical samples in qualitative research. These are the snowball technique (obtaining units, such as informants, from other units), quota sampling (selecting units on the basis of their presence in the universe, proportional or not), and judgemental sampling (the researcher selecting the most appropriate instances of the unit for the topic at hand). Through these sampling strategies, qualitative researchers must sample the research case and site, the time frame spent there, and the events and people to be studied. This provides two benefits. First, it ensures the representativeness of the findings as instances that make up the case, and, secondly, it facilitates generalisations to other cases or fields.

Note

1 In some rare examples where the unit is small or unusual, it is possible to include a universal study of the unit, but mostly it is impossible to have complete coverage.

Suggested further reading

Miller, R.L., Acton, C.A., Fullerton, D. and Maltby, J. (2002) *Social Research with SPSS*. 'Introduction' and 'Module 4'. London: Palgrave.

Hammersley, M. (1992) *What's Wrong with Ethnography?* Chapter 5. London: Routledge.

Reference

Denzin, N. (1970) *The Research Act*. Chicago: Aldine.

See also **Grounded theory**, **Sampling**, **Probability** and **Social Surveys**.

JOHN BREWER AND ROBERT MILLER

Geographic Information Systems (GIS)

There are many definitions of Geographic Information Systems (GIS) – systems for linking and analysing wide varieties of data together by common geographical referents. The Committee of Enquiry into the Handling of Geographic Information, chaired by Lord Chorley, succinctly described a GIS as:

> A system for capturing, storing, checking, integrating, manipulating, analysing and displaying data which are spatially referenced to the Earth. This is normally considered to involve a spatially referenced computer database and appropriate applications software. (Department of the Environment, 1987)

This definition still holds true today.

Since there is no explicit definition of a GIS, there have been misconceptions about what a GIS is. In particular, there can be confusion between computer assisted cartography (CAC), computer assisted drafting (CAD) and GIS. While all three of these systems use graphic displays, there are basic differences in the type of information that they can process (DeMers, 2000).

- Computer assisted cartography automates the production of maps, but lacks the analytical capabilities of a GIS.
- Computer assisted drafting produces graphic images, but is not usually tied to external descriptive data files.
- Geographic Information Systems can analyse as well as manipulate the information behind a map.

Advantages of using GIS

GIS is a multi-faceted technique, or tool within a broader research/computing context for supporting decisions and monitoring the use of resources. At a basic level, there are four main advantages of using GIS:

(1) *Data accessibility*. One big advantage is that GIS can link or integrate a variety of datasets together via a geographical locator, for example, addresses, post code or zip code, which helps departments and agencies share their data, both internally and externally. Such data may previously have been inaccessible to other departments or organisations.

(2) *Improved decision making*. GIS is not merely an automated decision making system – its strength lies in being a tool to query, analyse and map data in support of the decision making process. GIS can allow multiple scenarios to be displayed and examined. The most up-to-date information is available, for example, daily changes to map features can be incorporated. GIS can also include 'real time' information, such as systems developed for ambulance dispatch, which utilise a continuous stream of real-time information.

(3) *Making maps.* GIS can make maps with any type of geographic data, in a much more flexible way than traditional manual or automated cartography. For example, maps can be centred at any location, produced at any scale, and can be created at any time. Problems associated with traditional cartography, for example, the limited durability and storage needs of paper maps, are avoided.

(4) *Data output.* Data can be produced in map or tabular form, at a variety of scales, and formats. Output can often be imported into other computer applications for dissemination.

Barriers to using GIS

On the negative side, there are several barriers which inhibit the development of appropriate Geographic Information Systems. Most of these relate to data. In particular, users may not be aware of the existence of appropriate geographical or attribute data. If they are, then the availability or cost may be an issue.

A GIS analyst must also be aware of the quality of the data, as well as data standards. For example, geographical coordinates in Ireland are based on the Irish Grid, whereas Britain uses the National Grid system. Other issues include the format of the data and the need to convert data files according to the software used. However, the development of national and international standards of data portability have helped in this respect.

Geographic information

Objects in geographic space can be described on two levels:

- Spatial data, that is, their location in space
- Attribute data, that is, properties of the object apart from its location. This can be nominal, ordinal, interval, or ratio data, such as the height of a sign, the population within a town boundary, or the majority political affiliation of a borough.

Objects themselves have traditionally been categorised as points, lines, areas and surfaces. Another classification is based on the number of dimensions of an object: points have a value of zero, lines have a value of one, areas have a value of two, and surfaces have a value of three. More recently, space-time has been regarded as a fourth dimension.

While GIS offers greater power for manipulation and analysis of data than had previously been available, it also places greater demands on data accuracy and availability. As with all information systems, a GIS is only as accurate as the least accurate dataset contained within it. Issues to be aware of include the currency of the data and the scale at which it is collected.

For example, Northern Ireland consists of 26 District Councils, which are further subdivided into a system of electoral wards. The latter scale is often used in socio-economic research. However, when examining differences between data from different Censuses of Population, the analyst needs to be aware of the change in the boundaries of electoral wards. In 1981 there were 526 wards, while boundary changes in 1984 meant that the 1991 Census was administered in 566 wards. Since there is no exact overlay between the two boundary systems, changes within the inter-census period must be calculated using other imputational methods.

Systems in GIS

DeMers (2000) defines the following subsystems operating within GIS:

(1) A data input system to collect and process spatial data from various sources. Different types of spatial data can also be transformed, for example, the transformation of contour lines to point elevations.
(2) A data storage and retrieval system which allows the retrieval, updating and editing of spatial data.
(3) A data manipulation and analysis system to perform tasks on the data, and perform modelling.
(4) A reporting system that displays data in tabular, graphic or map form.

Many GIS software packages provide all or some of these functions, for example, ARC/INFO and MapInfo.

Applications

Historically, typical applications highlighted in academic and commercial litera-ture concentrated on land resources and utility management. However, GIS is equally important for all types of data, including social and environmental data. In particular, the growth of census mapping and socio-economic modelling in the 1990s have meant that socio-economic applications of GIS are now commonplace. Examples of GIS using socio-economic data include health care monitoring, risk assessment and population mapping. GIS has increasingly played a key role in the development of crime pattern analysis. One obvious advantage is being able to display the distribution of crime incidents and rates in order to expose spatial clusters.

What is the future of GIS?

One facet of GIS that is likely to increase is that of Distributed Geographic Information (DGI), which uses the Internet to distribute geographic information to a wider audience than is possible using a traditional GIS. The Internet has the potential for increasing the efficiency and effectiveness of the ways in which we obtain, use and share geographic information (which includes maps, graphics, text and data) (Plewe, 1997). DGI ranges from the display of pre-existing maps on a web page to network-based collaborative GIS in which users at different locations share common data and communicate with each other in real time .

References

DeMers, Michael N. (2000) *Fundamentals of Geographic Information Systems*. New York: John Wiley and Sons, Inc.

Department of the Environment (1987) *Handling Geographic Information*. London: HMSO.

Plewe, Brandon (1997) *GIS Online: Information Retrieval, Mapping and the Internet*. Albany, NY: OnWord Press, Thomson Learning.

PAULA DEVINE

Grounded theory

Grounded theory is a set of fully integrated and practical steps aimed at guiding the research process to completion, the end product of which is the generation of theoretical statements about the data. The chief mark is that this theory is grounded in data and built up from the bottom. It is a classic form of induction and is frequently invoked as a form of qualitative data analysis, although rarely practised properly. Grounded theory originated in the work of Barney Glaser and Anslem Strauss as a method of enquiry in qualitative research developed from their collaborative work in medical sociology (1965). This reinforces the point that grounded theory began itself as a bottom-up method, based upon actual research experience. The method was subsequently written up and published in the 1967 book *The Discovery of Grounded Theory*. The original ideas were later developed and extended by Glaser (1978) and by Strauss and Juliet Corbin (1990).

Grounded theory has its roots in the traditions and background of its co-founders. Glaser was trained at the Colombia School of Applied Social Research under the direction of Paul Lazarsfeld, with the result that grounded theory has been formed with some of the influences of this largely quantitative tradition. Strauss on the other hand was trained in the Chicago School of sociology and was heavily influenced by the basic tenets of symbolic interactionism. Given this latter influence, it is not surprising that grounded theory is often said to be a qualitative research method. However, in their separate developments of grounded theory, Glaser and Strauss have come into conflict. The result of this split at the heart of the method has been the emergence of two 'schools' of grounded theory and it is possible that some of the inherent tensions in the method have appeared because it was originally developed from two very different conceptual backgrounds.

Along with Merton's well-known middle range theories, grounded theory was developed in direct contrast to 'grand' theories, associated with the American sociology of the time, such as Parsons' Structural Functionalism. Glaser and Strauss argued that the general preoccupation of sociologists with grand theories was an imbalance and that sociologists should get back to collecting and analysing data. A key argument was that it is possible to generate smaller scale theories which were fully 'grounded' in data and therefore in some respects more legitimate than those grand designs which bore no relation to what was going on in the 'real' world.

Grounded theory is not an easy method to apply and most people invoke it as an approach without following its demanding strictures. Grounded theories typically emerge as analyses of how a problem is resolved or processed by participants in a particular problem area. For example, the original grounded theory in *Awareness of Dying* (Glaser and Strauss, 1965) seeks to explain how people resolve the problems associated with being or becoming aware that one is dying. The analysis and resulting theory was largely based on data that was collected in hospital settings. After identifying the substantive area to be studied and defining the problem of analysis, the grounded theory researcher aims to suspend belief in any preconceived ideas that may exist with respect to the problem at hand. The researcher is generally not required to do a literature review until much later in the research process. This aspect of grounded theory has been criticised quite severely since it gives the appearance that grounded theories are produced *tabula rasa* from data. This has led a number of commentators to state that the grounded theory method is in fact a form of positivism. Such criticisms are not unfounded but are nonetheless inaccurate. The language of grounded theory is close to the language used in quantitative traditions in sociology and reflects not only Lazarsfeld's influence on Glaser but also that the method was produced at a time when quantitative sociology was the dominant tradition. Grounded theory addressed this environment and hence used terminology such as coding and coding families. It more accurate to situate grounded theory in the post-positivist era of research enquiry.

After identifying the area to be studied the researcher is then required to commence collecting and analysing data simultaneously. The data are 'constantly compared' to each other across cases, within cases, as well as to the emerging categories. This initial stage of grounded theory is called *open coding*. Open coding is basically the development of as many codes as possible, which help summarise the differences and similarities between 'incidents' in the data. Incidents are basically data bits or chunks discerned by the researcher as being discrete entities. The codes should reflect the substance and flavour of the incidents being observed. Examples of codes from *Awareness of Dying* (Glaser and Strauss, 1965) include 'dying trajectory', 'mothering', 'emerging recognition', 'awakening to death', 'accommodating uncertainty' and 'awareness context'. As the researcher compares the differences and similarities between incidents, codes will jump out at them, and these observations are written down in memos about the codes. Such memos are simple notes about patterns observed in the data. As the analysis proceeds the idea is to capture all these raw ideas. In this way the researcher builds a data bank of observations about the emerging theory. Open coding typically generates many substantive codes; these in turn may develop complexity or not depending on how they recur in the data. The goal of this stage of data collection and analysis is to generate as many open codes as possible. Over time however some codes may develop greater variance and become more central than others. Essentially the idea is that from these open codes there will emerge more general 'categories' that have greater analytical power and the capacity to group together more data.

The method for deciding which category to use as the core category involves a process of *theoretical coding*. Theoretical coding occurs when the researcher chooses between a series of possible theoretical structures. The chosen structure is then used to organise the emergent theory. After selecting the core category the researcher has to check to see if it 'works'. The benchmark for doing so is to see if it successfully groups together all the other codes and categories. This stage is called 'selective coding' and involves selectively sampling and coding around the emerging core category. This is called theoretical sampling[1] and involves the researcher looking selectively at the development of the emerging categories and how they relate to the core category. The researcher is required to continue data analysis until less and less variation is observed in the relationship between the codes, categories and the core category. At this point the categories, codes and emergent theory are said to have reached 'saturation'.

Grounded theory is a powerful method that stresses the importance of data in research enquiry and forces researchers to be ever conscious of how they observe the data patterning out. Albeit difficult, it provides practical guidance for the researcher to produce a conceptually rich and pervasively dense theory which is directly applicable to the area under investigation. It is, however, a method for which there is as yet no detailed epistemology. The result is that it tends to be used in many varied and applied fields with varying degrees of sophistication. Grounded theory has been used in nursing, business management, marketing and even architecture. The result is that many grounded theories are social without being entirely sociological. The extent to which applications actually follow the original guidelines is also questionable. That is, grounded theory has tended to become whatever people claim it to be.

Note

1 Theoretical sampling is distinct from probability and other forms of survey sampling.

Suggested further reading

Dey, Ian (1999) *Grounding Grounded Theory: Guidelines for Qualitative Inquiry.* California: Academic Press.

References

Glaser, Barney (1978) *Theoretical Sensitivity*. Sociology Press.
Glaser, Barney and Strauss, Anselm (1965) *Awareness of Dying*. Chicago: Aldine.

Glaser, Barney and Strauss, Anselm (1967) *The Discovery of Grounded Theory*. Chicago: Aldine.
Strauss, Anselm and Corbin, Juliet (1990) *The Basics of Qualitative Research: Grounded Theory Procedures and Techniques*. London: Sage.

BARRY GIBSON

Hawthorne Effect

Originating from studies conducted at the Hawthorne Plant of the Western Electric Company in the 1920s and 30s, the term 'Hawthorne Effect' now has come to mean changes in the behaviour of subjects that originate solely from their being the subject of research.

The Hawthorne Studies began in 1924 at the Hawthorne Works of the Western Electric Company in Chicago, and continued until 1932. The company manufactured equipment for the Bell Telephone system, and at the time of the experiments there had been a good deal of dissatisfaction amongst the 30,000 employees of the firm. It should be noted that for its time, the Western Electric Company was quite progressive, with pension schemes, health schemes and numerous recreational facilities. The initial studies were carried out by engineers in the company, and followed a scientific management approach. The researchers worked on the assumption that workers should be treated as machines, and that the main factors affecting productivity would be environmental conditions such as lighting, inadequate heating, excessive humidity, and fatigue as a result of these factors.

In order to study the effects of altered illumination, two groups of employees were selected. In one, the control group, lighting remained unaltered. In the other, illumination was increased in intensity. As expected, productivity in the latter group increased. What was unforeseen was that the productivity in the control group also increased. This puzzled the investigators, as lighting in the control group had remained unchanged. When they reduced lighting in the test group, productivity again increased, once more puzzling the researchers. In addition, productivity in the control group continued to increase. The experiments were repeated with different groups of workers with the same results.

In 1927, Western Electric called on the Harvard Business School to try and make sense of their findings. Fritz Roethlisberger of the Hawthorne Plant, and William Dickson of the Harvard Business School (Roethlisberger and Dickson, 1939) carried out the bulk of the subsequent research. However the Hawthorne Studies are most closely associated with Elton Mayo who was at that time the director of the Harvard Business School, and oversaw the research (Mayo, 1945). Two studies carried out at the Hawthorne Plant are particularly famous; the study of the First Relay Assembly Test Room, and the study of the Bank Wiring Room.

In the Relay Assembly Test Room, six women were selected, and an observer charted their output. Although officially an observer, the recorder became in effect a 'surrogate supervisor' acting on behalf of the group. It was believed that the 'surrogate supervisor' role indicated the importance of good management and leadership, and how supervisors could play a crucial role mediating between the demands of the company and the desires of the workers in order to increase satisfaction and hence productivity.

Regardless of variations in light, rest pauses and the length of the working day, however, productivity increased. The conclusion drawn was that the work group was not responding to variations in conditions, but rather that it was actually the experiment *itself*, rather than feeling positive about increased attention or good management, which induced the results (Bryman, 1989). In other words, what caused the women in the Relay Assembly Room to increase productivity was that they knew they were part of an experiment. It is this that has become known as the 'Hawthorne Effect'. So, the Hawthorne Effect is a classic example of Experimenter Effect.

In the Bank Wiring Room experiments, more anthropological and non-interventionist methods were employed. Fourteen men, who had worked together as a group before the experiments, were closely observed for six months. No environmental conditions were altered, but rather a group bonus scheme was introduced. The group appeared to establish their own interpretation of 'a good day's work', and social norms within the group prevented any members exceeding or failing to maintain the norm, even though the group could easily have produced more than the limit they imposed. The conclusion drawn from this experiment was that group relations affected productivity. Organisation of work exists within informal groups, and if management can identify and work with these groups, it will be possible to align the group's goals with those of the company.

The Hawthorne Studies signalled the first attempt to introduce sociological explanations into the study of workers' behaviour. Heavily influenced by Durkheim and Pareto, Mayo argued that industrialisation causes social disorganisation and that the solution in an industrialised society lay in the plant as a harmonious unit with well integrated formal and informal organisation where the worker would find emotional security and the social satisfactions that could no longer be found in the family or the other decaying social institutions outside of the plant. Treating workers as important human beings, and recognising and working with informal structures would lead both to more satisfied workers and to the achievement of the firm's objective of high productivity. The Hawthorne Studies pioneered a whole branch of industrial sociology which became known as the 'Human Relations School', which investigates leadership, group relations, and other factors that increase worker satisfaction and productivity.

Criticisms

Despite their enormous influence, the Hawthorne Studies have been subjected to heavy criticism, at both methodological and ideological levels. Many subsequent studies have questioned the causal relationship between satisfaction and productivity, asking whether satisfaction does in fact lead to increased productivity, or whether increased productivity leads to increased satisfaction, if the worker is rewarded for high performance (Perrow, 1972).

The Hawthorne Experiments also have been criticised for focusing on the individual and group level, and not paying much attention to the organisation as a whole, or the general social climate in which the organisation exists. Despite thousands of interviews with workers, the Hawthorne research made little reference to trade unions except to say that workers rarely mentioned them. Yet the Western Electric Company spent an enormous amount of money ensuring unionism did not occur (Brown, 1975). The studies were conducted during the Great Depression, and the Hawthorne Plant was laying off workers. The possible effects of this on the restricted productivity strategy of the Bank Wiring Room were not considered. The studies have also been charged with designing different experiments for men and women in the plant, and displaying gender bias (Acker and Van Houten, 1974).

At an ideological level, the Hawthorne Studies are criticised for their bias in favour of management. Management is presented as rational, with workers presented as non-rational. Through adopting certain procedures, management can massage worker behaviour to match the company's objectives and increase productivity. While the Hawthorne Studies and the subsequent Human Relations School came to see itself as antithetical to Scientific Management and the experiments of Frederick Winslow Taylor, they share the same objective of increasing worker productivity. The concern is not with 'human relations' as such, but rather with management's desire to increase productivity. Also at an ideological level, the Hawthorne Studies have been criticised for failing to recognise the existence of legitimate conflict between labour and management. Managers and workers may have such deep divisions of interests that no amount of communication and schemes for participation will secure harmony.

The Human Relations School has become increasingly sophisticated methodologically and theoretically. Whatever the flaws of the original studies, they remain important because they revolutionised the classical theory of management by introducing the whole problem area of human behaviour in the firm (Mouzelis, 1984). The initial Hawthorne Studies remain of interest because they gave rise to what came to be known as the 'Hawthorne Effect', which in itself went on to become the explanation for the outcome of the experiment. The Hawthorne Studies themselves have proved to be of lasting influence in industrial sociology. Scott maintains that it is only a small exaggeration to suggest that the academic field of industrial sociology first saw the light of day at the Hawthorne plant, with Elton Mayo serving as midwife (Scott, 1987: 61).

References

Acker, J. and Van Houten, D.R. (1974) 'Differential Recruitment and Control: The Sex Structuring of Organisations', *Administrative Science Quarterly*, 19: 152–63.

Brown, J. (1975) *The Social Psychology of Industry*. Middlesex: Penguin Books.

Bryman, A. (1989) *Research Methods and Organisation Studies*. London: Unwin Hyman.

Mayo, E. (1945) *The Social Problems of an Industrial Civilization*. Cambridge, MA: Harvard University Press.

Mouzelis, N. (1984) *Organisation and Bureaucracy – an Analysis of Modern Theories*. London: Routledge and Kegan Paul.

Perrow, C. (1972) *Complex Organizations: A Critical Essay*. Illinois: Scott, Foresman and Company.

Roethlisberger, F.J. and Dickson, W.J. (1939) *Management and the Worker.* Cambridge, MA: Harvard University Press.

Scott, W.R. (1987) *Organizations: Rational, Natural and Open Systems.* New Jersey: Prentice Hall, Inc.

SALLY SHORTALL

Hermeneutics

Hermeneutics is a term derived from the Greek for 'to translate and interpret' and has its roots in the mythological figure Hermes who was the messenger and interpreter of the gods. This etymology is reflected in its contemporary usage, where hermeneutics is the science or method of interpretation. It is in wide currency in theology where it is associated with a form of textual analysis that believes sacred texts contain material within them that reveals their 'true' meaning and interpretation. It was particularly associated with Protestant theologians at the time of the Reformation given the contention in reformed theology that each individual is capable of reading and interpreting Scripture. However, the term has come to be used loosely in social science discourse to describe an approach that studies people's social meanings, much like the term *Verstehen*. It is not appropriate to use either term as interchangeable with social meanings, although it is easy to see how the mistake occurs.

Hermeneutics came to have this distorted meaning as a result of the way the term was used in the tradition of German social philosophy known as the *Geisteswissenschaften*, roughly translated as the cultural and social sciences. Dilthey best represents this tradition. According to Dilthey, *Verstehen*, or understanding, was the proper subject matter of these sciences, not explanatory knowledge, and one part of this was interpretation of the meaning of texts, or hermeneutics. The idea of the 'hermeneutic circle' or 'double hermeneutic' suggests that texts should be interpreted in their historical context, tracing a circle from the text to the author's biography, the immediate social context of the text's production to the historical period in which it was written and back to the reader and his/her context, who then interprets it. There is thus a constant interaction between reader and author. Twentieth-century German social philosophers contributed to this idea, notably Heidegger and Gadamer. In Gadamer's *Truth and Method*, published in 1960, he suggested that readers are able to construct a meaning of the text by grasping the author's intentions as revealed in the subject matter of the text. Such an interpretation is both relative to the reader, since it is shaped by the reader's interpretative processes and prejudices, and can change over time on subsequent re-readings. Interpretations are thus not fixed. This allows the focus to shift on to analysis of the reader's partisan interpretation and the way in which the meaning of the text is conditioned by the factors that affect its interpretation. Gadamer was particularly interested in how these prejudices are socially patterned, evolve and reproduce in language over time.

The term hermeneutics entered the social research literature through the way the *Geisteswissenschaften* tradition was incorporated into the 1960s attack on *positivism* and the rediscovery of interpretative social theories as theoretical foundations for alternative models of social research. Chief amongst the interpretators of this tradition for a new generation of social scientists was Anthony Giddens (1976; 1977). Various interpretative social theories were formulated (*ethnomethodology*) or rediscovered (*phenomenology*, symbolic interactionism) to provide the conceptual framework and theoretical ideas for the practice of social research in a non-positivist mould, and their connection with the *Geisteswissenschaften* tradition was explored by Giddens in particular. Hermeneutics entered the lexicon on social research at that point; indeed, Giddens refers to the *Geisteswissenschaften* as the hermeneutical tradition and he has traced the debt the 1960s interpretative sociologies, like ethnomethodology, owe to hermeneutics.

Suggested further reading

Bleicher, J. (1980) *Contemporary Hermeneutics*. London: Routledge.

Giddens, J. (1977) 'Hermeneutics, Ethnomethodology and Problems of Interpretative Analysis', in *Studies in Social and Political Theory*. London: Hutchinson.

Palmer, R.E. (1979) *Hermeneutics*. Evaston: Northwestern University Press.

References

Gadamer, H. (1979/1960) *Truth and Method*. London: Sheed and Ward.

Giddens, A. (1976) *New Rules of Sociological Method*. London: Hutchinson.

Giddens, A. (1977) *Studies in Social and Political Theory*. London: Hutchinson.

JOHN BREWER

Historical methods

Within the multi-disciplinary context of the present-day social sciences, 'historical methods' refers to the adoption of a diverse array of source materials, methods and modes of analysis utilised within the discipline of history, and employed within social research. Though increasingly acceptable within the broad field of social research, the use of historical methods has not always been so welcome, and the precise relationship between social and historical research, and between history and the core social sciences, remains contested.

Historical research materials

The materials, methods and modes of analysis used within the discipline of history are a heterogeneous lot, spread across a variety of specialisms and sub-disciplines ranging across the whole gamut of historical human experience. This renders the task of providing a comprehensive and exhaustive definition somewhat problematic. Instead, a brief selective survey of some of the more commonly used sources and their associated uses will be provided here, in order to indicate the sheer diversity of source materials and the varieties of uses to which they are put.

Official published documentary sources are commonplace sources for historical research concentrating upon the state. They include such things as documents of governments and state departments, legislative texts, constitutions, treaties, official records of parliamentary debates, court judgements and reports of governmental enquiries and commissions. Moreover, such materials are usually supplemented by *unpublished and/or unofficial documentary sources*, such as written records of minutes and memos stored in archives, and the memoirs, diaries, correspondence and autobiographies of individuals associated with official institutions. These can provide additional information and fresh insights into the detailed operations of states, parliaments, the military, diplomacy, and their various personnel. Furthermore, depending upon the specific topic being investigated, such materials may also be combined with *quantitative documentary sources*. These include social statistics, official censuses of population and production, fiscal records and accounts of state revenues and expenditures, and even almanacs. These may enable the researcher to glean insight into the broader social and economic conditions pertaining at the time, and may in turn be augmented by *reporting and recording sources*, such as annals, chronicles, previous works of history, newspaper archives and periodical literature, which can provide a wealth of insight and information into a wider range of contemporary phenomena not provided by the other sources.

The specific range of source materials considered for use in historical research, however, will depend upon the topic under investigation and the particular interest of the researcher in that topic, and so for historical research that does not accord pride of place to the state, the use of an alternative range of sources is normally required. These include an ever more wide ranging set of materials, and encompass such things as *non-official documentary sources*, for example, letters of individuals, marriage settlement papers, wills, leases, rental contracts, travel literature, maps and commercial advertisements. To these may be added a host of *unwritten sources* surviving in popular memory, such as folklore, songs, legends and oral poetry. Moreover, *material artefacts* such as monuments, buildings, landscapes, architectural layouts, tools and machinery may be employed as sources, whether to substitute for alternative sources, or to provide insight, information and evidence that written sources are not likely to provide. And finally, a welter of *miscellaneous sources*, such as place names, tombstone inscriptions, and various contemporary ritual and ceremonial practices, may be put to use in efforts to uncover past life.

This unruly mass of source materials in principle available to historical researchers presents them with the task of identifying and selecting the most appropriate sources with which to work. Critical determinants in this process of selection are the specific subject matter of the research and the particular interest of the researcher. For example, a researcher interested in exploring aspects of European migration to the Americas in the late nineteenth century might be interested in the making of immigration laws and policy in, say, Canada or the USA. This would entail a focus upon the appropriate official documents of the governments in question. Another researcher might be interested in the experiences of migrants, as they embark on their trans-Atlantic journey and endeavour to adapt to their new life and circumstances. This might entail the use of the logbooks of commercial shipping ventures that transported migrants from Europe, combined with the reports of literate fellow travellers such as clergy or merchants, and augmented with the correspondence between migrants and their relatives 'back home'. However, as this example illustrates, historical research crucially depends upon the *survival* of sources. Immigration documents may have been shredded, and emigrants' letters home may have not have been preserved, and even if preserved by friends and family, they may never have been collected and stored for the use of future historians. This reveals the single most important factor involved in the selection of source materials: their *original production and subsequent survival*.

The fact that historical researchers are so dependent upon the vagaries of past humans and their predilections for producing records and/or leaving traces of themselves behind, places them in a position quite distinct from that of investigators of contemporary society. Historical researchers cannot address, influence or directly engage with their subject matter or objects of study, nor can historical research generate its own designer-made data. Not surprisingly, to many social researchers trained to prize representative samples and control groups this unavoidable dependence of the historical researcher upon the fickleness of surviving evidence renders historical research less than ideal. However, while the inherent flaws of available source materials needs to be recognised as a critical factor, qualifying historical claims and limiting the scope of historical enquiry and research, the qualms of a social researcher must not be exaggerated. Indeed, they may even, on occasion, be misplaced, deriving from a commitment to a specific conception of social research that many historical researchers would contest.

The use(s) of history in social research

Social researchers rarely dispute the value of historical research. They do, however, disagree over how it should be *used* for purposes of social-scientific enquiry, and over the question of its proper place within the broad field of social research. Of cardinal significance to these two issues are the questions of how to conceptualise the relationship between past and present, and how to assess the importance of a specifically *historical* understanding of social phenomena.

Separating past from present

One popular, if not dominant, conception of the relationship between past and present is that which conceives the past as something like a separate world: practically, empirically and conceptually insulated from the present. Within this conception there is a radical separation of past and present, and the past is conceived primarily as a *resource*, consisting of a vast repository of (historical) examples of social organisation(s), social interactions and social behaviour, and serving as an enormous storehouse that can then be utilised for purposes of social research. For example, the past may be thought of as housing crucial *empirical data* against which to test a specific hypothesis, or upon which to base a specific generalisation. Alternatively, it may be thought of as containing a host of noteworthy *samples* of social phenomena, which may be investigated and studied as 'cases', perhaps as part of social research projects aimed at the construction of 'ideal types', and/or geared towards the building of 'models'. Despite variations in specific versions of this conception, each envisages the task of historical research as that of supplying the necessary data and/or requisite historical details to facilitate the specific social research project at hand. Examples of such historical research would include: (i) investigating past cases of economic decline and trying to identify evidence of contemporaneous religious revival that might serve to test the hypothesis that economic slumps generate religious revivals; (ii) studying mid nineteenth-century Britain as an exemplary case of classical industrial capitalism, from which a model of capitalist industrialisation might begin to be built; and (iii) researching third century Christian communities as an example of a religious sect from which ideal types of church and sect might be constructed. As these examples indicate, the precise kind of historical research undertaken will depend upon the specific way in which the past is conceptualised as a resource, and on how the social researcher understands her task, whether that of constructing a collection of trans-historical law-like generalisations and associated hypotheses, or that of expanding and enhancing the social-scientific stock of types and models.

Continuity between past and present

This specific understanding of the relationship between past and present, and between historical and social research has not gone unchallenged. The radical separation of past from present and the associated conceptualisation of the past as (no more than) a resource, have been questioned. And the idea of social research as embodying, and aspiring to, an understanding which is itself not historical has also been challenged. In contrast to these positions, it has been pointed out that much of the present is the *product* of the past, the *outcome* of previous actions, activities and even accidents. In short, rather than being distant, dead and gone, much of the past remains around us, alive and well. From this perspective, the social world we inhabit is manifestly *not* insulated from the past, but is very much a 'hand-me-down' world, and one which is repeatedly (re-)inherited and passed-on by successive generations. Therefore, the argument continues, many current social phenomena are ineradicably *historical* in character: they frequently bear the marks of their origins, and require that they be understood in historical terms. This alternative viewpoint envisages a distinctive role for historical research, not simply as a 'handmaiden' supplying evidence and examples to 'proper' social research, but as a full partner in the broader social-scientific enterprise. Hence historical research may be conducted as a specific *form* of social research, for example where the research aims to identify, uncover and analyse the 'origins', 'sources', 'foundations' and 'causes' of current social phenomena. For example, social-scientific interest in the phenomenon of nationalism might be enhanced by research that seeks to identify and trace the creation and formation of minority nationalities through processes of geo-political re-structuring, whether via conferences of world powers re-drawing the world map, as in Versailles in 1919, or via the fortunes of war and military conquest.

Such research needs to tread carefully, however, in order to avoid confusing 'origins' understood simply as beginnings in time, and 'origins' understood as causal explanations. One set of factors may be responsible for bringing a particular situation into existence, while an entirely different set of factors may sustain and maintain its subsequent survival. Weber's 'Protestant Ethic' may have played its part in bringing about a form of behaviour conducive to capitalistic activities, yet once established these activities may continue independently of their alleged 'source'. Indeed, the controversies that surrounded the debate over Weber's thesis on the origins of capitalism reveals some of the pitfalls and the scope for misunderstanding which commonly accompany attempts to provide historical accounts and explanations of current social phenomena.

The historicist challenge

A more radical challenge to the view of past and present as separate spheres is provided by historicism. Both weak and strong versions exist, with neither being simply content to highlight the historical character of many social phenomena investigated through social research. Instead, each seeks to emphasise the historical character of *social research* itself. It is not simply that the topics and objects of social research are frequently historical in character and demand to be understood in historical terms, but that the very concepts, categories, frameworks, propositions and practices which constitute social research are regarded as historical creations.

The strong version of historicism claims that due recognition of the historical character of social research requires that aspirations to a social-scientific understanding which is 'outside' history need to be abandoned: all that can be reasonably hoped for is an understanding within the terms of the inherited conceptual and theoretical frameworks available at the time of research. Hence, all social research will remain relative to those historical frameworks within which it operates. A royal road to relativism is thus opened up by strong versions of historicism, if rarely completely travelled.

The weaker version of historicism seeks to avoid abandoning classical scientific ideals and aspirations, and the associated turn towards relativism. Insisting that the historical character of social research must be recognised, it claims that such recognition is simply the first step towards a social scientific understanding by facilitating criticism of the taken-for-granted assumptions that may be smuggled into social research by an unhistorical conception of social reality and social research. It remains committed to classical scientific ideals, but stresses that historical self-criticism and reflexivity are required of social researchers when pursuing their social-scientific projects.

Suggested further reading

Hobsbawm, Eric (1997) *On History*. London: Weidenfeld & Nicholson.

Stern, Fritz (ed.) (1973) *The Varieties of History: From Voltaire to the Present*, 2nd edn. New York: Vintage Books. (1st edn, 1956.)

See also Documentary sources and **Social statistics**.

SEAN L'ESTRANGE

Hypothesis testing

The points covered in this entry are:

(1) the idea of the hypothesis
(2) hypothesis-testing in confirmatory statistical analysis
(3) Type I and Type II errors
(4) the idea of statistical significance.

Many basic statistics such as measures of central tendency (means, medians, modes etc.) and dispersion (standard deviation, variance, interquartile deviation etc.), as well as simple frequency counts and virtually all Exploratory Data Analysis statistics, are solely *descriptive*. While they allow us to see patterns in data and to establish their characteristics, this stage – orienting oneself and becoming familiar with the data – is just a preliminary stage to a proper analysis.

Researchers will have ideas (which we can call hypotheses) about the relation-ships in the data, and will want to *test* these ideas to see if they really hold true. In quantitative data analysis, this testing is carried out in a rigorous manner by *confirmatory statistical analysis*. Confirmatory statistical tests allow the researcher to test or evaluate the validity of results and then to report the results in ways that will be meaningful to anyone with a knowledge of the statistical procedures used.

Let's take an example from a survey of attitudes towards the police.

The survey has a scale variable that gives a score to people's evaluation of the impartiality of the police. The *higher* a person's score on the scale, the *more impartial* they think the police are. The mean score for whites is **11.3**, for non-whites, the mean is **10.8**. So, the non-whites appear to think the police are less impartial than the whites. But is this really so? After all, the difference really isn't all that great, only one-half a unit, and, remember, the data come from a survey and it is possible that, by chance, we might have picked up non-whites with unusually poor opinions of the police and/or whites with unusually good opinions. If this is the case, our difference may not be a real one. We must carry out a confirmatory statistical test that will tell us if the difference is real or not.

The difference between looking at the characteristics of data with descriptive statistics and then actually testing a hypothesis using confirmatory statistics can be seen as analogous to detecting a crime and then trying the accused person in a court. Seeing the difference in the impartiality scale scores between the whites and non-whites and deciding to test it with a confirmatory statistic is like a detective poking about and finding enough evidence to make an arrest. Then, carrying out the confirmatory statistical test to establish whether the difference is large enough to be considered real is analogous the extremely formal proceedings in a court trial in which the accused is found guilty or not guilty.

The hypothesis is like the formal indictment read out in court – a precise statement of exactly what the researcher expects to find. A hypothesis is a statement of a relationship between population parameters or variables and typically takes the form of predicting *differences* between groups or *relationships* between variables.

Using our example, the hypothesis could be: *The mean assessment of whites about the impartiality of the police is **higher** than the mean opinion of non-whites about the impartiality of the police.*

The researcher attempts to prove a hypothesis by *disproving* its logical opposite. This logical opposite is called the *null hypothesis* – a statement of *no difference or the opposite difference or no relationship or the opposite relationship* from that predicted by the hypothesis. Using our example, the null would be: *The mean assessment of whites about the impartiality of the police is **not different or lower** than the mean opinion of non-whites about the impartiality of the police.*

In this case, the researcher can carry out a statistical test called the *t*-test of significant difference between means. It will tell us whether the difference we see in fact *is* a real one – that the higher impartiality score of the whites is real. (In fact – as shown below – the *t*-test will find that the difference is real.) So, the researcher rejects the null hypothesis (of no difference between the groups or a difference in the opposite direction (non-whites having the lower mean score)) and thereby accepts the hypothesis.

Type I and Type II errors

That's the way it should work, but mistakes can be made. Statistical tests are not infallible. The researcher can make two types of errors.

(1) The researcher can *accept* a hypothesis as being *correct* when it is actually *false*. This is called a Type I error and is the worse type of error to make.
(2) The researcher can *reject* a hypothesis as being *wrong* when it is actually *true*. This is called a Type II error.

We can put this into a chart.

	Hypothesis is really . . .	
Researcher decides to:	INCORRECT	CORRECT
Accept hypothesis	**TYPE I ERROR** (the worst!)	Researcher accepted an hypothesis that is true – a correct decision
Reject hypothesis	Researcher rejected an hypothesis that is wrong – a correct decision	**TYPE II ERROR**

The reason a Type I error is worse than a Type II error becomes clear when you note that a researcher will act upon the results of his or her statistical test. If a Type I error is made, the researcher will continue with their investigation, only working with the belief that something is true that actually is not. They will become more and more confused when subsequent results fail to take the form they should. However, if only a Type II error is made, the researcher is stuck, but they will not carry on working under false premises. The cost of the error will be much less and the chance of realising that an error has taken place is much higher. An analogy would be coming to a crossroads. If you choose the wrong road (a Type I error) and start driving down it, things get very confusing as you become more and more lost. If you remain stuck at the intersection, unable to decide which road is the right one (a Type II error), at least you aren't getting more lost!

Statistical significance

Now, let us move back to how one actually uses statistics to test hypotheses and how to avoid making Type I and Type II errors. Returning to our example, remember the hypothesis is: *The mean assessment of whites about the impartiality of the police is **higher** than the mean opinion of non-whites about the impartiality of the police*, and the non-white impartiality score is higher. What we need is a statistical test that tells us whether this higher mean is a large enough difference to be genuine or whether it could be just due to chance. *t*-test is a confirmatory statistic that tests whether the differences between means are real, or *statistically signi-ficant*.[1] Without going into the details of how the test is calculated, the result is that the difference is statistically significant at a probability of 0.007 ($p < 0.007$). What this means, exactly, is that the odds that the difference we see between the mean impartiality scores for the whites and the non-whites being due only to chance is only 7 out of 1,000. These are pretty good odds, so we accept the hypothesis.[2]

Some important features of statistical testing, which both students and professionals often forget, follow on from this:

(1) The results of *all* confirmatory statistical tests are expressed in these terms of probability (for example, $p < 0.007$) . . . in effect, the odds that a Type I error has been made.

(2) The *smaller* the size of the level of significance, the *less likely* it is that a Type I error has been made and the *more likely* it is that our hypothesis really is true.

(3) There are 'standard' cut-off points for accepting hypotheses:
   $p < 0.05$ means a 5 in 100 (1 in 20) chance of a Type I error;
   $p < 0.01$ means a 1 in 100 chance that a Type I error has been made;
   $p < 0.001$ means less than a 1 in 1,000 chance of a Type I error.
   But note that these are only conventions that have been set arbitrarily.

(4) Usually, levels of significance greater than 0.05 are not considered good enough to reject the null hypothesis. For instance, even though $p < 0.10$ means only a 1 in 10 chance of a Type I error, we usually would not accept the hypothesis. The reason for this is that it is much less of a calamity to make a Type II error (rejecting a true hypothesis) than it is to make a Type I

error (accepting a false hypothesis). Hence, the odds of probability testing are highly skewed against making Type I errors.

(5) Really important research often adopts a stricter level of confidence cut-off than the 0.05 level.

All confirmatory statistics share these features, their results will be expressed in terms of statistical significance; in effect, the odds that the results are only due to chance.

Notes

1 The *t*-test is closely related to the Z-test.
2 Note that, since we are using sampling, there is always some possibility (though it may be tiny like here) that our significant result is due solely to a chance fluke (the much-dreaded Type I error).

Suggested further reading

Erickson, B.H. and Nosanchuk, T.A. (1992) *Understanding Data.* Buckingham: Open University Press. Especially Chapter 8.

Pawson, Ray (1989) *A Measure for Measures: a Manifesto for Empirical Sociology.* London: Routledge. Especially Chapter 1.

ROBERT MILLER

Ideal type

Ideal types are methods of investigation (heuristic devices) in which researchers construct concepts or ideas in their pure and essential form, mostly with the intent of then comparing them against the real world. Ideal types do not represent the average or typical features of the phenomenon they describe but what the researcher considers its essence. Nor do they represent normatively the ideal or most desirable features of the phenomenon. Ideal types are not descriptions of real phenomena as they appear in the social world but are representations constructed on the basis of what the researcher considers their character in some pure essential form. Thus, ideal types should not be confused with the typologies and taxonomies that are often developed in data analysis for these are real types based on the substantive data. It is very important therefore that when developing typologies and taxonomies researchers make clear whether they are real or ideal types.

In as much as they are not real there is only limited value to the use of ideal types as methods of investigation in social research. However, comparisons between the ideal type and its real world equivalent can offer useful glimpses of the phenomenon in the empirical world. In economics, for example, it is possible to compare the ideal type of the perfect market against markets as they operate in practice. In sociology it is possible to compare bureaucracies in real life against the ideal type 'bureaucracy'. While useful, this heuristic device is clearly restricted. In social science the term is most commonly associated with the German sociologist Max Weber who constructed ideal types for concepts like 'bureaucracy' and for processes like 'meaningful social action'. A considerable amount of work on organisations has been developed from Weber's ideal type of bureaucracy to show its departure from what organisations are like in real life. However, it is probably for his conceptualisation of the *meaning* of social action through the construction of ideal types of meaningful action that Weber is most well known in qualitative research.

Weber's penchant for ideal types needs to be located in the methodological debates within German philosophy at the time and which formed an intellectual pillar to his sociological writings. The tradition of hermeneutics popular within Germany at the time argued that interpretation (the literal translation of the term hermeneutics) and understanding (the English translation of Weber's famous term *Verstehen*) is the primary goal of the cultural or human sciences (called the *Geisteswissenschaften* tradition). The problem is that this approach can leave us with the historically specific and particular, which runs counter to the observed regularities that are evident in social life and the need to develop social *theory* through which these social regularities are explained in a systematic way. For its part, the *Geisteswissenschaften* tradition wished to avoid the dangers it perceived in the natural sciences (*Naturwissenschaften*) which emulated the goal to produce law-like general statements through deduction and the hypothetico-deductive method. The tension between the particular and the general, the unique and the regular, and the individual self and the social self was managed in Weber by means of the ideal type. By constructing ideal types that formed Weber's representation of the essence of meaningful social action, he was able to focus on (hypothesised) socially patterned regularities of meaning rather than potentially solipsistic and idiosyncratic meaning. Alfred Schutz in his formulation of social *phenomenology* faced the same problem and came up with the same solution of focusing on ideal types of meaning rather than on the potentially unique meanings of real individuals in real settings (something Robert Gorman once called Schutz's 'dual vision' (Gorman, 1977). This is the advantage *ethnomethodology* has over both Weber and Schutz's sociologies of meaning.

Suggested further reading

Hekman, S.J. (1986) *Weber, the Ideal Type and Contemporary Social Theory*. Notre Dame, IL: University of Notre Dame Press.

Reference

Gorman, R. (1977) *The Dual Vision*. London: Routledge.

JOHN BREWER

Impact Assessment

Since the early 1970s impact assessment procedures have continued to grow in popularity. While originally the focus fell exclusively on environmental concerns, a diversity of methodologies are now subsumed under this umbrella term. When first introduced, environmental impact assessments caused considerable controversy but they have since become well established and now provide the template to which other forms of impact assessment refer. The contemporary literature is peppered with examples of impact assessment procedures. Included in this literature will be found the following terms:

- Environmental Impact Assessment
- Social Impact Assessment
- Technology Assessment
- Policy Assessment
- Economic and Fiscal Impact Assessment
- Demographic Impact Assessment
- Health Impact Assessment
- Regulatory Impact Assessment
- Climate Impact Assessment
- Equality Impact Assessment
- Development Impact Assessment
- Environmental Auditing.

At first glance it may seem that impact assessments routinely address a wide array of social issues. In reality the primary focus of this work continues to be the environment, with the alternative procedures often representing adjuncts to a primary environmental impact assessment. The characteristics of a number of the more influential impact assessment procedures will now be outlined.

Environmental Impact Assessment (EIA)

The earliest environmental impact assessment system was introduced under the provisions of the US National Environmental Policy Act of 1969, along with the establishment of the Environmental Protection Agency in 1970. Within two years several high profile legal cases had helped to confirm the significance of these procedures. Internationally, there are now numerous systems in place, almost all of which are governed by legislation and in turn have taken their lead from the US system.

As the title suggests, the procedure is designed to consider how certain actions or events will impact on the environment, for example, new building. Beyond this it is accepted that an environmental impact assessment should not be construed primarily as a procedure for preventing actions with significant environmental impacts. Instead it is acknowledged that an environmental assessment will not take place in a political vacuum and consequently economic, social or political factors may outweigh environmental factors. Hence the purpose of an assessment may be to authorise actions in the full knowledge of their environmental consequences.

An EIA would typically involve the following eight iterative steps:

(1) Consideration of alternative means of achieving objectives
(2) Designing the selected protocol
(3) Determining whether an impact assessment is necessary in a particular case (screening)
(4) Deciding on the topics to be covered in the assessment (scoping)
(5) Preparing the report (that is, *inter alia*, describing the proposal and the environment affected by it and assessing the magnitude and significance of impacts)
(6) Reviewing the report to check its adequacy
(7) Making a decision on the proposal, using the report and opinions expressed about it
(8) Monitoring the impacts of the proposal if it is implemented.

In terms of techniques or methodologies, three principal methods have tended to be employed in order to indicate environmental effects and impacts, namely:

*   Checklists – Comprehensive lists of effects and impact indicators designed to stimulate the analyst to think broadly about consequences of contemplated actions
*   Matrices – lists of (a) human actions and (b) impact indicators are related in a matrix which can be used to identify causal relationships
*   Flow diagrams – used to identify action–effect–impact relationships in a visual form

In turn, three principal methods often have been employed to compare impact indicators:

*   Display of sets of values on individual impact indicators (for example, the Leopold matrix, which typically displays 17,600 pieces of information simultaneously (project actions listed horizontally; environmental characteristics and conditions listed vertically))
*   Ranking of alternatives within impact categories (which permits the determination of alternatives that have the least adverse impact but does not allow for weighting of impact indicators and so does not aid comparison between alternatives)
*   Normalisation and mathematical weighting (which places impact indicators into comparable forms, based on objective method for assigning numerical weights).

Despite the long experience of EIAs there remain a number of areas of concern and inconsistencies in relation to the process of impact assessment, primarily relating to how the results obtained from many diverse qualitative and quantitative methods are able to be combined in a decision-making process leading to the assessment statement. The role and scope of consultation is also a matter for debate, particulary in relation to scoping.

Social Impact Assessment (SIA)

SIAs have become commonplace since the mid-1980s. While some have encompassed topics including rural resource development, technological change, crime, transportation, rural migration and community projects, the majority involve environmental issues. The stages to be followed when conducting an SIA generally mirror those which characterise an EIA and include the following elements:

(1) Consultation/Public involvement – developing an effective public involvement plan to involve all potentially affected individuals and groups
(2) Identification of alternatives – describing the proposed action or policy change and reasonable alternatives
(3) Baseline conditions – describing the relevant human environment/area of influence and baseline conditions
(4) Scoping – identifying the full range of probable social impacts that will be addressed
(5) Projection of estimated effects – investigating the probable impacts
(6) Predicting responses to impacts – determining the significance of the identified social impacts
(7) Indirect and cumulative impacts – estimating subsequent impacts and cumulative impacts
(8) Changes in alternatives – recommending new or changed alternatives and estimating or projecting their consequences
(9) Mitigation – developing a mitigation plan
(10) Monitoring – developing a monitoring programme.

A number of research methods typically inform SIA, including:

- Comparative statistical methods (with or without inferential statistics)
- Straight line trend projections
- Population multiplier methods
- Scenarios ('imagination scenarios' of hypothetical futures based on either logical deduction or 'fitted empirical scenarios' where existing trends are used to predict future)
- Expert testimony
- Computer modelling (involving mathematical formulation of premises and quantitative weighting of variables)
- Calculation of 'futures foregone' (for example, loss of recreational facilities).

Typically an SIA will focus attention on defined social categories or variables. By way of illustration, Burdge et al. (1998) listed these social variables under five headings:

1   *Population characteristics*
Population change
Ethnic and racial distribution
Relocated populations
Influx or outflow of temporary workers
Seasonal residents

2   *Community and institutional structures*
Voluntary associations
Interest group activity
Size and structure of local government
Historical experience of change
Employment/income characteristics
Employment equity of minority groups
Local/regional/national linkages
Industrial/commercial diversity
Presence of planning and zoning activity

3   *Political and social resources*
Distribution of power and authority
Identification of stakeholders
Interested and affected parties
Leadership capability and characteristics

4   *Individual and family changes*
Perception of risk, health and safety
Displacement/relocation conerns
Trust in political and social institutions
Residential stability
Density of acquaintanceship
Attitudes toward policy/project
Family and friendship networks
Concerns about social well-being

5   *Community resources*
Change in community infrastructure
Native American tribes
Land use patterns
Effects on cultural, historical and archaeological resources

As should be apparent, an effective SIA requires considerable resources and will draw on a wide range of research methods, both qualitiative and quantitative.

Health Risk Assessment (HRA)

An HRA is distinct from either of the assessment preocedures decribed above. HRAs were first developed in the US in the 1980s, initially to help doctors communicate health risks more effectively to their patients. Very quickly HRAs became more widespread and now, for example, employers, insurance companies and health care bodies would use HRAs to project and prioritise group risks, and to plan health intervention programmes accordingly. One of the key benefits of HRAs has been the identification of high risk individuals whose health status can then be closely monitored. An HRA would typically employ the following elements:

(1) A self-report questionnaire
(2) A computation of risk
(3) Educational messages and individual risk reports.

The self-report questionnaire often gathers data in relation to family history, general health parameters (weight, blood pressure, cholesterol levels, etc.) and lifestyle (diet, tobacco and alcohol use, recreational activities, safety precautions, etc.). The risk computation would then compare responses to the questionnaire with data gathered from larger populations. Individual risk factors are then able to be compared with disease 'precursors' such as diet and lifestyle. Each precursor would be assigned a numerical 'relative risk' for every associated disease so as to indicate how much that precursor contributes to the disease.

An HRA report would often detail the individual's chronological age, his or her calculated risk age (meaning how old the general population is that matches the individual's health status), a target or achievable age (meaning the age of the general population that has the characteristics the individual could achieve with improvements), and a summary of the person's various health risks and lifestyle behaviours with suggestions on how to reduce risk for disease.

Equality Impact Assessment (EQIA)

While earlier assessments may have included an equality agenda, a deliberate focus on equality has only characterised the field of impact assessment relatively recently. To date the focus of this work has tended to be on a small number of equality categories, normally either gender or race. For example, Status of Women Canada has produced materials designed to assist policy makers in carrying out gender-based analyses. The methodology reflects EIA procedures, for example, the policy development/analysis cycle is represented as eight steps, with a series of structured questions associated with each step:

(1) Identifying, defining and refining the issue
(2) Defining desired/anticipated outcomes
(3) Defining the information and consultation inputs
(4) Conducting research
(5) Developing and analysing options
(6) Making recommendations/decision seeking
(7) Communicating policy
(8) Assessing the quality of analysis.

Likewise, the New Zealand Ministry of Women's Affairs has also produced a set of guidelines which provide a framework for gender analysis, based again on impact assessment procedures. Within Europe the primary focus has been on the mainstreaming of the gender perspective into general policies, with The Netherlands, Finland, Norway, Belgium, Sweden, Denmark and Northern Ireland all having such schemes in place. The method of EQIA draws heavily on environmental impact assessment procedures.

Suggested further reading

Glasson, J. (1999) *Introduction to Environmental Impact Assessment: Principles and Procedures, Process, Practice and Prospects.* London: Taylor and Francis.

Wathern, P. (1998) *Environmental Impact Assessment: Theory and Practice.* London: Routledge.

Wood, C. (1995) *Environmental Impact Assessment: a Comparative Review.* New York: Addison-Wesley.

Reference

Burdge, R.J. et al. (1998) *A Conceptual Approach to Social Impact Assessment.* Wisconson: Social Ecology Press.

JOHN KREMER

Induction

Induction is an approach in social research which argues that empirical generalisations and theoretical statements should be derived from the data. It is the inverse of deduction, in which hypotheses are derived from theory and then tested against data. Induction is associated with qualitative research and naturalism, where the intent is to be 'true to the data themselves', allowing the data 'to speak for themselves'. That is, a priori assumptions and theoretical ideas should not be used to interpret data, rather the social meaning inherent in the data alone should be used as the basis for any empirical generalisation or theoretical statement. As an approach to *theory* building it is associated with Glaser and Strauss' formulation of grounded theory in which theory is the outcome of the research. As an approach to qualitative data analysis it is expressed by the idea of 'analytic induction' in which empirical generalisations develop from the data instead of being used to interpret findings.

In the 1960s induction became part of the critique of positivism, which stresses deduction as an approach to theory and data analysis. Like many methodological developments in this period, induction had roots in earlier philosophical debates which had been rediscovered and were becoming part of the lexicon of practising social researchers. The ancient philosophical position of idealism gives support to induction, and the long-standing philosophical contrast between realism and idealism parallels that between deduction and induction. Various other antinomies, such as materialism versus free will and mind versus matter, are also parallel contrasts. Idealism suggests that ideas are more important than the material world and, moreover, that the mind is the source of all ideas. This focus on the perceptual apparatus and ideas of people fits induction as an approach in social research. Induction in philosophy describes the cognitive process by which human beings pass from the perception of things and events to knowledge of the world and this became translated in the discourse of anti-positivist social researchers to impact their understanding of methodology and practice. Methodologically it came to mean that knowledge of the social world must be based on people's perceptions of it, the stance taken in naturalism and which validates qualitative research. In terms of method it was translated into the practice of basing empirical generalisations and theoretical statements about the social world on the data themselves free of preconceptions, allowing subjects' perceptions, ideas and social meanings not only to speak for themselves but to speak in a broader way by generalisation and theory without contamination. In practice however, induction and deduction are not so mutually exclusive, in that social researchers often sway between the two when refining inductively developed theories by means of deducing new empirical questions that are put to further empirical research.

Grounded theory gave expression to this in terms of theory generation and analytic induction in data analysis. The irony is that both practices have quite positivist features, particularly analytic induction, but they are almost impossible to apply in a pure form. Indeed, the end result of analytic induction, were it possible to operate, is the development of deductive explanations.

Analytic induction was first formulated in 1943 by Florian Znaniecki, one of the founding generation of the Chicago School of sociology that was instrumental in the development of ethnography and other qualitative methods in sociology. It formed part of Znaniecki's attempt to systematise and codify the methods of research in sociology (the title of his book was *The Method of Sociology*). Analytic induction was defined as the process of deriving laws from a deep analysis of experimentally isolated instances. The goal of research was defined in very positivist terms and was conceived as making universal statements that are comprehensive, exhaustive and have causal implications. As conceived by Znaniecki analytic induction was a process for making general statements that is rooted in the data themselves and involves several steps: definition of the problem in tentative terms; development of a hypothesis about the problem; examination of a single instance of the phenomenon to test the hypothesis; reformulation of the hypothesis against the data based on the case; examination of additional cases to test the revised hypothesis; and further reformulation of the hypothesis against the data, leading to further data collection. Negative cases require the hypothesis be reformulated until there are no exceptions. Empirical observations orient the process and lead to improved hypotheses that better fit reality. Once no negative cases are found, the hypothesis is confirmed and the development of deductive statements about the phenomenon thus becomes possible.

Later supporters of analytic induction withdrew from some of the implications of this formulation. They particularly avoided the inference that there are universal laws of social behaviour, something completely out of step with the ideas of qualitative researchers who took up induction as part of their attack on positivism's claim to do likewise.

These ideas are curiously out of place in the post-structuralist and postmodern era when belief in an objective reality has given way to the belief that there are multiple versions of reality and the goal of research is to capture the variety of 'truths' held by different people. But even if one is not persuaded by postmodernism, analytic induction has serious deficiencies. No knowledge can be confirmed given the theoretical possibility of negative cases as yet undiscovered, thus any knowledge remains fallible. It also requires constant returns to the field to collect data against the revised hypotheses (Glaser and Strauss's approach in grounded theory merely requires data collection to the point where the category is 'saturated' with cases). The judgements that no further entries into the field are needed and data collection is finished because negative cases have been exhausted are subjective assessments. It is also doubtful that researchers are capable of bracketing off their theoretical preferences, ideas and preconceptions from the process of data collection and hypothesis testing. The philosophy of social research shows that the very methods researchers used to collect data against revised hypotheses were replete with implicit theoretical preferences. Most textbooks which use examples to illustrate the use of the method of analytic induction draw on early studies from Znaniecki's era of research. Seale recently described loyalty to the approach of analytic induction as of the 'bumper sticker' kind, something declared in public but not so much practised in private. Induction, however, as the more general principle, remains the foundation of qualitative research.

Suggested further reading

Robinson, W.S. (1951) 'The Logical Structure of Analytic Induction', *American Sociological Review*, 16: 812–18.

Seale, C. (1999) *The Quality of Qualitative Research*. London: Sage.

Znaniecki, F. (1934) *The Method of Sociology*. New York: Farrar and Rinehart.

See also
Deduction.

JOHN BREWER

Intellectual property rights

The term Intellectual Property Rights (IPR) is commonly associated with patents while in fact the term encompasses the expression of all ideas and information.

IPR are generated on a daily basis. Their careful management is critical, particularly where external persons, such as other researchers, companies, government departments or local authorities, have access to the information. IPR issues occur in projects such as collaborative research, contract research, consultancy, and specialist and other services.

There are five main types of IPR:

- Patents
- Confidential information and know-how
- Copyright
- Trade marks
- Design rights.

A single project may generate more than one type of IPR. While certain IPR can arise almost automatically, other types of IPR only arise through a formal registration procedure.

Patents

Patents are the best known form of IPR and are potentially the most valuable. Formal steps are required to obtain protection. In return for a *complete disclosure* to the state (patent authority) of a technical invention, the patent holder receives a 20-year monopoly over the use of the invention. The commercial exploitation of a patented invention may be undertaken by licensees who purchase rights to the invention from the patent holder.

In order to be patentable, the idea or invention must have certain qualifying conditions:

- It must be industrially applicable.
- It requires to be new, that is, different from what has gone before and not previously disclosed in any form and not in the public domain.
- There must be an inventive step. This step does not need to be a quantum leap since the majority of patents are granted for incremental improvements to existing technology which are not obvious routine developments.
- The invention must not be of a type excluded by law.

The following types of innovation are specifically excluded from patent protection:

- a discovery, scientific theory or mathematical method
- a literary, dramatic, musical or artistic work
- a scheme, rule or method for performing a mental act, playing a game or doing business
- inventions encouraging offensive, antisocial or immoral behaviour
- certain animal, plant or biological processes (although microbiology can be protected)
- methods of treatment or therapy of the human or animal body
- computer programs as such.

It should be noted, however, that these exclusions are not so sweeping as they appear at first sight. For example, it is possible to patent a manufacturing process where the novelty lies in the computer program controlling it.

The timing of the first filing of a patent applicaton is important – file an application too quickly and there is a risk of early disclosure to competitors, but file too slowly and there is a risk of other similar or overlapping patents being sought by competitors or other businesses.

When should patenting be considered?

This issue is a key feature of patent applications. Patents are only valid if *no prior disclosures* have been made concerning the invention. (Note that this includes any published papers, conference papers, speeches and even general discussions with anyone who is not bound by a Confidentiality Agreement.) Generally speaking, the sooner patenting is considered the more likely the applicant is to secure a strong patent that will give a commercial return for the inventive work.

What protection and other benefits does a patent give?

A patent holder can prevent anyone from making, importing, using or selling the invention protected by the patent in a given territory. Permission is granted in the form of licences, which generally produce royalty payments and, usually, also initial licence fees to the patent holder. Patents are effective on a national basis, but there are various international arrangements to simplify the procedure for patenting the same invention in more than one country. The duration of a patent in most countries is a maximum of 20 years from the filing date subject to the payment of annual renewal fees during this period. After a patent has lapsed or expired, the technical information falls into the public domain and is then freely available for use by anyone.

Why is the priority date important?

The priority date refers to the date of the first application for the invention. Foreign applications can be filed within the 12-month period following the first filing, claiming the benefit of the priority date, which means that the foreign applications will be effectively backdated to the date of the filing of the original case. This 12-month period cannot be extended. Modifications and developments of the original disclosure can be incorporated during the 12-month period, but not subsequently. Once the priority date has been established, the technical information contained in the application can be published.

Confidential information and know-how

Confidential information or know-how includes any information owned by someone which they wish to be regarded as confidential or secret. This includes commercially or technically valuable information. The management of confidential information must be tailored to protect the following:

• information created by you
• information disclosed by you.

In practice an obligation to keep information confidential entails not disclosing or using the information without permission of the person to whom the obligation is owed. There are three ways that someone can become subject to an obligation of confidentiality, namely:

- expressly by a contractual obligation
- implied by a contractual obligation
- from the nature of the relationship between discloser and recipient.

Where information is being disclosed, an obligation of confidentiality can only be created if all parties are aware of the obligation and agree to it. In all cases, disclosure should be controlled by parties first entering into a written Confidentiality or Non-Disclosure Agreement.

The principle of prior disclosure is at the very cornerstone of the patent system. Basically, prior disclosure to anyone who is not subject to an obligation of confidentiality could lead to the failure of an application for patent protection.

Copyright

Copyright, as the name suggests, gives the right to act to prevent others from copying without permission from the copyright holder and protects works including text, drawings, parts lists, graphic design in packaging, corporate logos, publicity material, computer programs etc. Copyright is an automatic right that arises whenever a literary, dramatic, musical or artistic work is expressed in a tangible form. Where possible the ownership should be indicated by the legend © with name and date. Unlike patents, copyright requires no formal registration and currently lasts for the lifetime of the author plus 70 years, in some cases as a result of European harmonisation.

It is important to secure ownership of copyright in any work which you would like to prevent anyone else copying. The first owner of copyright is the author, but if the author creates the work in the course of employment duties, then the first owner is the employer. If the copyright is commissioned work it will not normally belong to the commissioner unless there is a written agreement to that effect.

Trade marks

Trade Marks are any 'sign', for example, word, device, logo, legend, label, container etc., that usually identifies goods or services as coming from a particular source. They therefore serve to distinguish between different sources. As trade marks are associated with image and reputation, they can be expensive to develop and a very expensive loss if devalued by counterfeiters or the competition. It is useful to use the symbol ® if the mark is registered and ™ if you wish to indicate merely propriety rights. These have little legal importance, but are very useful as deterrents (although ® should not be used if the mark is not registered).

Before you adopt a trade mark, it is also advisable to carry out a clearance search to ensure that you are not infringing someone else's registered trade mark rights.

Patent agents can very quickly carry out searches of registered trade marks and pending applications to clear the trade mark for use.

Design rights

The area of design rights is complex and expert advice is essential. In essence, design rights relate to the visual appearance of an industrially produced article. There are two types of design rights – *registered* and *unregistered*.

Registered designs

Registered designs relate (as the name suggests) to designs which are determined to be registrable by a formal application procedure to the state; the design must be material to the customer in its shape, pattern or ornament. Registered rights give a monopoly right, as with patents and registered trade marks. A registered design, however, lasts for 25 years, providing renewal fees are paid at five yearly periods.

Unregistered design rights

Unregistered design rights are a less formal right; as the name suggests there is no formal application procedure. The right only gives protection against copying of features of shape, and is not a monopoly right. Furthermore, it lasts for a shorter period – 10 years from first marketing, and during the last five years anyone is entitled to obtain a licence to use the protected design on payment of royalties (Licences of Right).

Note

I acknowledge the assistance of Murgitroyd & Co. in the writing of this entry.

PHILIP GRAHAM

Internet

The Internet or World Wide Web[1] is an invaluable tool for locating information. By August 2001 almost 60% of the US and Canadian population used the web, in the UK, the figure was 55% (http://www.nua.ie/surveys/how_many_online/index.html). It is now generally accepted that it is not possible to complete thorough research without using the web.

Information on the web is either free or fee based and both categories should be addressed in order to obtain the full picture. From the academic researcher's point of view the most important types of information include the full text of documents, sources for bibliographic records and statistical data.

Search engines

The first step is to open a web browser. From here it is possible to use a variety of free 'search engines', specialist web sites which permit comprehensive searching across the whole of the net. It is worth noting that the robotic nature of search engines mean that even subtle differences in the search logic can misconstrue results. Online help within each search engine or database will advise on search strategy.

No one search engine covers the whole web. So, while Google (http://www.google.com/) or Excite (http://www.excite.com) etc. can be searched individually, meta search engines will search many all at once, for example, Profusion (http://www.profusion.com/) or All4One (http://all4one.com/). Judging the quality of web sites can be aided by the Internet Detective (http://www.sosig.ac.uk/desire/internet-detective.html) or The Virtual Training Suite (http://www.vts.rdn.ac.uk/).

Catalogues and directories

Web catalogues and directories can provide direct access to high quality web resources. For instance, the Social Science Information Gateway (http://www.sosig.ac.uk/) catalogues sites evaluated by professionals in the field and so is quality assured. It can be searched using keywords or browsed by subject to find research reports and papers, journals, statistics, software and databases. The US equivalent is The Scout Report (http://scout.cs.wisc.edu/), that also publishes weekly updates via email. Academic Info (http://academicinfo.net/), BUBL (http://www.bubl.ac.uk/), NISS (http://www.niss.ac.uk) and REGARD (http://www.regard.ac.uk) are multidisciplinary and worth considering, as, like SOSIG, they are particularly effective in focusing on quality resources. The Grapevine section (http://www.sosig.ac.uk/gv/), LISTSERV (http://www.lsoft.com/products/default.asp?item=listserv) and Mailbase services (http://www.mailbase.ac.uk/) make it possible to join online discussion groups and chat to people with similar interests. Another source for locating academics and researchers is the Directory of Scholarly and Professional E-Conferences (http://www.n2h2.com/).

Most university library catalogues are available over the web via their university home page. A comprehensive list of library catalogues world wide is available via the University of Saskatchewan library pages (http://library.usask.ca/catalogs/world.html). Legal deposit library catalogues are also obvious solutions to finding out what has been published in social research fields. The Library of Congress (http://www.loc.gov/) and the British Library (http://www.bl.uk/) can be a one stop shop in this respect.

Archives and sources of information

An increasing number of authoritative information providers and organisations are posting their information on their web sites. Most list their publications or research work and at their best some provide full text of their work, for example annual reports and working papers. The United Nations (http://www.unog.ch/library/pub/pub.htm) and the International Labour Organisation (http://

www.ilo.org/public/english/info/index.htm) fall into this category as do many government web sites. In 2000 the FirstGov portal (http://www.firstgov.gov/) was launched. Its aim is to connect the world to US government information and services. The UK government had a similar mission during the 1990s with the creation of the CCTA Government Information Service (http://www.ukonline.-gov.uk/online/ukonline/home). Both services provide an index to all government departments and agencies via a 'clickable' alphabetical or functional index. The US House of Representatives (http://www.house.gov/), the US Senate and the UK Parliament site (http://www.parliament.uk/) provide direct access to their respective government sites with daily updates. The US Government Printing Office[2] (http://www.gpo.gov/) and the UK Stationery Office[3] (http://www.clickt-so.com/) catalogues are available on the web as well.

The Gunner Anzinger site will help trace government web sites world wide (http://www.gksoft.com/govt/en/) while the complex Europa site (http://Europa.eu.int/) can be viewed as a gateway to the major EU institutions.

A vast array of statistical information is also available. The UK National Statistics' StatBase and Databank (http://www.statistics.gov.uk/) provide access to key official statistics and over 55,000 datasets respectively. FedStats (http://www.fedstats.gov/) is the gateway to US government statistics, including more than 70 statistical agencies. The main source of EU statistics is EUROSTAT (http://europa.eu.int/comm/eurostat/).

Fee based databases on the web are usually administered by the organisation which pays the bill. They are either 'i.p. authenticated' (the address of the computer you are using is recognised by the database provider when you try to gain access) or password authenticated (a username and password are provided to legitimate users).

There are several data archives on the web. The Economic and Social Research Council (ESRC) in the UK has a data archive (http://www.data-archive.ac.uk/) which stores the largest collection of computer readable data in the social sciences in the UK. American equivalents include the University of California's Social Science Data Extraction site (http://sun3.lib.uci.edu/~dtsang/ext.htm) and NORC[4] (http://www.norc.uchicago.edu/) which was established in 1941, claims to be at the forefront of survey research methodology. Of relevance to qualitative research is the Qualitative Data Archive, QUALIDATA (http://www.essex.ac.uk/qualidata/index.htm) at the University of Essex in the UK that preserves primary qualitative data that can be used for secondary research. In planning research, it is wise to carry out a search of these archives just to see what has been done.

The Manchester Information and Associated Services (MIMAS) (http://www.mimas.ac.uk), based at the University of Manchester in the UK provides access to complex datasets, key bibliographic information, software packages and large scale computing resources. The key services for the social researcher include census and related datasets, government and continuous surveys, time series databanks and digital map datasets. The Centre for Applied Social Surveys (CASS) (http://www.natcen.ac.uk/cass/docs/fr_casshome.htm) is improving standards in UK survey research by providing access to questionnaires from major surveys, as does the Question Bank (http://qb.soc.surrey.ac.uk/).

For European statistical data, r.cade (http://www-rcade.dur.ac.uk/), the Resouces Centre for Access to Data on Europe, works in collaboration with National Statistics and the UK Datashop network. Free accounts can be set up to gain access to statistics relating to EU members.

e-journals

Growth in 'e-journals' began in the early 1990s. Many journal publishers are making their titles available online in full text. In addition, new journals are appearing which only exist in an electronic online version. Both types of electronic journal are usually accessible via library catalogues for registered users or via provider interfaces. In 1995 there were 250 titles available online. By 2000 this had risen to 8,500. From the social researcher's point of view access will depend on publishing deals and how institutions route to the provider interfaces such as SwetsNet and ScienceDirect.

As is the case for most full text online documents, e-journals are easier and quicker to produce and update compared to print-only subscriptions. Contents can be freely searched, usually include multimedia content, do not take up shelf space and most importantly for the researcher, provide 24 hour/7 day, multiple and remote access. The main problem is that archiving, although secure, is still developing. Most universities now incorporate e-journals into their web catalogue. By searching for the journal title the catalogue will indicate full holdings, often with a link direct to the e-journal or at least to the provider's interface which itself is usually fully searchable. Additional services are also available, for example, ScienceDirect provides for search alerts and new issue alerts. To identify journals, PubList.com (http://www.publist.com/), lists subject specific journals using keyword searching. For free full text journals try All Academic Incorporated (http://www.allacademic.com/).

Bibliographic information

Most of the key bibliographic information databases are available on the web. The International Bibliography of the Social Sciences (http://www.lse.ac.uk/IBSS/) includes articles, abstracts, books and reviews. It is multilingual, updated weekly and with an international focus, dates back to 1950. The Institute for Scientific Information (ISI) Social Sciences Citation Index (SSCI) covers articles, editorials, letters, reviews and other published material. Covering publications back to 1981, it indexes more than 1,725 journals and adds 2,700 new records per week to its current holding of 3.15 million records. FirstSearch (http://www.oclc.org/firstsearch/) provides access to multidisciplinary databases. As they embrace social science subjects the following are worth checking in order to be thorough: ArticleFirst and ContentsFirst index journals dating back to 1990; ProceedingsFirst and PapersFirst together cover every congress, conference, exposition, workshop, symposium and meeting received at the British Library since 1993. WorldCat offers access to over 40 million bibliographic records of various types other than journals. Conference papers are also indexed on the fee-based InsideWeb database produced by the British Library Document Supply Centre. The Index to Social

Sciences and Humanities Proceedings covers conference papers globally. PolicyFile indexes research and practice reports covering a wide range of public policy. In most bibliographic databases, the results of a search for references can be either printed, e-mailed and/or saved to disk.

Notes

1 Referred to as the net or web from this point on.
2 The Government Printing Office produces and distributes Federal Government information products
3 The Stationery Office holds the contract to publish UK Parliamentary material.
4 National Opinion Research Centre at the University of Chicago.

Suggested further reading

Gibbs, G.R. (1997) *SocInfo Guide to IT Resources in Sociology, Politics and Social Policy*. Stirling: University of Stirling.

Hock, Randolph (2001) *The Extreme Searcher's Guide to Web Search Engines*, 2nd edn. New Jersey: CyberAge Books.

Jellinek, Dan (2000) *Official UK: The Essential Guide to Government Websites*, 2nd edn. London: Stationery Office.

Notess, Greg R. (2000) *Government Information on the Internet*, 2nd edn. London: Bernan Press.

Winship, Ian and McNab, Alison (2000) *The Student's Guide to the Internet 2000–2001*. London: Library Association.

See also **Literature searching**.

NORMA MENABNEY

Interpretation

Interpretation is the process by which meaning is attached to data. Interpretation is a creative enterprise that depends on the insight and imagination of the researcher, regardless of whether he/she is a qualitative analyst working closely with rich in-depth interview transcripts or 'thick description' based upon intense observation[1] or, at the other extreme, a quantitative researcher carrying out a complex multivariate statistical analysis of a massive dataset. In both instances, interpretation, the way in which the researcher attaches meaning to the data, is not mechanical but requires skill, imagination and creativity; Norman Denzin once described it as an art. As such there have been no attempts to codify the process of interpretation as there have been for analysis. However, it is important to distinguish between two kinds of interpretation: that generated by the analyst, and that supplied by the respondents themselves. Sometimes disclosure of the latter is the sole point of the research, other times respondents' interpretations and understandings are a starting point only, but rarely, however, are they something to be completely ignored. Qualitative researchers particularly will make reference in their interpretations of data to the understandings possessed by their subjects, even if they believe their findings and conclusions go beyond them. This requires the qualitative researcher in particular to be aware of some procedures for the process of interpretation.

Researchers should check their interpretations with members of the public to ensure people in the field find them credible and feasible. While giving credence to what people say, they must develop and maintain a critical attitude towards what respondents tell them (since some people may deliberately try to deceive). Checking is important because people's accounts, even if truthful, are often full of contradictions and inconsistencies that need to be represented and explored. There is a more fundamental reason for doing this, however, called member validation. Member validation forms a significant part of qualitative research practice. There are three main types of member validation: checking one's interpretations by their power to predict members' future behaviour; trying out one's interpretations by engaging in behaviour that passes as a member of the setting; and directly asking members to judge the adequacy of one's interpretations, either by their evaluation of the final report, or getting them to comment on the interpretations. These procedures apply primarily, but not exclusively, to qualitative researchers but there are other warnings worth bearing in mind when interpreting results that apply to all styles of social research. All data are socially situated and constructed in that time and place limit them. They are impacted by the methods used to collect them and the social interaction between the people involved in the research process, researchers and respondents alike. These limitations need to be borne in mind when attaching meaning to the data and interpretation should be constrained by them.

Note

1 Although some programmes for *qualitative data analysis by computer* make claims that they also assist in interpretation by developing concept and theory formation.

Suggested further reading

Denzin, N. (1998) 'The Art and Politics of Interpretation', in N. Denzin and Y. Lincoln (eds), *Strategies of Qualitative Enquiry*. London: Sage.

Seale, C. (1999) *The Quality of Qualitative Research*. London: Sage.

JOHN BREWER

Interviewer effects

See **Interviews**.

Interview schedule

See **Questionnaires and structured interview schedules**.

Interviews

Interviews are one of the most widely used and abused research methods. They provide a way of generating data by asking people to talk about their everyday lives. Their main function is to provide a framework in which respondents can express their own thoughts in their own words. They generally take the form of a conversation between two people (although they can involve larger groups – see the entry on **Focus groups**). Since everyone has experience of talking to people, there is a tendency to assume that conducting interviews is easy to do and requires little skill. This leads to the notion that anyone can do an interview. Nothing could be further from the truth. Interviews are not just conversations. They are conversations with a purpose – to collect information about a certain topic or research question. These 'conversations' do not just happen by chance, rather they are deliberately set up and follow certain rules and procedures. The interviewer initiates contact and the interviewee consents. Both parties know the general areas the interview will cover. The interviewer establishes the right to ask questions and the interviewee agrees to answer these questions. The interviewee also should be aware that the conversation will be recorded in some way and is therefore 'on record'.

Establishing trust and familiarity, demonstrating genuine interest in what the respondent says and appearing non-judgemental are all necessary skills for conducting effective interviews. The interviewer has to develop an effective balance between talking and listening. This involves remembering what the respondent has said and knowing when and when not to interrupt. The interviewer also has to decide whether to use a tape-recorder to record the data and/or to take notes. Both yield advantages and disadvantages. In other words, interviews are rarely straightforward. They involve the interviewer considering different options and often making difficult choices. The interview itself requires the interviewer to possess, or learn, a number of skills and to be able to apply these skills effectively during the interaction with respondents. Interviews can yield rich and valid data but they are by no means an easy option.

Interviews are used both in quantitative and qualitative research. However, there are key differences between the two approaches. Quantitative interviews typically involve the use of a structured survey instrument that asks all respondents the same questions in the same order and the responses are amenable to statistical analysis. Qualitative interviews are more flexible and open-ended. They are often used to develop ideas and research hypotheses rather than to gather facts and statistics. While the qualitative researcher may want to count or enumerate certain aspects of the data, there is less focus on quantification. Qualitative researchers are more concerned with trying to understand how ordinary people think and feel about the topics of concern to the research. Moreover, whereas quantitative research methods gather a narrow amount of information from a large number of respondents, qualitative interviews gather broader, more in-depth information from fewer respondents. In this sense, qualitative interviews are concerned with micro-analysis. Interviews are more or less taken at face value for what they have to tell the researcher about the particular issue being discussed. They can be used as a stand-alone data collection method to provide rich information in the respondent's own words. They allow respondents to say what they think and to do so with greater richness and spontaneity. Often interviews are combined or 'triangulated' with other methods. Sometimes they are used to ensure that the questions that will appear in a widely circulated questionnaire are valid and understandable. Alternatively they may be used as follow-up to a questionnaire. This allows the researcher to explore in more depth interesting issues that may have emerged from the standard questionnaire. Interviews can thus lead to the development of new ideas and hypotheses and throw up new dimensions to be studied. In this way, interviews may complement questionnaire data.

There are three main types of interview: structured, semi-structured and unstructured. These three types are generally differentiated by the degree of structure imposed on their format. Structured interviews are very similar to questionnaires in that they use a standard format consisting of pre-determined questions in a fixed order. Here the concern is with flexible forms of interviewing so the focus will be on semi-structured and unstructured interviews.

Semi-structured interviews

Semi-structured interviews involve the interviewer deciding in advance what broad topics are to be covered and what main questions are to be asked. Flexibility plays a key part in structuring the interaction. The interviewer may ask certain major questions the same way each time but may alter their sequence and probe for more information. Most interviewers conducting semi-structured interviews use an *aide-mémoire* to remind them of the key topics and issues they are broadly interested in and to assist them in making connections between different parts of the interaction. The interviewer is therefore able to adapt the research instrument to the individuality of the research respondent. While semi-structured interviews contain a set of specific topics, interviewees are allowed sufficient freedom to digress. Questions are generally open-ended in order to gain richer information about attitudes and behaviour. The format is therefore mainly discursive, allowing the respondent to develop their answers in their own terms and at their own length and depth.

Unstructured interviews

Unstructured interviews allow the researcher to adopt a non-directive almost conversational style that allows the interviewee largely to determine the course of the discussion. Interviewers begin with the assumption that they do not know in advance what all the necessary questions are. They are particularly useful when the researcher is unfamiliar with the respondent's life style, religion or ethnic culture. They enable the interviewer to see the world through the eyes of the interviewee and discover how they make sense of their experiences. Unstructured interviews are excellent for establishing rapport and allow researchers to gain rich information about various phenomena. During the interview, the researcher continually develops, adapts and generates questions and follow-up probes appropriate to the general area of investigation. Interviewers are therefore given the freedom to phrase the questions as they see appropriate and ask them in any order that seems pertinent at the time. The interviewer may try to adopt as unobtrusive a role as possible and allow interviewees to develop their own thoughts or on occasion may join in the interaction by discussing what they think of the topic themselves to aid the flow of the conversation.

Advantages of interviews

(1) *Flexibility*. One major advantage of the interview is its flexibility. The less standard the format the more scope there is for flexibility. Interviewers can ask questions on the spot, change the order of questions, follow up interesting leads and allow respondents varying levels of control during the interaction.

(2) *High response rate*. Most people if approached properly will agree to be interviewed. People are often more confident of their speaking ability than their writing ability and those unwilling to write out answers to questionnaires may be more willing to talk to interviewers.

(3) *Check on questions*. The interview format allows the interviewer to explain any ambiguities and correct any misunderstandings in the questions.

(4) *Probes*. These may be used to get the interviewee to expand on their answer in more detail. This may result in more extensive answers to questions. Probes may be non-verbal as well as verbal. An expectant glance may function just as effectively as a probe as a follow-up question.

(5) *Clarification*. The interviewer may obtain clarification from the interviewee concerning what is said and how it is being interpreted. This is particularly relevant when the respondent's answers are imprecise. Interviews allow researchers to clarify ambiguous answers.

(6) *Confirmation*. The interviewer can repeat what is being said in order to confirm what is being said and the accuracy of their own interpretation of what is being said.

(7) *Prompts*. These can be used to encourage the interviewee to answer questions. They can help jog people's memory.

(8) *Connecting*. The interviewer can make connections between different parts of the conversation and check with the interviewee that the connections made are valid.

(9) *Non-verbal communication*. Interviewers not only hear what the subjects say but see how they say it. Body gestures, facial expressions, and so on, may

provide a rich source of data in their own right. They allow interviewers to assess the validity of the respondent's answers.

(10) *Timing of interview*. The interviewer can record the exact time, date and place of the interview. If an important event takes place, the researcher can check if this influenced the respondent's answers. It also enables the researcher to compare answers before and after the event, if appropriate.

Disadvantages of Interviews

(1) *Reliability*. Since unstructured and semi-structured interviews are not standardised, this may affect the reliability ('reproducibility') of the data produced. Interviewers may have to introduce a number of quality control measures in order to deal with the various potential sources of error or bias (see below) that this method entails.

(2) *Lack of comparability*. Since the interviewer may change the order of questions, ask different questions of different people or phrase the same question differently, this makes it difficult for the researcher to compare answers.

(3) *Time consuming*. The transcribing of data (particularly tape-recorded interviews) can be extremely laborious and time-consuming. Researchers have to decide whether to introduce verbatim or selective transcription. Verbatim transcription has the advantage of ensuring that all possible analytic uses of the data are allowed for. Significant aspects of the data may only become significant during verbatim transcription. Selective transcription involves the researcher making judgements about which aspects of the data are particularly relevant to the research question. While a number of technological aids are now available to speed up and systematically deal with this process, it remains extremely time consuming. Interviews may also take a long time to arrange and conduct. This is particularly problematic if respondents are geographically widespread. The interviewer must arrange their time to suit the interviewee. Often only one or two interviews can be conducted in one day even though the actual interview time may be brief.

(4) *Costly*. Interviews can be very costly to carry out. Travel costs may be incurred if respondents live far apart. The larger or more dispersed the sample, the greater the total costs of the interviewing process. It may also be costly to employ someone to transcribe tape-recorded interviews.

(5) *Interruptions*. It may be difficult to conduct the interview in private. People either coming in or going out may disrupt the interaction. The interviewee may be called away to the telephone or have to deal with other demands. These interruptions may affect the quality of the respondents' answers.

(6) *Lack of anonymity*. The interviewer typically knows the respondent's name and address. Moreover, since interviews take place face-to-face, this reduces the respondent's anonymity. If the information is incriminating, embarrassing or sensitive in some way, then respondents may find it difficult

to participate honestly in the interview and may withhold information or give partial answers.

Interviewer effects

One of the greatest disadvantages of interviews is the possibility that the interview may be biased. First appearances are very important as they may influence how people respond to one another. During the process of interaction, the interviewer and interviewee may have expectations of one another. Interviewers, therefore have to examine whether these expectations affect the data that are collected and whether one can control these expectations. In the 'classic' model, interviewers are expected to neutrally record elicited information, however many qualitative researchers are critical of the 'classic' approach and argue that interviewing should be as open a method as possible involving a genuine interplay between the researcher and interviewee.

The interviewer may have general expectations about what the respondent knows or feels about a particular situation. These preconceived notions may affect the quality of the interview. Moreover, prompting, probing, and so on, require great skill. The interviewer has to ensure that the usage of these techniques is accomplished in a way that does not incline the interviewee towards a particular response.

Preconceived notions may also exist among interviewees. The interviewee may have certain conceptions of the interviewer based on appearance and demeanour. Overt, observable characteristics such as age, race, gender, ethnicity may be used by an interviewee to construct an image of what the interviewer is like. Other characteristics such as dress, manner and general demeanour may be used to confirm or deny these assumptions. Depending on how sensitive or personal the issue being discussed is to the respondent, these preconceptions may influence how honest the respondent is during the interview and what they decide to divulge or keep secret. Sometimes interviewees might supply answers that they feel fit in with the interviewer's view of the world (or, alternatively, give answers deliberately calculated to antagonise the interviewer). Sometimes they may assume that the interviewer expects them to answer in certain ways. Either way, the validity of the data can be affected. There is a limit on the extent to which interviewers can alter this situation. Characteristics such as age, gender and so on are fixed and cannot be changed although some interviewers try to minimise the potential effect by matching as far as possible the demographic characteristics of interviewer and interviewee. Other less definitive characteristics such as demeanour and appearance can be dealt with but this involves an element of judgement on behalf of the interviewer that may not always be accurate. Research textbooks give differing advice on how to dress for interviewing. Some suggest dressing to look like an interviewer so as to legitimate the role taken. Others suggest dressing neutrally so as not to bias respondents' answers, or dressing as unobtrusively as possible so that the emphasis will be on the interview rather than the interviewer's appearance. The interviewer needs to be reflective in assessing the extent to which interaction during the interview may have been influenced by these factors and acknowledge their potential impact when writing up the research.

Suggested further reading

Burgess, R. (1982) *Field Research.* London: Allen and Unwin.

Denzin, N. (1989) *The Research Act: a Theoretical Introduction to Sociological Methods.* Englewood Cliffs, NJ: Prentice Hall.

Silverman, D. (1985) *Qualitative Methodology and Sociology.* Aldershot: Gower.

MADELEINE LEONARD

> *See also* **CAPI Computer assisted personal interviewing** and **Focus groups**.

L

Literature searching

Identifying relevant previous work is an essential skill in social research. The massive expansion in the volume and type of information, together with the increasing complexity of interrelated branches of knowledge, has given added importance to the need for systematic searching, and for critical appraisal and synthesised accounts of previous research. This entry addresses the task of searching for relevant literature in the 'information age' and will focus primarily on a systematic and logical approach to literature searching using electronic databases. The emphasis will be on identifying research published in peer-reviewed journals, although similar principles and practices apply to searching for 'gray literature' (such as conference papers and theses) and indexes of current research.

Clarity of focus

The first consideration in effective searching is to be clear about the question, topic or set of issues of interest. This will then guide the rationale for the search. In general terms, options include: canvassing colleagues who are knowledgeable in the area of interest; contacting recognised experts or research groups working in the field to request reports and papers; 'hand-searching' and library work by following up references in research publications; and, in recent decades, using computer-based search strategies – the main focus of this entry.

Using a computer linked to the World Wide Web, you can search electronic databases for: (1) words in the title or abstract of items on the database related to your topic of interest; or (2) words by which an item has been indexed in the database.

Although databases may include books, the vast majority of items are articles in journals, and the term 'article' will be used here. Some journals require authors to provide keywords as well as an abstract, and some databases will search these keywords also, at the same time as the titles and abstracts.

Electronic databases

There are a number of nationally networked electronic databases of interest to social researchers and accessible through the World Wide Web. Each contains details of publications from a range of relevant journals. Some of the main databases for specific disciplines are listed in the table. Note, however, that this is a continually changing field. The details on databases usually include abstracts (but

Table 1 *Some major databases for social researchers seeking publications of previous research (There are additional sources for original data and official publications.)*

Subject Area	Database
Anthropology	Anthropological Index Online
Community development	CommunityWise
Criminology	Criminal Justice Abstracts
Business and Economics	ABI – Inform
	EconLit
Education	British Education Index (BIDS Education Service)
	ERIC (Educational Research Information Clearing House)
Health care management	HMIC (Health Management Information Consortium)
Law	CELEX (European Community Law)
	Current Legal Information
	JUSTIS
	LEXIS
Planning and Urban Development	AVERY (Architectural Design and Urban Planning)
	URBADISC (Planning, Construction and Social Policy)
	PADDI (Planning Architecture and Design Database Ireland)
Politics	International Political Science Abstracts
	Parliament
Psychology	Behaviour Analysis
	PsycINFO (Psychology Information)
	PsycLIT (Psychology Literature)
Public affairs	PAIS International
Social sciences, general	Applied Social Sciences Index & Abstracts (ASSIA)
	International Bibliography of the Social Sciences
	Social Sciences Citation Index
	Wilson Social Sciences Abstracts
Social policy	PolicyFile
Social work	CareData
	ChildData
	Social Services Abstracts
	Social Work Abstracts
Sociology	Sociological Abstracts

not always), and sometimes include the full text of articles. Most databases are in English and concentrate on the major journals published in English, although their international scope is expanding. Some databases carry abstracts in English of articles in other languages. Each database will indicate the date from which abstracting of a particular journal began.

Terminology for searching

One issue facing the literature reviewer is the different terminology and spelling used in different countries and disciplines. Also, language changes over time, and with new topics the terminology may not yet have reached a standardised consensus. A way is needed to retrieve all the varieties of a term. Databases usually help in addressing this by using 'wild-card' characters (usually '*' or '?'), which represent any letter of the alphabet or any group of letters. Thus a search for 'teach*' is a common form to pick up 'teaching', 'teacher' and 'teachers' as well as 'teach'. It may also pick up 'teacher's' and 'teachers'', although the retrieval of punctuation marks varies between databases. This term will not of course pick up 'taught'.

Combining search terms

Databases use an extension of standard Boolean algebra for combining search terms. Four main Boolean operators are used: AND, OR, NOT and brackets or parentheses ( ); many databases also use the operators: quotation marks " " and NEAR.

As an example, a search of a database of bibliographic entries for the terms 'stimulus OR response' will produce a list of 'hits' of all articles that have *either* the word 'stimulus' *or* the word 'response' (or both) anywhere in their title or abstract. This will be much too general for your purpose if you are searching for articles *only* on responses to stimuli rather than stimuli in general or responses in general. A search using the phrase 'stimul* AND response*' will narrow the focus to a list of 'hits' of articles containing *both* of these words (in singular or plural form) somewhere in the title or abstract.

The principles of Boolean algebra can be used for more sophisticated searches. For example, a simple search for 'gangs AND violence' could be narrowed to articles that discuss a particular type of gang violence by using the more restricted search 'racism AND gang* AND violence'. The search could be broadened to include either of the first two terms with 'violence' by using the phrase '(racism OR gang*) AND violence', in order to seek articles about violence related to gangs and articles about violence related to racism (including articles that refer to both).

The operations on terms inside brackets are carried out first before combining the result with terms outside brackets. This is an essential part of the logic of Boolean algebra. For instance, the expression 'racism OR (gang* AND violence)' has the same words as the last example, but with the different position of the brackets would give *all* articles on racism, and also those that referred to violence and gang(s). Note that although most databases use these common words for these operations, some specify upper or lower case, and some use particular symbols instead, such as '&' for 'AND'.

On most databases, inserting a phrase within quotation marks will restrict the search to that phrase *exactly* as you have typed it in, rather than searching for the individual words. For instance, while the phrase 'community AND care' would retrieve all articles in which both words occur anywhere in the title or abstract (but not necessarily together or in that order), typing inside quotes as: ''community care'' will narrow the search to articles where that exact phrase occurs.

On some databases, the operator NEAR can be used to search for terms that are within a given number of terms of each other, but not necessarily as a defined phrase. Thus 'devolution NEAR/5 (government OR governance)' might be the style of search for the word 'devolution' within five words of 'government' or 'governance', thereby picking up their use in a phrase even though they are unlikely to be next to each other.

The term 'NOT' should be used with caution, as it will exclude any article that mentions the term in the abstract, even if that term is not the focus of the article. One important use of the term 'NOT' is to check a formula that is being developed, in order to identify the impact of a new term that is being added. Thus, for example, '(co-ownership housing OR housing association* OR housing scheme*) NOT (co-ownership housing OR housing association*)' will identify the number of additional articles that have been retrieved by including the term 'housing scheme*'. In algebraic language this can be written as '(A or B or C) not (A or B)' as a formula to test the impact of adding term 'C' to an existing search involving 'A or B'. This method can be repeated for each new term being considered, with any number of terms in the existing formula.

Indexed systems

Some databases have an index system such that each article is indexed using a defined thesaurus of terms. This facility greatly simplifies the task, as one can search for these index words instead of (or as well as) the text searching described above. One is less likely to miss items due to an unconventional use of language, or the author's omission of significant words from the title or abstract. The thesaurus used by the database can be checked to see the nearest terms to your topic, and for the appropriate terminology. As an example, searching for the single thesaurus term 'Homes for the Aged' on Medline (an indexed system for medicine) is more straightforward than the equivalent (but similarly productive) search on a non-indexed system such as Social Science Citation Index, where the search might have to include a range of terms such as: 'care home* OR home* for the aged OR institutional care OR old people's home* OR old peoples home* OR out of home placement*'.

It is of course possible to combine searches of indexed systems using the same principles as for non-indexed systems, as described above. Indexed databases are prey to errors of indexers, although systems are continually improving in this regard. If an article has not been indexed appropriately, a search using the index terms may not find the article, whereas a text search might.

Citation searching

Some databases have a citation searching system that makes it possible to access earlier articles referenced by the article that you have identified, enabling you to trace back the history or sources of a topic. It is also possible to access subsequent articles that have cited the article at which you are looking. This feature is helpful if you wish to track the later development of an idea from its beginnings in a recognised seminal publication. The citation searching is of course limited to other publications that are on the same database, making it a useful facility for scanning within a well-defined sphere of knowledge embraced by a single database. Unfortunately, for a number of social science disciplines it is necessary to use more than one database at the present time for effective searching.

Additional search features

On many databases it is possible to limit the search by various aspects such as language, year of publication, age of subjects and publication type. The facility to search by the type of research methods employed is particularly useful, but depends on authors including this information in their abstracts, and on the level of agreed terminology in the social science discipline. Although searching generally focuses on topics, if you have identified a certain author as a key authority in the field, one approach to overcoming the limitations of present search facilities is to search for the person's name, thereby retrieving material written by him or her that may not have been picked up by your text search or index terms. Some databases also provide an 'alerting service', which typically means that your search formula will be re-run automatically every month and the results sent to you via e-mail.

Sensitivity and precision of searches

A key issue is the sensitivity of the search, that is its capacity to identify as many as possible of the total available relevant articles. Sensitivity may be defined as the number of relevant items identified by a search divided by the total number of relevant articles existing on the topic. A researcher wanting to retrieve all relevant research will design the search for high sensitivity.

Every search also yields articles that are irrelevant, even on indexed systems. Because there is wide variation in the use of language, and limited standardisation of abstracts in the social sciences, it is easy for a search to be swamped by irrelevant material. Thus, the precision of the search is also important, usually defined as the number of items identified by the search that are relevant divided by the total number of items retrieved by the search. This is a measure of the positive predictive value of the search. Although the focus in designing a search formula is normally on sensitivity, if too many irrelevant items are being retrieved it may be helpful to address precision also in the design. Although the ideal might be to aim for 100% sensitivity, in some cases sensitivity and precision of searching must be balanced against each other for a manageable search.

Conclusion and a word of caution

Online searching of abstracts is a highly efficient and cost-effective way of scanning a vast amount of bibliographic material, which is almost certain to uncover references that would be missed by 'traditional' methods. However the techniques for electronic searching should not be thought of as totally complete or foolproof. It is always possible that an important reference does not have the words you have used in your search in its title or abstract, or that the database that you are using may not have indexed the journal in which it appears. Taking the advice of colleagues and experts, and developing a 'feel' for the important publications in an area by noting what authors and articles are cited regularly are also helpful to build a comprehensive overview of the literature as an essential step towards a meaningful synthesis of the most important findings.

It will be apparent to the reader that there is a developing art and science of literature searching. Use of nationally networked electronic databases designed for academic and professional purposes is clearly the way forward, adding a systematic sophistication to more ad hoc approaches used in the past. This is a rapidly developing field, influenced by a range of factors such as newly emerging fields of knowledge, technological innovation, the economics of database provision, the steady advance of indexing systems, editorial influences on the content of abstracts and keywords, and (hopefully) increasing mutual understanding and agreement on terminology across social science disciplines. Social researchers in all disciplines need to keep abreast of these developments.

Suggested further reading

Grimshaw, J. (2000) *How to Find Information: Social Science*. London: The British Library Board.

Hart, C. (2001) *Doing a Literature Search: a Comprehensive Guide for the Social Sciences*. London: Sage.

Herron, N.L. (1989) *The Social Sciences: a Cross-Disciplinary Guide to Selected Sources*. Colorado: Englewood.

Taylor, B.J., Dempster, M. and Donnelly, M. (forthcoming) 'Hidden Gems: Systematically Searching Electronic Databases for Research Publications for Social Work and Social Care', *British Journal of Social Work*.

Thomas, P.A. and Knowles, J. (2001) *Dane and Thomas: How to Use a Law Library – an Introduction to Legal Skills*. London: Sweet & Maxwell.

See also
Internet and
Systematic
review.

BRIAN J. TAYLOR

Loglinear analysis

This entry gives a general introduction to the reasoning underlying the loglinear analysis technique. First, the types of problem that loglinear analysis can answer will be discussed in a general manner. Second, the 'logic' underlying the loglinear analysis procedure will be presented in non-statistical terms.

Problems that loglinear analysis can answer

The loglinear analysis technique makes possible the multivariate analysis of data in which all the variables in the analysis are made up of categories; either nominal data in which the categories do not fall into any particular order or ordinal data in which they do. The technique can address two basic types of issues.

Firstly, loglinear analysis can be thought of as an extension of contingency table analysis in which there are several control variables. Let us take a very basic and general example in order to illustrate this first type of problem. Assume that we have four categorical or ordinal variables, which we call: A, B, C and D. Each of these four variables can take three distinct values or levels: 1, 2 or 3. We can indicate a variable and level by a subscript. For instance, the three values that variable A can take would be indicated by: A_1, A_2 and A_3; and the three values that variable B can take would be: B_1, B_2 and B_3 and so on. If we think there may be an association between variables A and B, we could put them into a crosstabulation table of A by B and test for an association applying a statistical test like Chi-square. If a significant association is found, we can work out which cells in the table cause the association by looking at the differences in the number of cases we would expect to find in each cell of the table in comparison to the number we actually find.[1] If we think the form of the association between A and B might be different depending upon the level of variable C, we could produce three crosstabulation tables of A by B, one for each level of variable C (that is, variable C would be a control variable). Each table could be checked in turn for whether it had a significant association and what the pattern of association in the table's cells might be.

Problems begin to arise, however, if we also suspect that the pattern of associations we find in the A by B tables with C as a control *also* might vary depending upon the value that D takes. If we use both C and D as control variables, we will end up with *nine* separate A by B tables, one for each of the combinations of the variables C and D. Each table could have a different pattern of association, with some of these tables perhaps having statistically significant associations while others do not. Also, there may be no real reason why we should not present the data in the form of C *by* D tables with A and B as control variables (or A by C tables with B and D as controls . . . or B by D tables with A and C as control variables and so on). This is a multivariate problem – we require a means of deciding which of the many possible associations between these four categorical variables are important so we can concentrate on them and ignore the many other insignificant associations. Loglinear analysis can provide an answer to this problem.

A second version of loglinear analysis can be thought of as a categorical parallel to multiple regression analysis. Staying with our 'A to D variables' format, let us say that variable A can be considered possibly affected or caused by variables B to D. (For example, A could be whether a person had decided to take early retirement; B could be a person's sex; C whether the person's health had been good, average or poor; and D whether the person had a pension plan or not. B, C and D could be thought of as existing prior to the decision about early retirement and possibly to have affected the decision.) We could produce individual crosstabulation tables of A by B, A by C, and A by D with the association in each table considered on its own apparently statistically significant. But if we also suspect or know that B, C and D are strongly associated with each other, the apparent significant links of one or more of these variables with A could in fact be illusory. Again, this is a multivariate problem – we require a means of deciding which of the three associations are important and which are statistical artefacts. A special case of loglinear analysis called logit analysis can provide an answer to this problem.

A non-statistical presentation of the 'logic' of loglinear analysis

The basic idea of loglinear analysis is in fact an extension of the reasoning behind Chi-square. Let us take another example using four variables – A, B, C and D – only simplify the example even further and have only two levels for each of the four variables so that, for instance, variable A will have two values: A_1 and A_2. So, taking all four of the variables together, there will be 16 possible combinations (or possible cells) of the variables.[2] Also, let us say we have a small dataset with 144 people.

Loglinear analysis builds up a model based upon the effects of distribution. These effects can be broken down in the following manner.

(1) Cell frequency/Gross effect

First, we would expect to find on average 9 people in each of the sixteen cells (144 / 16 = 9). That is, holding everything else equal, if the 144 people are scattered completely at random across the sixteen cells, by chance each cell should have 9 people in it.

(2) Marginal effects

For the sake of argument, let us assume that for each of our variables A, B, C and D, level 2 has twice as many people as level 1. So, for example, level A_1 will have 48 people and level A_2 will have 96 people (a 1 : 2 ratio), variable B will be the same (B_1 = 48 people and B_2 = 96 people) as will C_1 and C_2, and D_1 and D_2. Holding everything else equal, that means that you would expect to find that any cell associated with level A_2 should have twice as many cases as any equivalent cell associated with level A_1. The same should hold for B_1 cells contrasted with B_2 cells, C_1 cells contrasted with C_2 cells, and D_1 contrasted with D_2 cells. These are called *marginal effects*.

(3) Two-way interactions

If any two variables are crosstabulated together, say A by B, the actual, observed distribution of cases in the cells of the crosstabulation may differ significantly from that which would be expected by chance. If this is the case, we have a *two-way interaction* between the two variables, as depicted in the table below:

A by B, 'chance' and 'actual' distributions

Expected ratio of cases If A & B are not associated			A hypothetical ratio of cases If A & B are associated		
	B_1	B_2		B_1	B_2
A_1	1	2	A_1	3	1
A_2	2	4	A_2	2	2

On the left-hand side, you can see the ratio of how the cases would be distributed by chance in the table, A by B, if there was no association between the two variables. If there is an association, the actual distribution would differ significantly from that expected by chance, yielding a different distribution across the cells of the crosstabulation table. The right-hand table illustrates one such possible different form that this distribution could take.

So, the basic logic of loglinear modelling parallels that which underlies Chi-square; the actual distribution of cases in cells is contrasted with that which you would expect to find by chance.

(4) *Three-way interactions*

It is also possible that the distribution of cases in the A by B crosstabulation can be different depending upon the level taken by a third variable. If this is the case, that the A by B association varies for different values of a third variable, C, we have a *three-way interaction*. The table below illustrates the possible appearance that the absence and presence of a three-way interaction could have.

A by B for two levels of C, 'three-way' interaction absent

C_1			C_2		
	B_1	B_2		B_1	B_2
A_1	3	1	A_1	3	1
A_2	2	2	A_2	2	2

A by B for two levels of C, 'three-way' interaction present

C_1			C_2		
	B_1	B_2		B_1	B_2
A_1	2	3	A_1	3	1
A_2	2	7	A_2	2	2

Note that the ratio of cell numbers in the 'three-way' interaction absent table are exactly the same regardless of which value is taken by the third variable, C. In contrast, note that the ratio of cell numbers in the 'three-way' interaction present table *vary* depending upon the value taken by the third variable, C. That is, when the pattern of association between A and B varies depending upon the value taken by C, there is a three-way interaction between A, B and C.

(5) Four- or N-way interactions

The distribution of cases in the A by B crosstabulation tables that are different for each value of C could also vary for each value of a fourth variable, D, yielding *four-way interactions*. This pattern of increasingly complex interactions can be extended for an additional number of N extra variables.

All this ends up in a linear equation that can be expressed like this:

Any cell's frequency = Gross effect × Marginal effects × Interaction effects

To make the computation easier, the effects are put into terms of logs so they can be added rather than multiplied, hence the name of the procedure, *Loglinear analysis*.

The goal of a loglinear analysis usually is *parsimony* – to establish the simplest possible loglinear equation that manages to produce predicted frequencies for each cell that do not vary significantly from the actual cell frequencies. This is accomplished by eliminating the most complex interactions in turn. If the cell frequencies predicted after the most complex interaction is removed do not diverge significantly from the actual cell frequencies, the next most complex interaction term is removed and again the predicted frequencies are compared with those that actually occur. This process is repeated until eventually no more interaction terms can be removed without producing a model whose predicted values do not 'fit' the actual cell frequencies well. For instance, taking our A × B × C × D example, it may be possible to remove the most complex four-way interaction term (A × B × C × D) and all of the three-way interactions before arriving at the simplest model that still gives a good 'fit' – a model that includes only two-way interactions. If such a result can be obtained, the interpretation of associations is comparatively easy. You would not need to worry about complex tables with one or more control variables and instead would only need to describe what is going on in a series of relatively simple two-variable crosstabulation tables.

The 'regression' style of loglinear analysis follows the same logic, only ignoring[3] the interactions between the independent/causal variables and concentrating upon finding the simplest set of interactions between the independent variables and the dependent variable.

Notes

1 That is, by examining the *residuals*.
2 $2 \times 2 \times 2 \times 2 = 16$.
3 In fact, allowing them to retain all possible interactions.

Suggested further reading

Christensen, Ronald (1997) *Log-linear Models and Logistic Regression*. New York: Springer.

Hout, Michael (1983) 'Mobility Tables', Number 31 in the Sage series *Quantitative Applications in the Social Sciences*. Beverly Hills, CA: Sage.

Knoke, David and Burke, Peter J. (1980) 'Log-linear Models', Number 20 in the Sage series *Quantitative Applications in the Social Sciences*. Beverly Hills, CA: Sage.

**See also
Contingency
tables**.

ROBERT MILLER

Longitudinal research

'Longitudinal' is a broad term. It can be defined as research in which: (1) data are collected for two or more distinct periods (implying the notion of repeated measurements); (2) the subjects or cases analysed are the same, or at least comparable, from one period to the next; and (3) the analysis involves some comparison of data between or among periods (Menard, 1991: 4).

Longitudinal designs

There are a number of different designs for the construction of longitudinal evidence: repeated cross-sectional studies; prospective studies, such as household panel surveys or cohort panels; and retrospective studies, such as life and work histories and oral histories.

Repeated cross-sectional studies

In the social sciences, cross-sectional observations are the form of data most commonly used for assessing the determinants of behaviour (Davies, 1994; Blossfeld and Rohwer, 1995). However, the cross-sectional survey, because it is conducted at just one point in time, is not suited for the study of social change. It is therefore common for cross-sectional data to be recorded in a succession of surveys at two or more points in time, with a new sample on each occasion. These samples either contain entirely different sets of cases for each period, or the overlap is so small as to be considered negligible. Where cross-sectional data are repeated over time with a high level of consistency between questions, it is possible to incorporate a time trend into the analysis. Examples of repeated cross-sectional social surveys are: the UK's *General Household Survey* and *Family Expenditure Survey*, and the EU's *Eurobarometer Surveys*.

Prospective designs

The temporal data most often available to social researchers are panel data, in which the same individuals are interviewed repeatedly across time. Variations of this design (Buck et al., 1994: 21–2; Ruspini, 2002) include:

Household Panel Studies (HPS). A random sample of respondents with repeated data collections from the same individuals at fixed intervals (usually, but not necessarily, annually). HPS trace individuals at regular discrete points in time: they seek to discover what happens/has happened to the same subjects over a certain period of time. Thus, the fundamental feature they offer is that they make it possible to detect and establish the nature of individual change. For this reason, they are well-suited to the statistical analysis of both social change and dynamic behaviour. Among the best known prospective panel studies are the US *Panel Study of Income Dynamics* (PSID), the *British Household Panel Study* (BHPS) and the German *Socio-Economic Panel* (SOEP).

Cohort Panels. A specific form of panel study that takes the process of generation replacement explicitly into account. A cohort is defined as those people within a geographically or otherwise delineated population who experienced the same significant life event or events within a given period of time. A random sample of the individuals in the cohort is followed over time. Usually a researcher will choose one or more birth cohorts and administer a questionnaire to a sample drawn from within that group: thus longitudinal analysis is used on groups that are homogeneous and a number of generations are followed, over time, throughout their life courses. The interest is usually in the study of long-term change and in individual development processes. Such studies typically re-interview every five years. If, in each particular generation the same people are investigated, a cohort study amounts to a series of panel studies; if, in each generation, at each period of observation, a new sample is drawn, a cohort study consists of a series of trend studies (Hagenaars, 1990). Examples are the UK *National Child Development Study* and the German *Life History Study*.

Linked or Administrative Panels. In these cases data items which are not collected primarily for panel purposes (census or administrative data) are linked together using unique personal identifiers (the combination of name, birthdate and place of birth is normally enough to identify individuals and enable linkage of administrative and/or other records). This is the least intrusive method of collecting longitudinal data (Buck et al., 1994).

Retrospective Studies (event oriented observation design)

All the data types discussed so far have been recorded with reference to fixed and predetermined time points. But, for many processes within the social sciences, continuous measurement may be the most suitable method of empirically assessing social change. When data are recorded in a continuous time, the number and sequence of events and the duration between them can all be calculated. Data recorded in continuous time are often collected *retrospectively* via life history studies that question backwards over the whole life course of individuals. The main advantage of this approach lies in the greater detail and precision of information (Blossfeld and Rohwer, 1995). A good example is the UK 1980 *Women and Employment Survey*, which obtained very detailed past work histories from a nationally representative sample of women of working age in Britain.[1]

Advantages and limitations of longitudinal data

Longitudinal data: allow the analysis of duration of social phenomena; permit the measurement of differences or change from one period to another in the values of one or more variables; explain the changes in terms of certain other characteristics (these characteristics can be stable, such as gender) or unstable (that is, time-varying, such as income) (van der Kamp and Bijleveld, 1998: 3); can be used to locate the causes of social phenomena and 'sleeper effects', that is, connections between events that are widely separated in time (Hakim, 1987).

Insights into processes of social change can thus be greatly enhanced by making more extensive use of longitudinal data. Dynamic data are the necessary empirical basis for a new type of dynamic thinking about the processes of social change (Gershuny, 1998). The possibility of developing research based on longitudinal data also builds a bridge between 'quantitative' and 'qualitative' research traditions and enables re-shaping of the concepts of qualitative and quantitative (Ruspini, 1999). Longitudinal surveys usually combine both extensive and intensive approaches (Davies and Dale, 1994). Life history surveys facilitate the construction of individual trajectories since they collect continuous information throughout the life course. Panel data trace individuals and households through historical time: information is gathered about them at regular intervals. Moreover, they often include relevant retrospective information, so that the respondents have continuous records in key fields from the beginning of their lives. As an example, the *British Household Panel Study* took the opportunity (over the first three waves) to get a very good picture of respondents' previous lives by asking for life-time retrospective work, marital and fertility histories. Longitudinal analysis thus presupposes the development of a methodological mix where neither of the two aspects alone is sufficient to produce an accurate picture of social dynamics (Mingione, 1999).

However, although dynamic data have the potential to provide richer information about individual behaviour, their use poses theoretical and methodological problems. In addition, longitudinal research typically costs more and can be very time-consuming.

The principal limitations of the repeated cross-sectional design are its inappropriateness for studying developmental patterns within cohorts and its inability to resolve issues of causal order. Both of these limitations result directly from the fact that in a repeated cross-sectional design, the same cases are neither measured repeatedly nor for multiple periods (Menard, 1991). Thus, more data are required to characterise empirically the dynamic process that lies behind the cross-sectional snapshot (Davies, 1994).

Concerning panel data, the main operational problems with prospective studies (other than linked panels) (Magnusson and Bergmann, 1990; Menard, 1991; Duncan, 1992, Blossfeld and Rohwer, 1995; Rose, 2000) are:

Panel attrition. If the same set of cases is used in each period, there may be some variation from one period to another as a result of missing data (due to refusals, changes of residence or death of the respondent). Such systematic differences between waves cause biased estimates. For example, a major problem in most surveys on poverty is the under-sampling of poor people: they are hard to contact (and therefore usually undersampled in the first wave of data) and hard to retain for successive annual interviews. Even though weight variables could be used to mitigate under-representation, it is difficult to assess the real efficiency of such weights.

Course of events. Since there is only information on the states of the units at predetermined survey points (discrete time points), the course of the events between the discrete points in time remains unknown.

Panel conditioning. Precisely because they are repeated, panel studies tend to influence the phenomena that they are hoping to observe. It is possible that responses given in one wave will be influenced by participation in previous waves (Trivellato, 1999). During subsequent waves, interviewees often answer differently from how they answered at the first wave due solely to their experience of being interviewed previously. For example, this may occur because they have lost some of their inhibitions or, because they have been sensitised by the questioning in previous waves, respondents to a panel study may acquire new information that they would not have done otherwise (Duncan, 2000).

Consequently, the potential of panel data can only be fully realised if such data meet high quality standards (Duncan, 1992). In particular, Trivellato (1999) stated that for a panel survey to be successful, the key ingredients are a good initial sample and appropriate following rules, that is, a set of rules that permit mimicking the population that almost always changes in composition over time. Taking the *British Household Panel Survey* as an example, because the BHPS tracks household formation and dissolution, individuals may join and leave the sample. Thus, the study has a number of following rules determining who is eligible to be interviewed at each wave. New eligibility for sample inclusion could occur between waves in the following ways: (a) a baby is born to an Original Sample Member (OSM); (b) an OSM moves into a household with one or more new people; (c) one or more new people move in with an OSM (Freed Taylor et al., 1995).

The drawback of linked panels is that they can only provide a very limited range of information and often on a highly discontinuous temporal basis (as in the case of a census). Moreover, such panels suffer from problems of confidentiality and of data protection legislation, so there is often only very limited access (Buck et al., 1994).

Even if retrospective studies have the advantage of usually being cheaper to collect than panel data, they suffer from several limitations (Davies and Dale, 1994; Blossfeld and Rohwer, 1995):

Recall bias. Many subjects simply forget things about events, feelings, or considerations, and even when an event has not been wholly forgotten, they may have trouble recalling it (memory loss and retrieval problems). Retrospective questions concerning motivational, attitudinal, cognitive or affective states are particularly problematic because respondents find it hard to accurately recall the timing of changes in these states.

Tolerance. Retrospective surveys tend to be quite lengthy. There is a limit to respondents' tolerance for the amount of data that can be collected on one occasion.

Reinterpretation. The way in which individuals interpret their own past behaviour will be influenced by subsequent events in their lives. Subjects tend to interpret and re-interpret events, opinions and feelings so that they fit in with their, the subjects' own, current perceptions of their lives and past lives and constitute a sequence of events that 'bears some logic' (van der Kamp and Bijleveld, 1998).

Misrepresentation. Like panel studies, retrospective studies too, are subject to distortions which are caused by changes within the sample, changes brought about by death, emigration or, even, a refusal to continue.

Conclusion

The use of longitudinal data (both prospective and retrospective) can ensure a more complete approach to empirical research. Longitudinal data are collected in a time sequence that clarifies the direction as well as the magnitude of change among variables. However, the world of longitudinal research is quite hetero-geneous. Some important general suggestions are (Menard, 1991):

- If the measurement of change is not a concern, if causal and temporal order are known, or if there is no concern with causal relationships, then cross-sectional data and analysis may be sufficient. Repeated cross-sectional designs may be appropriate if it is thought that the problem of panel conditioning may arise.
- If change is to be measured over a long span of time, then a prospective panel design is the most appropriate, because independent samples may differ from one another unless both formal and informal procedures for sampling and data collection are rigidly replicated for each wave of data. Within this context, it is important to remember that a period of time needs to occur before it is feasible to do an analysis of social change: a consistent number of waves is necessary to permit in-depth long-term analyses to be carried out.
- If change is to be measured over a relatively short time (weeks or months), then a retrospective design may be appropriate for data on events or behaviour (but probably not for attitudes or beliefs).
- In order to combine the strengths of panel designs and the virtues of retro-spective studies, a mixed design employing a follow-up and a follow-back strategy seems appropriate (Blossfeld and Rohwer 1995).

Finally, due to the complexity of longitudinal data sets, user documentation is crucial for the researcher. It should contain essential information required for the analysis of the data (including details of fieldwork, sampling, weighting and imputation procedures) and information to assist users in linking and aggregating data across waves. The documentation should both make the analysis easier and more straightforward and help evaluate data quality.

Notes

This is a revised and updated version of an article first published in *Social Research Update*, 28 (Department of Sociology, University of Surrey).

1 Strictly speaking, longitudinal studies are limited to prospective studies, while retrospective studies have been defined as a quasi-longitudinal design, since they do not offer the same strengths for research on causal processes because of distortions due to inaccuracies in memories (Hakim, 1987: 97).

Suggested further reading

Davies, R.B. and Dale, A. (1994) 'Introduction', in A. Dale and R.B. Davies (eds), *Analysing Social and Political Change: a Casebook of Methods*. London: Sage Publications.

Ruspini, E. (ed.) (1999) 'Longitudinal Analysis: a Bridge between Quantitative and Qualitative Social Research', Special Issue of *Quality and Quantity*, 33 (3), July–August.

Ruspini, E. (ed.) (2002) *Introduction to Longitudinal Research*. London: Routledge.

Ruspini, E. and Dale, A. (eds) (2002) *The Gender Dimension of Social Change: the Contribution of Dynamic Research to the Study of Women's Life Courses*. Bristol: The Policy Press.

References

Blossfeld, H.P. and Rohwer, G. (1995) *Techniques of Event History Modeling: New Approaches to Causal Analysis*. Hillsdale, NJ: Lawrence Erlbaum Associates.

Buck, N., Gershuny, J., Rose, D. and Scott, J. (eds) (1994) *Changing Households: the BHPS 1990 to 1992*, ESRC Research Centre on Micro-Social Change. Colchester: University of Essex.

Davies, R.B. (1994) 'From Cross-Sectional to Longitudinal Analysis', in A. Dale and R.B. Davies (eds), *Analysing Social and Political Change: a Casebook of Methods*. London: Sage Publications.

Davies, R.B. and Dale, A. (1994) 'Introduction', in A. Dale and R.B. Davies (eds), *Analysing Social and Political Change: a Casebook of Methods*. London: Sage Publications.

Duncan, G.J. (1992) *Household Panel Studies: Prospects and Problems*. Working Papers of the European Scientific Network on Household Panel Studies, Paper no. 54. Colchester: University of Essex.

Duncan, G.J. (2000) 'Using Panel Studies to Understand Household Behaviour and Well-Being', in D. Rose (ed.), *Researching Social and Economic Change: the Uses of Household Panel Studies*, Social Research Today Series. London: Routledge.

Freed Taylor M., Brice J. and Buck N. (eds) (1995) *BHPS User Manual*. Introduction, Technical Report and Appendices, Vol. A. Colchester: University of Essex.

Gershuny, J. (1998) 'Thinking Dynamically: Sociology and Narrative Data', in L. Leisering and R. Walker (eds), *The Dynamics of Modern Society*. Bristol: The Policy Press.

Hagenaars, J.A. (1990) *Categorical Longitudinal Data: Log-Linear Panel, Trend and Cohort Analysis*. London: Sage Publications.

Hakim, C. (1987) *Research Design: Strategies and Choices in the Design of Social Research*. London: Allen and Unwin.

Magnusson, D. and Bergmann, L.R. (eds) (1990) *Data Quality in Longitudinal Research*. Cambridge: Cambridge University Press.

Menard, S. (1991) *Longitudinal Research*. Newbury Park, CA: Sage Publications.

Mingione, E. (1999) 'Foreword', in E. Ruspini (ed.), 'Longitudinal Analysis: a Bridge between Quantitative and Qualitative Social Research', Special Issue of *Quality and Quantity*, 33 (3), July–August.

Rose, D. (2000) 'Household Panel Studies: an Overview', in D. Rose (ed.), *Researching Social and Economic Change: the Uses of Household Panel Studies*, Social Research Today Series. London: Routledge.

Ruspini, E. (1999) 'Longitudinal Research and the Analysis of Social Change', in E. Ruspini (ed.), 'Longitudinal Analysis: a Bridge between Quantitative and Qualitative Social Research', Special Issue of *Quality and Quantity*, 33 (3), July–August.

Ruspini, E. (ed.) (2002) *Introduction to Longitudinal Research*. London: Routledge.

Trivellato, U. (1999) 'Issues in the Design and Analysis of Panel Studies: a Cursory Review', in E. Ruspini (ed.), 'Longitudinal Analysis: a Bridge between Quantitative and Qualitative Social Research', Special Issue of *Quality and Quantity*, 33 (3), July–August.

van der Kamp, Leo J. Th. and Bijleveld, Catrien C.J.H. (1998) 'Methodological Issues in Longitudinal Research', in Catrien C.J.H., Bijleveld et al., *Longitudinal Data Analysis: Designs, Models and Methods*. London: Sage Publications.

ELISABETTA RUSPINI

Measurement, level of

The term level of measurement of a variable[1] refers to how the values of the variable relate to each other. We distinguish four levels of measurement. These are: the nominal/categorical; the ordinal; the interval; and the ratio. The nominal/categorical level is taken to be the 'lowest' level and the ratio level the 'highest' in terms of the amount of information conveyed about the way the values of the variable are related.

Nominal/categorical

At the nominal/categorical level of measurement numbers are used merely as labels for the values of a variable. Nominal/categorical variables can either be *binary*, or *multi-categorical*. In the case of binary nominal/categorical variables, the variable takes on two values, where one value implies the opposite or lack of the other. Examples would be questionnaire responses where the answer to each question is either 'Yes' or 'No'. Another example would be a variable called 'Sex' with the categories 'Male' and 'Female'. We could assign these categories the numeric codes 1 and 2 respectively. Note that we can only say that the categories, and the numbers used to code them, are different. We cannot present mathematical relationships between them. We cannot rank the categories in any order; for instance, we cannot say that one gender is more of a sex than the other. (After all, we could just as easily have coded female as '1' and male as '2'.)

A nominal/categorical variable can be multi-categorical and have more than two categories; for example, a variable 'Religion' could be coded '1' for 'Catholic', '2' for 'Protestant', '3' for 'Islamic', '4' for 'Hindu' and so forth. As with binary variables, the categories, and the numbers used to code them, are different but the values of the numbers have no meaning. We cannot present mathematical relationships between the numbers and we cannot rank the categories in any order; for instance, we cannot say that 'Catholic' is more of a religion than 'Islamic'.

Ordinal

Next, there is the ordinal level of measurement. This applies to variables where we can place the values in an order of rank by some characteristic. We can rank order the values into higher or lower, or say that one value is greater than or less than the other. We can assign numeric codes which reflect this rank order. In the example below, the values are in rank order and this is reflected in their numeric codes.

Ranking of values	Numeric code
Very often	1
Quite often	2
Rarely	3
Never	4

In this example we have ranked the values along a characteristic of 'frequency of occurrence' from 'Very often' (1) to 'Never' (4). Alternatively, we could have ranked them from 'Never' (1) to 'Very often' (4). In either case, it is the ranking that is meaningful and the numeric codes only reflect this ordering.

At the ordinal level of measurement, we can only say that one category is greater than or less than another, but we cannot say by how much. The differences between the ranks need not be equal. For example, the difference between ranks 1 and 2 above is not necessarily the same as the difference between ranks 3 and 4. This distinguishes the ordinal level from the next two levels of interval and ratio. In the interval and ratio levels of measurement each point in the scale is the same distance from the preceding one.

Interval level

At the interval level of measurement, not only can the values be ranked but differences between the values of the variables have the same meaning at different points on the scale. Consider the following example of the values of the variable 'year of birth'.

Values
1980
1982
1975
1977

The difference (of 2 units) between 1980 and 1982 has the same numeric meaning as the difference between 1975 and 1977. It is meaningful to add and subtract values and so we can give the exact differences between points on the scale. There is, however, no meaningful zero point on the scale. Therefore, meaningful ratios cannot be produced. Another example of a variable measured at the interval level is that of the Celsius scale.

Ratio level

The ratio level includes the features of interval level plus there is an absolute zero on the scale. Variables such as age, weight, time, length have natural zero points and are measured at the ratio level. It is possible to multiply and divide and form ratios. Comparisons such as twice as long make sense at the ratio level of measurement.

The ratio is the 'highest' level of measurement. By 'higher', we mean that a variable at a higher level of measurement contains all of the information of all the levels of measurement below it, *plus* the extra characteristic that distinguishes it from 'lower' levels of measurement. For example, consider a person whose age has been coded as '38'. 'Age' is at the ratio level of measurement because a new-born person could have the genuine age of '0'. As well as being ratio, 'age' contains the information of the interval level of measurement because the difference between two people's ages has an exact meaning; for example, a person aged 40 will be 2 years older than our 38-year-old. Also, 'age' contains the information of the ordinal level of measurement; for example the 40-year-old is 'older' than our 38-year-old (that is, ranked above the younger person). Finally, 'age' is a nominal/categorical 'label' of the person (a '38-year-old').

The importance of levels of measurement

In collecting data, for example through a questionnaire, we can decide which level of measurement is required and feasible to collect. Note that data collected at a higher level can later be recoded 'down' into the lower level (for instance, from the ratio down to ordinal level) but not vice versa. So, while we can see from the above that you could develop a set of ordinal age categories from a ratio variable of age in years (for example, 'Young adults' (18 to 29); 'Adults' (30 to 45); 'Middle-age (46 to 64); 'Old' (65 and up)), the reverse would not be possible. If you coded age as four ordinal age categories when the data were collected, it would be impossible later on to work out a person's actual age in years. Hence, if possible, *always* code variables at the 'highest' feasible level of measurement.

Why is level of measurement important? The reason is that statistical procedures are only appropriate for certain levels of measurement. For example, it is meaningless to try to calculate a mean for a variable at the nominal level of measurement. (Remember the binary variable 'Sex'? If we calculated the mean 'Sex' for a survey drawn from the general population, the result would be about 1.55; literally, that the typical sex of people is hermaphroditic! A nonsensical result.)[2]

Notes

1 Sometimes also called a variable's scale.
2 Note that for more complex statistical procedures, there can be debate about which statistics can be used for variables at particular levels of measurement.

Suggested further reading

De Vaus, D.A. (1996) *Surveys in Social Research*, 4th edn. London: UCL Press.

Frankfort-Nachmias, C. and Nachmias, D. (1996) *Research Methods in the Social Sciences*, 5th edn. London: St. Martin's Press.

RICHARD O'LEARY

Meaning

This is an uncomplicated non-technical term used to describe all those qualities human beings have that make them different from animals – people have views, constructions, interpretations, beliefs, feelings, perceptions, thoughts, moods, emotions, ideas and conceptions of themselves, others and the social and natural worlds generally. These qualities are called 'social meanings' or 'interpretative processes' and comprise the stuff that qualitative research and interpretative social theories like phenomenology and ethnomethodology seek to study and discover. More technical terms for 'social meanings' exist associated with German social and philosophical thought, such as *Verstehen* (translated as understanding) and hermeneutics (translated as interpretation). These terms, however, are technical terms and best not used interchangeably between themselves or with the non-technical term 'meaning'.

It is not just that people are seen as 'meaning endowing', that is, that they have the capacity to endow meaning to all features of the world, people are also discursive. That is, human beings have the capacity for language and are able to formulate their meanings into language and articulate them. This leads some researchers to adopt a fairly simple approach to research: if they want to know why something is happening they ask the people behaving in that way. It is the view within the methodological position of *naturalism* that knowledge of the social world is incomplete unless people's social meanings are disclosed.

This is rarely the end point, however, since analysts often wish to go beyond the discovery of people's meanings. The meanings people apply to their behaviour do not reveal all there is to know about social life. Unintended consequences, for example, are critical to understanding social life. People's accounts of their actions and motives are often one-sided and restricted. They often lie, dissemble or exaggerate. Furthermore, the meanings that people consciously ascribe to their own actions may be incomplete, not taking account of deeper motivations, inhibitions or humankind's capacity for self-deception. People are not islands unto themselves because they must take into account other people's views and interpretations.

Nonetheless, while not the end point, qualitative researchers place the study of social meanings as, at least, the departure point. There are some schools of thought within the social sciences, however, that argue that the social world is socially constructed by people's interpretative processes and that this is all there is to know. These radical social constructionist views can be tempered by a claim that if not constructed, the social world is at least interpreted and reinterpreted by people. Schwartz and Jacobs refer to this more tempered view as 'reality recon-struction' – that messy, tortuous business of trying to see the world as it looks to people. Both standpoints require attention on the disclosure of people's social meanings, in one case as the whole point of social research, in the other as the starting point.

Disclosure of these meanings is no easy thing. People's views, beliefs, inter-pretations, perceptions and the like are often taken-for-granted and deeply embedded in the context of their lives. They are often not superficially tapped and require data collection techniques that penetrate past people's unwillingness to talk, their reluctance to engage in personal disclosures and natural reserve or inhibitions. For this reason the focus on social meanings is associated with tech-niques like ethnography, unstructured interviews, personal documents, vignettes and participant observation. These methods successfully meet the imperatives for social research that derive from the methodological stance of naturalism: that people are asked their meanings; that when asked they are allowed to speak in their own terms; that they are asked in such a way that they can talk in depth; and that the social context in which these meanings are developed and applied is addressed.

Suggested further reading

Lincoln, Y. and Guba, E. (1985) *Naturalistic Inquiry*. London: Sage.

Schwartz, H. and Jacobs, J. (1979) *Qualitative Sociology*. New York: Free Press.

Wallis, R. and Bruce, S. (1986) 'Accounting for Action', in *Sociological Theory, Religion and Social Action*. Belfast: Queen's University of Belfast.

See also
Ethnography, **Participant observation**, **Verstehen** and **Vignette**.

JOHN BREWER

Methodology

Methodology connotes a set of rules and procedures to guide research and against which its claims can be evaluated. It is therefore fundamental to the construction of all forms of knowledge. While it is too simplistic to liken it to a recipe, it could be thought of as a set of guidelines that are widely known and generally adhered to. These procedures as they have been built up over time help both to define a subject discipline and to differentiate it from others. These rules and conventions give the researcher a structure of enquiry and a set of rules of inference (drawing conclusions from evidence). They derive from the logical or philosophical basis of the discipline. Overall, methodology provides the tools whereby understanding is created. Hence, emphasis is on the broad approach rather than, as often (mis)understood, just techniques for data gathering and analysis. One is normally speaking of the design of the research. Methodology is as centrally concerned with how we conceptualise, theorise and make abstractions as it is with the techniques or methods which we utilise to assemble and analyse information. These conventions are neither fixed nor infallible, although they might appear so at times.

I find it helpful to think of methodology in a two-fold way. It is first of all a set of rules and procedures for reasoning, a set of logical structures. Facts do *not* 'speak for themselves' but must be reasoned. Conventions for classification and definition, deduction, induction, sampling procedures and so forth allow one to proceed systematically through the evidence. The second way of thinking about methodology is as a form of communication, a language. In order to be able to communicate with others, especially one's peers, one follows certain conventions. Looked at in this light, methodology provides not just a way of organising ideas and evidence but a language and format for communicating what one has found in one's research. It is in this view an essential part of establishing legitimacy for oneself as a researcher and also for one's work.

The quantitative and the qualitative approaches

There are two general methodological approaches in the social sciences: quantitative and qualitative. While they are not totally understandable as opposing approaches, they do adopt a very different position on the fundamentals of the relationship between ideas and evidence.

The departure point of quantitative research, as its name suggests, is numerical measurement of specific aspects of phenomena. It is a very structured approach; in it competing explanations must be formulated in terms of the relationship between variables. The first step is to condense what one is studying into a number of key attributes or dimensions. These are generally taken as indicators or variables. Measurement is not only very important in this approach but it has to be as exact as possible. Hence, when choosing indicators it is very important in quantitative research that one searches after variables which are: (a) representative of what they are a proxy for (that is, the valid operationalisation of concepts); and (b) able to take a numerical form (that is, they vary either absolutely or by level of degree). These variables then become the basic building blocks of analysis. In a next step, the researcher elaborates a set of competing explanations and propositions (in terms of postulating differences between or relationships among variables). Thirdly, statistical analysis is performed to establish whether these differences or relationships can be identified. The ultimate goal in this type of work is to find as small a set of variables as possible which explain as much as possible. The broader philosophical thinking which informs this approach is that to know something one must establish general sets of relationships which are robust across as many instances or cases as possible. Generalisation is the goal – the main reason why the researcher is interested in establishing relationships is to demonstrate that these are general features of social life. As Ragin (1987) points out, this kind of approach is well suited to testing theories, identifying general patterns and making predictions. It is therefore deductive in nature.

The qualitative approach is based on intensive study of as many features as possible of one or a small number of phenomena. Instead of condensing information, it seeks to build understanding by depth. It is not so much that qualitative research is not interested in breadth but rather that it defines breadth holistically to refer to the 'all roundedness' of one or a number of social phenomena (rather as in the quantitative approach to study as many different instances as possible). Qualitative research seeks *meaning* (rather than generality as with its quantitative counterpart) and contributes to theory development by proceeding inductively. Meaning is achieved not by looking at particular features of many instances of a phenomenon but rather by looking at all aspects of the same phenomenon to see their inter-relationships and establish how they come together to form a whole. To establish the distinctiveness of what one is studying can be an achievement in this approach. One does not in qualitative work separate out something from its context. Rather the phenomenon is studied in its context with the view that it is impossible to understand it apart from it. 'Context' could refer to different things though. It could mean, for example, the setting within which something occurs, or it could refer to the meanings and understandings which the people involved have about something. Diversity, which includes similarities as well as differences, is considered interesting for its own sake, whereas in the quantitative approach diversity can cause the researcher problems because it may challenge the existence of general relationships (the demonstration of which is the goal of this kind of research). The focus in qualitative research is on configurations – how combinations of attributes and conditions come together.

An opposition between quantitative and qualitative approaches to understanding underlies much of the discussion and development within social research. Contrast postmodernism with, say, functionalism. The former emphasises the specificity of each situation, fragmentation as a general feature of society and the search after value and meaning as one of the motors of social life. It will be obvious therefore that postmodernism subscribes to a qualitative methodology. Functionalism, on the other hand, considers that society can be meaningfully understood in terms of the relationship between the parts and the whole. Whereas postmodernism would question whether such a whole exists, functionalism holds not just that it is possible to see parts as being integrated into an overall whole but that it is possible to identify these and study them in isolation. Its preferred methodological approach is quantitative.

Both qualitative and quantitative methodologies are developing very fast. This is especially the case because information technology is being brought to bear on the techniques of analysis. For example, in quantitative work statistical techniques are becoming ever more sophisticated and, similarly, computer programmes for the analysis of qualitative information also are developing rapidly.

Overall it is very important to realise that the methods and techniques one chooses are part of a broader package. It is quite widely accepted that methodology involves a set of standards which should be aspired to. Less widely acknowledged is the fact that assumptions and values underlie all methodologies as well as a particular view of how we are to understand the social world. We need to be as conscious of the assumptions and conditions attaching to our methodology, as we are in applying and using them.

Suggested further reading

See also
Philosophy of
social research

King, G., Keohane, R.O. and Verba, S. (1994) *Designing Social Enquiry*. Princeton, NJ: Princeton University Press.

Nachmias, C. and Nachmias D. (1996) *Research Methods in the Social Sciences*. London: Edward Arnold.

Reference

Ragin, C. (1987) *The Comparative Method*. Berkeley: University of California Press.

MARY DALY

'Micro' sampling techniques

After the main features of a probability sample design have been established a particular problem can develop at the last stage – the selection of individual elements. Often, information about the individuals located within the units that are being sampled is not available and the researcher has to set up procedures so that the interviewer on the site can select individuals while at the same time retaining the principles of random selection. A number of techniques have been developed for maintaining 'randomness' in the selection of individuals while 'out in the field'.

The random walk

This technique is used to introduce an element of chance into the selection of interviewees by interviewers working 'on the street'. Experienced interviewers quickly develop a 'radar' that allows them to anticipate the likely reaction of a person if they approach him or her for an interview. Given the opportunity, interviewers understandably will prefer to approach people who are likely to be cooperative. While this may be more pleasant for the interviewer, it can introduce a powerful bias (towards nice people?) that can have unpredictable effects upon the responses obtained by a street survey.

The interviewer on the street picks a person 'at random' *but* then does not interview that person but rather *nth* next person that comes along. For example, the interviewer picks a person exiting a store, but then has to wait for the seventh person after that who comes out; this seventh person is the one who is approached. Once a person is determined as a candidate, every reasonable effort should be made to secure the interview. If the interviewer is being honest in applying the technique, there should be no unconscious prior selection of those approached.

The listing method

A list of addresses may be available but no accurate list of who may be living at the addresses. The interviewer goes from door-to-door and compiles a list of the eligible individuals living at the addresses, ordering them by some predetermined criteria (such as listing from oldest to youngest) and writing the names on a special listing sheet. The numbered spaces on the list have a random series of 'stars' and whenever a person is listed by a 'starred' space, they are to be targeted for an interview. This is equivalent to a simple random sample only with the interviewer making up the final list of individuals as they go along.

The Kish selection table

A problem with the listing method is that if no one is at home at one of the addresses on a street, the interviewer is 'stuck'; they can't continue making up the list until they discover how many people are living in the house where no one is at home. A way around this is to have a separate 'selection sheet' for each address. The interviewer lists the eligible people at an address by a predetermined ordering method and the sheet indicates which person is to be interviewed. Since the sheets indicate which person is to be interviewed in a random order, the sample remains random. Because the interviewer doesn't have to keep the list 'running' from house to house, he/she can skip over those houses where no one is at home and call back another time. Kish selection sheets look like this:

If the number of people at the address is:	Interview person number:					
	A	B	C	D	E	F
1	1	1	1	1	1	1
2	1	2	1	2	1	2
3	1	2	3	1	2	3
4	1	2	3	4	3	4
5	1	2	3	4	5	5
6+	1	2	3	4	5	6

Only one column of numbers, A through F, will be on any selection sheet, thereby ensuring the random selection of one individual from each address.[1]

Note

See also
Sampling,
probability and
Sampling,
snowball.

1   Note that the Kish selection procedure requires that a sampling weight must be applied to each person selected. At addresses where only one person resides, the odds are 100% that that person will be chosen once that address is chosen. However, if two eligible people live there, the odds are only 50% for either of them that they will be chosen; for three people, 33.3% and so on.

ROBERT MILLER

Modernity

In the discourse on the nature of contemporary society the terms modernisation, modernity and modernism are often used promiscuously. There is clearly an overlap in meaning between the three concepts as they do share a common root in the idea of the modern which stretches back to antiquity as implying a break, or a discontinuity, with the past. The reality of the 'shock of the new' is an integral part of contemporary culture and consciousness in a world where, as Marx put it, '*All that is solid melts into air*'.

In an effort to unravel the complex process of turbulent change which has been a characteristic of all parts of the world to a greater or lesser degree for nearly two centuries it is useful to make an analytical distinction between three interrelated processes. *Modernisation* is a process of change driven by the idea of reason and the process of industrialisation. *Modernity* is a state in which people are exposed to the uncertainty and opportunity brought about by the destruction of traditional society. *Modernism* is a movement, most influential in the cultural sphere, which has both responded to change and moulded its cultural forms.

The emergence of modern science and secular thought under the philosophical banner of reason in the sixteenth and seventeenth centuries separated the idea of reason from the theological realm and redefined it as a secular and human orientated force: a force without God. This form of reason, scientific and secular, is the motor of modernisation as a linear, historically driven process that unleashes impersonal and rule governed forces, subject to human control, and dissociated from the transcendental. Modernisation is the conquest and harnessing of nature through science and the disenchantment of the social world. This process did not begin at any fixed point, but attained critical mass with the onset of industrial capitalism. In retrospect it is possible to distinguish developments the consequences of which were not visible for centuries. The invention of double entry bookkeeping in the monastic demesnes of southern Europe in the late middle ages was one such development, allowing the principles of profit and loss to be applied to agriculture, as was Galileo's revolutionary contention that the world could be understood through mathematics.

In the seventeenth and eighteenth centuries in particular, the idea that humans had the innate capacity to apply reason and logical thought to achieve progress and perpetual peace took firm root and permeated the ideas of Hobbes, Rousseau, Kant, St Simon, Comte, Spencer and Marx. Where philosophy led, social thought was quick to follow. The founders of modern social theory, such as Weber, Durkheim, Tönnies and Simmel were steeped in the tradition of continental philosophical thought which tended to view the world as a totality in need of a grand theory. The influence of both Freud – in particular the theory of the unconscious which challenged the rational basis of human behaviour – and Marx's synthesis of English political economy, French socialism and German philosophy, was considerable. It was the crisis of reason, exposed in the contradictions of capitalist modernisation, which fuelled this first wave of sociological thinking. The depredations of capitalism, the wanton destruction of traditional life worlds and cultures forced a reassessment of the role of the irrational in human life and a focus on the need to create a meaningful world amid the flux and change of modernity. Weber's pessimistic prognosis of the negative outcome of the rationalisation of the world is counterpoised with a repressed nostalgia for a world less disenchanted. Weber's bitter disillusionment with the hopes of the Enlightenment sprung from his belief that the 'iron cage' of bureaucratic rationality would stifle and suffocate the dream of universal freedom. Tönnies expresses a more overt nostalgia for the lost world of community solidarity and Durkheim uncovers the problems of creating meaning in a world that seems bent on its destruction. Within the German speaking world a form of romantic and conservative anti-capitalism emerged which had strong nationalist overtones.

The crisis of modernity was seen in terms of an opposition between *Kultur* and *Zivilisation* where the latter embodied the values of the Anglo-French love affair with material and technical progress. *Kultur* is characterised by a life driven by aesthetic, ethical and spiritual values centred upon an organic spiritual universe capable of resisting the excesses of capitalist materialism.[1]

Simmel comes closer to expressing the conflicting realities of modernity than any of his contemporaries. Simmel focused upon the fluid and transitory nature of the experience of modernity and was convinced that modern life could not be understood in its totality, but only in a contingent and transitory fashion. Examining the fragments of modernity was the only way of making it accessible.

Simmel sees Marx's theory of commodity fetishism as a particular case of the tragedy of culture as a whole. He viewed his own work as an 'attempt to construct a new storey beneath historical materialism' which would expose economic forms as a result of 'metaphysical preconditions'. Despite his philosophical escapism Simmel had a profound influence on Marxist writers such as Georg Lukács. Simmel's focus upon the tragedy of a culture where the culture of things was to dominate totally the culture of persons, and his contention that contained in each of life's details was the 'totality of its meaning', led him to look at the transitory and the fleeting and use the essay form as the main vehicle of his writing.

This connects Simmel, more than any of his academic contemporaries, to the current of modernism that emerged with such force in the latter decades of the nineteenth century. Indeed, the icon of *fin de siècle* Paris, the epicentre of the modernism movement, was the *Flâneur*, that observer of urban life , detached and cynical as he strolled the boulevards in search of transitory pleasures, appearing in the writings of Baudelaire and ever present in the paintings of the impressionist Manet. Simmel's famous pieces on urban life, *The Stranger* and *The Metropolis and Modern Life* deal with the same concerns of the nature of the individual in a society where uncertainty rules. Berman vividly describes the condition of modernity:

> There is a mode of vital experience – experience of space and time, of the self and others, of life's possibility and perils – that is shared by men and women all over the world today. I will call this body of experience 'modernity' . . . modernity can be said to unite all mankind. But it is a paradoxical unity, a unity of disunity; it pours us all into a maelstrom of perpetual disintegration and renewal, of struggle and contradiction, of ambiguity and anguish. (Berman, 1983: 163)

Modernism confronted this crisis of representation. The linear and chronological form of the nineteenth-century novel, the realist form of much visual art and the declamatory tone of poetry were the art forms of a dying age. New forms of representation were experimented with in the effort to grasp the contingent and fleeting nature of modern life. Cultural producers were faced with strategic choices about the representation of modern life and some retreated before the challenge, simply carrying on as before. Writers such as Joyce and Proust, poets like Yeats and Aragon, along with Picasso, Manet and Braque and many other artists tried to develop new cultural codes and languages to grasp the ephemeral and chaotic reality which surrounded them. Writing of the parochial experience of the war of independence in Ireland the poet William Butler Yeats expressed a deeper truth about western culture in general:

> Things fall apart; the centre cannot hold
> Mere anarchy is loosed upon the world.

The sense of disillusion with the idea of progress set in early among European intellectuals. As early as 1905 Weber wrote that the 'rosy blush of the Enlightenment [is] irretrievably fading' and the First World War led to terminal disillusionment with the project of modernisation and progress for many. Durkheim, Weber and Simmel died within a few years of the armistice in 1918.

German social thought, in particular, adopted a profoundly pessimistic stance in the shape of the Institute for Social Research in Frankfurt founded by Theodor Adorno and Max Horkheimer. For them, the dream of reason had become the nightmare of domination. Using a synthesis of the thought of Hegel, Marx and Freud, members of the Frankfurt School analysed how reason had become technological rationality, a means of domination that clothed itself in the rhetoric of freedom. Culture itself had become progressively industrialised and commodified as capital penetrated and colonised the everyday world of cultural practices. When the leading lights of the School fled from the horror of fascism to the USA in the 1930s they found their worst suspicions confirmed: here was a society where modernity meant the subjection of all aspects of life to the regime of capital accumulation.

The USA after the Second World War was for some, such as Herbert Marcuse, C.W. Mills and David Riesman, a profoundly undemocratic and repressive society ruled by power elites and kept under control by the blandishments of consumption. For others, and the vast majority of sociologists and political scientists, the triumph of the American way of life was the realisation of the project of the Enlightenment, which could, and should, be carried to all parts of the globe. This ambitious ideological and practical project was carried by modernisation theory which was to dominate social theory in the US – and wield a disproportionate influence in the rest of the world – for two decades after the Second World War.

The highly influential sociologist, Talcott Parsons, disinterred the theoretical cadavers of Weber and Durkheim and made them palatable to the new theoretical order. The idea of a modern society was redefined to dovetail with the perceived characteristics of western societies – the USA in particular – and encompassed terms such as 'secular', 'democratic', 'individualistic' and 'capitalist' to describe a society that was inherently stable both politically and socially. The breathtaking claims of modernisation theory to have uncovered the secret of progress became a template for research in the social sciences. The influential cross-cultural study carried out by Murdock, *Social Structure*, concluded that the nuclear family was the basic building block of all societies, therefore the essential social basis for the transition from traditional to modern society was a universal presence. Modernisation theory was the key to understanding the world, it explained the logic of the transition from backwardness to modernity in a rational way and presented an interpretation of the world which linked being modern with economic growth and the culture of mass consumption. The theory seeped down from academia to all forms of popular culture, from the Hollywood movie to popular music, instructing people across the globe on the proper way to live. Parsons' objective, to use modernisation theory as the basis of a scientific theory of development that would apply to any and every country and culture, seemed achievable in the heady years of the Cold War.

In the field of aesthetics and artistic production, modernism was also losing its cutting edge and revolutionary aspirations. Modern architecture, once seen as embodying a fundamental break with the past and offering technocratic and aesthetic solutions to social problems (form follows function) descended into the bland International Style demanded by corporations to both hide and celebrate their anonymous power. The world of modernist literature and art, both in the US and Europe, was infiltrated by American political interests and directed towards the objectives of cold war politics.

If both the arts and the social sciences were concerned with the complex reality of modernity, their starting points were, and remain, fundamentally different. The arts articulated with society in terms of the place of humans in society and in the twentieth century and, in broad terms, dealt with the universal problems faced by Baudelaire's *Flâneur* '. . . you're not at home but you feel at home everywhere; you see everyone, you're at the centre of everything, yet you remain hidden from everybody.' The social sciences, on the other hand, produce the concepts, the theoretical structures, which attempt to explain how the human world works. While it may well be that, for instance, American abstract expressionism was promoted by the CIA and other state agencies as a celebration of the values of US society, there is no evidence that the movement itself, centred around the artists de Koonig and Jackson Pollock, produced a particular type of art under political direction.

The social sciences, however, stand in a different relationship to political and economic power structures, a relationship that contains and circumscribes their autonomy. The development of a Fordist type society where the growth of capitalist production depended upon the habituation of whole populations to the new creed of consumption and the extension of this new confluence of production and consumption across the world was one side of the equation. The other was the emergence of what President Eisenhower described as the military industrial complex. Both processes had an omnivorous appetite for research clothed in the mantle of science. The grand narrative of modernisation directed social science research in a direction that dovetailed with both the ideological and economic interests of the burgeoning American *Imperium*.

The state became seriously involved in the funding of academic research, and the code word for access to the new realm of academic privilege and preferment was 'science'. As many had feared, reason was harnessed for dubious scientific and political ends. The idea that the social sciences could, and should, provide the state with 'neutral' research results to be used as the basis for policy decisions, took hold. Parsons called this the ethos of cognitive rationality. In the social sciences, the production of theories of the middle range, limited in scope and subject to empirical verification, dominated research. But this golden age of theoretical complacency and professional monopoly was not to last.

Criticism of the failures of the modern project first began to appear in critical appraisals of the built environment. As early as 1961 Jane Jacobs in her book *The Death and Life of Great American Cities* sought to redefine the nature of urban life by pointing to the terrible social costs of modernist inspired urban planning. The architectural critic Charles Jencks went so far as to locate the symbolic end of modernism to a precise time and date: 3.32 p.m. on July 15 1972, when a prize festooned housing project in St Louis, lauded as a 'machine for living' for its low income tenants, was blown up and levelled as being a disastrous failure.

There is probably no such defining moment in the fragmentation of the social sciences under the postmodern onslaught, but by the middle of the 1960s, modernisation theory, and the logic of instrumentalist rationality which under-pinned it, was under attack from a number of directions. The process of capitalist modernisation had led to both an increasingly sterile and subservient aesthetic modernism as well as the exclusion and marginalisation of substantial social groups. Women, ethnic, nationalist and gay liberation groups were becoming vocal in their condemnation of the exclusionary nature of Fordist society. The first cracks in the hegemonic structure began to appear in the academic study of English literature where the emphasis on a canon of great books was derided as ethno-centric, patriarchal and elitist. Postmodernism emerged as a new set of literary and artistic practices, critical of modernism and directed at the erosion of the distinc-tion between 'high art' and 'popular' culture.

The very motor of modernisation theory, the expansionist dynamic of industrial production, was gradually giving way to a new information-led global economy. As the term postmodern began to gain currency in the 1970s two broad positions began to emerge.

Fredric Jameson viewed postmodernism as a radically new experience of space and time as well as an erosion of the difference between 'high' and 'low' culture.

Applying a Marxist analysis to the changes taking place in the economic sphere, Jameson concluded that postmodernism, while a significant cultural phenomenon, was not the harbinger of a new historical epoch, but instead the intensification and restructuring of late capitalism.

The French philosopher Jean François Lyotard, in his book *The Postmodern Condition*, located the problem in the form of 'grand narratives' which were no longer credible or adequate. Both the Enlightenment narrative of a progressive instrumental reason and the Marxist narrative of human and social emancipation were fatally and tragically flawed.

For sociology the advent of postmodernism was a particular challenge. If capitalism had permeated the very pores of society obliterating the old distinctions between culture and economy and between public and private, then the very nature of the subject was in question. Sociology had traditionally been preoccupied with the problem of order and integration whereas the central tenet of postmodernism was the idea of difference. The idea of difference was used in France to deconstruct the genesis and legacy of French colonialism and to demolish the master narrative of modernisation. Other social movements, the feminist, postcolonial, ethnic and civil rights movements made the idea of difference central to their attempts to deconstruct the legacy of the Enlightenment.

The effects of these broad social and cultural changes on the academy were not long in coming. Across the range of carefully constructed and jealously guarded academic disciplines siege was laid to the idea of a particular canon and subservience to the ideas of (mostly dead) white European males. The theoretical charge was led by theorists (mostly French) whose work defied easy classification. Was the work of Foucault, Baudrillard, Bourdieu or even Habermas to be defined as philosophy, social theory, political science or sociology? No one seemed to know. In the 1970s, however, the work of Giddens, Runciman and Mann attempted, from different perspectives, to reconstruct a theoretical basis for the understanding of contemporary society. It can be argued now that this project has run out of steam, and that the fragmentation of the social sciences is a *fait accompli* given the reality of the informational revolution and the global commodification of culture in the twenty-first century. Perhaps the poet Paul Valéry was correct when he wrote: 'Le moderne se contende de peu' (the modern contends with very little).

Note

1 This line of thought was to inform the support of many German intellectuals for plunging Europe into the Great War.

Suggested further reading

Berman, M. (1983) *All That is Said Melts into Air: The experience of modernity.* London: Verso.

Clark, T.J. (1999) *Farewell to an Idea.* London: Yale University Press.

Giddens, A. (2000) *The Consequences of Modernity.* Cambridge: Polity Press.

Harvey, D. (1989) *The Condition of Postmodernity.* Oxford: Basil Blackwell.

See also
Structuralism

JIM SMYTH

Multilevel models

- Multilevel modelling extends more traditional statistical techniques by explicitly modelling social context. This introduces a degree of realism often absent from single-level models such as multiple regression.
- Many of the populations of interest to social scientists have a hierarchical, or nested structure. Some have a cross-classified structure. Multilevel models analyse the levels of these structures simultaneously. Consequently, questions about the appropriate level of analysis are redundant.
- Multilevel modelling techniques can fruitfully be applied to repeated measures data and to multivariate data, and are especially valuable in these situations when data are missing.
- There is a range of software which enables multilevel models to be fitted easily.

Many social scientists aim to explain variability in human behaviour and attitudes, and how these behaviours are modified and constrained by shared membership of social contexts – the family, the school, the workplace and so on. One way in which social scientists further their understanding of social behaviour is by using statistical models to analyse quantitative data. A weakness of the way in which these models are often applied to social data is that they focus too much on the individual and too little on the social and institutional contexts in which individuals are located. Multilevel modelling aims to redress the balance, by emphasising both individuals and their social contexts.

Population structure

Commonly, populations of interest to social scientists have a hierarchical or nested structure. To give two examples: (1) individuals live in households which, in turn, are located in geographically defined communities; and (2) pupils are taught in classes within schools within Local Education Authorities. Hierarchically structured populations can be thought of as pyramids with different numbers of levels. In the first example, there are three levels: (1) individuals as the base level or level one; (2) households as an intermediate level (level two); and (3) communities as the highest level or apex (level three). In the second example, there are four levels: pupils; classes; schools; and LEAs. In a nested structure, each individual belongs to just one household, each pupil to just one class, and so on up the hierarchy. In principle, there is no limit to the number of levels of a hierarchy but, in practice, we are rarely in the position to carry out analyses with more than four levels of nesting.

Most of the developments in multilevel modelling up to now have been concerned with analysing data with a nested structure. However, some populations have a cross-classified structure. For example, patients can be defined by their family doctor and by the hospital they attend. However, GPs can refer their patients to a number of different hospitals, and hospitals draw their patients from a number of GPs, and so GPs and hospitals form a cross-classification within which patients are nested.

Extending Multiple Regression

The aim of most statistical models is to account for variation in a response variable by a set of one or more explanatory variables. The actual model used will be influenced by a number of considerations, foremost being the nature of the response – whether it is binary, categorical or continuous. Multilevel modelling techniques have been developed for each of these cases, but we will confine ourselves here to continuously measured responses, those situations where multiple regression methods have traditionally been used.

Let us build up the ideas by way of a simple example. Suppose a researcher is interested in the relation between educational attainment at age 16 (the response) and household income (the explanatory variable), for all pupils in England. Suppose a large sample is selected which, for convenience, has been clustered by secondary school. Hence, we have just two levels – pupil and school.

A traditional regression model is specified as:

$$\text{ATTAINMENT} = a + b\ \text{INCOME} + e_i \tag{1}$$

with e_i the residual term for pupil i, and interest is in the size of b, the effect of income on attainment.

This model does not, however, recognise that pupils are taught in schools. Hence, the specification is incomplete and potentially misleading because the institutional context is missing. For example, it is possible that mean attainment varies from school to school, after allowing for the effect of income on attainment. One implication of this is that pupils' attainments within schools are more alike, on average, than attainments in different schools, and this might lead to some interesting findings about the effect of schools. One penalty for ignoring the effect of school in Model (1) is that the standard error of the regression coefficient, b, is too low. Essentially the same problem arises in survey research if we base our estimates of the precision of any estimated parameter on the assumption of simple random sampling, rather than accounting for the clustered nature of our sample.

We should therefore extend model (1) to:

$$\text{ATTAINMENT} = a_j + b\ \text{INCOME} + e_{ij} \tag{2}$$

We now have two subscripts, one for each of the two levels – i for pupils and j for schools. Also, we have a_j rather than just a to represent the variability in the intercept from school to school. This can be referred to as the 'school effect', which we treat as a random effect and which we represent as a variance. Consequently, we now have a multilevel model; in fact, a simple two-level model which is sometimes known as a variance components model.

Random slopes

The simple two-level model – Model (2) – allows the intercept to vary from school to school. We might also like the slope, b, to vary from school to school, because schools might influence the relation of income to attainment, with some schools reinforcing it and others reducing it. Hence, we can write:

$$\text{ATTAINMENT} = a_j + b_j \text{ INCOME} + e_{ij} \qquad (3)$$

and we now have two random effects – a_j as before and now b_j to represent the variability in slopes from school to school. We must also allow the schools' intercepts and slopes to be correlated. This more complicated model is sometimes called a random slopes, or a random coefficients model.

The three panels of Figure 1 show how we have introduced complexity into our model, and hence made it more realistic. Panel (a) illustrates the simple regression model, Model (1). In panel (b), the intercepts are allowed to vary but the slopes are constant, Model (2). In panel (c), corresponding to Model (3), both the intercepts and slopes vary from school to school, and, in this case, there is a negative correlation between intercept and slope.

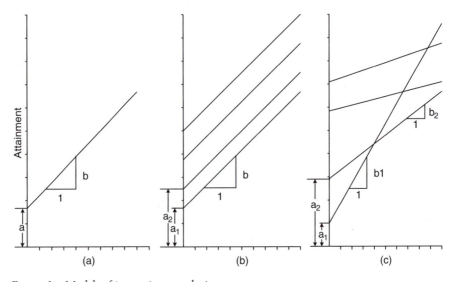

Figure 1   *Models of increasing complexity*

Fixed and random effects

The distinction between fixed and random effects is an important one in multilevel modelling. We could represent the effect of school on attainment as a set of dummy variables, the size of this set being one less than the number of schools. However, with many schools, estimating so many fixed effects (a_1, a_2 etc.) is inefficient. It is much more efficient to estimate just one variance.

The distinction can be illustrated by another example. Suppose a researcher is interested in the effects of ethnic group on an attitude for two kinds of social contexts – the effect of belonging to a particular social class, and the effect of living in different geographically defined communities. Social class is a fixed effect; we are interested in the effects of each class and it does not make sense to sample from a 'population' of social classes. We introduce the social context by including social class in our model, usually as a small set of dummy variables, and by estimating the size of the interaction between ethnic group and social class to allow for the possibility that the relation between attitude and ethnic group varies across social classes. These interaction terms are also fixed effects. However, community is a random effect; we sample from the population of communities and we are interested in saying something about communities in general, rather than about one particular community. The effect of community can be represented by a set of random effects, a random intercept and a collection of random slopes, one for each ethnic group.

An illustration

Suppose we have estimated the random slopes Model (3) on a large sample, both of pupils (5000, say) and, importantly, of schools (200, say). Our response is a score generated from pupils' GCSE results and household income is measured in thousands of pounds and, for convenience, as deviations from the sample mean. Suppose the between school, or level-two variance in the intercept is 4, and the between school variance in the slopes is 0.04. This implies that, at mean income, about 95% of the schools' intercepts lie within 4 units of the mean intercept (i.e within two standard deviations, twice 4), and about 95% of the school slopes lie within 0.4 units of the mean slope (twice 0.04). Finally, if the variance of the pupil residual, e_{ij}, is 8 then, at mean income, one third of the total variation in GCSE results is between schools (4/(4+8)) and two thirds within schools. We can see, from Figure 1(c), that between school variation varies by income in a random slopes model.

Using multilevel modelling techniques with these data gives us more information about the relation between attainment and income than we would have had if we had used a single-level model. (It is, of course, possible, that the school random effects turn out to be small. In these cases, which only become apparent after the event, a single-level model is sufficient.) On the other hand, results such as these are tantalising because they give no indication why, for example, the relation between attainment and income varies as much as it does from school to school. One possibility is that variables measured at the school level account for some of the between school variation. For example, suppose we can divide the sample schools into two groups – those which use some form of selection at age 11 and those which do not. Our multilevel model can be extended to incorporate these 'school-level' variables, which vary from school to school but not from pupil to pupil within a school.

The existence of variables measured at different levels sometimes leads researchers to ask 'at which level should I analyse my data?' A strength of the multilevel approach is that it renders such questions redundant. Data can, and should, be collected and analysed at all levels simultaneously. This avoids the pitfalls associated with aggregation. Suppose, for example, we only had measures of school mean attainment and school mean household income, and we fitted a simple regression to these aggregated data. We would typically find that the relation between attainment and income is much stronger at the school level than it is, on average, at the pupil level. This is often referred to as the ecological fallacy. Attainment and income are, however, individual-level (or level-one) variables, and should be measured and modelled at that level, within a multilevel model which allows for institutional effects.

Other extensions

There are two other situations for which a multilevel approach is particularly useful. The first is with repeated measures data. Suppose we have a sample of individuals whose income is measured annually over a number of years. We can think of this as a nested structure with the occasions of measurement defining level one and the individuals defining level two. (Not all multilevel structures have individuals at the lowest level.) We can now model income as a smooth function of time, and see how, and why, the parameters of this function vary from individual to individual. It is not necessary for each individual to have the same number of measurements, and so the approach can encompass missing data. Multivariate data can also be modelled as multilevel data. Then, the different variables measured for each individual define level one, with the individuals themselves defining level two. And if these individuals are, in turn, members of different social or geo-graphical groups, then we can discover whether the structure of associations between the variables is different at different levels.

Conclusion

Multilevel modelling techniques offer quantitative social researchers the opportunity not only to analyse their data in a technically more appropriate way than traditional single-level methods do, but also to extend the kinds of questions they can ask of their data, and hence the opportunity to model contextual richness and complexity. But like all statistical techniques, they cannot replace social theory (although the results might add to it), interpretation is usually more of a challenge than computation, and they must be used with due attention paid to their assumptions. We do require, however, reasonably large numbers of higher-level units to carry out satisfactory analyses.

Note

This entry first appeared as *Social Research Update* 23 (Department of Sociology, University of Surrey).

Software and resources

There are two main specialist packages for multilevel modelling. These are MLwiN, produced by the Multilevel Models Project at the Institute of Education,

University of London with ESRC support, and, from the United States, HLM (HLM stands for Hierarchical Linear Modelling). Both operate in a Windows environment. In addition, some multilevel modelling is possible within major statistical packages such as SAS (PROC MIXED). Rapid developments in statistical computing, and methodological advances in modelling mean that further software developments are likely.

In addition, there is an electronic multilevel discussion list, which can be joined by sending a message: join multilevel '*firstname lastname*' to jiscmail@jiscmail.a-c.uk. There is also a *Multilevel Models Newsletter*, published twice yearly with ESRC support by the Multilevel Models Project (e-mail: m.yang@ioe.ac.uk). Further details about MLwiN can be found on the Project web site (http://www.ioe.ac.uk/mlwin/) and general information about multilevel modelling at: http://www.ioe.ac.uk/multilevel/.

Suggested further reading

There are a number of textbooks and expository articles on multilevel modelling. Useful introductions can be found in:

Hox, J.J. (1994) *Applied Multilevel Analysis*. Amsterdam: TT-Publikaties.
Kreft, I. and De Leeuw, J. (1998) *Introducing Multilevel Modelling*. London: Sage.

Plewis, I. (1997) *Statistics in Education*. London: Edward Arnold.
Raudenbush, S.W. and Willms, J.D. (eds) (1991) *Schools, Classrooms and Pupils*. San Diego: Academic Press.

For advanced reading, there are three major texts:

Bryk, A.S. and Raudenbush, S.W. (1992) *Hierarchical Linear Models*. Newbury Park, CA: Sage.

Goldstein, H. (1995) *Multilevel Statistical Models*, 2nd edn. London: Edward Arnold.
Longford, N. (1993) *Random Coefficient Models*. Oxford: Oxford University Press.

IAN PLEWIS

N

Narrative approach

The narrative approach to interviews and their analysis bases itself upon the ongoing development of the respondent's viewpoint during the course of the interview. Understanding the individual's unique and changing perspective as it is mediated by context takes precedence over questions of fact. In the narrative perspective, 'context' includes both positioning in social structure and time and, just as important, the social context of the interview itself. The interplay between the interview partnership of interviewee and interviewer is at the core of this approach. 'The two together are collaborators, composing and constructing a story the teller can be pleased with. As collaborator in a open-ended process, the researcher-guide is never really in control of the story actually told' (Atkinson, 1998: 9). The narrative approach can be labelled 'postmodern', in that reality is seen to be situational and fluid – jointly constructed by the interview partnership during the conduct of the interview. The personal characteristics of the interviewer can constitute one of the main stimuli to the interviewee and there is not a blanket prohibition against the interviewer either reacting openly to the statements of the interviewee and/or revealing personal details of their own. In fact, the ethnomethodological question of 'How the interview context is constituted' (Silverman and Gubrium, 1994; Holstein and Gubrium, 1995) is central to the narrative approach. How the interview partnership generates the context and flow of the interview is used to provide insight into social life. In 'normal' life actors generate their ongoing perceptions of their social environments through interaction with others and with their structural contexts – and the interview situation is seen as no more than a special instance of the general. The interplay of reactions between the interviewee and interviewer – the tensions, negotiations, agreements, accommodations, etc. – provide insight into the only available social reality, the one that is ongoing at that time.

Since the narrative approach views 'reality' as being situational, dependent upon how the interviewee perceives and constructs at the time of the interview, it ultimately stands in opposition to 'realist' views which purport that there is a single true underlying perspective. In contrast to 'narrativists', 'realists' would purport that there is a genuine 'true' reality and the goal of the researcher is to attempt to come as close as possible to understanding that reality.[1] The contrast between realist approaches and the core of the narrative approach is fundamental. For narrativists, there is not a single objective reality that is factual and existing at a level of abstraction beyond the current situation. Reality is (at least potentially) chaotic and in constant flux. What constitutes reality will be dependent upon the temporary joint perceptions generated by the interaction of social actors. Hence, the idea of a single 'meta-reality' which can be apprehended through the use of empirical information is nonsensical to a pure narrativist. Information about structure and process is obtained, but it is of a special nature – direct information about structure and process is only revealed in the relative statuses and interactions between the interview partners themselves at the time and place of the interview. The postmodern view of 'structure' held by the narrative approach does not see it as a single reality that may be successively approached as it can be in realist or neo-positivist approaches, but, nevertheless, 'structure' is real in its consequences. The interplay between the two actors in the interview partnership provides insights into a fluctuating reality of shifting positions and the subjective perceptions of this impermanent structure. Hence, information about any wider context is indirect, mediated through the perceptions generated during the course of interview interaction.

While the narrative approach is tightly located in the 'present moment' of the interview, the process of reflection encouraged during the relation of a narrative story in an interview encourages the respondent to bring in issues of change over time. Biographical interviewing through the collection of life histories and life stories employs methods of eliciting an interview that encourage respondents to give narratives. Analysts of biographical material are aware that the collection of a life history/story prompts processes of remembrance of the past and anticipation of the future in which the interviewee's viewpoint of reality is reconstructed continuously through the lens of the present (Kohli, 1981).

For the narrative approach the interview situation, in particular the interplay between interviewed and interviewer, is the core source of information. Realist life and family *histories* may be contrasted with narrativist life and family *stories*. In the narrative approach it is the manner in which the life or family story develops and is related during the course of interview, that which realist and neo-positivist approaches strive to eliminate, that provides the essential avenue to understanding. It is the interplay between the interview partners as information is generated that gives clues to social processes and to structures.

Note

1 Albeit accepting the idealistic nature of this goal and that attaining a complete vision of 'the truth' is not feasible. Realist researchers recognise that the many obstacles to attaining a complete vision include the shifting perceptions of reality that narra-tivists centre upon.

Suggested further reading

Miller, Robert L. (2000) *Researching Life Stories and Family Histories*. London: Sage.

Reissman, Catherine Kohler (1993) 'Narrative Analysis', Vol. 30, *Qualitative Research Methods*. Newbury Park, CA: Sage.

References

Atkinson, Robert (1998) 'The Life Story Interview', *Qualitative Research Methods*. Vol. 44, Thousand Oaks, CA: Sage.

Holstein, J.A. and Gubrium, J.F. (1995) *The Active Interview*. Sage Qualitative Research Methods Series 37. Thousand Oaks, CA: Sage.

Kohli, Martin (1981) 'Biography: Account, Text, Method', in Daniel Bertaux (ed.), *Biography and Society: the Life History Approach in the Social Sciences*. London: Sage.

Silverman, David and Gubrium, Jaber F. (1994) 'Competing Strategies for Analyzing the Contexts of Social Interaction', *Sociological Inquiry*, 64 (2): 179–98.

ROBERT MILLER

Naturalism

It is rare that concepts or terms in social science currency have directly opposite meanings but naturalism is one. Conceptual definitions are often nuanced but never contradictory, except in this case. To some naturalism refers to the adoption of natural science models of research to the social sciences, a position more commonly known as *positivism*, naturalism being preferred as a term because it lacks the pejorative connotations of the term positivism. This usage is associated with a few leading social scientists like Giddens and Bhasker (see Bhasker, 1989). However, the more common usage is to describe the trenchantly opposed methodological position, where the social sciences are modelled not on the natural sciences but stand apart as humanistic or hermeneutical disciplines devoted to exploring social meanings. This is the definition adopted here.

Naturalism has theoretical roots in nineteenth-century German social philosophy where the hermeneutical tradition developed and has been infused by all the twentieth-century interpretative social theories based on this tradition, like phenomenology, ethnomethodology, symbolic interactionism and social action theory. It is because of this association that naturalism as a methodological position is also sometimes called the hermeneutical or interpretative tradition. Theoretical ideas from this tradition were used in the attack on positivism and the natural science model of social research from the 1960s onwards, and gave legitimacy to alternative practices in social research. In his account of the philosophy of social research, John Hughes calls this alternative approach the humanistic model of social research, drawing on an idea common in the 1960s amongst sociologists like Berger and Bruyn where the social sciences were presented as humanistic disciplines (see Berger's famous *Invitation to Sociology*). It is more accurate to see this alternative model as having survived in low profile in many areas of research, such as in the modern heirs to the Chicago School tradition of ethnography, and then being rediscovered in the 1960s attack on positivism.

Naturalism is an orientation concerned with the study of social life in real, naturally occurring settings; the experiencing, observing, describing, understanding and analysing of the features of social life in concrete situations as they occur independently of scientific manipulation. It is the focus on natural situations that leads to the sobriquet 'naturalism', and it is signified by attention to what human beings feel, perceive, think and do in natural situations that are not experimentally contrived or controlled. These naturally occurring situations are also sometimes called 'face-to-face' situations, mundane interaction, micro-interaction or everyday life. Stress is laid on experiencing and observing what is happening naturally rather than hypothesising about it beforehand, mostly by achieving first-hand contact with it, although researchers minimise their effect on the setting as much as possible. Stress is also laid on the analysis of people's meanings from their own standpoint, the feelings, perceptions, emotions, thoughts, moods, ideas, beliefs and interpretative processes of members of society as they themselves understand and articulate them. Naturalism presents this as 'being true to the natural phenomena', as Jack Douglas termed it, and from this is it easy to see why naturalism as a methodological position is partnered in research practice by a commitment to ethnography and other qualitative methods.

There are ontological and epistemological assumptions within this stance, which further highlight its contrast with positivism as a methodological position. Central to naturalism is the argument, going back to the *Geisteswissenschaften* (roughly translated as the cultural and social sciences) tradition of German philosophy in the nineteenth century, that human beings and social behaviour are different from the behaviour of physical and inanimate objects. People are meaning-endowing, in that they have the capacity to interpret and construct their social world and setting rather than respond in a simplistic and automatic way to any particular stimuli. Moreover, people are discursive, in that they have the capacity for language and the linguistic formulation of their ideas, and possess sufficient knowledge about discourse in order to articulate their meanings. Society, thus, is seen as either wholly or partially constructed and reconstructed on the basis of these interpretative processes, and people are seen as having the ability to tell others what they mean by some behaviour, idea or remark and to offer their own explanation of it or motive for it. Society is not presented as a fixed and unchanging entity, 'out there' somewhere and external to the person, but is a shifting, changing entity that is constructed or reconstructed by people them-selves. People live in material and bounded structures and locations, and these contexts shape their interpretative processes, so that we are not free to define the social world as if we existed as islands each one inhabited by ourselves alone. All social life is partially interdependent on the concrete situations and structures in which it exists, so 'society' is not a complete invention (or reinvention) every time. But knowledge of the social world, in this methodological position, is inadequate if we do not also document, observe, describe and analyse the meanings of the people who live in it. This must be the starting point of any social science study of society according to naturalism, although it may clearly not be the end point, in that the researcher may want to extend the analysis beyond people's own accounts, explanations and meanings. The theory of knowledge within naturalism thus sees it as essential for understanding the freely constructed character of human actions and institutions in the natural settings and contexts that influence and shape people's meanings. Thus, knowledge must be inductive not deductive.

Naturalism is thus also closely associated with grounded theory as an analytical approach in the social sciences.

The three essential tenets of naturalism are therefore clear. The social world is not reducible to that which can be externally observed, but is something created or recreated, perceived and interpreted by people themselves. Knowledge of the social world must give access to actors' own accounts of it, among other things, at least as a starting point, and sometimes as the sole point. People live in a bounded social context, and are best studied in, and their meanings are best revealed in, the natural settings of the real world in which they live.

What is relevant here is the impact of these theoretical ideas on research practice. Four imperatives or requirements for social research follow from this methodological position. Social researchers in the humanistic model of social research need to meet one or more of these: (1) to ask people for their views, meanings and constructions; (2) to ask people in such a way that they can tell them in their own words; (3) to ask them in depth because these meanings are often complex, taken-for-granted and problematic; and (4) to address the social context which gives meaning and substance to their views and constructions. These research imperatives go toward defining the attitude and approach of naturalist social researchers, predisposing them to focus on topics that can be approached through the exploration of people's meaning and giving them a preference for data collection techniques that can access these meanings.

Suggested further reading

Brewer, J.D. (2000) *Ethnography*. Buckingham: Open University Press.
Douglas, J. (1971) *Understanding Everyday Life*. London: Routledge.

Hughes, J.A. (1990) *The Philosophy of Social Research*. London: Longman.

See also
Philosophy of social research.

References

Berger, P. (1963) *Invitation to Sociology*. Penguin.

Bhaskar, R. (1989) *The Possibility of Naturalism*. Harvester.

JOHN BREWER

O

Observation, overt and covert

Observation is a fundamental part of social life and is critical to many forms of social interaction and work. Thus, it is necessary to distinguish between observation done to accomplish everyday life and work and that done to understand them. Here again, observation is an inherent part of many types of research; it forms part of laboratory experiments as mice are observed in mazes or chemicals in test tubes. In social research there are two parameters along which observation can be categorised as a research tool. The more familiar typology is based on the degree of participation by the researcher in what is being studied; the other is structured around the level of awareness subjects have of being observed. In the first case the normal contrast is between unobtrusive and participant observation, in the latter, covert and overt observation, and the two sets of distinctions are related.

In participant observation observers participate in the everyday life they are trying to understand. This contrasts with observation where the researcher stands aloof, a form of observation that is part of unobtrusive research, where the intention is to engage in research unknown to subjects in order to avoid the reactive effect. Unobtrusive observation is mostly covert, where subjects do not know they are being observed or are part of a researcher project. But this is not always the case. Unobtrusive observation plays a great part in psychology, where the observation is managed by means of a two-way mirror, and subjects are put in experimental situations where, although the observer does not participate, the observation can be overt in that people may know they are involved in research. Unobtrusive observation therefore does not always eliminate the reactive effect. However, with sociology's focus on naturally occurring behaviour, where subjects tend not to be placed in experimental situations, unobtrusive observation tends to be mostly covert. Nonetheless, it provides a very limited form of data. With participant observation data obtained as a result of watching the phenomenon under study is augmented by data generated through introspection on the part of the researcher. That is, by the observer reflecting on the internal experiences arising from doing and sharing the same everyday life as those under study, a process sometimes also called 'auto-observation'. In this way, data collected by participant observation are not external stimuli unaffected by the intervention of the observer: the experiences, attitude changes and feelings of the observer form a central part of his or her understanding. Unobtrusive observation avoids this reactive effect but at the cost of reliance on very limited forms of data – that which is garnered by watching. Thus in social research unobtrusive observation either requires no attention to be given to the social meanings involved in the phenomenon, and thus to the study of fairly unambiguous phenomena, or observation of phenomena known to the researcher where these taken-for-granted social meanings already shape their understanding. Unobtrusive observation, for example, would be impossible in social anthropological research of new and different cultures and people groups; which is why classic social anthropology was one of the intellectual pillars of participant observation. Overt unobtrusive observation is popular in psychology where the actual behaviour is the focus – such as what toys children use in playrooms – rather than the social meanings of the behaviour to the participants. There are occasions in sociology when unambiguous behaviour needs to be studied and for which covert unobtrusive observation is suitable, such as study of pedestrian behaviour, the social formation of queues, and even, as in one study by Stone, the behaviour of men outside pornographic bookstores. Most of these topics, however, involve phenomena whose social meaning can be understood as a result of familiarity. Where this familiarity is lacking, or where the researcher does not want to rely on taken-for-granted knowledge, participant observation comes into its own.

Participant observation can also be done either overtly or covertly. In classic anthropological studies with 'foreign' and 'exotic' people groups and cultures, where the researcher was white and the subjects not, overt observation was the norm. Among other things, the use of translators where researchers did not know the local language perforce required that subjects know they were being researched. As anthropology has moved into analysing modern and industrialised settings in which researchers can 'pass' as ordinary members, it has been possible to engage in covert research. Not all participant observation is covert but a lot has been, particularly when the focus has been on sensitive groups, settings and behaviour in which a pronounced reactive effect is anticipated. Overt participant observation is essential in situations where is it impossible to 'pass' as an ordinary member, and when specialised forms of behaviour are required, particularly in occupational settings, such as when studying police forces. This is why work-based ethnography has been done covertly mostly in settings where the occupational tasks are menial and low skilled. Specialised occupational tasks have tended to require members themselves to undertake observation, overtly or covertly, such as Holdaway's ethnography of policing done while as a serving member of the police (1983), or researchers coming in to do overt research (Brewer, 1991) and having to remain distant as a result. One American sociologist decided to enlist in the air force to undertake participant observation in a highly specialised occupational setting rather than come in overtly as an outsider, although this degree of dedication and time commitment is rarely possible.

The participant–unobtrusive dichotomy is not as sharp as the contrast suggests. Often non-participative forms of observation involve the observer in some manipulation or construction of the setting, such as the arrangement of furniture or the positioning of artifacts, and in experimental situations the observer intrudes without participating in the activity. It is thus sometimes necessary to distinguish between level of participation and level of control, for some forms of non-participative observation still involve high degrees of intervention to standardise and manipulate the observation. Likewise, the presence of the participant observer may be unknown or unseen by subjects in some instances and contexts as they are caught unawares. The level of participation in forms of observation is best perceived as a continuum, around the middle of which there is much blurring and overlap. The same is true for the overt–covert distinction. Overt participant observation requires the permission of the gatekeeper but not everyone in the setting may know of the research or be aware that at that time they are being observed. Some forms of covert research often involve the complicity of one or more members of the field in order to manage the fieldwork and maintain the pretence. Sometimes participant observers let some groups know of the research and others not, by design (to test the impact of their presence) or by accident (in that the pretence can be discovered by some), although this creates difficult relations in the field and can be problematic to maintain. The level of knowledge subjects have of the observation again should be understood as a continuum with blurring in the middle.

It is possible nonetheless to list the respective advantages and disadvantages of overt and covert observation in ideal type terms. Overt observation, for example, assists in researchers maintaining their objectivity precisely because of the detachment and distance involved as a result of subjects knowing they are being studied. It prevents the problem of 'going native', of over-identification with the subjects, that can arise when the researcher has almost to become an 'insider' in order to pass as an ordinary member to avoid disclosure of the observation. Access to some settings, people or groups may have to be negotiated with a gatekeeper because of the impossibility of entry in some disguised role, and some may even find a special status in being the object of research and grant permission because of it. If members know of the observation, they can assist the observer by treating him or her as an incompetent, a non-initiate, and thus better explain things. Members are often assumed to share the same tacit knowledge and thus outsiders can have things made explicit that members are thought to know already. There can be advantages in overt observation because the people or groups in the setting perceive the researcher as neutral, as above members' conflicts and partisanship, and this can facilitate access to decision-making processes within the field. Above all, overt observation permits use of other data collection techniques alongside observation; interviews can be conducted, questionnaires sent out and natural conversations openly recorded, all things impossible if the research is disguised. However, the gatekeeper or subjects in the field can impose constraints when the observation is overt, the researcher becomes an intervening variable in the field, influencing what is observed, and the data becomes distorted by an unknown 'reactive effect' which can restrict the ability of the researcher to get close to the people and capture life from an insider's point of view.

In reverse mirror image, with covert observation, closeness with the group and immersion in the setting can be more easily generated (although still not guaranteed) because it avoids the distance created by knowledge of the research. It avoids the problem of having to get permission, and it removes the possibility of constraints being imposed by subjects in the field. Nonetheless, special personal skills are needed to take on a disguised role and researchers can become so self-conscious about not revealing their identity that their observation is seriously handicapped. The covertness may or may not involve the researcher pretending to be a full member of the group or setting, in that some other role may be utilised from which to observe rather than ordinary member. But if the role involves passing as a full member of the group or setting, there is the problem of over-identification – 'going native' – and associated problems arising from lack of detachment. Moreover, there is the problem of collecting data from the role as ordinary member. Covert observation requires the researcher to appear typical and since ordinary members may not ask probing questions, make notes or utilise data collection techniques, the research either risks disclosure or is severely restricted.

Above all, covert observation raises serious ethical concerns since it involves people being deceived and fails to obtain their informed consent. Not only does this breach the dignity of the subjects, it risks harm to the researcher and the discipline as a whole should deceit be shown to be involved. This can make withdrawal from the field very difficult for the covert observer once people become aware of the deception and it cuts off future opportunities for research by someone else. For this reason, covert observation is not encouraged; codes of conduct from ethical committees or professional associations either disallow or discourage it. While much of the ethical debate has focused on covert observation, it is important to note that other methods also breach the principle of informed consent and even where permission is obtained for observational research, this often involves someone else higher up the hierarchy giving permission on a person's behalf lower down. Sometimes however, it can be the only method if the group or setting is closed or hostile to research, although suspicion often surrounds this defence since covert observation can be too readily resorted to.

These distinctions between types of observation belong to realism as an approach to social research since they represent alternative ideas for improving the correspondence between social reality 'as it is' and the observer's representation of it. Post-structuralist and postmodern notions of research dispute that there is unadulterated 'objective' reality anyway to be affected by whether the observation involves participation or not or whether subjects know of the research or not. All research is contaminated and socially situated by the people involved and the methods used, amongst other things. Such an approach tends to make irrelevant most of the tortured judgements around what type of observation to use.

Suggested further reading

Brewer, J.D. (2000) *Ethnography*. Buckingham: Open University Press.
Burgess, R. (1984) *In the Field*. London: Routledge.

Spradley, J.P. (1980) *Participant Observation*. Orlando, FL: Harcourt, Brace Jovanovich.

See also
Participant observation and **Unobtrusive measures**.

References

Brewer, J. (1991) *Inside the RUC*. Oxford: Clarendon Press.

Holdaway, S. (1983) *Inside the British Police*. Oxford: Blackwell.

JOHN BREWER

Online methods

Recent years have witnessed the Internet rapidly come to the forefront of people's working and personal lives. In some respects the term 'World-Wide-Web' is indicative and reflects the essence of online activity, as surfing the net allows us to glean information about anything and anyone; essentially we can find out about *who* we want, *what* we want, *whenever* we want. The proliferation of the Internet more generally is also in vogue with greater and increasing globalisation wherein the rest of the world is no longer 'out there' but accessible in cyberspace at the mere touch of a button. But what are the implications of the Internet for conducting social research?

Up to now, market research has taken the lead, finding its niche online as virtually every type of industry is realising the potential of the Internet as a primary tool to evaluate customer attitudes to a particular product and/or service. However, social researchers are extending their data collection activities to the web. Arguably, quantitative methods (for example, surveys) are more conducive to online research because the data required does not rely so much on 'quality' interaction between researcher and respondent. Qualitative methods such as focus groups and/or interviews are much more contingent upon the social dynamics between the researcher and research respondent(s) and this can be inhibited in online interaction. Nevertheless, qualitative methods are also beginning to be used on the web. The remainder of this discussion will consider the use of online focus groups and online surveying and the aim is to provide a brief general overview of the issues relating to the usage of these methodologies online. As will become clear, using the Internet as a research tool has its limitations and merits in common with any other method of social enquiry.

Focus groups

Focus groups generally provide a platform for discussion and/or debate around the research topic at hand and are an effective means by which the attitudes, perceptions and/or experiences of participants can be gained. Moreover, they can feed into the research process by identifying further issues to be addressed, for example in subsequent in-depth interviews or questionnaires.

It is possible to run the equivalent of a focus group online. 'Electronic' focus groups can be conducted in two ways:

(1) *Synchronously* – respondents take part in a 'live' online discussion, in a manner analogous to participating in a chatroom.
(2) *Asynchronously* – respondents can read others' comments and contribute to the discussion at any time, but not necessarily immediately or even when anyone else is online. That is, the mode of participation can be analogous to belonging to an e-mail discussion group.

Online focus groups have some clear advantages over the 'traditional' approach:

- The researcher can recruit respondents from a wide geographic area, even from around the globe if required. Since participants do not have to be convened in one geographical location, many of the costs associated with the traditional group are eliminated (for example, travel, rent of facility, catering).
- Respondents participating in online focus groups tend to be more objective and straight to the point; therefore, discussions may be less likely to veer off on tangents and/or be dominated by a particular individual.
- Since respondents communicate by typing there is no room for transcription error(s) and a transcription of the session can be made available more quickly.
- Respondents may be more willing to speak their minds if they have the anonymity that an online focus group can facilitate.

Whilst there are merits of holding focus groups online, there are also drawbacks:

- Actions often speak louder than words and the researcher loses the significance of non-verbal cues if he/she facilitates a focus group online.
- The identity of respondents cannot be known for sure. Therefore the researcher cannot always be sure that the respondent is whom he/she claims to be and/or to represent.
- A key reason for using focus groups is to exploit face-to-face group dynamics as respondents 'bounce' off each other in a lively conversation. This can often provide the researcher with additional key insights. This is less likely to happen online. Moreover, there is less liklihood of spontaneity of comments online.
- In the traditional focus group, respondents understand that they are expected to participate fully in the session while it is going on. It is very difficult however to prevent the online respondent losing interest or being distracted from the proceedings.
- In the traditional setting, the researcher can use his/her own interpersonal skills in order to influence the participation of respondents. The researcher is much more restricted online in how, for example, he/she can encourage respondents to participate more fully.
- If the session is asynchronous, participation may be sporadic and/or lengthy and therefore consistency to the issues at hand may be lost.

While it is clear that online focus groups cannot totally replace traditional focus groups, each have their own strengths that can be used to augment the other.

Online surveying

Conducting surveys online is an effective and inexpensive method of gathering data from a wide variety of respondents. Like focus groups, however, online surveying does not constitute an overall replacement of traditional methods and should only be utilised if compatible with the overall research design. It is therefore important to evaluate the research objectives and determine the most appropriate sampling and research methodology.

The sample required will be a major determinant of whether or not the survey should be conducted online. The online option may seem ideal if a large sample is required in so far as there are few limits to the potential number of respondents who can participate. On the other hand, if a sample that is representative of the general population is required, then the utility of an online survey is compromised. In particular, conducting a survey online *immediately* places limitations on the potential sample, in so far as the researcher can only access population(s) that:

- have access to the Internet
- are IT literate
- are willing to participate.

Bearing these points in mind, conducting a survey online can exclude a large portion of a given target population; for example, if the aim is to survey individuals of lower class backgrounds, it is unlikely that they will have access to a PC.

Using the online method also means that the researcher has less control over who responds to the questionnaire and therefore must take adequate measures to safeguard against any one person masquerading as a legitimate respondent as this again would skew the sample. If conducting the survey manually, the researcher at least has control over the distribution and return of questionnaires.

Interviewing online

Similar to the benefits of conducting focus groups and/or surveys online, the Internet opens up unique opportunities for carrying out one-to-one in-depth interviews. Since the Internet transcends distance, it is possible to access 'hard to reach' populations at a global level. Many of the costs involved with traditional interviewing are reduced, or, with regard to the cost of transcribing interviews and the expense of travel to the interview, eliminated altogether. Online interviews can be conducted 'live', wherein researcher and interviewee communicate via e-mail in a designated session. Alternatively, the interview can take place where messages are exchanged over a longer time period. The latter method, whilst allowing a degree of flexibility may however be detrimental to consistency of thought between interviewer and respondent and furthermore compromise spontaneity in so far as there is more time to think about responses and/or reactions.

There are also drawbacks to online interviewing. Similarly to working with focus groups online, the Internet interviewer cannot capture the non-verbal cues of interviewees that often are important indicators of opinions and attitudes. Furthermore, the researcher is restricted in his/her interpersonal skills that are often vital to eliciting important information during the course of an interview.

More generally, a disadvantage of online interviewing for the social researcher is that the researcher cannot be sure that the interviewee is who he/she claims to be. This anonymity at the same time, however, can help procure a good interview, as the interviewee may be more open since she/he is not face-to-face with the interviewer. However, if confronted with a question that they would rather not answer or if they become uninterested or bored with the interview, online interviewees can break off contact at any time.

The anonymity of the Internet also intensifies some ethical problems for the researcher. An online researcher could be tempted to become an academic version of an Internet 'predator'; for instance, 'lurking' within a chatroom, eavesdropping on participants' virtual conversations without their knowledge, or carrying on an e-mail conversation without informing the other party that they are being exploited as a research subject.

Conclusion

Overall, the Internet does have a role within social research, albeit a rather tentative one for the reasons highlighted above. It has become a truly massive communication medium and the fact it is projected that there will be over 490 million users by the end of 2002 cannot go unnoticed. New electronic technologies will no doubt progress and emerge in the twenty-first century and this will invariably have implications for the facilitation of social research online. In the meantime however, the social researcher should be cautious about the use of the Internet for the application of social enquiry and be aware of its limitations, as well, of course, as its potential advantages. Like any other method of carrying out social research, there are both benefits and drawbacks involved with carrying out research online. Ultimately, the suitability of online research methods will be determined by the particular research aims and objectives and/or the resources available to the researcher.

See also **Focus groups** and **Internet**.

Suggested further reading

Hine, C. (2001) *Virtual Ethnography*. London: Sage.

CAROLINE MCAULEY

Paradigm

Paradigm, from the Greek 'paradigma', meaning pattern, is a theoretical structure or a framework of thought that acts as a template or example to be followed. Thomas Kuhn applied the term to a critique of scientific research practice. In *The Structure of Scientific Revolutions* (1962), he describes a paradigm as a set of scientific and metaphysical beliefs that make up a theoretical framework in which scientific theories can be tested, evaluated and, if necessary, revised. Additionally, a paradigm is 'an entire constellation of beliefs, values, techniques and so on, shared by a given [scientific] community' in which 'universally recognised scientific achievements . . . for a time provide model problems and solutions to a community of practitioners' (Kuhn, 1962: 175).

Kuhn argues that, contrary to a model of the slow refinement and accumulation of scientific knowledge, genuine dramatic progress takes place when the scientist steps out of the accepted paradigm and discovers something new. He also challenged the idea that a scientific community is disinterested and rational, and would therefore reject old theories in favour of new ones that fit with the facts.

Kuhn focused on the processes of historical change. Most disciplines have a dominant approach to research that has been developed as practitioners reach a consensus, and eliminate other alternative options – a paradigm. The 'routine problem solving' of 'normal science' occurs within a paradigm. Problems are solved, but only within this framework; the framework itself is not questioned. Eventually, some problems that are intractable within the framework become persistent and in turn challenge the validity of the paradigm. These anomalies can lead to a crisis. This can only be resolved by addressing the problems and creating a new framework. Then normal science continues within the new paradigm.

However, new paradigms are often met with hostility. There are no independent rational criteria for discriminating between competing scientific paradigms. The evidence of what counts as rational knowledge is dependent on the paradigm itself. A new paradigm does not build on past achievements and in fact it often rejects these. Hence, vested interests within a scientific discipline will resist their established positions being threatened. Rather than being supplanted by rational argument, a new paradigm gradually gains adherents amongst new scholars and those located outside the periphery of power. Eventually, through the attrition of mortality and almost a guerilla campaign of academic dispute, the new paradigm supplants the old. From this viewpoint, science appears as a series of peaceful interludes punctuated by intellectually violent revolutions.

Concerning the social sciences, Kuhn saw them as 'preparadigmatic' since no consensus has emerged and a collection of basic orientations are in fundamental dispute with each other. Other commentators have argued that the mutually incommensurate viewpoints of the social sciences are 'multiparadigmatic' (Ritzer, 1981).

Kuhn opened the way for new ways of thinking and did much to advance the cause of relativism although he himself was not a relativist. Foucault claimed that knowledge and power are inextricably linked. Some social theorists have attempted to use Kuhn's ideas alongside Foucault's ideas of discourse and discursive regime. Jean François Lyotard (1984), another postmodern writer, says that meta-narratives (grand theories) operate like Kuhnian paradigms and impose meanings on historical events rather than empirical exploration. Kuhn's idea of paradigms has been revolutionary and debate continues today on its validity as a paradigm itself.

Suggested further reading

Benton, T. and Craib, I. (2001) *Philosophy of Social Science.* Houndsmills, Basingstoke: Palgrave.

Snizek, W.E., Fuhrman, E.R. and Miller, M.K. (1979) *Contemporary Issues in Theory and Research: a Metasociological Perspective.* London: Aldwych Press.

References

Kuhn, Thomas S. (1962) *The Structure of Scientific Revolutions*. Chicago: University of Chicago Press.

Lyotard, Jean François (1984) *The Postmodern Condition: a Report on Knowledge.*

Ritzer, George (1981) *Toward an Integrated Sociological Paradigm.*

SANDRA BAILLIE AND ROBERT MILLER

Participant observation

Participant observation is at one level self-explanatory, in that it involves research-led observation of the social world while simultaneously participating in it. This observation can be done overtly or covertly. Sometimes a distinction is drawn between classic participant observation, where the researcher utilises a new and unfamiliar participative role from which to observe, and 'observant participation', where observation is done from a role the researcher already possesses and which is familiar and known. In the former case it is essential that researchers develop an insider status in order to come close to understanding the initially strange situation; in the latter, that they remain distant from taken-for-granted knowledge and cultural assumptions associated with the role and become relative strangers.

The key to the observation done with either kind of participation is that the data obtained from watching the phenomena under study are enhanced through introspection by the researcher who undergoes the same experiences, attitude changes and events as people under study. The balance of this data may therefore yield a richness of detail that other methods may not achieve. Introspection, however, is criticised as unscientific, and participation in the field under study ensures that the researcher is an intervening variable in the research. While unobtrusive observation, done purely by watching, may avoid the complications that arise from the researcher's own presence in the field, it relies on a more limited form of observational data.

Participant observation is associated with qualitative research, and particularly ethnography, although the latter is much broader and uses a range of other data collection techniques. The 'participant observer' field technique has been well established in social and cultural anthropology since Malinowski, where it has mostly been associated with studying pre-literate and pre-industrial societies. It has also been adopted as a method of research by sociologists in such fields as education, medicine, deviance and religion. It was the Chicago School of sociology at the beginning of the twentieth century that first used participant observation, amongst other methods, to study an urban environment.

One of the main justifications for this method of data collection is that there are everyday processes that cannot be studied in depth without the researcher being in close proximity to the individuals involved. The reactive effect associated with most kinds of social research gives added value to covert participant observation since co-participants are unaware that they are subjects of research and thus their behaviour is unaffected by knowledge of the research, although the researcher's presence still intervenes. This impulse to gain intimacy and closeness highlights the intellectual authority that participant observation gets from the methodological position known as naturalism. The second generation of Chicago sociologists, like Herbert Blumer, pioneered this methodological position in the mid-twentieth century and, together with the rebirth of interpretative sociology in the 1960s, brought to more prominence the necessity of gaining access to the world-view of individuals in different situations by means of participant observation. Participant observation therefore concentrates on research topics that expose the beliefs and social *meanings* held by individuals and groups. The intent is to 'be true to the things themselves'; to study the social world from 'the inside' and to offer 'thick descriptions' richly and deeply embedded in the setting under study.

Postmodernist notions of social research, which involve an attack on realism, challenge the view that it is ever possible to get close to 'the inside', because of all sorts of selection processes which filter out much of what is seen, or that there is a single 'reality' that can be faithfully captured by intimacy and closeness. The participant observer's view is seen as only one amongst a number of competing accounts. Under the impulse of postmodern deconstruction of the method, participant observers are now encouraged to capture the multiple voices in the field and to be reflexive in socially situating their own data to the time, location and people involved. Thus, while it is a common method of data collection, participant observation is also one of the most demanding on the researcher.

Researching a group whilst entering it from the outside offers up immediate problems with access as well as understanding. Researchers who become participant observers have to develop certain personal skills, primarily to balance the demands of their simultaneous 'insider' and 'outsider' status; to identify with the people under study and get close to them, while maintaining a professional distance which permits adequate observation and data collection. It is a fine balance. 'Going native' is a constant danger, wherein observers lose their critical faculties and become an ordinary member of the field; while remaining an 'outsider', cold and distant from people in the field, with professional identities preserved and no rapport, negates the method. Participant observers also need to be able to share in the lives and activities of other people; to learn their language and meanings, to remember actions and speech, and to interact with a range of individuals in different social situations. And where the observation is covert, the participant observer needs to be able to maintain the pretence and disguise in order not to reveal their surreptitious research. Time commitment is also necessary. The observer reflects on the experiences arising from sharing the same everyday features of life as those being studied and, in order to achieve this, the participant observation may require many months or years of intense work with the observer immersed in the culture under study. Of course, this is why observant participation is also popular, for in as much as the social world under study is known and familiar, there is no long period of socialisation and immersion necessary, although the problem here becomes one of establishing sufficient distance.

The most common objection to participant observation is its lack of objectivity. The participant observer is a member of the group under study whilst simultaneously reporter, interviewer and scientist all at once, requiring a level of sympathy with subjects whilst retaining a measure of detachment. Within this delicate balance participant observation may seem unstructured, too flexible and open-ended. Indeed documentation can be difficult and field notes may contain too much information on one area and too little on another. To balance this it is always hoped that intimacy and closeness glean data that is otherwise unobtainable. As Winch (1958) maintained, when the researcher has entered into the world of meanings which characterise a sub-culture and begun to understand members' activities on their own terms it is then not possible to engage in the analyses recommended by natural science. Just as a historian loves to read a new manuscript that no one else has seen before, the area of observation for social scientists opens up and offers the intimacy and privilege of studying people at first hand.

However, it is important not to claim more than the evidence will support. While this is true for all data collection techniques, the limits of participant observation make this especially true. The scope of a participant observer's observations is constrained by the physical limits of their role and location, which is normally one field site amongst a vast universe of other settings. From an unknown universe of events, the observer records only a small selection. The basis of this selection is often non-random and influenced by various conditions of a non-scientific kind. Lone observers are bound to be selective because of the impossibility of taking everything in, which is why multiple observers can sometimes be used. Lone observers are particularly susceptible to focusing on the abnormal, aberrant and exceptional. There is also the problem of personal perspective. Participant observation can only be a partial portrait of a way of life compiled from selective records, and is thus highly autobiographical. It is partial because it is one person's personalised view (or several people's personalised views), and because it is a vignette whose representativeness is unsure. Postmodern social researchers recognise that the participant observer's view is *a* view, and a view is sometimes better than no view, and there are occasions when there is no alternative to a period of participant observation, but it should never stand alone as a research method for these sorts of reasons.

Suggested further reading

Atkinson, Paul (1990) *The Ethnographic Imagination*. London: Routledge.
Brewer, John D. (2000) *Ethnography*. Buckingham: Open University Press.

Spradley, J.P. (1980) *Participant Observation*. Orlando, FL: Harcourt Brace and Janovich.

See also
Observation
and
Naturalism.

Reference

Winch, P. (1958) *The Idea of a Social Science*. London: Routledge.

LINDA THOMPSON AND JOHN BREWER

Participatory action research

Participatory action research considers itself to be a radical alternative to mainstream research. Its objective is to transcend the distinctions between activism and research, common sense understanding and academic expertise. Participatory action research has a double objective; it aims to produce knowledge and action directly useful to people, and also to empower people through the process of constructing and using their own knowledge. Participatory action research is reminiscent of liberation theology in the way that it addresses issues of power and powerlessness. While it is used in the western world, it is an approach to research that identifies itself primarily with the developing world. It views itself as a more holistic, pluralist and egalitarian approach to research, based upon the active involvement of 'participants' rather than the exploitation of research 'subjects'. The commitment to participation means that considerable emphasis is given to the process of research as well as to its outcomes. Participants are engaged in the research process actively, and the research aims to provide tools for the improvement of the lives of participants. Participatory action research is committed to honouring and valuing the knowledge and experience of people, usually oppressed people (Reason, 1994). It is believed that attending to and valuing popular knowledge advances scientific knowledge.

Participatory action research identifies itself with Habermas' (1972) articulation of the need for a critical science which serves emancipatory interests. It represents a rejection of positivism and holds a deep-seated aversion to empiricism, which suggests only neutral 'experience' can provide an acceptable foundation for valid knowledge. In addition, it rejects what Habermas calls the 'objectivist illusion' of pure theory. Habermas argues that knowledge, methodology and human interests are inextricably linked (1972); a position taken by participatory action researchers (Carr, 1994). They also utilise Habermas' argument that empirical-analytic research and interpretative research unintentionally establish a hierarchical relationship between researcher and researched because they do not have an explicit politics. Instead, participatory action research aims to dismantle an academic monopoly on the definition and employment of knowledge, arguing that 'democracy in knowledge production gives the participants a stake in the quality of the results, increasing the reliability of information and the likelihood that results will be put into practice' (Greenwood et al., 1993). Dialogue and reflexivity are central to participatory action research. Through dialogue the subject–object relationship of traditional science gives way to a subject–subject one, in which the academic knowledge of formally educated people works in a dialectical tension with the popular knowledge of the people to produce a more profound understanding of the situation. Reflexivity furthers the reunification of theory and practice as, on the one hand, researchers reflect on and examine their assumptions and methods following dialogue with popular knowledge and, on the other hand, participants reflect on and examine the value of knowledge generated for their everyday lives.

Reason, a prominent participatory action researcher, has noted that it is far easier to discover the ideology of this approach rather than a detailed description of how it actually works (Reason, 1994). He suggests that participatory action research is a methodology for an alternative system of knowledge production based on 'the people's' role in setting agendas, participating in data gathering and analysis, and controlling the use of outcomes (1994: 329). In theory, participatory action research can use diverse methods, both quantitative and qualitative, but in practice, it is primarily qualitative research methods that are used. Information is usually collected by participant observation, interviews, compilation of field notes and document analysis. In keeping with the commitment to value popular knowledge, vernacular, usually oral, traditions of communication and dissemination of knowledge are used. The emphasis on inquiry as empowerment means that for participatory action researchers; 'the methodologies that in orthodox research would be called research design, data gathering, data analysis and so on are secondary to the emergent processes of collaboration and dialogue that empower, motivate, increase self-esteem and develop community solidarity' (Reason, 1994: 329). Community meetings and events are an important part of participatory action research. These events are seen as a way of reclaiming a sense of solidarity, making sense of information collected, and developing the skills of the community. Storytelling, sociodrama, plays and songs are used to encourage communities to engage with and contribute to the research.

Criticisms

The literature on participatory action research tends to be written in an ideological and romantic tone. So, for example, it is claimed that: 'Those who adopt participatory action research have tried to practice with a radical commitment that has gone beyond usual institutional boundaries, reminiscent of the challenging tradition of Chartists, utopians, and other social movements of the nineteenth century' (Fals-Borda and Rahman, 1991: vii). Unfortunately, while participatory action research provides an attractive ideological alternative to traditional research approaches that tend to objectify their research subjects, it has yet to develop a concomitant epistemological basis. Its tendency to focus almost exclusively on specific cases has left it open to the claim that its findings are specific and do not lead to defensible generalisation. Participatory action research raises pivotal questions about the relationship between theory and action. However, as a form of research, it is argued that it relies more on ideological justification than theoretical and methodological sophistication.

The extent to which participants who are unfamiliar with the basic techniques of research can be involved in the research has been questioned. The involvement of untrained participants has led to charges of it being unsophisticated research, practised (and not very well) by amateurs. The most serious criticism of participatory action research, which attacks its ideological base, argues that it presents a naïve understanding of power and powerlessness, and processes of empowerment. While the objective is to include and empower participants through the research, it remains the case that the research question is formulated by the researcher, rather than the participants approaching the researchers with a particular social problem. More seriously, critics assert that participatory action research pays little attention to the macro-economic, social and political structures of society. The notion of empowerment is limited to the particular case in hand. This weakness is sometimes acknowledged, and sometimes, rather weakly, defended:

> Does this assume that all problems of society can be solved by applied social research, without major changes in the macro-economic and social structure of society? Not at all. In principle, I am not opposed to such major changes – including revolutions – but I can only imagine how changes of so drastic a nature may come about. Meanwhile, I find it useful scientifically and practically to study what can be done here and now under the existing social and economic conditions. (Whyte, 1986: 562)

Suggested further reading

Truman, Carole, Mertens, Donna M. and Humphries, Beth (eds) (2000) *Research and Inequality*. London: UCL Press.

References

Carr, W. (1994) 'Whatever Happened to Action Research?', *Educational Action Research*, 2 (3): 427–37.

Fals-Borda, O. and Rahman, M. (eds) (1991) *Action and Knowledge: Breaking the Monopoly with Participatory Action Research*. New York: Intermediate Technology/Apex.

Greenwood D., Whyte, W.F. and Harkavy, I. (1993) 'Participatory Action Research as a Process and as a Goal'. Special Issue on Action Research, *Human Relations*, 46 (2): 177–89.

Habermas, J. (1972) *Knowledge and Human Interests: Theory and Practice; Communication and the Evolution of Society*, J.J. Shapiro, trans. London: Heinemann.

Reason, P. (1994) 'Three Approaches to Participative Inquiry', in N. Denzin and Y. Lincoln (eds), *Handbook of Qualitative Research*. Thousand Oaks, CA: Sage Publications. pp. 324–40.

Whyte, W.F. (1986) 'On the Uses of Social Science Research', *American Sociological Review*, 51: 555–63.

See also **Action research** and **Policy research**.

SALLY SHORTALL

Phenomenology

In the words of Edmund Husserl (1859–1938), the German philosopher who founded phenomenology as a new method of inquiry, we must be true to the nature of phenomena themselves, free of preconceptions and prior assumptions. Phenomenology is about bracketing off preconceived ideas about phenomena, through a process called phenomenological reduction, in order to achieve a state of pure knowledge and understanding uncontaminated by a priori beliefs. As such it is easy to see the attraction of phenomenology in the post-empiricist, post-positivist climate of the 1960s, when Hermino Martins argued there was a 'cognitivist revolution' in the social sciences. Once freed from the constraints of natural science models of social research with the attack on positivism, the focus shifted to issues like people's cognition, perceptions, beliefs, interpretations and social meanings (a tradition also known as interpretative sociology or hermeneutics). The social science focus on subjectivity fitted the cultural ethos of the time, with the decade of the 1960s seeing a burgeoning of similar traditions, such as existential sociology and ethnomethodology. Ernest Gellner abused the latter as a particularly Californian style of subjectivity, parodying San Francisco as the centre of the hippie culture and the search for new subjective experiences (through 'free love' and psychedelic drugs mostly).

Despite this fit of time and ideas, the cognitivist revolution in the social sciences mostly drew on ideas formulated decades before. This is particularly true of phenomenology. Edmund Husserl was far removed in time and ethos from the cultural climate that made his ideas popular in the 1960s and, at first sight, his writings seem also removed from usual social scientific inquiry. Like most German philosophers, Husserl was really debating with the ghost of Kant, and was interested in basic philosophical problems about what is real and how it is possible to know what exists. He was thus interested in the nature of knowledge and this led him into studying the nature of consciousness. Husserl argued that human beings know about the world only through experience and all our understandings of the world are thereby mediated through the senses as we interpret them in the human mind or what he called consciousness. People live in a taken-for-granted 'life world' (*Lebenswelt*), in which they use familiar and ordinary ideas, beliefs and knowledge to understand the world. This must be bracketed off in order to understand the true essence of the phenomena. At this point one reaches 'pure consciousness' in which one suspends the substance of one's ordinary understandings and leaves behind what Schutz later called 'practical consciousness'.

These ideas entered social science through the work of one of Husserl's disciples, Alfred Schutz (1899–1959), and it is Schutz's writings that primarily impacted on the cognitivist revolution in the 1960s through interpreters like Berger and Luckmann, whose book *The Social Construction of Reality* in 1966 first popularised phenomenology.[1] Schutz fled Nazi persecution and moved to New York in 1939, where he combined his work as a social philosopher with merchant banking. His main work on phenomenological sociology was written much earlier however. His *Phenomenology of the Social World* was published in 1932 and reprinted at the height of the cognitivist revolution in 1967. Schutz tried to combine the phenomenology of Husserl with the sociology of Weber in a radical programme that Gorman called Schutz's 'dual vision'. From Husserl he took the focus on individual subjectivity, from Weber the requirement to develop an 'objective' social science understanding of social meanings. This required a departure from both and critics see him falling between two stools.

If it could be said that Marx turned his mentor Hegel on his head, so too did Schutz with respect to Husserl, for Schutz was interested in exploring the very thing that Husserl thought secondary, the nature of common sense knowledge in the everyday life world. Schutz rejected the attention on pure consciousness and turned the focus on the sociological dynamics of people's taken-for-granted 'natural attitude' in the life world. He placed emphasis, like Weber, on general social patterns of action and meaning, looking at the regularities in social meaning that permitted the development of a regularising and 'objective' social science. Schutz has unkindly been referred to as a one point man, that *idée fixe* being the nature and use of common sense knowledge. Reality for people – their natural attitude towards the external world – consists of their common sense stock of knowledge; it is their paramount reality, the form of knowledge they draw on first to make sense of the world. It is not scientific knowledge but common sense knowledge that people use in the first instance to understand the external world. Common sense knowledge comprises the taken-for-granted assumptions, beliefs, ideas and interpretations socially disseminated and prevalent in their everyday life. Since this life world is shared, this knowledge is both common and it makes sense. We assume others share our understandings and social meanings and as we develop evidence of them acting and believing in ways we expect, so the social world comes to develop what Schutz called a 'standardised sameness'. It becomes seen as a 'factual reality', existing as an objective reality in our *sense* that there is an external social world beyond us; later ethnomethodologists called this people's sense of social structure. People thus appear to 'know' and 'understand' in the same way, to act socially in expected ways, and appear to form part of a broader social collectivity that we become aware of through the deployment of common sense knowledge. People therefore develop regularities of social meaning and social action that permitted Schutz, like Weber, to focus on general features rather than each individual's personal social action and social meanings. It is not sub-jectivity that is important to them both but intersubjectivity, the maintenance of a common world amongst different interacting individuals. Schutz, if you like, was dealing with the same problem that dominated American sociology at this time, particularly in the writings of Talcott Parsons, of how social order was possible in society. But he finds the solution not in the dominance of cultural values over individual action and meaning, as did Parsons, but in the development of common sense knowledge routinely used by us all to act and think which gives a standard-ised sameness to the social world and leaves us all with the impression that the world exists beyond us as a constraining influence. The social world is real but only in our sense that it is real.

Like Husserl before him however, Schutz remained at the abstract level and did not develop a programme of research to operationalise these ideas; Weber often undertook substantive studies, giving us classics like *The Protestant Ethic and the Spirit of Capitalism*. Besides his work on 'the stranger' and 'the homecomer', people divorced or separated from common sense knowledge and thus out of place in thought, behaviour and meanings, Schutz was like Parsons in remaining a theorist. Nonetheless, social phenomenology has been important to social research in several ways. In a general way, these ideas formed part of the critique of empiricist and positivist models of social research for neglecting people's inter-pretative and cognitivist abilities. They also gave validity and authority to the arguments of qualitative researchers that if social science wants to understand the social world it must, in part if not in whole, understand the way that world is understood by ordinary people. In more specific ways, these ideas shaped later interpretative approaches that were more empirically oriented. For example Kenneth Leiter (1980) stresses the influence of Schutz on Garfinkel's development of ethnomethodology and its programme of research, and subsequent writers have drawn attention to the development of a wide number of empirical studies that they label 'ethnomethodological ethnographies' (Travers, 2001). Conversation analysis, for example, is rooted firmly in Schutz's idea that taken-for-granted common sense knowledge is used routinely in social behaviour, in this case the social organisation of conversation. While it is a backdrop to many other kinds of study, social phenomenology lends itself more directly to empirical social research within the qualitative tradition. There have been several studies that have intended to implement Schutz's ideas and they have supported qualitative studies of the social meanings and common sense knowledge surrounding many and varied social topics. These include studies of the membership of the British Union of Fascists, the educational under-achievement of West Indian youths, and the development of racism in Britain, amongst many others.

Note

1 An equivalent book in Britain in 1972 was Filmer, Philipson, Silverman and Walsh's *New Directions in Sociological Theory*.

Suggested further reading

Berger, Peter and Luckmann, Thomas (1966) *The Social Construction of Reality*. New York: Doubleday.

Brewer, John (1984) 'Looking Back at Fascism: a Phenomenological Analysis of BUF Membership', *Sociological Review*, 32: 742–70.

Brewer, John (1984) 'Competing Understandings of Common Sense Understanding: a Brief Comment on "common sense racism"', *British Journal of Sociology*, 35: 66–74.

Gorman, Robert (1976) *The Dual Vision*. London: Routledge and Kegan Paul.

References

Leiter, Kenneth (1980) *A Primer on Ethnomethodology*. Oxford: Oxford University Press.

Travers, Max (2001) *Qualitative Research Through Case Studies*. London: Sage.

JOHN BREWER

Philosophy of social research

The philosophy of science is an ancient sub-discipline that has addressed very broad-ranging issues about the nature of knowledge, known as epistemology, as well as concerns like the nature of causality, logic and understanding. The philosophy of the social sciences applies these concerns to the nature of social scientific knowledge, and explores the special considerations concerning the nature of proof, evidence, causality and understanding in knowledge about social life. Recognising some of the special features of the disciplines in this area, the philosophy of the social sciences concerns itself in addition with issues like the place of values in knowledge, ethics and the nature of human motivation. Two of its central preoccupations are the desirability of applying natural science models of research to the study of social life and the related question of the possibility of value freedom within the social sciences.

The philosophy of social research is a more recent development, and was first used as a term in the title of a book written by John Hughes in 1980. It describes the application to social research practice of the same philosophical concerns with the nature of knowledge. There is thus some synergy with the more ancient field. In the philosophy of social research, research practice is deconstructed and attention focused on how social researchers make evidential claims, present 'facts', interpret the data and engage in all those other practices that make up the process of social research. As such the approach slots easily into its time, the post-1960s attack on positivism and the emergence of post-structuralist social theories, like postmodernism, that tended to deconstruct all shibboleths, intellectual or otherwise. Its central argument is that all social research is partisan in that it is conceived and conducted within philosophical and theoretical frameworks that validate and give authority to its practice. Thus, it is possible to define the philosophy of social research as the study of the theories of knowledge which validate particular research practices. In his explication of the philosophy of social research, Hughes outlined two models of social research, which were premised on two different theoretical positions, the natural science model based on positivism and the humanistic model based on naturalism. These were counterpoised as mutually exclusive (indeed, as if they were in a 'paradigm war') and set up almost as ideal types. Nonetheless, the different research practices associated with these models were located in terms of the contrasting theories of knowledge and general philosophical ideas within the two positions of positivism and naturalism.

These methodological positions involve the researcher in commitments whether or not they are aware of it, for they entail assumptions about the nature of society (*'ontological'* assumptions) and assumptions about the nature of knowledge (*'epistemological'* assumptions). These methodological positions can also entail different sorts of research practices, since they predispose the use of different data collection techniques. Positivism in social research is associated with questionnaires, social surveys and experimental design, while naturalism favours ethnography, unstructured interviews and other qualitative techniques. They thus end up producing quite different kinds of data; the one 'hard', numerate and statistical, the other 'soft', rich and taking the form of extracts of natural language. The philosophy of social research is thus a useful way to understand the differences in research practice between styles of social research.

Rooting these differences in theories of knowledge, however, is problematic. The most contentious claim in this argument is not that research methods get their authority and legitimacy from particular theories of knowledge, but that researchers choose the data collection techniques to employ in any piece of research because of a prior commitment to this methodological position rather than out of practical expediency. Early notions of social research tended to portray research tools as neutral techniques, the choice between them being determined by the problem at hand, which is why earlier research method textbooks tended to list the respective advantages and disadvantages of a series of techniques so as better to choose the right one for the topic. Post-structuralist deconstruction changed that. One kind of deconstruction is that proffered by the philosophy of social research when Hughes argues that research practice derives from methodological preferences.

It is possible to envisage that this preference can be scientifically based – in that researchers believe one methodology and its related set of methods and techniques to be more scientific than another – or it can be subjective and personal. The researcher may lack the competence to understand and apply one or other technique: since we cannot all count or some people are frightened by computers or do not like talking to people, we avoid those methods that involve our short-comings. According to Hughes, however, these biases arise from our preference for particular theories of knowledge and we end up by design engaging in the social research practices associated with that philosophical framework. These practices range from formulation of the research problem, development of the research design, the use of particular data collection techniques and the types of analysis and interpretation used, to ways of presenting the results. Some of the impli-cations that follow from this argument are worth highlighting. In this view, the data collection methods used to make the social world amenable are not neutral tools that somehow exist within a vacuum, but operate within a given methodo-logical position. Since methodologies lay down the procedures by which reliable and objective knowledge is said to be obtained, the choice of data collection technique is not dictated by the problem at hand, but largely by prior preferences in the researcher for a given methodological position with which those techniques or rules are associated. Differences in the kinds of data produced, between 'hard' numerate data and data that comprise extracts of natural language, have to be located in methodological choices by the researcher rather than decisions about the problem at hand. When there are competing methodological positions vali-dating different rules or methods for collecting data, there is no consensus about the value or merit of particular research methods and the use of particular methods is a source of contention.

This has important implications for the debate about combining qualitative and quantitative methods in the one research design. At a technical level it may be desirable, even necessary, to use triangulation of methods, but at an ontological and epistemological level, this can result in marrying incompatible methodological positions. The choice of whether or not to use quantitative and qualitative methods thus depends on whether technical expediency is a higher priority than methodological purity. Methodological pluralism, it has to be said, is not often the option chosen and while researchers railed against the heuristic construction of a mutually exclusive binary divide, this does describe the practice of many people.

Suggested further reading

Ackroyd, S. and Hughes, J.A. (1981) *Data Collection in Context*. London: Longman.

Brewer, J.D. (2000) *Ethnography*. Buckingham: Open University Press.

Hughes, J.A. (1990) *The Philosophy of Social Research*, 2nd edn. London: Longman.

See also
Methodology.

JOHN BREWER

Policy research

Within social scientific research a distinction is often made between theoretical research ('pure') and policy research ('applied'). Broadly speaking, theoretical research aims to enhance an academic social science discipline's understanding of the world while the concerns of policy research are principally with knowledge for action and with the practical application of research. That is, policy research is *applied* research intended to inform or to effect changes in social policy. Further- more, while academic 'ivy-tower' research often holds up the neutrality of the researcher as an ideal, in contrast, policy research is not value-free. Social policies are intended to realise valued goals and, hence, the results of all policy research can be interpreted in terms of being 'good' or 'bad'; that is, whether the research finds that the positive goals of a social policy are being met. As such, policy research deals with actionable social factors and often makes recommendations for action to be taken. Finally, policy research, by its nature, is multi-disciplinary in its approach in contrast to theoretical research whose principal audience tends toward aca- demics within each single discipline.

As policy research is rarely grounded in a single discipline it can examine a problem or issue using a variety of social scientific perspectives – 'hybrid' fields such as social policy draw on sociology, political science, psychology, law and economics. Policy research addresses itself to those involved in making and implementing policy and those campaigning for policy change – that is, those with a direct and immediate stake in the results of the research. Both theoretical and policy research can be carried out by researchers based inside universities, but policy research is also undertaken outside the 'ivy tower' either by policy-making bodies and government or by consultants or commercial firms working on a com- mercial basis. Though there are are distinctions between theoretical and policy research, the similarities and overlaps between them are substantial. Thus, theor- etical research may draw out the practical, policy implications of research, while policy research approaches are informed by theoretical insights.

Policy research includes the analysis of causation and consequences. That is, it may focus on whether a particular antecedant is a necessary or sufficient cause of a known behaviour, attitude or other social phenomenon or it may focus on the effects of a given social phenomenon (Hakim, 1987). Policy research may vary in the extent to which it seeks to apply a theoretical or analytical framework to data collection and analysis. It uses a variety of methods – both quantitative and qualitative – to obtain a balanced picture on any topic. It is strongly evidence- based; both gathering *primary data* and analysing *secondary data*, and making use of social statistics. Policy research favours representative samples because of the policy implications and the intense public interest in the findings.

The range of policy research includes whole welfare systems or particular elements of them: the measurement or evaluation of a new or existing policy, programme or project at the level of inputs, outputs and outcomes; description and analysis of best practice (either in the home country or abroad) and the policy lessons to be learned from it; projections on the basis of modelling techniques; large-scale experimental research in real-life settings. Policy research is funded by research councils and foundations, by governments, and by non-governmental agencies such as charities, community groups and trades unions which are interested in effecting changes to (usually government) policy and/or practice to the benefit of particular groups or to society as a whole. Comparative cross-national policy research is increasingly favoured by governments and international governmental organisations such as the EU and OECD. Governments favour this type of policy research because they are interested in learning about what goes on in other countries, whether these policies are effective and, if so, whether there are any policy lessons that can then be applied domestically.

Policy research is related to a number of other types of research. It is related to *advocacy research* in that it seeks to provide a catalyst to the development of policy proposals by measuring social problems and generating greater public awareness of them. Like *action research*, it also seeks to steer the course of social (policy) action and measure the effects or consequences of this. Policy research is also closely related to *evaluation research* as both are commissioned particularly by governments and other bodies disbursing public funds to ensure accountability in the use of these funds, i.e. to ensure that resources invested in the programme represent best value for money, and that appropriate policy lessons are learnt from the research.

Although publicly funded policy research may provide an 'inside track' to government resources that permits access to statistics and people which may not otherwise be accessible or publicly available and provide resources to undertake more expensive research, this is not without costs. The source of funding for policy research has implications for research ethics, particularly if the research seeks direct access to past, current or potential users of welfare services who may be vulnerable. There may be conflicting interests between the policy researcher and the funder/customer. This may particularly be the case for policy research undertaken in the commercial sector as consultancy work. For example, the findings of policy research may reveal the ineffectiveness or incompetence of a funder's own policy or programme. While findings may not end up being falsified deliberately, they easily can be distorted through selective citation or the report may be 'shelved', not published or circulated only to a restricted internal audience. Because of the close relationship between policy researchers and their customers, policy research, particularly that which is undertaken commercially, may be accused of being biased in favour of the funding body's interests. The task for policy research is to ensure that the range of potentially conflicting interests, or stakeholders (that is, those with an interest in policy decisions) are represented to avoid the allegation that it is partial or biased. Hence, while the source of funding – whether for theoretical or policy research – has implications for who has ultimate responsibility for, and control over, a project's design and its findings, this is particularly acute in the case of policy research. This is because the political motives and interests of the funders may be more directly affected. Whenever the interests of individuals or institutions are likely to be affected for good or ill by research findings, the research can be said to have a *political* dimension. When research findings are debated in a polticised context, issues to do with the type of research and evidence that are most likely to carry conviction may not be just those of an impartial disinterested consideration of the worth of the findings. Instead, questions of academic veracity may be eclipsed by the power of interests to impose their own gloss upon the results. Hence, it is important to remember that no policy research is ever going to be totally free from the assumptions and values that the individual researcher, or indeed the individual funder, brings to a project.

Suggested further reading

Bulmer, Martin (ed.) (1978) *Social Policy Research*. London: Macmillan.

Reference

Hakim, Catherine (1987) *Research Design: Strategies and Choices in the Design of Social Research*. Unwin Hyman: London.

NICOLA YEATES

See also **Action research** and **Action research, participatory**.

Positivism

Positivism subscribes to the application of natural science methods and practice to the social sciences, a position sometimes also confusingly called naturalism, which usually describes the complete opposite position (notably Bhasker and Giddens mistakenly use it this way). Positivism is a greatly used and abused term, traversing several disciplines and sets of literature, such as the philosophy of social science, sociological theory and the research methodology literature. At one time positivism was the orthodoxy in mainstream social science and the principal understanding of how social science research should be undertaken, although by the 1960s it had become a derogatory term as a result of sustained attack by philosophers of science, such as Thomas Kuhn (*The Structure of Scientific Revolutions*) and Karl Popper (*The Poverty of Historicism, The Logic of Scientific Discovery* and *Conjectures and Refutations*). Their attack was enthusiastically taken up by social scientists in the 1960s and later, especially by sociologists, who criticised natural science models of social research and who advocated more humanistic models of social research. This critique showed itself in attacks on particular methods associated with the positivist orthodoxy, such as official *social statistics* and *questionnaires*, and advocacy for new approaches and methods.

Positivism began as a body of social theory that originated with the French sociologist Auguste Comte in the nineteenth century, where it was used it to describe the application of science to study society rather than metaphysical or theological speculation. Another intellectual pillar is the 'Vienna Circle' of philosophers of science at the beginning of the twentieth century that rooted science in empirical observation rather than speculation. Comte has shaped sociological theory but not social research practice, but the Vienna Circle found a route into the social research literature through the philosophers of social science who adopted their ideas, such as Nagel (1961) and Hempel (1966). They used the term 'logical positivism' to describe an approach to social research that has come to be called abstract empiricism. The meaning of the term has undergone further revision. In the social research literature, through key figures within the philosophy of social science and the philosophy of social research, positivism has now come to refer to a methodological position, the essential attributes of which are summed up in the word 'positive', which in the English language conjures up an image of 'certainty', 'precision' and 'objectivity'.

The principal characteristic of this methodology is the contention that the methods, concepts and procedural rules of the natural sciences can and should be applied to the study of social life. This involves ontological assumptions about the nature of society, for social life is perceived to comprise objective structures independent of the people concerned, and to consist of wholes and systems which go beyond the consciousness of individuals. There is thus a 'real world' out there independent of people's perceptions of it: the social world is revealed to us, not constructed by us. For this reason positivism and realism are sometimes used, mistakenly, as interchangeable terms. It follows from this ontology that objective knowledge is possible, for there is a fixed and unchanging reality which research can accurately access and tap. There is thus also an epistemology inherent in positivism. Further epistemological assumptions follow: knowledge of social life can reveal only that which is externally observable through the senses, and positivism can disclose the causal relationships that exist within social life. From this follows the epistemological assumption that it is possible and desirable to develop law-like statements about the social world by means of *deductive analysis*, where vocabulary is used like the 'hypothetico-deductive method' and 'nomological-deductive explanations'. These phrases essentially mean the deduction of general statements from a theory or law, from which hypotheses are formed, which are then tested against prediction and observation.

Three beliefs thus characterise positivism: that the social sciences address problems similar to those of the natural sciences; that the social sciences should search for social causation when explaining human activity and aspire to deductive explanations; and that they should deal with systems and wholes. The best example remains Durkheim's theory of suicide developed in 1905, well before the heyday of positivism in social research later in the twentieth century. His general statement was that suicide varied inversely with the degree to which individuals were integrated with the group. From this he deduced less general statements, to the effect, for example, that Catholics have lower suicide rates than Protestants because Catholicism is a more communal religion and integrates believers into a more collective group. Factual statements could be deduced from this which could be tested against prediction and observation, to the effect that the suicide rate will be lower, for example, in Catholic countries than Protestant ones. Suicide statistics for Italy compared to those for Holland could then confirm or refute the original general law-like statement. It is the original law-like general statement or theory that provides the explanation, below which comes descriptive data that are revealed through sense-experience observation. Confirmation or refutation cannot be achieved by data revealed through people's interpretative or meaning-endowing capacities (by studying, say, the meanings of suicides as revealed in their suicide notes) but only data revealed externally through the way the world is observed and experienced via our senses (in this case 'objective', official statistics).

Data for the positivist model of social research is thus called 'hard', wishing to imply that it is untainted by the interpretative and meaning-endowing processes of people, whether these people are the subjects of the research or the researchers themselves. And such data is numerate, seeking to measure and describe social phenomena by the attribution of numbers. This gives an elective affinity, as Weber would say, between the natural science model of social research and those data collection techniques which give best access to sense-experience data, notably questionnaires, social surveys and experiments. Positivism believes the world to be an external, knowable entity, existing 'out there' independent of what people believe or perceive it to be. In a world made known to us through our sense experience, people contribute very little to knowledge in this way, simply receiving the sensory stimuli and recounting the response. Questionnaires and surveys are exemplary at doing this. They collect numerate data that supposedly render social phenomena 'objective' and untouched by people's interpretative and reality-constructing capacities. Hence, for example, textbooks identify the procedural rules for, say, constructing and applying a standardised interview schedule (advice on prompting and probing by means of standardised phrases to be used by the interviewer, the elimination of the *'interviewer effect'*, and practices to standardise the instrument), the following of which supposedly allows researchers to eliminate personal and interpersonal variables that distort what is seen as a direct relationship between stimulus (the question) and response (the answer). Since the stimulus takes the same form for everyone, if respondents give different responses the differences are assumed to be 'real' not artificially created by variations in the way the question was asked. The data thus become 'real', 'hard' and 'objective' since they are seen as untainted by the personal considerations of the interviewer or the respondent. Positivism, however, is the orthodoxy no longer and research models based on naturalism vie in importance and significance.

Suggested further reading

Bhasker, Roy (1993) *The Possibility of Naturalism*. Hemel Hempstead: Harvester.

Giddens, Anthony (1974) *Positivism and Sociology*. London: Heinemann.

Hughes, J.A. (1990) *The Philosophy of Social Research*, 2nd edn. London: Longman.

References

Hempel, K (1966) *Philosophy of Natural Science*. Prentice-Hall.

Nagel, E (1961) *The Structure of Science*. Hackett Publishing Co.

JOHN BREWER

Primary data

See **Secondary data analysis**.

Post-modernism

See **Modernity**.

Qualitative

See **Methodology**.

Qualitative research

Qualitative research goes under several sobriquets, such as the humanistic model of social research, unobtrusive methods and ethnographic approaches. 'Qualitative research' is the preferred term for most people. It is a term used to describe an approach to research than stresses 'quality' not 'quantity', that is, social meanings rather than the collection of numerate statistical data. For example, qualitative research might explore how an individual who voted for the Green Party in the United Kingdom sees themselves as a member of a minority party dealing with environmental issues rather than, say, exploring overall voting trends over time for the Green Party and other minority parties within Britain's two-party system. It is normally contrasted with quantitative research, an approach to research that stresses the reverse dimension. For example, if one wanted to explore what being vegetarian means to someone, the focus would be on the social meanings around organic food use and animal welfare and so on, resulting in the use of qualitative research. If one wanted to know how many people in an area were vegetarian, and perhaps voted for the Green Party as well, one would use a questionnaire and social survey to generate numerate data. Both kinds of data are valuable for their respective purposes.

However, the focus on social meanings through the use of qualitative research is often seen as less reliable than numerate data given the preference of governments, civil servants, policy makers and other users of research for 'hard facts'. Popular culture also gives status and authority to numbers, with meanings appearing ephemeral and elusive. Qualitative research accordingly struggles for legitimacy compared to quantitative research. Nonetheless, qualitative research is premised on important philosophical ideas concerning human nature, society and the nature of knowledge associated with the methodological position of naturalism. In naturalism people are seen as 'meaning endowing' and discursive, such that they have the capacity to endow the world with meaning and are able to articulate these meanings when asked. Society is seen in part as composed of people's perceptions of the social world, which means that knowledge of the social world is incomplete unless we also understand people's social meanings. These ideas have been well established by the German *Geisteswissenschaften* tradition and the American pragmatic philosophy of people like John Dewey and George Herbert Mead. Thus, qualitative research can draw on philosophical ideas in phenomenology, symbolic interactionism, hermeneutics and other traditions to support the attention on 'quality' rather than 'quantity'. Qualitative research is also closely associated with a variety of data collection techniques that have a long history of use and which over the years have developed authority and reputation. These include techniques like ethnography, unstructured interviewing, participant observation, discourse analysis and vignettes that give privileged access to people's social meanings. These methods gather data that is said to be 'soft', 'rich' and 'deep' and which comprises extracts of natural language, such as verbatim transcripts of interview material and extracts from texts, discourse, personal documents, field notebooks and the like.

Summary statements of the nature of qualitative research tend to mention some or all of the above features. For example, Alan Bryman (2001: 264) writes that three characteristics are noteworthy of the qualitative tradition: an inductive view of the relationship between theory and research in which theory is built up from the bottom through the data themselves; an epistemological position which sees knowledge as obtained through understanding how the social world is interpreted by its participants; and an ontological position which sees social phenomena as outcomes of the interactions of people. Martyn Hammersley (1992: 160–72) describes five essential traits of qualitative research: data come in the form of words and images rather than numbers; these are naturally occurring data rather than artificial experimental data; the focus is on meanings that document the world from the point of view of those under study; natural science models of social research are rejected; and induction is used in data analysis and theory generation. Both are good basic statements of what Clive Seale calls the quality of qualitative research (1999).

There is very little limit on the range of topics which qualitative research can be used to study, so long as they can be rendered in terms of the social meanings, perceptions and beliefs of participants and others involved in, or implicated by, the topic. However, consideration of the surrounding social meanings is not always necessarily the most important question to ask about the topic. Thus while virtually all topics can be defined in terms that make qualitative research possible, it is not always appropriate to do so. It is therefore rare today for qualitative researchers to argue against the desirability of approaching some topics through the collection of numerate data. What limit there is on the scope and scale of qualitative research is imposed by the data collection techniques used – some, like ethnography, are very restricted by the nature of the method itself – but qualitative research tends to sacrifice breadth of scope and scale for richness and depth because of the techniques used in the research.

The contrast between data that is 'soft' versus 'hard', 'flexible' or 'fixed', 'deep' or 'broad', 'rich' versus 'abstract' tended to be the terms used to place qualitative and quantitative research in opposition to each other. Qualitative research was normally contrasted in simple heuristic, ideal type terms with quantitative research with respect to methods of data collection, the type of data collected, the breadth and geographical coverage of the data, the forms of data analysis and the kind of evidential claims made. In the immediate post-positivist climate of the 1960s it was fashionable to opt for either qualitative or quantitative research and to denounce the other. Later it became common to argue for combining the two in a triangulation of method and methodology. The use of multiple methods was strongly urged as a technical expediency irrespective of the arguments in the philosophy of social research that suggested an incompatibility of philosophical positions between the two styles of research. It is now more in vogue to decon-struct the contrast and show that 'quality' and 'quantity' presuppose each other. At one level, 'numbers' and 'meaning' are interrelated at all levels, often requiring each other or being implicit in each other. Elementary forms of enumeration (such as counting) depend on the meanings of the unit reckoned together (we need a concept 'apple' whose meaning is understood before we can count them), and social meanings are often better understood when articulated in relation to the number of observations referred to or the number of the experiences they describe. It sets a poor example in qualitative research to use phrases like 'many people believe this' or 'most people said this' as a measure of proportion without being more specific. Qualitative data analysis by computer is extolled as cementing the rapprochement between 'quality' and 'quantity'.

In *The New Language of Qualitative Method*, Gubrium and Holstein (1997) argue that there are four types or 'language idioms' in qualitative research, with each having limitations. They distinguish naturalism (which tends to pursue deep insights into what is happening at the exclusion of how it occurs), ethnomethodo-logy (which focuses on how common sense practices work in the organisation of talk but excludes contextual factors), emotionalism (which privileges closeness with research subjects and the search for their narratives and biography at the expense of other experiences) and postmodernism (which seeks to deconstruct the research process to reveal the representation of different versions of reality but at the cost of denying any certainty or definitiveness). In another account, Max Travers (2001) classified four types of qualitative research based on their methodologi-cal position: positivism, interpretivism, realism and post-structuralism. Positivist qualitative researchers like to adhere to as many features of natural science research as is possible within a qualitative approach, such as collecting large amounts of data, the use of scientific criteria to assess qualitative data, the deployment of computer assisted analysis packages to manage the data and representational techniques generally which remove us from the specific voices of the people themselves. Interpretative qualitative researchers focus on people's understandings of the social world in their own words through small scale case studies. Realists tend not to take people's voices uncritically and want to look at some of the structures, forces and circumstances that people may not be aware of but which nonetheless impinge on their behaviour and beliefs. People's voices are captured but only in the context of the structures and circumstances that shape them. Post-structuralist qualitative researchers deny that there is a knowable and objective social world or that it is possible to unproblematically represent that world in a text. Therefore, they adopt what is often called 'postmodern ethnography' and try to capture the multiplicity of versions of reality in a textual form that does not give the author's voice any status or authority above that of the multiple voices of people themselves. If somewhat basic and arbitrary in the choice of axis along which qualitative research is classified, these typologies are useful in illustrating that qualitative research covers a wide range of different activities, methods and practices.

Suggested further reading

Bryman, Alan (1988) *Quantity and Quality in Social Research*. London: Allen and Unwin.

Seale, Clive (1999) *The Quality of Qualitative Research*. London: Sage.
Travers, Max (2001) *Qualitative Research through Case Studies*. London: Sage.

References

Bryman, Alan (2001) *Social Research Methods*. Oxford.
Gubrium, J. and Holstein, J. (1997) *The New Language of Qualitative Method*. New York: Oxford University Press.

Hammersley, Martyn (1992) *What's Wrong with Ethnography?* London: Routledge.

JOHN BREWER

Qualitative research data, archiving

Although publicly funded social science data archives have provided repositories for machine-readable datasets since the 1960s, there had been no similar initiative for preserving social science research data in other media, primarily that generated by qualitative research methods. As a result, although huge resources have been devoted to qualitative interviews and ethnographic, case and anthropological studies, the data are often inaccessible, untraceable or have been destroyed. Results from surveys of United Kingdom Economic and Social Research Council

(ESRC) grant holders across all social science disciplines back to the 1960s suggest that, after completing their research projects, about two-thirds of researchers store their data, either at home or at work, very few archive their data, and about a fifth destroy their material.

Researchers' concerns about archiving qualitative material

A significant number of researchers are resistant to archiving their research material for a variety of reasons. The main areas of concern follow.

Preservation of confidentiality and informed consent

Many researchers promise informants, usually orally, that their contribution will remain confidential to the research project. In some cases, they obtain written consent from informants. However, there are instances, such as a participant observation study, where neither is consent obtained nor are promises given to the observed. While not necessarily involving a legal requirement, promises to preserve confidentiality do carry a moral obligation. Also, there are some studies, for example those dealing with illicit or criminal behaviour or certain sexual activities, where the informants could be put at risk by breaches of confidentiality, and others, for example covert investigations of paramilitary groups or religious cults, where the researcher could be at risk. Also studies involving readily identifiable public figures present major difficulties in preserving confidentiality. Social research practitioners have addressed some of the problems of research ethics and most of the professional and commercial associations provide basic codes of practice. It is important for a recipient repository to be fully informed about consent given by informants or undertakings given by the investigators either at the time of the project or subsequently.

Measures that can be taken to help with preserving confidentiality once material has been deposited include:

(1) closure of the material for a specified period
(2) restricted access, where the material is only available to certain types of researcher. This may be combined with requests for access being vetted by the depositor
(3) anonymisation, where all personal identifiers are removed
(4) users undertaking not to breach confidentiality by publishing identifiable information
(5) recontacting the informants to obtain consent for deposit in a public archive.

For current research it may be possible to secure permission from informants for material to be archived at the time of interview.

Doubts about usefulness to secondary researchers

Some researchers are concerned that their material cannot be used sensibly without the background knowledge which they have accumulated during its collection. This is particularly so with longitudinal studies of a group where the researcher feels that a special rapport has been developed without which the material may be meaningless. However, the researchers' documentation of the material should provide its context and there are uses other than re-analysis such as comparative research, provision of teaching or illustrative material, methodological studies and historical information.

Continuing use of the material by the researcher

Researchers may feel that they are not ready to deposit their data because they have not yet realised its full potential for their own work. This is often the case for anthropologists who continue to use material from field trips early in their career throughout their working life. However, depositing material secures its preservation and does not prevent the originator from continuing to use it. It may also be possible to copy the data, allowing the researcher to retain the originals, or delay depositing part of the collection.

Criticism of research methods

Some researchers are concerned about exposing their research methods and conclusions to criticism by making their material publicly available. While this concern is understandable, it is probable that secondary users will be more interested in using the data for their own specific research rather than replicating the original analysis. Also there is a benefit to depositors because users will be required to cite both the materials and the original investigator in any publications.

Copyright and ownership of research material

As the law stands today, ownership of copyright depends primarily on when and where the research was conducted, the form of the material and who sponsored or commissioned the work. In the United Kingdom the Copyright, Designs and Patents Act (1988) specifies that the first owner of the copyright in a work is usually the person who brought the work into existence. In the majority of cases in academic research, it is the principal investigator (or employer or sponsor) who owns copyright and who may transfer it if he or she wishes. Qualidata has produced guidelines on copyright detailing the rights of copyright holders of qualitative interview data (Qualidata, 2000).

Some principal investigators wish to retain copyright themselves, whereas others are prepared to transfer rights to a recipient repository. Either option can be included in an agreement of transfer between the depositor and the repository. Fieldwork carried out after the 1988 UK Act is more problematic for archiving because interviewees are now entitled to copyright in their own words. This may, but in most circumstances will not, have implications for subsequent publishing and quotation of material from interviews. If the intention is to archive recorded interview data it is advisable for researchers to get informants to sign a copyright clearance form (an example is given in Qualidata, 2000).

Time involved in preparing material retrospectively for archiving

The amount of time and resources required to document material from a qualitative study may appear to make archiving an impossible task. However, handwritten material such as field notes can be archived and it is not necessary to type everything before a repository will accept it. Grant-awarding bodies are being encouraged to provide financial support for these activities.

Criteria for archiving qualitative data

Material should be accorded a higher priority for archiving to the extent to which it meets the following criteria:

- the research is recognised to have had a major influence in its field and/or representing the whole working life of a researcher
- it is complementary to existing holdings in repositories
- there is a high level of perceived re-analysis or comparative use potential
- it is at risk of destruction.

In addition, material is more suitable for archiving if:

- there is documentation of the original research proposal, aims, methods and outcome sufficient to enable informed re-use
- it can generally be made freely available for academic use
- it is in a reasonably accessible condition, for example, good tape sound quality, shorthand or other abbreviations explained
- copyright and confidentiality restrictions and depositor's conditions of access allow reasonable access
- the resources needed to make the material available do not outweigh its potential for re-use
- a suitable repository can be found.

Repositories for qualitative data

Qualidata: a centre funded by the British Economic and Social Research Council and hosted by the UK Data Archive at the University of Essex, UK. The Centre's aims are to locate, assess and document qualitative data and arrange for their deposit in the UK Data Archive and other public archive repositories, to disseminate information about such data and raise awareness among the social science research community. A key objective is to improve access to qualitative data for researchers. The Centre maintains a database about the extent and availability of qualitative research material in general, whether deposited in public repositories or remaining with the researcher and can be accessed at: http://www.essex.ac.uk/ qualidata/.

British Library, Special Collections Department: national politics, economic and social policy and cultural material arising from the work of any person of more than local significance.

National Sound Archive, British Library: life story and personal testimony tapes of national significance which will broaden the collection and increase research interest; gay and lesbian material.

London School of Economics: British political, economic and social history and social anthropology; material must be relevant to research within the School.

School of Scottish Studies, University of Edinburgh: oral history in a national Scottish context including newly arrived inhabitants and Scots overseas; human content is a primary criterion.

University of Warwick, Modern Records Centre: industrial relations and politics at the national level including management and business/entrepreneurial activities; motor and related industries; interest groups and political movements, especially left-wing and radical.

Wellcome History of Medicine Library: founded in 1979 to concentrate on acquiring material relating to twentieth-century medical science and healthcare in all its aspects.

Contemporary Medical Archives Centre (CMAC): now holds nearly 600 separate collections of archives and papers of organisations and individuals, and the number is constantly increasing.

Further details of these and other repositories can be obtained from Qualidata and found in Foster and Sheppard (1995).

Note

An earlier version of this entry appeared as 'Archiving Qualitative Research Data' in *Social Research Update*, 10.

Suggested further reading

Barnes, J.A. (1980) *Who Should Know What? Social Science, Privacy and Ethics*. Cambridge: Cambridge University Press.

British Sociological Association (2001) *BSA Statement of Ethical Procedures*.

Bulmer, M. (ed.) (1982) *Social Research Ethics*. London: Macmillan.

Burgess, R. (1984) *In the Field: an Introduction to Field Research*. London: Allen and Unwin.

Corti, Louise, Day, Annette and Backhouse, Gill (2000, December). 'Confidentiality and Informed Consent: Issues for Consideration in the Preservation of and Provision of Access to Qualitative Data Archives', *Forum Qualitative Sozialforschung/Forum: Qualitative Social Research* (online journal), 1 (3). Available at: http://qualitative-research.net/fqs/fqs-eng.htm.

Fielding, N (2000), 'Resistance and Adaptation to Criminal Identity: Using Secondary Analysis to Evaluate Classic Studies of Crime and Deviance', *Sociology*, 34 (4): 671–89.

Hammersley, M. and Atkinson, P. (1983) *Ethnography, Principles in Practice*. London: Tavistock Press.

Hammersley, M. (1989) *The Dilemma of the Qualitative Method*. London: Routledge.

Market Research Society (2000) *MRS Code of Conduct*. London: Market Research Society.

Qualidata (2000) *Confidentiality, Research Ethics and Copyright*. Qualidata website.

Social Research Association (2000) *Social Research Association Ethical Guidelines*. London: Social Research Association.

Thorne, S. (1994) 'Secondary Analysis in Qualitative Research: Issues and Implications', in J.M. Morse (ed.), *Critical Issues in Qualitative Research Methods*. London: Sage.

See also
Confidentiality,
Research
ethics and
Copyright.

References

Foster, J. and Sheppard, J. (1995) *British Archives: a Guide to Archive Resources in the UK*, 3rd edn. London: Macmillan.

Qualidata (2000) *Guidelines on Confidentiality and Copyright with Respect to Archiving Qualitative Data*. Colchester: University of Essex.

LOUISE CORTI, JANET FOSTER AND PAUL THOMPSON

Quantitative

See **Methodology**.

Queer research

Although queer research is a relatively new form of social research, the last 10 years have witnessed a veritable explosion of theoretical and empirical explorations in this area. Queer research is based upon the theoretical perspective known as *queer theory*. Queer theory draws from many disciplines including sociology, history, literature, cultural studies, anthropology, politics and health. There is clearly overlap between queer and *lesbian and gay studies*, and the nature of the distinction between these studies (if in fact there is one) remains controversial. Queer, lesbian and gay studies all take as their starting point a radical questioning of heteronormativity. Heteronormativity refers to the hegemonic position that heterosexuality has both in academic discourse and in society more generally. Thus, lesbian, gay and queer research necessarily involves a fundamental questioning of heterosexuality as normative. For lesbian, gay and queer researchers, heteronormativity leads to homophobia and heterosexism, and a significant dimension of this research is a commitment to political action to confront these forms of discrimination.

Perhaps what most distinguishes queer from lesbian and gay theory is the status of 'sex' within each theory. Lesbian and gay identities are most often formulated from the assumption that 'lesbian' refers to female bodies and 'gay' refers to male bodies. This often leads to concerns with the 'authenticity' of gender expression. For instance, some studies within lesbian and gay theory have focused on the extent to which transsexual individuals are 'authentic' members of one sex or the other. Queer research, on the other hand, rejects the assumption that there is a stable morphological basis for discerning sexual difference. Thus, in queer theory, we find a shift from an analytic emphasis on the authenticity of sexed identity to a more malleable notion of sexed identity as 'performativity'. This shift is propelled by a combination of transsexual rights claims, post-structural and postmodern feminist theory's critique of essentialism, and an increasing focus on identity. The most prominent and commonly cited text referring to performativity is Judith Butler's *Gender Trouble* (1990). Butler argues that 'we never experience or know ourselves as a body pure and simple, i.e. as our "sex", because we never know our sex outside of its expression of gender' (1986: 39). Butler reverses the naturalised understanding of sex existing prior to gender and argues that gender produces the effect of sex:

> Acts, gestures, and desire produce the effect of an internal core or substance, but produce this *on the surface of the body*, through the play of signifying absences that suggest, but never reveal, the organising principle of identity as a cause. Such acts, gestures, enactments, generally construed, are *performative* in the sense that the essence or identity that they otherwise purport to express are *fabrications* manufactured and sustained through corporeal signs and other discursive means. That the gendered body is performative suggests that it has no ontological status apart from the various acts which constitute its reality. (1990: 136, original emphasis)

Drawing upon Foucault's insight that dominant discourses reinforce the idea that nature has already determined the 'truth' of our bodies, and that our bodies define for us our gender, Butler argues that gender does not alter from some locatable starting point, but is much more an activity, enactment or performance in constant movement. Butler joins other queer theorists in arguing that rather than ontology, sex is no more than an 'effect'. Put another way, 'biological, psychological and social differences do not lead to our seeing two genders. Our seeing two genders leads to the "discovery" of biological, psychological, and social differences' (Kessler and McKenna, 1978: 163).

Butler's account of gender producing sex through performative enactment is a contemporary development of distinguished and distinctly sociological theories of *symbolic interactionism* and *ethnomethodology*. Defining one of the fundamental precepts of symbolic interactionism, George Herbert Mead (1934) forcefully argued that the self cannot exist without society – the continuous interactive process between individuals establishes and maintains conceptions of self by reflecting back images of the self as object. What is now discussed in terms of performativity, symbolic interactionism emphasised decades ago as the continually renegotiated character of social action, which produces malleable identities, both allowing and compelling the possibility of contradiction and conflict.

Erving Goffman developed many of Mead's ideas to argue that human inter-action is fragile and maintained through social performances. In *The Presentation of*

Self in Everyday Life (1971) Goffman theorises the self as a process and effect rather than an 'object' with prior ontological status. He notes, however, that social interaction is largely governed by a deep belief that objects produce signs that are self-informing. In *Gender Advertisements* (1976), Goffman explores gender as a particularly powerful object which does not in any essential way exist, but whose 'schedule' for portrayal does, and this portrayal is often mistaken as 'essentially real' (1976).

As much as the ontological status of 'sex' differentiates queer theory from lesbian and gay studies, each is united in the political goal to disrupt hegemonic performances of gender. For instance, two excellent examples of queer research challenge the assumption that an individual must possess particular genitals to 'know' and experience themselves as gendered. Prosser (1998) argues transsexuals phantasmatically feel surgically constructed genitals as 'real' – in the same way that people who have lost limbs maintain the 'feeling' of those limbs phantasmatically. In another effort, Stoltenberg reverses the claim that bodies produce gender to argue that ideas about gender produce feelings attached to particular body parts:

> Most people born with a penis between their legs grow up aspiring to feel and act unambiguously male, longing to belong to the sex that is male and not to belong to the sex that is not, and feeling this urgency for a visceral and constant verification of their male sexual identity – for a fleshy connection to manhood – as the driving force of their life. *The drive does not originate in the anatomy. The sensations derive from the idea. The idea gives the feelings social meaning; the idea determines which sensations shall be sought.* (1989: 112, my emphasis)

Because queer research is specifically interested in disrupting heteronormativity, and the sex/gender binary that underpins it, it often employs transsexualism as a key queer trope in challenging claims concerning the immutability of sex and gender. As such, transgender studies invest heavily in transsexualism's 'transgressive' potential. As Zita writes 'queer scramble[s] the categories of heterosexual sex/gender ontology and open[s] up the possibility of playing against the edge of meaning with the body' (1998: 55). However, the degree to which queer research is able to effect this challenge is disputed. One critique of queer research is that although queer theory contests the attribution of any character to masculinity and femininity, performing or 'doing' gender seems to consist principally in combining or parodying existing gender practices, for instance in assertions of a 'third sex'. Butler asks whether 'parodying the dominant norms is enough to displace them; indeed, whether the denaturalisation of gender cannot be the very vehicle for a reconsolidation of hegemonic norms' (1990: 125). Put another way, imitation is always implicated in the power that it opposes. The overarching concern is that *all* modern expressions of sex and gender identity depend upon the current two-gender system, and subversion is not guaranteed through imitation, particularly if that imitation remains focused on femininity and masculinity.

Another critique is that, by contesting homosexuality and the sex/gender binary as much as heterosexuality, queer research fragments feminist, lesbian, gay and transgendered communities at a time when there is much greater political purchase to be gained in unifying around real, material oppression. This critique is concerned with the consequences of eroding a community that is already under constant threat from the dominant heteronormative society.

Suggested further reading

Beemyn, B. and Eliason, M. (eds) (1996) *Queer Studies: A Lesbian, Gay, Bisexual and Transgender Anthology*. New York and London: New York University Press.

Seidman, S. (ed.) (1996) *Queer Theory/ Sociology*. Oxford: Blackwell Publishers.

Weed, E. and Schor, N. (eds) (1997) *Feminism Meets Queer Theory*. Bloomington and Indianapolis: Indiana University Press.

See also **Sex surveys**.

MYRA H. HIRD

Questionnaire and structured interview schedule design

The design of each questionnaire or structured interview schedule poses its own challenges but there are some common considerations:

- being clear about the purpose of the questionnaire/interview schedule and deciding what to include
- choosing the appropriate type of research instrument
- deciding on open or closed formats for questions
- the order in which questions are asked
- the suitable wording of questions
- pretesting and piloting of the draft questionnaire or interview schedule.

What to include

As regards what to include in the questionnaire or interview schedule, the researcher must be clear about the purpose. The researcher must decide whether the instrument is intended to be primarily descriptive or explanatory. If the questionnaire/interview schedule is explanatory in purpose the researcher needs to have clear hypotheses which will determine which variables need to be included. A thorough knowledge of the research literature on the topic will be a good guide to suitable hypotheses and to which variables are relevant. The researcher will need to view the variables in terms of whether they are dependent, independent, intervening or control variables and to think ahead to the type of analysis that might be conducted. Time invested in thinking ahead at this stage will be repaid handsomely when the researcher is later faced with a dataset to be analysed.

A consideration here is the type of questions to be included. There are two main types. One is the factual type which may be about socio-demographic characteristics or routine behaviour. The second type is more subjective and is concerned with experiences and attitudes. The latter type is more problematic to measure and may require the use of a scale made up of multiple items on the questionnaire or interview schedule.

All essential questions need to be included as the researcher will only get one chance to administer it. The first draft of the instrument may be rather long. So a decision may have to be made as to which subject areas to exclude. Deciding on what to include or exclude demands that the researcher refine the research focus. It is all too easy to avoid this issue by simply extending the length of the data collection instrument. However, there can be a price paid for this when respondents refuse to complete a too-long interview or questionnaire, with a resultant negative impact on survey response rate. Ruthless editing and shortening the questions forces the researcher to prioritise and to start to think ahead to what he/she will actually do when the time comes to analyse the data. A useful analogy is packing for a holiday. Fill the suitcase, then throw out the non-essentials.

Type of research instrument

There are two main types of research instrument to choose from, reflecting the different types of survey:

- the formal *structured interview schedule* in which the questions are administered on a face-to-face basis by the researcher or a trained interviewer
- the *self-completion questionnaire*, such as the postal questionnaire.

The decision on which type of data collection instrument to use will be influenced by the nature of the research topic and it will have profound implications for design. With the formal structured interview schedule, the use of a trained interviewer means that elaborate complicated sets of questions can be used; allowing for the investigation of more complex topics. In contrast, for the self-completion questionnaire without the backup of an interviewer on the scene, what needs to be done in order to fill in the questionnaire must be very clear and complicated structures of questions should be avoided.

The suitability of the survey approach for sensitive topics varies depending on the topic. Often it is felt that very sensitive topics require an unstructured in-depth interview approach. Low response to particular questions in a questionnaire or structured interview schedule can be an indication that the formal approach may not be working. On the other hand, questionnaires can offer the important advantage of anonymity – an essential condition for co-operation by some respondents.

Open and closed formats

A *closed question* presents the respondent with a pre-determined selection of responses. Closed questions have an advantage in that they are more straightforward to answer and the responses are faster to code. However, the researcher needs to be confident that the limited set of responses provides adequate coverage of the range of possible responses. In contrast, *open-ended* questions give the respondents the opportunity to give an answer to the question in their own words.

Open-ended questions have an advantage in that they allow for elaboration in a response and so can provide insights into the meanings which respondents attach to their actions and beliefs. However, coding open-ended responses and comparisons between respondents are more difficult. Furthermore, there may be a bias in the kinds of respondents who complete open-ended questions.

Question order

The order in which questions are asked in a questionnaire or during a formal structured interview can affect the pattern of response significantly. Questions measuring attitudes can be particularly sensitive to context. This is a particular problem for time-series surveys where a proportion of the questions will be repeated word for word in each survey sweep, but the questions *surrounding* the replicated questions may change year on year. Consistency effects occur when two questions are asked in fairly close succession on the same topic and the respondent feels under pressure to be (or appear to be) consistent in his/her answers. An often-cited example from the 1940s (Rugg and Cantril, 1944) involves the two questions:

> *Should the United States permit its citizens to join the French and British armies?* (Yes: 45%)
> *Should the United States permit its citizens to join the German army?* (Yes: 31%)

When the question order is reversed, the percentage saying that citizens should be permitted to join the German army drops by nine percentage points to 22%.

Other order-effects can arise where one question measures attitudes towards a *general* issue and the other to a *specific* aspect or instance of that issue. This is sometimes referred to as a 'part-whole effect'. Schuman and Presser (1996) report on responses to a general question on the legalisation of abortion followed by a specific question on the availability of abortion if there is a strong chance of a serious defect in the baby. Support for legalised abortion is greater if the questions are asked in the above order. The authors hypothesise that when the more general item is asked first, some respondents' answers will support this – but with just such a specific example in mind (the possibility of a serious defect in the baby). When the item on abortion because of a serious defect is asked first, however, this indicates to respondents that the general item that follows does not cover this instance. Thus respondents 'subtract' the more specific rationale and a lower proportion end up agreeing with the general legalisation question.

Wording

The choice of wording in questions is never as easy as it might first appear. Indeed there is an advantage in, where possible, using or adapting questions which have previously been used successfully. This strategy also has the advantage of facilitating comparisons between different surveys. In designing new questions, the wording needs to be as unambiguous as possible. This is best achieved by using short questions and by always editing out double-barrelled questions. Leading questions, that is, those that suggest a particular response, must be excluded, as should 'loaded' (prejudiced) statements. Above all, we must avoid making unrealistic assumptions about the level of literacy of the respondents. The safest way to proceed is to pitch the language usage at the lowest common denominator; that is, word the questionnaire with your least literate respondents in mind.

Pretesting and piloting

Before a survey is ready to administer its research instrument needs to be tested. The first stages of this process will be *pretesting* – trying out alternative versions of questions or interview schedules informally with a small number of individuals to uncover problems with comprehension and non-response on particular questions. It can be tempting under time pressure to skip this stage. This is extremely inadvisable since without pretesting serious flaws may slip through and not be identified until too late. The initial pretesting work may include conducting some in-depth interviews and may involve testing and revising attitudinal scales. The 'grand finale' of the pretesting stage will be a *pilot* – carrying out a miniature version of the whole survey by administering the final draft questionnaire or interview schedule to a small number of test respondents. The pilot survey should mimic the full survey in as many aspects as possible, including drawing a sample before the actual interviewing, and coding the question data afterwards, perhaps even going so far as a dummy analysis.

Conclusion

Although surveys are not always appropriate and have some limitations they have tremendous advantages and are the mainstay of much research in the social sciences. There is of course no perfect survey and each must be judged in the light of its own specified goals. Nevertheless, there are too many unnecessarily flawed surveys whose problems can be addressed by prior thought and thorough piloting.

Suggested further reading

De Vaus, D.A. (1996) *Surveys in Social Research*, 4th edn. London: UCL Press.

Oppenheim, A.N. (1992) *Questionnaire Design, Interviewing and Attitude Measurement*. London: Pinter.

See also
Questionnaires and structured interview schedules and **Social surveys**.

References

Rugg, D. and Cantril, H. (1944) 'The Wording of Questions', in H. Cantril (ed.), *Gauging Public Opinion*. Princeton: Princeton University Press.

Schuman, H. and Presser, S. (1996) *Questions and Answers in Attitude Surveys*. California: Sage.

RICHARD O'LEARY AND LIZANNE DOWDS

Questionnaires and structured interview schedules

The questionnaire or structured interview schedule is the data collection technique most commonly used by social surveys. It is traditionally in the form of a printed document and is essentially a list of questions. The defining features of the questionnaire/structured interview schedule are that the design itself is highly structured and that the same instrument is administered to all the participants in the survey. When respondents fill in the instrument on their own without the help of an interviewer, as is the case in a postal survey, the research instrument is called a *questionnaire*. When interviewers are present, asking the questions and helping the respondent, as in face-to-face-interviews or a telephone survey, the research instrument is known as a *structured interview schedule*. The design and way the questionnaire is administered depend on the type of survey. Questionnaires and structured interview schedules are used in social surveys by market research companies, by government agencies and by academics. The content is as diverse as the purposes set by the users but almost always includes some questions on demographic characteristics such as gender and age. The main body of questions, however, is likely to cover the activities, opinions or attitudes of respondents and will vary according to the topic under investigation.

The use of a highly structured interview schedule or questionnaire has many attractions. It enables the collection of large quantities of data from large numbers of people. This can be done relatively easily, depending on the way it is administered, and in a relatively short space of time. Because each respondent is asked exactly the same questions, and in the same way, the responses score high on reliability. Due to the standardised form of questioning, it is assumed that bias due to the effect of the researcher is minimised. Because it collects information from respondents about the same characteristics and in a form that can be coded systematically, it is an ideal way of producing data that is suitable for quantitative data analysis. If the questionnaire/interview schedule is being used on a survey that has a valid sample design, it is possible to make reliable generalisations from survey figures (sample estimates) to the whole population (population parameters).

Relative advantages of questionnaires and interview schedules

The advantages of one type of structured interview instrument constitute the disadvantages of the other and vice versa.

First, let us consider the advantages of questionnaires:

(1) Cheapness – questionnaires are relatively cheap. Interviewers are very expensive creatures as one must pay for interview time and the travel expenses of the interviewer. You cannot mail interviewers but you can mail questionnaires. As a rough rule of thumb, the cost of an interview procured

via a questionnaire will be about one twenty-fifth that of the same information obtained through a face-to-face interview.

(2) Problems associated with interviewers are avoided with a questionnaire survey. Interviewers have to be trained, briefed and supervised. These problems can be much worse for a researcher using volunteer interviewers since the sanction of non-payment for poor work is absent. With questionnaires you just address them and send them out.

(3) When the respondent must go and look up information, a mailed questionnaire is better because they can do this at their leisure.

(4) Respondents may been shown to be more willing to give out personal or embarrassing information or to admit to 'unsocial' opinions when filling out an anonymous questionnaire rather than telling the lurid facts face-to-face to an interviewer who is, after all, a complete stranger. Researchers routinely find more extreme political attitudes with postal surveys than with personal interview surveys.

Reflecting their higher costs, structured interview schedules offer many advantages:

(1) More complexity is possible. With an interview schedule, you can be sure that questions will be understood, will be answered and will be answered in the correct manner. The interviewer is there to help the respondent and to see that nothing goes wrong. On the other hand, when a person receives a questionnaire, they have to be able to understand it and fill it out completely unaided. Therefore, questions must be unambiguous, short and simple and designed to cater for unmotivated, disinterested respondents. (Students tend to design questionnaires with the average person in mind forgetting that half of the population by definition is *below* average. Note that some people are illiterate – how can they fill in a questionnaire? While the poorer classes don't have any monopoly on stupidity, they are less educated and, hence, a postal questionnaire survey can be biased against the lower social strata.)

(2) Related to this, interview schedules are superior to questionnaires because the interviewer can *probe* for more information or a fuller answer to a question, whereas with a questionnaire, you just have to accept whatever comes in.

(3) Interview schedules are better for obtaining spontaneous answers or discovering what the respondent really thinks or knows about a topic. With a questionnaire, the respondent has time to deliberate over what they will say, or even look up the information, or discuss with other people (like their spouse) what to put down.

(4) Answers can be considered to be independent of each other. That is, with an interview schedule, the researcher controls the order in which the questions are asked. With a questionnaire, the respondent can look over the whole form before answering any question, make sure that their answers are all consistent with each other and so forth.

(5) One can ensure that the correct (sampled) person gives the responses. A respondent can easily hand a questionnaire to someone else and ask them to fill it in for them.

(6) The validity of the responses can be checked by the interviewer through observation. Interviewers can tell a lot about a person by their physical appearance and manner and by seeing their house. The interviewer may realise that the person is obviously lying when this could not be known from a questionnaire, for example, people who deliberately exaggerate or understate their income.

(7) Direct interviews produce a lower rate of non-response than questionnaire surveys. In contrast to refusing an interviewer, it is much easier to put off and eventually throw away a questionnaire. High response rates are important because survey non-respondents tend to differ *systematically* from the respondents in ways that are, by definition, unknown. Non-respondents tend to be, for example, male, less educated, poorer, younger (the elderly are at home and have the time to be interviewed), belong to minority groups, have more extreme politics, and generally be 'nasty rather than nice'. Arguably, it is better to have a smaller sample with a very high response rate than to have more interviews from a larger sample with a low response rate.

Criticisms

The main criticism of the use of questionnaires and highly structured interview schedules is that the data collected may lack validity. Especially in the case of questionnaires where an interviewer is not present to provide help, respondents may interpret the questions posed and the response options in different ways, making the interpretation of the responses by the researcher problematic. This is particularly an issue when people are asked to give ranked responses (for example, 'not much', 'a little' or 'a lot'), the meaning of which may vary from person to person.

In addition it is argued that respondents may not always be honest in their answers or even capable of answering a particular question. Critics may argue that these issues can be identified and addressed more easily in more in-depth approaches to data collection, such as unstructured interviews. (Of course, the two approaches need not be exclusive. For instance, it may be possible at the end of a questionnaire survey to recruit a sub-set of respondents for more in-depth interviewing.)

Suggested further reading

De Vaus, D.A. (1996) *Surveys in Social Research*, 4th edn. London: UCL Press.
Moser, C.A. and Kalton, G. (1971) *Survey Methods in Social Investigation*. London: Heinemann.

Oppenheim, A.N. (1992) *Questionnaire Design, Interviewing and Attitude Measurement*. London: Pinter.

See also
Questionnaire and structured interview schedule design and **Social surveys**.

RICHARD O'LEARY AND ROBERT MILLER

R

Realism

Realism, at its most basic, is the philosophical doctrine that some things exist independently of the mind. As such, it is the antonymic position to philosophical idealism, which holds that the world is created by the mind. At a sociological level, realism involves the assertion of the existence of a social reality over and above the existence of individuals. This can be contrasted with *constructionism*, which holds that society is constructed by individual subjectivities. This onto-logical dichotomy has profound implications for the focus of social research, apropos whether that research should be focusing on the subjective motivations that lead to the social actions of individuals or whether it should be focusing on the social structures that determine or influence the actions of individuals. How-ever, as we shall see, contemporary realists argue that it is possible, and indeed profitable, to do both.

Realism has a long history in the social sciences. Both Durkheim's notion of the **social fact** and Marx's historical materialism were based on realist assumptions that there was something more out there in society than individuals. Con-temporary realism, in its most explicitly worked through form, which is termed critical realism, owes much to the ideas of these two social theorists. However, before examining the links between classical and critical realisms, it is important to note that critical realism is only one form of realism that has been adopted by social researchers. Other forms include the more qualified 'subtle realism' of Martyn Hammersley (1992).

From Durkheim, critical realists have taken ontological justifications for assert-ing the existence of social structures. These involve two arguments about the nature of reality. The first argument is termed the *emergent theory of reality*, because it involves the observation that more complex forms of reality emerge from the interactions of simpler forms. Each emergent form requires, in turn, a different approach to its examination if we are to understand it. Thus, from the interactions of organic chemicals emerged living organisms. While all living organisms are composed of organic chemicals, they possess something distinct that those chemicals do not have on their own – life. If the study of living things were to be restricted to chemistry, it would be impossible to explain the very thing that makes them unique. Hence the need for the discipline of biology. Durkheim likened the domain distinction between chemistry and biology to that between psychology and sociology. He argued that individuals, in their interactions with each other, form a social system that has its own specific characteristics that cannot be reduced to the sum of those individuals (Durkheim, 1982 [1895]). It was these emergent properties of the social world that distinguished the object-domain of sociology from that of psychology.

The second argument involves the *causal criterion of reality*, which seeks to ascribe reality to forces. The most commonly held criterion for reality is the perceptual criterion, which holds that if a 'thing' cannot in principle be perceived, then it cannot be real, therefore if social structures do not exist as perceptible things, then they do not exist except in the minds of individuals. Realists counter this argument by adding a new criterion, which turns on the capacity of an entity to bring about changes in material things. On this criterion, to be is not to be perceived, but to be able to do (Bhaskar, 1989). Once again, appeal is made to the domains of other sciences to demonstrate the acceptability of such a notion. Thus it is observed that in physics, forces such as gravity and magnetism are accepted as having a reality despite the fact that we can only know of their existence through their effects upon objects. Given that human behaviour is to a greater or lesser degree patterned, it is argued that analogous forces must be operating in the social realm.

There is a problem here for realists that does not confront those who confine their research to empirically amenable social interactions. How are they to investigate a structural reality that cannot be directly perceived? Certainly, it rules out *empiricism* as a basis for realist social research. Observation of social events needs to be supplemented by other intellectual tools that enable researchers to understand the deeper reality of social structures. In response to this requirement, critical realists have adopted the position of *transcendentalism*. It is called that because it involves asking what Immanuel Kant (1964 [1781]) termed the transcendental question. This question asks what must be the case in order for events to occur in the way that they are observed to occur. Thus, in relation to society, it asks what factors must exist in order for human understanding and actions to be patterned in the ways they are observed to be patterned. This is not to say that empirical research is rejected, rather it is seen as part of the research process. It is needed both to establish the manner in which events are patterned, in order to provide the substantive basis upon which to apply the transcendental question, and also to test whether the answers that the researcher makes to the transcendental question have explanatory purchase.

Where critical realists differ sharply from Durkheim and the structural-functionalist approach that succeeded him is in their view of what social reality consists of. To wit, they reject the structural-functionalist assumption that sees groups as having a fundamental reality that can provide the bedrock of social explanation. Instead, they adopt a *relational model of society*, which sees social structures as structures of relations. This echoes the position of Marx, who stated that 'Society does not consist of individuals, but expresses the sum of interrelations, the relations within which these individuals stand' (Marx, 1973 [1857/8]: 265). Thus, one can only be a wife by dint of one's relationship with a husband, or a worker because of one's relationship with an employer. It follows from this that the initial purpose of social research is to uncover how these social relations are structured.

The uncovering of structural relations is only seen as the initial purpose of social research by critical realists because, along with Marx, they seek to go further than this: 'The philosophers have only *interpreted* the world, in various ways, the point is to *change* it (Marx and Engels, 1970 [1846]: 123). In a similar fashion to *critical theory*, critical realism rejects the pretension that science can and should be value-neutral. Instead, it examines the structuring of human relations using the criterion of whether they promote or constrain the human freedom and dignity of those involved in them. This information can then be used as a resource for those who wish to act in a way that will transform oppressive social structures.

It follows from this belief in the capacity of social action to alter structures that critical realists also reject Durkheim's determinist view of society. Instead, they assert that the existence of structured relations are dependent upon social actions, which will have the effect of either transforming or maintaining those structures. However, this does not lead them to accept models of society which see structures as the creations of individuals, for the reason that the structures we experience pre-exist us, and are rarely instantaneously changed by our actions (Archer, 1995). Instead, realists plot a middle course, which regards structure and action as distinct but interdependent entities. This means that realist social research focuses on the interpolations of structure and action, attempting to plot the conditions that structured relations place upon social action, along with the effects that social action has upon those structures.

What formally distinguishes critical realism from other models of social research is the requirement to combine empirical research with transcendental theorising. This does not entail any prescription about the methods of empirical research that should be used. Indeed, perhaps counter-intuitively given the macro-sociological aspects of critical realism, the use of qualitative methods in the empirical moment of realist research is far from rare. Critical realist ethnographers argue that the adoption of such a theoretical basis for qualitative research enables the researcher to move beyond ideographic descriptions of particular social interactions, and to provide information that will be, to a greater or lesser degree, generalisable. Moreover, it allows for that generalisability to be tested by subsequent research (something that is impossible if ethnographic studies are seen as pertaining solely to the unique social milieux examined). It is also argued that it enables ethnographic research to move from the description to the explanation of social interactions (Porter, 1993). Nor is it just in terms of method that critical realism takes a heterodox approach, but also in terms of discipline. Critical realist studies have been conducted in sociology, economics, psychology, linguistics, political science and organisation studies, to name a selection.

It can been seen that realism provides the potential for a broad basis for the conduct of social research. Those who adopt it claim that its importance lies in its capacity to provide a sound foundation for research, given the decay of empiricism as a viable model, and the concomitant rise of scepticism in the form of post-modernism.

References

Archer, M. (1995) *Realist Social Theory: the Morphogenetic Approach*. Cambridge: Cambridge University Press.

Bhaskar, R. (1989) *Reclaiming Reality: a Critical Introduction to Contemporary Philosophy*. London: Verso.

Durkheim, E. (1982 [1895]) *The Rules of Sociological Method*. London: Macmillan.

Hammersley, M. (1992) *What's Wrong with Ethnography?* London: Routledge.

Kant, I. (1964 [1781]) *Critique of Pure Reason*. London: Macmillan.

Marx, K. (1973 [1857/8]) *Grundrisse*. Harmondsworth: Penguin.

Marx, K. and Engels, F. (1970 [1846]) *The German Ideology*. London: Lawrence and Wishart.

Porter, S. (1993) 'Critical Realist Ethnography: the Case of Racism and Professionalism in a Medical Setting', *Sociology*, 27 (4): 591–609.

SAM PORTER

Reflexivity

Reflexivity is a term that has been in currency since the 1960s and has several different meanings, but it has become most closely connected with the crises facing ethnography, where it is seen as both the problem and the solution to ethnography's difficulties. The 'problem' is that ethnographers are part of the social world they study and do not collect uncontaminated data, the 'solution' is that they should situate the data by reflecting on how their presence and other contingencies helped to create the data. Reflexivity requires a critical attitude towards data, and recognition of the influence on the research of such factors as the location of the setting, the sensitivity of the topic, power relations in the field and the nature of the social interaction between researcher and researched. Reflexivity thus affects both writing up the data, known as *the crisis of representation*, and the data's status, standing and authority, known as *the crisis of legitimation*. It is associated with the idea that ethnographic representations of reality are partial, partisan and selective, and thus with anti-realist and postmodernist denials that there is a perfectly transparent or neutral way to represent the social world (or the natural one). Reflexivity in this sense constitutes a problem because ethnographic accounts reflect the social world that produced them. By being reflexive however, ethnographers are said to be able to contextualise and situate the data, making explicit the ways in which their account is socially constructed. In this way reflexivity is simultaneously also the solution. Reflexivity is now a much used and abused term. We currently live in what is known as the 'reflexive turn' within ethnography. Critics who wish to reassert some of the old certainties in ethnography contend that this is a card now being played too regularly in the social sciences.

Origins

The variety of its usage owes a lot to the diverse origins of the term, for it is associated with the 1960s radical critique of sociology, feminist critiques of research methodology, social studies of scientific knowledge, and only more recently with anti-realism and postmodernism in ethnography. There were three sorts of radical critique in sociology in the 1960s into which reflexivity fits. One began with Garfinkel and ethnomethodology, in which reflexivity was understood to describe the situated nature of all social knowledge, and was meant as an attack on abstract, general theorising. Descriptions of the social world are within and part of the world they describe, so that they reflect something of the social situation in which they are situated. This reflection or reflexivity could be of the social relationships behind the description, the moral evaluations embedded in them, or the political, moral or social consequences they contain. An entirely different radical critique emerged at roughly the same time in the work of Gouldner, where practitioners of sociology were told to cast a cold eye on their own activities and come to view their own beliefs with the same critical attitude as they do those held by others. In truth he was attacking the myth of value free research. Gouldner (1973) came later to write that a reflexive sociology required us to establish the relationship in one's work between our identity as social scientist and as person, which was meant as an attack on the notion of objectivity and the belief that there can be uncontaminated research. The third critique that was to emerge at this time was feminism. Feminist theory and praxis questioned the privileged position accorded to the social scientist's observations against those of the voiceless (female) subjects, and encouraged a self-critical approach on the part of the researcher. This was a concern over representation to ensure that female subjects were not rendered voiceless in the writing-up of the text, and with legitimation to ensure feminist researchers identified the procedures by which evaluations, interpretations and conclusions were reached.

The contribution that social studies of science made to reflexivity should not be overlooked. The point these studies made was that even natural science produces socially situated knowledge. The reflexive turn these studies later took, in work such as Woolgar (1988) amounted to a recognition that the studies which demonstrate science to be a social product are themselves social products, contingent on various social processes into which their data must be located to affect their authority and status. This required experimentation with textual forms in order to demonstrate both the multi-vocal character of any analysis and interpretation, and the fallacy that there is a single reading. This approach reinforced the association of reflexivity with both representation and legitimation. From the 1980s anti-realism and postmodernism cemented the reflexive turn in ethnography. Postmodern cultural anthropologists deconstructed the practice of ethnography and the ethnographic text and reduced the data to that of one narrative among many (the crisis of legitimation) and the text to telling a story (the crisis of representation). Probably the first ethnographers in Britain to expound the implications of reflexivity were Hammersley and Atkinson (1983). Social research, they wrote, had a reflexive character – by which they meant that researchers are part of the social world they study. The implication of reflexivity for the practice of social research made it futile to eliminate the effects of the researcher; rather, we should set about understanding them. The upshot now is that we are encouraged to be reflexive in our account of the research process, the data collected, and the way we write it up because reflexivity shows the partial nature of our representation of reality and the multiplicity of competing versions of reality.

Descriptive and analytical reflexivity

In a recent exposition, Stanley usefully distinguished between 'descriptive' and 'analytical' reflexivity. The former involves reflecting on the impact that various contingencies had on the outcome of the research, such as a description of the social location of the research, the preconceptions of the researcher, power relations in the field, and the nature of the interaction between the researcher and subjects. It requires the development of a critical attitude toward the data. Ethnographers who seek to rescue their craft from the extremes of postmodernist deconstruction and retain some form of realism, normally end their reflexivity with this type. Descriptive reflexivity can be used to provide a secure realist-like foundation to the research, but it can also be used as part of the postmodern project. If the latter, it is normally done in conjunction with 'analytical reflexivity'. 'Analytical reflexivity' is a much tougher requirement. It deals with epistemological matters and knowledge claims, and requires a form of intellectual autobiography in which researchers explicate the processes by which understanding and interpretation was reached and how any changed understanding from prior preconceptions came about.

Being reflexive in the descriptive sense requires that ethnographers ask themselves a series of questions and reflect on how the answers impinged upon and helped to situate and shape the data and their analysis and interpretation of it. Reflexive ethnographers should thus account for themselves and their social relations, as well as the substantive findings and construction of the text. Analytical reflexivity requires yet more difficult reflection. In this sense ethnographers should ask themselves questions about the theoretical framework and methodology they are working within, the broader values, commitments and preconceptions they bring to their work, the ontological assumptions they have about the nature of society and social reality, and what Stanley calls the 'felt necessities' the researcher has about the topic and their approach to it that resonates with them passionately.

In brief, reflexivity rejects the notion of the detached, aloof and objective researcher who produces knowledge claims as if in a vacuum. Instead the researcher should not only engage with their subjects but also reflect upon the processes by which conclusions are reached and display these argumentative procedures in ways that readers can reconstruct. In this way, the data is situated rather than presented as if produced by what van Maanen calls a process of immaculate perception.

Suggested further reading

Babcock, B. (1980) 'Reflexivity: Definitions and Discrimination', *Semiotica*, 30: 1–14.

May, T. (1999) 'Reflexivity and Sociological Practice', *Sociological Research Online*, 4 (3). http://www.socresonline.org.uk/socresonline/4/3may.html.

Stanley, L. (1996) 'The Mother of Invention: Necessity, Writing and Representation', *Feminism and Psychology*, 6: 45–51.

References

Gouldner, A. (1973) *For Sociology*. Harmondsworth: Penguin.

Hammersley, M. and Atkinson, P. (1983) *Ethnography*. Tavistock.

Woolgar, S. (1988) *Knowledge and Reflexivity*. London: Sage.

See also **Ethno-methodology**.

JOHN BREWER

Research design

Research design is the model used by the researcher to discharge 'the burden of proof' – the logical organisation that allows him or her to feel that whatever they have done in their research allows them to reach valid conclusions.

Research design is *not* the step-by-step procedures one goes through in carrying out a piece of research (such as the tasks that have to be carried out to design and implement a social survey or an observation study).

The classic research design is the *randomised experiment* that may be diagrammed like this:

Group	Pretest		Stimulus		Post-test
Control	O_1	$\longrightarrow$	Yes	$\longrightarrow$	O_2
Experimental	O_3	$\longrightarrow$	No	$\longrightarrow$	O_4

Two groups, a *control group* and an *experimental group* are selected that should be fundamentally the same at the beginning of the experiment (O_1 should equal O_3). During the experiment, the experience of both groups is identical, except that the experimental group is exposed to some 'stimulus' that the control group does not experience. At the end of the experiment, *if everything has been carried out correctly* and if the experimental group differs in some way from the control group (O_2 not equalling O_4), the difference should have come from the stimulus that only the experimental group was exposed to.

To take an example: suppose that a researcher wishes to test whether encouragement from teachers will cause students to do better on IQ tests. The students are randomly divided into two groups and their IQs are tested. Then, after the experimental group alone has been given encouragement from its teacher, the two groups take a second IQ test. If the students in the experimental group show a greater improvement than the unencouraged students in the control group *and* if there have been no flaws in the experiment's design, logically the only source of the experimental group's greater improvement should be the encouragement they received.

The big advantage of the randomised experiment is that, if it is carried out correctly, the researcher can infer *causality*. The experimental and control groups are the same beforehand. During the course of the experiment the only difference is that the experimental group is exposed to the experimental stimulus (in this case, teacher encouragement), so that any difference in the end must be due to (caused by) the experimental stimulus.

The essence of the true experiment is *control* – the researcher controls everything except the experimental stimulus so that any difference between the experimental and control groups must arise from the experimental stimulus.

In reality, however, achieving complete experimental control is very difficult; control can break down or not be complete. There are a number of factors that can cause experimenters to lose control of their experiments, creating problems of *internal* and *external* validity.

Internal validity

There are at least 5 intrinsic factors that can cause validity problems:

(1)   history
(2)   maturation
(3)   mortality
(4)   instrumentation
(5)   testing effects.

Continuing with our fictitious example of an IQ experiment, let's see how each of these possible intrinsic flaws could occur.

History

The events that happen to the experimental and control group could vary over the course of the experiment. For example, the experimental group's teacher could fall ill and have to be replaced by a substitute teacher. While the students still receive encouragement, it will not be coming from the teacher they are accustomed to. In effect, there is now more than one stimulus in the experimental design. If the experimental group shows a greater improvement in IQ scores than the control group, the researcher cannot be sure that it comes from the encouragement, or from the class having a new teacher, or from both in some combination. If the experimental group in fact is not doing any better (or even worse), the researcher cannot be sure whether this comes from the disruption caused by a change in teachers.

Maturation

Biological or psychological processes may become plausible alternative explanations for differences found between the experimental and control groups.

Staying with our example, if by chance one group happens to have more boys and the other more girls, changes in the average IQ scores of the groups over time could be due to gender-based differing rates of maturation of the pupils. (In effect, the two groups were not identical at the beginning in an essential characteristic.)

If the control group becomes aware that it is not receiving the encouragement that other classes are getting, it could react as a group and decide to try harder, thereby producing greater improvement in IQ scores. While this technically could still be considered a genuine experimental effect brought on solely by the unique stimulus, the dynamics of the causality is more complex than the simple A (encouragement) causes $\rightarrow B$ (high IQ scores) that the experiment is supposed to be testing.

Mortality

More or different drop-outs in the two groups may cause an artificial difference to emerge. For example, if some of the smarter students in the experimental group moved away before the second IQ test was administered, the average score of the experimental group would fall even if encouragement was raising IQ test performance.

Instrumentation

Differences in the measurement procedures applied to the two groups may cause artificial differences to appear. For example, inaccuracies in measurement may cause spurious results. If the researcher believes strongly that encouragement is bound to raise IQ test performance and the same researcher is scoring the tests, it is quite possible for an unconscious bias in favour of the students in the experimental group to creep in. Positive results in the experiment are then in fact being generated by the researchers themselves. 'Double blind' experimental designs, where the researcher recording the data does not know which group received the experimental stimulus, are intended to avoid this problem of biased recording producing spurious results.

Testing effects

The fact that measurements are being taken can in itself create false results. For instance, if the students in the control group know they are part of an important experiment, they may feel 'special' and perform better on subsequent IQ tests even without any encouragement. This phenomenon is sometimes called 'the Hawthorne effect' after a famous series of experiments and observations.

The problem is well known in medical drug research where patients often appear to improve when given a new drug solely because they are receiving a new 'wonder' cure and not in fact due to any genuine effect of the drug itself. To guard against this, researchers add in a third group which are given a fake pill – a 'placebo' – that has no physiological effects. The true effect of the drug can be assessed by comparing the improvement of the 'placebo group' patients with that shown by the experimental group who did receive the genuine drug.

All of these are problems with the internal validity of an experiment. If the experiment is carried out correctly, they can be avoided, but they are pitfalls that must be avoided.

External validity

There are also three problems that pertain to the *external validity* of the experiment:

(1) *The experimental and control groups may not in fact be identical to start with.* For instance, it could be possible that the two groups of pupils differed from each other at the beginning of the IQ experiment – so any different results found for the groups at the end are useless. There are strategies for avoiding this problem:

  (i) The research subjects may be *randomly assigned* to the experimental and control groups. By chance, there should be no differences between the two groups. The problem is that, by chance, it is quite possible that the two groups will end up being randomly different. For example, most of the brighter students may by chance end up in one group while all the rest end up in the other.

  (ii) The alternative is to *match subjects* in the two groups. For example, if the researchers have a 12-year-old middle class boy in the experimental group, they find another student with the same characteristics for the control group. However, there can be two problems with matching: first, the researchers may not be able to find the perfect match; second, they may have matched on the wrong characteristics so that the two groups still differ in important ways unknown to them that will change the outcome of the experiment.

(2) *Population validity.* Experimental groups tend not to be random selections from the general population. For instance, one of the gibes directed against psychology is that it is really only a science of first-year undergraduates since these are the people who are usually the experimental subjects. This is a problem of generalisability.

(3) *Artificiality.* Similarly, experiments, being highly controlled, tend to be artificial. One must always wonder if what is observed in the laboratory would take place in the real world. For example, Milgram carried out a famous experiment where he tricked people into believing that they were punishing other experimental subjects with ever stronger electrical shocks. Did the subjects really believe that they were causing so much pain (and death)?

Broader issues

Most of the social sciences use the experimental method only rarely. The main reason for this is that many of the topics and issues that interest social scientists may not be amenable to experimentation for practical or ethical reasons. It may be impossible to control the situation adequately to allow for experimentation. For example, consider the case of the dangers of cigarette smoking. We all 'know' that cigarette smoking is a cause of a variety of human diseases. But tobacco companies persist in refusing to acknowledge this fact. QUESTION: How can they do this?

ANSWER: Because no one has been able to demonstrate by experimental means in humans a direct, unambiguous causal link between cigarette smoking and disease.

In fact, it would be quite simple to design an experiment that would resolve the question once and for all. All one would need to do would be to take about 10,000 newborn babies and randomly divide them into control and experimental groups of 5,000 each. The children in the experimental group would be required to gradually take up smoking from the age of 10 on, so that by the time they were aged 30, all were smoking a pack or more of cigarettes daily. At the same time, the control group would have to never smoke (no cheating allowed!). After 40 years, the data would begin to come in and, by the end of this century, the link would be incontrovertibly established.

This counterfactual example does illustrate in an exaggerated way, the ethical and practical considerations that can rule out experiments. Ethically, researchers could not require 5,000 children to develop a dangerous, probably fatal, addiction.[1] Practically, while the experiment would resolve the debate, it would be very expensive to carry out and, more to the point, pointless if one had to wait literally a lifetime for the solution.[2]

Alternative research designs

Most research in the social sciences employs research designs other than that of the classical experiment. Furthermore, social scientists investigate issues all the time where the application of the true experimental method is ruled out completely either for ethical reasons or on practical grounds of cost and time. What kinds of research designs do they rely on instead?

'Natural' experiments

Sometimes chance circumstances will combine in a way that produces a situation that resembles an experimenter generating an experimental and a control group. If researchers realise this and are quick off the mark, they can benefit.

For example, say two very similar social services offices are located next to each other in the same city and serve very similar areas. Due to cutbacks being unevenly imposed (while near each other, the offices are in different administrative jurisdictions), one office suffers a severe cutback in funding while that of the other is left intact. We have a 'natural experiment' where the 'experimental stimulus' is the cutback. Researchers decide to take advantage of the situation and monitor the two offices for a year to see what sort of effects the cutbacks cause. Since the only thing different about the two offices is the cutback, the logic is that any differences must somehow arise from that cutback.

However, while 'natural experiments' can provide opportunities for research, these opportunities have to be recognised and seized when they occur. Since the conditions for a natural experiment depend on chance and luck they may never happen. Also, the 'control' is unlikely to be as good as what a researcher would desire in a real experiment.[3]

So, if social scientists often cannot do real, controlled experiments and neither can they wait around for natural experiments to occur; what do they do?

Correlational designs

Most researchers, quantitative or qualitative, collect their information or data from the world *as is*, without any attempt at experimental manipulation. *Any research method other than the true experiment*, whether it is a survey, a qualitative ethnographic study or whatever, is an example of correlational research. The researcher investigates the apparent linkages or associations between the factors or variables in his or her data in order to try and infer what the relationships or causal linkages might be.

For example, a qualitative researcher carrying out a study of unemployment may be trying to see how the fact of being unemployed affects the way that the subjects see the world and how they behave. But, unless the researchers are using a *longitudinal design* and following their subjects over time from before they lost their jobs, while they may form opinions that are correct about the effect of unemployment upon their subjects, they have no way of really being sure that these apparent effects of unemployment are in fact due to the subjects being unemployed and not due to something else. The main guide to validity is the researchers' own subjective, intuitive understanding of the situation of the unemployed subjects. In experimental terms, there is no control.

Quantitative researchers also have the same problem of lack of control even though their techniques and approaches will differ radically from those of the qualitative researcher. The quantitative researcher will employ what is known as *statistical control*. For instance, if quantitative researchers are investigating the effect of cigarette smoking upon health, they will try to allow for (that is, control) the effects of other things that are also known to raise a person's chances of dying (for example, being older, being overweight, being unfit, being poor, having parents who died young, living in an area that has a higher than average chance of mortality, etc.). If, after the researchers have allowed for the effects of all these other factors, they still find that smokers have a higher mortality than non-smokers, they can conclude that it is the fact of smoking and not something else that has caused the higher mortality for the smokers. What the quantitative researchers are attempting to do, in fact, is to impose an after-the-fact experimental design upon their data.

Hence, for ethical and practical reasons the only realistic choice of research design for most researchers on most topics is the correlational research design. Correlational research designs do have one crucial advantage over experimental designs that compensates for their lack of control – correlational designs obtain their data from real people in real situations in the real world. That is, in comparison to experiments, correlational designs are much more validly *generalisable* to the real world and to the population as a whole.

Notes

1 Note, however, that medical researchers routinely face this type of ethical dilemma where they have to withhold potentially life-saving treatments from control groups in order to establish the genuine efficacy of new treatments and drugs.
2 And *control* would be impossible. As many parents know, simply forbidding young people to take up smoking is not guaranteed to work.

3 In the example of the social services offices, it is unlikely that they were *exactly* identical before the cuts hit one of them.

Suggested further reading

Kidder, Louise (ed.) (1981) 'Experimental Design', in *Sellitz, Wrightsman and Cook's Research Methods in Social Relations*, 4th edn. New York: Society for the Psychological Study of Social Issues (original author Claire Sellitz).

ROBERT MILLER

Sampling, probability

The social sciences sample in quantitative research in order to:

(1) *Minimise the costs* of collecting data (costs in terms of money, time and energy)
(2) *Increase precision* in the data collected.

The reason for this apparent paradox becomes clear when one notes that it is possible to control the quality of a few hundred or even a few thousand interviews. With enormous surveys, the *real* precision will be less because good quality control becomes unfeasible (for example, the census can be seen as a very big (100%) sample survey in which quality control is terrible).

Randomness

Probability or scientific sampling is based upon the idea of random sampling, that each person or unit selected should have a completely random chance of being selected or (in jargon) *Each element within the population should have an equal and/ or measurable chance of random selection*. Elements are the units that are sampled. These may be persons, households, schools or whatever. The population is all of the elements from which a sample is drawn.

The rationale behind random sampling is that the characteristics of the good random sample (the *sample estimates*) should mirror the characteristics of the population as a whole (the 'true' *population parameters*). The big advantage of probability sampling is that, if you have carried out all of your sampling procedures correctly (a very big if), you can calculate the possible amount of error in the sample. (That is, how far your sample estimates may vary from the true parameters of the whole population.) This is an important point. The ability to estimate the amount of potential sampling error can *only* be done with probability sampling and is its main advantage over other kinds of sampling. All confirmatory statistical tests are based upon the assumption of a random probability sample. This ability to reliably estimate sampling error is the reason that probability sampling is also sometimes called '*scientific*' sampling.

The Simple Random Sample

A Simple Random Sample has three requirements:

(1) *A clear definition of the population to be sampled*; that is, one must be able to sample exactly those in the target population and no one else. It can be surprisingly difficult to define exactly who is in the target population, for example, the population of the United States (what about 'resident aliens', illegal immigrants, temporary visitors to the country, expatriate American citizens living abroad, or just the fact that people are constantly being born or dying etc.?).

(2) *A complete listing of all the elements in the population*. This also can be surprisingly difficult to produce (a complete and accurate listing of all the people in the United States?).

(3) *Statistical independence* (somewhat less obvious). One must be able to assume that all the elements in the sampling frame are statistically independent of each other. That is, the selection of any one element should in no way affect the chances of any other element being selected or not selected. This can also cause difficulties, for example, one is selecting individual people from a population of households and deciding to take only one person from each house – the elements (people) are *not* statistically independent since once you have chosen one person from a house, everyone else's chances of selection *are* affected (they drop to zero).

How to select a simple random sample:

(1) After defining the target population exactly, list all of the elements in the population and assign them consecutive numbers from *1 to N*

(2) Decide on the sample size, *n*

(3) With a table of random numbers, select *n* different numbers that fall between *1 and N*

(4) The elements in your population that have those numbers are the simple random sample.

The systematic sample

With a sample of any size, taking a simple random sample can be a long and tedious process; so researchers often use a modification called systematic sampling.

How to select a systematic sample

Steps (1) and (2) in selecting a systematic sample are the same as for the simple random sample, then:

(3)   The researcher computes a *selection interval* (sometimes called the *sampling fraction*) by dividing the population size by the sample size, *N/n*.

(4)   The researcher then selects a random starting point in the first selection interval. That element and every element in the equivalent place in the rest of the selection intervals is the systematic sample.

Stratified sampling

There are two basic elaborations of probability sampling. The first of these is *stratified sampling*. Stratified sampling involves dividing ('stratifying') the whole population into two or more separate, more homogeneous, groups and then sampling separately from within each of these groups (that is, after stratification, each group is treated like a population on its own).

There are two advantages to stratified sampling. Firstly, if the criteria chosen to divide the population into strata has been chosen wisely, a stratified sample will be *more representative than a simple random sample*. An example will help to explain how this can be so. In Northern Ireland, the single variable most crucial for a person's political opinion is their religion; Protestants overwhelmingly hold 'unionist' opinions (that Northern Ireland should remain part of the United Kingdom in one way or another) and virtually all support for Irish nationalism (that Northern Ireland should become part of the Irish Republic) comes from Catholics. If one was carrying out a survey on political opinion in Northern Ireland, it would be crucial that the proportions of Protestants and Catholics in the survey's sample matched the actual proportions of Protestants and Catholics in the population. However, a worrying feature of simple random sampling is that, even when the sample is drawn exactly correctly, while random chance dictates that the proportions in the sample will closely resemble the 'true' population proportions, random chance *also* dictates that there will be a significant chance that the proportions in the sample will *not* exactly match the proportions in the population from which the sample is drawn. Table 1 illustrates the different results that could occur if three simple random samples were drawn. There is absolutely nothing wrong with the sampling procedure, but the researcher has been a bit unlucky each time and sometimes the sample has oversampled Protestants and undersampled Catholics and other times the reverse has happened.

Table 1

	Catholic	Protestant
Population figure	40%	60%
Simple random sample 1	39%	61%
Simple random sample 2	41%	59%
Simple random sample 3	37%	63%
Proportionate stratified sample	40%	60%

However, with a *proportionate stratified sample*, the population is divided into its Protestant and Catholic groups before any sample is drawn and then 40% of the sample is taken from the Catholic population and 60% of the sample is taken from the Protestant population.[1] Hence, the proportionate stratified sample is forced to match the 'true' population proportions on the very important (for political opinion) characteristic of religion. To put it technically, the variance of the sample from the population on the stratification criteria is reduced to nil.

Since the sample proportions must fit the population proportions exactly, this sort of stratified sample is called a *proportionate stratified sample* or a *self-weighting sample*.

Secondly, sometimes one may have a different sort of problem and be interested in comparing fairly rare groups in a population with more numerous groups. For example, to stick with religion in Ireland, one might want to compare the political opinions of the 4% of Protestants in the Irish Republic with the other 96% of Roman Catholics.

With a Simple Random Sample, the important rare group will appear in too small numbers even with a large sample. The solution is *disproportionate stratified sampling* where the researcher deliberately takes a larger sample from the rare group(s) thus ensuring that they appear in the sample in adequate numbers for an analysis (see Table 2).

Table 2

	RC	Protestant
Population	96%	4%
Simple random sample (of 1,000)	96%	4%
	(960)	(40)
Disproportionate stratified sample (of 1,000)	50%	50%
	(500)	(500)

This disproportionate stratified sampling procedure is legitimate as long as one only wants to compare one group with the other. Obviously, however, the numbers in the sample from the two strata do not match the population proportions in any way. That is, the chances of individual selection vary depending upon which strata an element belongs to (in our example, Protestants have a 24 times greater chance of being selected) – the sampling fractions of a disproportionate stratified sample vary from strata to strata. To be able to make statements about the sample as a whole, one has to *weight* the undersampled group more (that is, count them more than once in order to make the proportions of the strata/groups artificially match the true population proportions).

Cluster sampling

Stratified sampling is a technique for getting closer to the ideal – a sample exactly representative of a population. But, anyone faced with doing a real survey, whether it is a student carrying out a small-scale research project or an academic researcher with a million in research funds, also will find themselves faced with a variety of purely practical problems, such as:

(1) as noted above, amassing the lists of individual elements from which to draw a sample
(2) transport to and from the interview area
(3) getting from one interview to another.

The main strategy for minimising the practical difficulties of survey sampling is called *cluster sampling*. In cluster sampling, complete blocks of elements are randomly chosen prior to the selection of individual elements from within the blocks. *Area sampling* is the most typical example of cluster sample; specific geographic areas are chosen from within the whole geographic area covered by the population. These blocks of elements are called *clusters*.

For example, a team of researchers may want to carry out 500 interviews in a medium-sized city which has 100 electoral wards. Without clustering, they will on average have five interviews in each of the wards. If they randomly select 20 wards for the survey, the practical problems will ease dramatically. They will need to procure the electoral rolls for only 20 wards. There will be about 25 interviews located in each ward, thereby drastically cutting down the time needed to travel to the interview sites. Since the 25 sampled addresses in a ward will be 'clustered' close together, the time spent going from house to house in order to obtain interviews will be much less.

Note that these advantages, which are considerable, are *solely* practical advantages. The *dis*advantage, which is also considerable, is that 'randomness' is much lessened with a cluster sample. Even with completely random selection of clusters, there is a good chance that the researchers will end up with a selection of 20 wards that are not very typical of the population of the city as a whole. For instance, they could by chance easily choose the 20 poorest wards in the city and end up concluding that the city is much less prosperous that it really is. Technically, once a cluster has not been selected, the chance of anyone in the cluster appearing in the sample drops to zero; so the odds of getting an unrepresentative sample rises dramatically with cluster sampling. The larger the number of clusters one picks, the *greater* the chance that they will be representative of the population – BUT – the larger the number of clusters one picks, the *less* will be the advantages gained through concentrating interviews. This can be depicted in a diagram:

	Number of clusters	
Large	← – – – – – →	Small
Accurate	← – – – – – →	Inaccurate
Few practical advantages	← – – – – – →	Lots of practical advantages

So, with cluster sampling, the researcher has to try to strike a compromise between obtaining a representative sample and a practical sample.

Multi-stage sampling

A complete sample design will combine all three of these techniques together into what is called a multi-stage sample in order to exploit the advantages of each:

(1) *Clustering* to reduce the practical difficulties of sample surveying
(2) *Stratification* to make the sample more accurate by either forcing the sample to match the population exactly on an important characteristic (proportionate stratified sampling) or to ensure that a small group is present in numbers adequate for analysis (disproportionate stratified sampling)
(3) *Random selection* at all times to maintain 'probability' in the sampling process.

There is no such thing as a single 'best' sample design for all purposes. The manner in which the researcher chooses to combine these procedures together into his or her sample design will depend upon the unique needs and resources of the research.

Note

1 Note that this example is for the purposes of illustration only. It would be very difficult to be able to divide the Northern Irish population into its Protestant and Catholic components prior to taking a sample. Also, the real relative size of the Protestant and Catholic components of the Northern Irish population is a matter of heated political debate. The 60/40 split here is solely for purposes of illustration.

Suggested further reading

Arber, Sara (2001) 'Designing Samples', in N. Gilbert (ed.), *Researching Social Life*. London: Sage.
Kish, Leslie (1965) *Survey Sampling*. New York: J. Wiley.

Moser, C.A. and Kalton, G. (1971) *Survey Methods in Social Investigation*. London: Heinemann. Chapters 4–7.

See also **Sampling, quota**, and **Social surveys**.

ROBERT MILLER

Sampling, quota

Quota sampling is a 'non-probability' sampling technique that can be important in social research. In a quota sample, rather than being given a specific list of named individuals or addresses to interview, the interviewer is told to find a number of people who match a set of characteristics determined by the market research firm. These characteristics should be relevant to the topic of the survey and should be at least broadly representative of their occurrence in the target population. For example, an interviewer may be told to interview 40 people:

- ten of whom are between the ages of 40 and 60 and male
- ten of whom are between the ages of 20 and 40 and male
- ten of whom are between 40 and 60 and female
- ten of whom are between 20 and 40 and female.

The big advantages of quota sampling are that it is quick and cheap. In contrast to a probability sample where the interviewer can only interview the people chosen in the sample and may spend a considerable amount of time travelling to the interview site and calling back until the target individual is found at home, all the interviewer needs to do to fulfil a quota sample is find people willing to be interviewed whose characteristics match those of the quota.

The big disadvantages of quota sampling are:

(1) Interviewers will use their ingenuity and go some place where they know they can easily find people who match the characteristics of their quota and who will be 'approachable'. This can result in a considerable bias in a quota sample. For example, an interviewer with a quota of young adults in their late teens and early twenties may go to a university campus where such people are found easily. The effect will be a considerable bias in favour of the more educated.

(2) Since there is nothing really random about the selection process, unlike probability sampling, there is no basis for estimating the amount of potential error in the sample.

Social science researchers are most likely to use quota sampling at the pretest stage of a survey, when they want to gauge the reactions of a variety of different types of people to their research instrument. Quota sampling is often used by market researchers because it is much quicker and therefore cheaper than probability sampling; this recommends it to market researchers who, after all, are in it for the money.

See also
Sampling,
probability.

ROBERT MILLER

Sampling, snowball: accessing hidden and hard-to-reach populations

Key Points

- In its simplest formulation snowball sampling consists of identifying respondents who are then used to refer researchers on to other respondents.

- Snowball sampling contradicts many of the assumptions underpinning conventional notions of sampling but has a number of advantages for sampling populations such as the deprived, the socially stigmatised and elites.
- Snowball sampling has advanced as a technique and the literature contains evidence of a trend toward more sophisticated methods of sampling frame and error estimation.
- Apart from violating common principles of sampling techniques, the use of snowball strategies provides a means of accessing the vulnerable and more impenetrable social groupings. However, the nature of similarity within social networks may mean that 'isolates' are ignored.

Treading an uneasy line between the dictates of replicable and representative research design and the more flowing and theoretically led sampling techniques of qualitative research, snowball sampling lies somewhat at the margins of research practice. However, the technique offers real benefits for studies which seek to access difficult to reach or hidden populations which are often obscured from the view of social researchers and policy makers who are increasingly keen to obtain evidence of the experiences of some of the more marginal excluded groups.

Policy makers and academics have long been aware that certain 'hidden' populations, such as the young, male and unemployed are often hard to locate. Other groups such as criminals, prostitutes, drug users and people with unusual or stigmatised conditions (for example, AIDS sufferers) pose a range of methodological challenges if we are to understand more about their lives. This entry describes the processes, advantages and difficulties with utilising snowball sampling techniques.

Snowball sampling may simply be defined as: 'A technique for finding research subjects. One subject gives the researcher the name of another subject, who in turn provides the name of a third, and so on' (Vogt, 1999). This strategy can be viewed as a response to overcoming the problems associated with sampling concealed populations such as the criminal and the isolated (Faugier and Sargeant, 1997). Snowball sampling can be placed within a wider set of link-tracing methodologies (Spreen, 1992) which seek to take advantage of the social networks of identified respondents and can be used to provide a researcher with an ever-expanding set of potential contacts (Thomson, 1997). This process is based on the assumption that a 'bond' or 'link' exists between the initial sample and others in the same target population, allowing a series of referrals to be made within a circle of acquaintance (Berg, 1988).

Snowball sampling can be applied for two primary purposes. Firstly, and most easily, as an 'informal' method to reach a target population. If the aim of a study is primarily explorative, qualitative and descriptive then snowball sampling offers practical advantages (Hendricks et al., 1992). Snowball sampling is used most frequently to conduct qualitative research, primarily through interviews. Secondly, snowball sampling may be applied as a more formal methodology for making inferences with regard to a population of individuals who have been difficult to enumerate through the use of descending methodologies such as household surveys (Snijders, 1992; Faugier and Sargeant, 1997).

An early example of the technique is Patrick's study of a Glasgow gang (1973) which utilised initial contacts to generate contexts and encounters that were used to study the gang dynamic. A general move away from participant observation of this kind towards the use of snowball sampling techniques primarily for interview-based research has been seen more recently. Snowball sampling has been used in studies of drug users (Avico et al., 1998, Griffiths et al., 1993; Kaplan et al., 1987); prostitution (McNamara, 1994); AIDS sufferers (Pollak and Schlitz, 1988); and the seriously ill (Sudman and Freeman, 1988).

While some may seek to characterise the areas often dealt with using snowball strategies as being trivial or obscure, the main value of snowball sampling is as a method for dealing with the difficult problem of obtaining respondents where they are few in number or where some degree of trust is required to initiate contact. Under these circumstances techniques of 'chain referral' may imbue the researcher with characteristics associated with being an insider or group member which can aid entry to settings that conventional approaches find difficult to succeed in.

A range of advantages have been claimed for snowball sampling. Firstly, it has enabled access to previously hidden populations. Often members of such populations may be involved in activities that are considered deviant, such as drug taking, or they may be vulnerable, such as the stigmatised in society, making them reluctant to take part in more formalised studies using traditional research methodologies. Trust may be developed as referrals are made by acquaintances or peers rather than other more formal methods of identification. Snowball sampling has been found to be economical, efficient and effective in various studies (Avico et al., 1988). It has been shown to be capable of producing internationally comparable data as in Avico et al.'s study of cocaine users in three European cities. It may also be used to examine changes over time. Snowball sampling can also produce in-depth results and can produce these relatively quickly.

Perhaps one of the strongest recommendations for the snowball strategy stems from a distinction between *descending* and *ascending* methodologies (Van Meter, 1990). Traditional techniques such as household surveys, descending strategies, are associated with a largely quantitative tradition of the measurement of social problems which often suffers from a lack of responses from particular groups. Ascending methodologies, such as the use of snowball techniques, can be used to work upwards and locate those on the ground who are needed to fill in the gaps in our knowledge on a variety of social contexts. In this sense snowball sampling can be considered as an alternative or as a complementary strategy for attaining more comprehensive data on a particular research question.

While many have considered snowball strategies primarily as an aid to accessing the vulnerable or the deviant it is also clear that other studies have used such an approach to engage with the 'hard to reach' in terms of urban elites. Saunders' (1973) study of urban politics gives us an example where a 'reputational' method was used in which respondents were asked who held power in the local arena. This led to a series of contacts and the establishment of a subjective indication of the relative local power bases. This suggests that snowball sampling has a wider application in sociological research than has been realised hitherto.

Difficulties

Snowball samples have a number of deficiencies. These are as follows.

1. *Problems of representativeness and sampling principles*

The quality of the data produced is the primary concern of recent snowball sampling research and in particular a selection bias which limits the validity of the sample (Van Meter, 1990; Kaplan et al., 1987). Because elements are not randomly drawn, but are dependent on the subjective choices of initially accessed respondents, most snowball samples will be *biased* and do not therefore allow researchers to make claims to any level of generality from a particular sample (Griffiths et al., 1993). Secondly, snowball samples will be biased towards the inclusion of individuals with inter-relationships, and therefore will over-emphasise cohesiveness in social networks (Griffiths et al., 1993) and potentially miss 'isolates' who are not connected to a network which the researcher has tapped into (Van Meter, 1990).

The problem of selection bias may be partially addressed, firstly through the generation of large sample sizes and secondly by the replication of results which may strengthen any generalisations claimed by snowball studies. At present, statistical formalisation of snowball sample biases are not available (Van Meter, 1990). However, larger sample sizes may reduce bias, for example Pollak and Schlitz's study of AIDS sufferers produced a sample with representative proportions for age, class and size of town of residence (Pollak and Schlitz, 1988).

In addition to selection bias there is also the issue of gatekeeper bias (see Groger et al., 1999). In their work they identified a difficulty when using nursing home staff as 'go-betweens' in obtaining the informed consent of caregivers. These 'gatekeepers' were sometimes reticent or protective toward those they cared for and sometimes hindered access for the researchers. Based on their experiences they make some attempt at drawing an equivalence between snowball sampling and 'scrounging sampling'. They describe the latter in terms of: 'desperate and continuing efforts, against mounting odds, to round out the collection of individuals with relevant types of experiences we know to exist but have not been able to capture' (Groger et al., 1999: 830).

While social scientists may vary in the degree to which they would accept such a viewpoint we can recognise similar traits in quantitative approaches such as household surveys. We often find struggles to obtain adequate numbers of respondents by making repeated visits to minimise biases derived from low response rates.

The ideal number of links in a referral chain will vary depending on the purposes of the study. More links in each chain will generate substantial data about a particular sample, and may also allow access to those most difficult to identify (that is, those respondents who require the greatest level of trust to be built up before participating). However, it is also more likely that members of such a large single chain sample will share similar and unique characteristics not shared by the wider population. Thus, there may be a case for initiating several discrete chains with fewer links, particularly where any inference about a wider hidden population is considered important.

Attempts have been made to consider the statistical accuracy of samples obtained by snowball techniques using 'mark-recapture' techniques (Fisher et al., 1994; Shaw et al., 1996) to estimate homeless populations. Mark-recapture techniques take their name from techniques used to estimate numbers of natural wild populations. A sample of animals is captured from the population and released, a second sample is taken and counted and the number of recaptures noted. In comparing registers, such as service agency data and police arrest data, the ratio of total agency population to the number of overlaps can similarly be used to estimate the size of an unknown population.

2. Finding respondents and initiating 'chain referral'

By their very nature members of a hidden population are difficult to locate. Often studies require some previous 'knowledge of insiders' in order to identify initial sample respondents. Such prior knowledge may not be readily available to researchers and it may be very time consuming and labour intensive to acquire. Under these circumstances it is possible that people in positions of relative authority or proximity may provide a route into the required population (for example, Groger et al., 1999). For example, housing officers might be able to introduce a researcher to a tenant on incapacity benefit if the tenant agrees to be identified. It should be stressed that there are clear ethical implications for such work and that informed consent should be considered a prerequisite.

Criteria for membership in a sample will depend on the nature of the research question being posed. In the case of deviant activities such as drug taking it may be that some referrals will not necessarily be accurate. Secondly, referrals will largely depend on the subjective perceptions of initial respondents about the involvement of others in the same activity. Thus particular individuals (those most popular, long-term residents or those with wider social networks) are more likely to be identified than others. Much of snowball sampling rests on the assumption that social networks consist of groups with relatively homogenous social traits. However, there are limits to this and it largely depends on what characteristics are considered to be the most important. In the case of a particular disability, for example, it is assumed that someone in this group would know others to whom a researcher could be directed. However, some groups may themselves consist of highly atomised and isolated individuals whose social network is relatively impaired. Young unemployed men have been viewed as a prime case in this respect. It is therefore apparent that snowball samples are both time consuming and labour intensive (Griffiths et al., 1993; Faugier and Sargeant, 1997).

3. Engaging respondents as informal research assistants

Researchers may encounter initial hostility and suspicion from targeted individuals. There is also evidence of research fatigue, particularly amongst marginalised groups who have been subject to previous research (Moore, 1996). Establishing the trust of respondents is therefore essential. Often trust can only be built up slowly as the purposes of the study and the consequences for respondents of taking part become clearer as the study develops (Berg, 1988; Faugier and Sargeant, 1997). In both an ethical and practical sense, respondents need to be reassured of the protection of the information they provide. This assurance of confidentiality can only be demonstrated over time. These points suggest that the initial respondents may act as invaluable assistants in obtaining the confidence or time of further respondents.

Conclusions

Snowball sampling techniques offer an established method for identifying and contacting hidden populations and, potentially, for their enumeration (although often this may be considered as a secondary concern). Hence, we may want to make a distinction between snowball strategies as a method of contact in a practical sense and as a method of sampling in a more formalised and statistical sense. This latter connotation has been viewed as problematic but statistical techniques are being used to improve the method. Snowball-based methodologies are a valuable tool in studying the lifestyles of groups often located outside mainstream social research. They may also be used to complement other research methodologies in the study of less stigmatised and even elite groups. Advances in the quantitative application of snowball techniques and the increasing need for ascending methodologies to fill in gaps in our knowledge of more obscure social situations suggest both a complementary and substitute role for snowball sampling. The real promise of snowball sampling lies in its ability to uncover aspects of social experience often hidden from both the researcher's and lay person's view of social life.

References

Avico, U., Kaplan, C., Korczak, D. and Van Meter, K. (1988) *Cocaine Epidemiology in Three European Community Cities: a Pilot Study using a Snowball Sampling Methodology.* Brussels: European Communities Health Directorate.

Berg, S. (1988) 'Snowball Sampling', in S. Kotz and N.L. Johnson (eds), *Encyclopaedia of Statistical Sciences Vol. 8.*

Faugier, J. and Sargeant, M. (1997) 'Sampling Hard to Reach Populations', *Journal of Advanced Nursing*, 26: 790–7.

Griffiths, P., Gossop, M., Powis, B. and Strang, J. (1993) 'Reaching Hidden Populations of Drug Users by Privileged Access Interviewers: Methodological and Practical Issues', *Addiction*, 88: 1617–26.

Hendricks, V.M., Blanken, P. and Adriaans, N. (1992) *Snowball Sampling: a Pilot Study on Cocaine Use.* Rotterdam: IVO.

Kaplan, C.D., Korf, D. and Sterk, C. (1987) 'Temporal and Social Contexts of Heroin-Using Populations: an Illustration of the Snowball Sampling Technique', *Journal of Mental and Nervous Disorders*, 175 (9): 566–74.

McNamara, R.P. (1994) *The Times Square Hustler: Male Prostitution in New York City.* Westport: Praeger.

Moore, R. (1996) 'Crown Street Revisited', *Sociological Research Online*, 1 (3) http://www.socresonline.org.uk/1/3/2.html.

Patrick, J. (1973) *A Glasgow Gang Observed.* London: Eyre Methuen.

Pollok, M. and Schlitz, M.A. (1988) 'Does Voluntary Testing Matter? How It Influences Homosexual Safer Sex', Paper presented at the Fourth International Conference on AIDS, Stockholm, Sweden, June 13 1998.

Saunders, P. (1979) *Urban Politics: a Sociological Interpretation.* London: Hutchinson.

Shaw, I., Bloor, M., Cormack, R. and Williamson, H. (1996) 'Estimating the Prevalence of Hard-to-Reach Populations: the Illustration of Mark-Recapture Methods in the Study of Homelessness', *Social Policy and Administration*, 30 (1): 69–85.

Spreen, M. (1992) 'Rare Populations, Hidden Populations and Link-tracing Designs: What and Why?', *Bulletin Methodologie Sociologique*, 36: 34–58.

Snijders, T. (1992) 'Estimation on the Basis of Snowball Samples: How to Weight', *Bulletin Methodologie Sociologique*, 36: 59–70.

Sudman, S. and Freeman, H. (1988) 'The Use of Network Sampling for Locating the Seriously Ill', *Medical Care*, 26 (10): 992–9.

Thomson, S. (1997) 'Adaptive Sampling in Behavioural Surveys', *NIDA Research Monograph*, 296–319.

Van Meter, K. (1990) 'Methodological and Design Issues: Techniques for Assessing the Representatives of Snowball Samples', *NIDA Research Monograph*, 31–43.

Vogt, W.P. (1999) *Dictionary of Statistics and Methodology: a Nontechnical Guide for the Social Sciences*. London: Sage.

See also
Sampling, probability and **Sampling, micro**.

ROWLAND ATKINSON AND JOHN FLINT

Scales, scaling

See **Attitudes**.

Secondary analysis of qualitative data

Although the secondary analysis of quantitative data is a common and generally accepted mode of inquiry, the same cannot be said of qualitative data. This entry outlines some of the forms that secondary analysis of qualitative data can take, the key methodological and ethical issues that arise, and how the approach might be developed further (Hinds et al., 1997).

What is secondary analysis?

Secondary analysis involves the use of existing data, collected for the purposes of a prior study, in order to pursue a research interest which is distinct from that of the original work; this may be a new research question or an alternative perspective on the original question (Hinds et al., 1997; Szabo and Strang 1997). In this respect, secondary analysis differs from systematic reviews and meta-analyses of qualitative studies that aim instead to compile and assess the evidence relating to a common concern or area of practice (Popay et al., 1998). As will be shown below, secondary analysis can involve the use of single or multiple qualitative data sets, as well as mixed qualitative and quantitative data sets. In addition, the approach may either be employed by researchers to re-use their own data or by independent analysts using previously established qualitative data sets.

Despite the fact that thus far secondary analysis of qualitative data has not been widely undertaken, there have been a few reviews of the approach (for example, Hinds et al., 1997; Thorne, 1994). Classification of different types of secondary analysis of qualitative data is not straightforward as there are almost as many types as there are examples. It is made more difficult by the fact that some researchers may not define their work as secondary analysis (Hinds et al., 1997).

These difficulties notwithstanding, forms of secondary analysis are cross-classified in Table 1 according to the focus of the analysis and the nature of the original data used. Examples of work classified in this way will be described; some cells remain empty (cells 1c, 2a and b, 3a and c) because appropriate examples have not yet been identified and it is not known if these forms of secondary analysis have ever been conducted (there are no a priori grounds for excluding them).

Table 1   *Forms of qualitative secondary analysis*

	Nature of original data		
Main focus of analysis	a: Single qualitative dataset	b: Multiple qualitative datasets	c: Mixed qualitative and quantitative datasets
1. Additional in-depth analysis	1a	1b	1c
2. Additional sub-set analysis	2a	2b	2c
3. New perspective/ conceptual focus	3a	3b	3c

(1)   *Additional in-depth analysis*: a more intensive focus on a particular finding or aspect than was undertaken as part of the primary work. For example, Szabo and Strang (1997) describe how they used secondary analysis of their previous study on informal carers of relatives with dementia to consider how carers' perceived 'control' enabled them to manage their care giving experience (cell 1a). Kirschbaum and Knafl (1996) combined data from two studies with which they had been involved to explore the nature and quality of parent–professional relationships across two different illness situations (cell 1b).

(2)   *Additional sub-set analysis*: a selective focus on a sub-set of the sample from the original study (or studies), sharing characteristics which warrant further analysis. For instance, in their secondary analysis of related quantitative and qualitative datasets about claimants of Invalid Care Allowance, McLaughlin and Ritchie (1994) concentrate on the ex-carers in the original sample in order to describe the socio-economic and psychological legacies of care giving among this group (cell 2c).

(3)   *New perspective/conceptual focus*: the retrospective analysis of the whole or part of a data set from a different perspective, to examine concepts which were not central to the original research. I have adopted this strategy in my ongoing doctoral research which involves re-examining qualitative data relating to people's experiences of hospital discharge in order to explore the temporal organisation of this process and associated aftercare regimes (cell 3b).

Why do qualitative secondary analysis?

There is growing interest in re-using qualitative data, reflected, for instance, in the establishment of the Qualidata in Britain (a national service for the acquisition, dessemination and re-use of social science qualitative research data).[1] More generally, limited opportunities for conducting primary research and the costs of qualitative work have prompted researchers to consider maximising use of the data available to them. The advent of software to aid the coding, retrieval and analysis of qualitative data is another development that is likely to facilitate both the archiving and availability of qualitative data for secondary analytic purposes. In these respects, the impetus behind the approach is similar to the one that informed the secondary analysis of quantitative data (Procter, 1993).

Various arguments in favour of developing secondary analysis of qualitative studies have been put forward (Hinds et al., 1997; Sandelowski, 1997; Szabo and Strang, 1997; Thorne, 1994). For example, it has been contended that the approach can be used to generate new knowledge, new hypotheses, or support for existing theories; that it reduces the burden placed on respondents by negating the need to recruit further subjects; and that it allows wider use of data from rare or inaccessible respondents.

In addition, it has been suggested that secondary analysis is a more convenient approach for particular researchers, notably students (Szabo and Strang, 1997). However, Thorne (1994) argues that where the researcher was not part of the original research team the approach is best only employed by experienced researchers because of the particular difficulties of doing secondary analysis in an independent capacity. It should also be noted that use of secondary data does not necessarily preclude the possibility of collecting primary data. This may, for example, be required to obtain additional data or to pursue in a more controlled way the findings emerging from the initial analysis. There may also be a need to consult the primary researcher(s) (assuming that they are available) in order to investigate the circumstances of the original data generation and processing.

Despite the interest in and arguments for developing secondary analysis of qualitative data, the approach has not been widely adopted to date. Furthermore, existing studies have mainly been conducted by researchers re-using their own data rather than by independent analysts using data collected by others. This raises questions about the desirability and feasibility of particular strategies for secondary analysis of qualitative data, discussed below.

Methodological and ethical considerations

Before highlighting some of the key practical and ethical issues that have been discussed in the literature, there are two fundamental methodological issues to be considered.

The first is whether the secondary analysis of qualitative studies is tenable, given that qualitative research is often thought to involve an inter-subjective relationship between the researcher and the researched. In response, it may be argued that even where primary data is gathered via interviews or observation in qualitative studies, there may be more than one researcher involved. Hence within the research team the data still has to be contextualised and interpreted by those who were not present. A more radical response is to argue that the design, conduct and analysis of both qualitative and quantitative research are always contingent upon the contextualisation and interpretation of subjects' situation and responses. Thus, secondary analysis is no more problematic than other forms of empirical inquiry, all of which at some stage depend on the researcher's ability to form critical insights based on inter-subjective understanding.

The second issue concerns the problem of where primary analysis stops and secondary analysis starts. Qualitative research is an iterative process and grounded theory in particular requires that questions undergo a process of formulation and refinement over time (Glaser, 1992). For primary researchers re-using their own data it may be difficult to determine whether the new research is part of the original enquiry or sufficiently distinct from it to qualify as secondary analysis. For independent analysts re-using other researchers' data but employing the same viewpoint or conceptual perspective there are also similar issues about the degree of overlap between their respective work.

Just as the above issues have received little attention in the literature to date, so the principles of, and guidelines for, the conduct of secondary analysis remain rather ill-defined (Thorne, 1994). However, commentators have highlighted a number of practical and ethical considerations (Hinds et al., 1997; Szabo and Strang, 1997; Thorne, 1994). Four key issues are summarised below.

(1) *Compatibility of the data with secondary analysis*: Are the data amenable to secondary analysis? This will depend on the 'fit' between the purpose of the analysis and the nature and quality of the original data (Thorne, 1994). Scope for additional in-depth analysis will vary depending on the nature of the data; for example, while tightly structured interviews tend to limit the range of responses, designs using semi-structured schedules may produce more rich and varied data. A check for the extent of missing data relevant to the secondary analysis but irrelevant to the original study may also be required; for example, where semi-structured interviews involved the discretionary use of probes. More generally, the quality of original data will also need to be assessed.[2]

(2) *Position of the secondary analyst*: Was the analyst part of the original research team? This will influence the decision over whether to undertake secondary analysis and, if so, the procedures to be followed. Secondary analysts require access to the original data, including tapes and field notes, in order to re-examine the data with the new focus in mind. This is likely to be easier if they were part of the original research team. If not, then ideally they should also be able to consult with the primary researcher(s) in order to assess the quality of the original work and to contextualise the material (rather than rely on field notes alone). Further consultation may also be helpful in terms of cross-checking the results of the secondary analysis. Finally, whether conducting secondary analysis in an independent capacity or not, some form of contractual agreement between the secondary analyst and the primary researcher(s), data archive managers, and colleagues involved in the primary research but not in the secondary analysis may have to be negotiated.

(3) *Reporting of original and secondary data analysis*: Such is the complexity of secondary analysis, that it is particularly important that the study design, methods

and issues involved are reported in full. Ideally this should include an outline of the original study and data collection procedures, together with a description of the processes involved in categorising and summarising the data for the secondary analysis, as well as an account of how methodological and ethical considerations were addressed (Thorne, 1994).

(4) *Ethical issues*: How was consent obtained in the original study? Where sensitive data is involved, informed consent cannot be presumed. Given that it is usually not feasible to seek additional consent, a professional judgement may have to be made about whether re-use of the data violates the contract made between subjects and the primary researchers (Hinds et al., 1997). Growing interest in re-using data make it imperative that researchers in general now consider obtaining consent which covers the possibility of secondary analysis as well as the research in hand; this is consistent with professional guidelines on ethical practice (British Sociological Association, 1996).[3]

Conclusion

Despite growing interest in the re-use of qualitative data, secondary analysis remains an under-developed and ill-defined approach. Various methodological and ethical considerations pose a challenge for the would-be secondary analyst, particularly those who were not part of the primary research team. Further work to develop this approach is required to see if the potential benefits can actually be realised in practice.

Notes

This is a revised and updated version of an article first published in *Social Research Update*, 22 (Department of Sociology, University of Surrey).

1 Qualidata can be visited on the web at: http://www.qualidata.essex.ac.uk/
2 Hinds et al. (1997, Appendix) provide a set of criteria for this task.
3 On this note, it is encouraging that Qualidata has worked with the British Economic and Social Research Council to produce guidelines on collecting and preparing data for archiving and on issues of confidentiality and copyright (Corti and Thompson 1998).

References

British Sociological Association (1996) 'Statement of Ethical Practice'.

Bull, M.J. and Kane, R.L. (1996) 'Gaps in Discharge Planning', *Journal of Applied Gerontology*, 15 (4): 486–500.

Corti, L. and Thompson, P. (1998) 'Are You Sitting on Your Qualitative Data? Qualidata's Mission', *International Journal of Social Research Methodology*, 1 (1): 85–9.

Glaser, B.G. (1992) *Basics of Grounded Theory Analysis*. Mill Valley, CA: Sociology Press.

Hinds, P.S., Vogel, R.J., Clarke-Steffen, L. (1997) 'The Possibilities and Pitfalls of Doing a Secondary Analysis of a Qualitative Data Set', *Qualitative Health Research*, 7 (3): 408–24.

Kirschbaum, M.S. and Knafl, K.A. (1996) 'Major Themes in Parent–provider Relationships: a Comparison of Life-threatening and Chronic Illness Experiences', *Journal of Family Nursing*, 2 (2): 195–216.

McLaughlin, E. and Ritchie, J. (1994) 'Legacies of Caring: the Experiences and Circumstances of Ex-carers', *Health and Social Care in the Community*, 2: 241–53.

Popay, J., Rogers, A., Williams, G. (1998) 'Rationale and Standards for the Systematic Review of Qualitative Literature in Health Services Research', *Qualitative Health Research*, 8 (3): 329–40.

Procter, M. (1993) 'Analysing Other Researchers' Data', in N. Gilbert (ed.), *Researching Social Life*. London: Sage.

Sandelowski, M. (1997) '"To Be of Use": Enhancing the Utility of Qualitative Research', *Nursing Outlook*, 45 (3): 125–32.

Szabo, V. and Strang, V.R. (1997) 'Secondary Analysis of Qualitative Data', *Advances in Nursing Science*, 20 (2): 66–74.

Thorne, S. (1994) 'Secondary Analysis in Qualitative Research: Issues and implications', in J.M. Morse (ed.), *Critical Issues in Qualitative Research Methods*. London: Sage.

JANET HEATON

Secondary data analysis

Secondary data analysis involves the analysis of an existing dataset, which had previously been collected by another researcher, usually for a different research question. The collection of original data by a researcher is called primary data collection. Secondary data analysis is widely used by researchers undertaking analysis of quantitative data, and has begun to be applied to qualitative data.

There are many advantages to undertaking secondary, rather than primary, analysis.

(1) *Savings* in relation to resources, in terms of time, money and personnel. To begin with, using data collected by someone else means that the data is available relatively quickly. The researcher does not have to go through the long and costly processes of obtaining funding, designing and implementing their own survey, or paying for a sampling frame, conducting fieldwork, data preparation and data cleaning. The main cost in undertaking secondary analysis is that of obtaining the data.

(2) *Increased data quality*. Many secondary data sets are of high quality, especially in terms of questionnaire and sample design. For example, question-naires may include standardised items and scales. Since the dataset has probably been analysed previously, obvious errors and biases should have been noted and rectified.

(3) *Larger sample size*. Large scale datasets will often use a larger sample than those that can be obtained or afforded by undertaking primary data collection. Larger samples, often drawing from a national population, mean that statistical inference becomes much more straightforward.

(4) The secondary analyst is also able to research topics and/or time periods that they would not otherwise have access to, for example, time-series analysis or cross-national studies.

(5) *Intellectual advancement*. Hinde (1991) notes that secondary analysis builds upon previous work, and thereby creates new knowledge. Another by-

product is that analysing data from a different perspective or theoretical framework may reveal unexpected relationships between variables.

Having outlined the advantages, it is important to note the following problems inherent in undertaking secondary analysis.

(1) *Location and accessibility of data*. The first step in undertaking secondary analysis obviously is locating and accessing a relevant dataset. For some topics, such as crime, there is a choice of easily available datasets, but not for others. For example, while the British Crime Survey series provides a regular source of data using a nationally representative sample, similar series are not readily available for other topics, such as religion.

However, data archives play a great role in making datasets known and available. While it may take time to access data from an archive and the archive may impose a 'handling charge', the amount of time and the cost are minimal compared to that which was required to collect the data in the first place.

(2) *Understanding the dataset*. Having accessed a dataset, the secondary analyst must spend time examining and learning to understand the data. This is greatly facilitated when the original primary researcher has provided comprehensive and accurate documentation of the data.

Also, the data may initially come in an unfamiliar format that the secondary researcher will need to adapt. However, there is a growing general tendency towards data structure formats that are more compatible across different systems. Also, data archives are becoming more adept at providing datasets in the format that will be most useful to the secondary analyst.

(3) *Different purposes of data collection*. Secondary analysis uses data for purposes other than that for which they were originally collected. Consequently, it is unlikely that the dataset will contain all the variables that the researcher wishes to examine. Data may only be available in scaled or aggregated form. For example, a social class variable may be included, but not the original raw information that was used to derive it. As a result, it may not be possible to derive other classifications of social class.

Particular questions may not have been asked of certain subgroups. This is exemplified by the 1991 Northern Ireland Census of Population, which only asked women who were married, widowed, separated or divorced about the number of children they had. The same question was not asked of single women. This gap in information meant that certain measures, such as fertility rates across all women, cannot be calculated.

(4) *Sample issues*. One issue to be aware of is that the sampling design or sample size of the dataset may mean that analysis of particular subgroups is not possible. For example, a survey may have a sample that is representative of a national population, but the sample design does not allow the disaggregation of the dataset into small regional areas.

(5) *Data quality*. While it is hoped that secondary data sources are of high quality, this may not always be the case. Often trivial sources of error will be magnified when a dataset is used in a different way.

The Census of Population in a country is frequently used for secondary data analysis. In most countries, a census is undertaken every 10 years. The main purpose of a national government census is to inform policy, and its limited range of questions reflects this. Questions are only included if there are good policy reasons for doing so. Furthermore, the number of questions that can be included is limited further by a census' sheer scale and expense.

While the census is probably the only survey that includes the whole population, confidentiality concerns require that the complete dataset of individual records is usually not available to researchers. However, in some nations, for instance the United Kingdom, data are available in other formats, such as a sample of anonymised records, or small area statistics. These can provide enough information for substantial secondary analysis.

Another main drawback to censuses is the currency of the information. Since the census in most nations normally takes place only every 10 years, much information gleaned from it is long out of date before the next census is carried out a decade later.

While most secondary data analysis involves the use of quantitative data sets, discussion of and the use of qualitative data for secondary analysis has begun. Heaton (1998) raises four issues that relate specifically to the analysis of qualitative data.

(1) *Compatabilty* of qualitative data with secondary analysis. The protocols for recording qualitative data, such as interviews, are in no way as standardised or established as those for quantitative data. Individual qualitative researchers will have used their own system which may be difficult to understand or even incomprehensible for secondary researchers.;

(2) *Position* of the secondary analyst. While the relationship between the original qualitative researcher and the research subjects from whom he or she collected information should have been quite clear,[1] this will not be the case for the secondary analyst, who probably will never encounter the original subjects of the research.

(3) *Reporting* of secondary data analysis. The original contact between the primary researcher and his/her subjects (hopefully) will have been covered by clearly established agreements about the use and publication of data and the access and right of comment that the subjects will have. The extent to which a secondary analyst will be bound by these agreements can be unclear.

(4) *Ethical issues.* In addition to the above, the secondary analysis of qualitative data raises or intensifies a number of ethical issues of which confidentiality is a particular concern. Even if guarantees of confidentiality or anonymity had been given originally, the access to detail on the subjects that the secondary analysis of qualitative data implies means that these guarantees can easily be breached.

Conclusion

Having reviewed the advantages and disadvantages of secondary analysis, it is useful to summarise Stewart and Kamins (1993), who proposed asking the following broad questions before using secondary data:

(1) What was the purpose of the study?
(2) Who was responsible for collecting the information – what qualifications, resources, and potential biases are represented in the conduct of the survey?

(3)   What information was actually collected?
(4)   When was the information collected?
(5)   How was the information obtained?
(6)   How consistent is the information obtained from one source with information from other sources?

Secondary analysis can be an effective and highly efficient means for carrying out high quality research.

Note

1   In addition, often being quite emotionally intense.

Suggested further reading

Hakim, Catherine (1982) *Secondary Analysis in Social Research: a Guide to Data Sources and Methods with Examples* (Contemporary Social Research: 5). London: George Allen & Unwin.

Kiecolt, K. Jill and Nathan, Laura E. (1985) *Secondary Analysis of Survey Data* (Quantitative Applications in the Social Sciences, Paper 53). Beverley Hills, CA: Sage Publications, Inc.

References

Heaton, Janet (1998) 'Secondary analysis of qualitative data', *Social Research Update*, Issue 22.

Hinde, Andy (1991) 'Secondary Analysis', in Graham Allan and Chris Skinner (eds), *Handbook for Research Students in the Social Sciences*. London: The Falmer Press.

Stewart, David W. and Kamins, Michael A. (1993) *Secondary Research: Information Sources and Methods* (Applied Social Research Methods Series, Vol. 4). Newbury Park, CA: Sage Publications, Inc.

See also **Data archives** and **Ecological fallacy**.

PAULA DEVINE

Sensitive research

Research can be sensitive because of its topic, its location or both. Sensitivity means one or both of two things in this context: the research has potential implications for society as a whole or some people within it; or it is threatening to the researcher or the subjects in terms of financial, political, social or psychological costs and dangers. Research done on police corruption, for example, has potential implications for society or social groups, as does research disclosing the extent of discrimination experienced by some group. Research on social security fraud or white-collar crime is threatening to the subjects, while information that is dangerous for the researcher to discover and disclose is not hard to imagine. Some researchers have been killed (one notably while studying the drug trade) and many are threatened physically or their findings impugned because their research is controversial. This has led researchers to become aware of the special implications of doing sensitive research and dangerous fieldwork. Clearly, what is sensitive about a topic or location can mostly be predicted beforehand but sometimes not, and what is sensitive is relative to the people concerned and can sometimes be different to the various parties involved. Careful thought is therefore needed when planning research in order to anticipate what might be considered sensitive about the topic or location and to whom. This is a recent recognition; for although sensitive research has always been done, it has been approached in the past mainly as a question of ethics, which we now realise is only one of the problems associated with research of this kind.

Advice to researchers studying sensitive topics or working in sensitive locations was initially addressed to the ethical implications of the research. The instructions were prosaic, although not less useful for that. It was discussed rarely in early research methods textbooks, but when it was, students were given advice such as: to keep the research secret or at least out of the public and media domain; to keep their data safe under secure conditions and away from prying eyes; to reassure respondents that confidentiality would be protected; and to be aware that on publication others may use the findings for their own ends and in ways that might have negative effects. Confidentiality is often impossible to guarantee but researchers were given the advice to ensure in all ways possible that they anonymised identities, locations and settings.

Researchers were also told of the potential 'research fatigue' that can come with sensitive research (although it is hardly restricted to it). With sensitive topics or locations, where there is controversy, fear about the research or perhaps hostility towards it, the interpersonal antagonisms between researcher and subjects or 'consumers of research' can lead to fatigue and disillusionment. Tough skins by sensitive researchers are what are needed, we were told, and researchers should guard against easy distraction by the flak they might encounter. The fact that the research may be overt and permission granted by a gatekeeper does not prevent subjects engaging in retrenchment from the bottom, by which through various dodges, devices and deviousness they restrict the researcher's access because they find the research sensitive. In some cases, permission by a senior figure in a bureaucracy can be a disadvantage because it makes workers worried about the management's motives in allowing access, which adds to their sensitivity about the research. Indeed, permission alone can make the research sensitive if it is seen as part of social control, which is why some favour covert observation.

Sensitive research tends to complicate at every stage the usual problems revolving around technique, methodology, fieldwork and dissemination involved in all research, and it brings unique problems of its own. The methodological implications of sensitive research therefore extend well beyond the issue of ethics. Problems of social context (the social, political and economic environment in which the research is carried out) and the physical security of researchers and subjects tend to be unique to sensitive research, but these special considerations impact on and complicate the general problems all research brings. Planning at the design stage needs to give attention to the difficulties that may arise from the social context and in terms of the physical security of the people involved. For example, at the planning stage, researchers who anticipate their topic and location will be sensitive need to reflect on how the research might be designed and presented to the gatekeeper in such a way that permission be granted. This requires consideration of what the gatekeeper might find controversial about the research. As another example, sensitivity impacts on the data collection methods used. Certain styles of research are better suited to overcoming the resistance of people at the bottom who might engage in retrenchment. Qualitative research and ethnographic techniques are specially suited to developing a rapport with subjects over a long time period in the hope of overcoming any retrenchment from below.

Sensitivity also affects relations in the field, the establishment of trust, the techniques used for recording data and the writing up of results. Agonising over prose is necessary to avoid revealing any details that might breach the promise of confidentiality; and sometimes guarantees cannot be delivered because, once in the public domain, matters are largely out of the researcher's control. Sponsors, gatekeepers and subjects can take exception to the way others have used the information rather than what the researcher has actually written, which can impact on future access.

The findings that arise from sensitive research also can be said to have an inherent *political* dimension. Whenever anyone – research subjects, research colleagues, funders, academic or lay 'consumers'of research etc. – disagrees with, or feels threatened by, research findings, political considerations can affect the evaluation, dissemination and impact of the research. The reason for this is that the research will be subject to considerations other than an impartial assessment of its academic worth. People who feel threatened by findings may unconsciously negatively evaluate the research that produced them. Worse, instances in which sound research is criticised unjustly solely to lessen its impact or to promote an opposing viewpoint are all too common. This political aspect of sensitive research can affect its conduct at all stages. Sponsors may deliberately avoid funding research that has the potential to produce 'difficult' findings or back research into 'safe' topics instead. Research subjects are not totally passive and can take umbrage at research they perceive as likely not to be to their benefit. The impartiality of the review process, either of funding applications or of the publications that come out of sensitive research, can be subverted. Contrary to its 'ivory tower' image, power is intrinsic to university life and many academics cynically will block legitimate lines of inquiry in order to promote their own careers or those of their proteges.

Sensitivity is now rightly recognised as an important research issue that warrants special attention and that has 'practical' as well as ethical dimensions. Where research is sensitive, pragmatic decisions often have to be made on the hoof as an issue can arise that was not anticipated to be controversial or sensitive. What is sensitive is highly situational and relative and tied to the wider context of the research, the setting of its location and the people involved. Researchers therefore need to give serious attention not only to what they believe to be sensitive about the research, its topic or location, but also to what their respondents, sponsors, potential gatekeepers and the community at large might make of it.

Suggested further reading

Lee, Ray (1994) *Doing Sensitive Research*. London: Sage.
Lee, Ray (1995) *Dangerous Fieldwork*. London: Sage.

Renzetti and Lee, R. (1993) *Researching Sensitive Topics*. London: Sage.

See also
Ethics.

JOHN BREWER

Sex surveys

Sex surveys in the United States and Britain emerged through sexology's shift in emphasis from 'pathology' to 'normality'. Whilst 'first wave' sexology had focused on 'negative' aspects of sexuality, 'second wave' sexology became interested in the sexual attitudes and behaviour of the general population. This shift deeply affected methodology. Sexology of the 'pathological' drew mainly from clinical case studies. In order to study the 'normal' population, sexologists needed a much broader database, and turned to large-scale survey methods.

By far the most important (and sensational) 'second wave' sexologist was Alfred Kinsey. In 1948 in the United States, Kinsey published one of the most famous contemporary sex surveys. Kinsey developed a coded questionnaire with which his researchers conducted 20,000 in-depth interviews with people about their sexual behaviour. Rather than focus on sexual attitudes, Kinsey sought to answer a simple, yet rarely asked question: what do people do sexually? The results were (at the time) startling. Despite conservative attitudes towards sexuality, Americans were actually engaged in a wide variety of sexual behaviours. Kinsey found that pre-marital sex and adultery were common. Americans regularly masturbated and engaged in oral sex. But the most unexpected result concerned the prevalence of homosexuality. The survey found that approximately 4–5% of the male population was exclusively homosexual; 50% of single men in their mid-thirties had engaged in explicit homosexual relations; and a significant proportion of married men had also engaged in homosexual sex before and/or during marriage. Kinsey used these results to create a seven-point heterosexuality-homosexuality continuum, arguing that most people are neither exclusively heterosexual nor exclusively homosexual.

The most interesting result of Kinsey's sex survey was that Americans actually engage in a wide variety of sexual behaviour, only a fraction of which is socially sanctioned. Put another way, an implication of Kinsey's results was that it is statistically invalid to label any sexual behaviour 'deviant' if people engage in that behaviour in large numbers. Kinsey's message was radical: rather than focus on people's attitudes, it is much more revealing to focus on what people actually do. Focusing on human behaviour reveals that people are sexually multidimensional.

News of Kinsey's sex survey travelled to Britain, and in 1949 'Little Kinsey' was carried out by a large survey organisation called Mass Observation. In its original form, Mass Observation was concerned with exploring the 'everyday' lives of British people through large surveys. World War II had brought massive political, economic and social changes to Britain, and researchers recognised that much of Britain's 'social fabric' was in major flux. So, from 1937 to 1949, Mass Observation explored public attitudes towards topics such as venereal disease, the declining birth rate, and public displays of sexual activity. For instance, in one early study, Mass Observation studied the sexual behaviour of working-class people who took their annual week's holiday in Blackpool, a seaside holiday resort. Mass Observations' researchers both observed and interviewed people about their sexual activity during this annual holiday. Like Kinsey's report, the results showed that people engaged in a wide variety of sexual behaviour, and that sexual morality was much more the product of social context than inalienable principle. Whilst the construction of the research was in line with what the researchers felt constitutes sexual behaviour, the results suggest that respondents emphasised their own and other people's *actual* behaviours. The results also suggested that whilst sexual activity is usually described as private and individual, people actually recognise that sexual activity is socially mediated. One of the most interesting findings of this study was that public sexual behaviour was common amongst holidaymakers, and much of this public sexual activity was sanctioned.

In the decades after Kinsey in the United States and 'Little Kinsey' in Britain, a number of other surveys were carried out. The AIDS epidemic gave urgency to research into sexual behaviour and prompted the most recent national sex surveys. In Britain, the Wellcome Trust funded the 'National Survey of Sexual Attitudes and Lifestyles' (1990) which produced two books: Johnson et al.'s *Sexual Attitudes and Lifestyles*, and Wellings et al.'s *Sexual Behaviour in Britain*. These sex surveys now coexist with an ever-increasing number of 'pop psychology' textbooks, newspaper and magazine articles, Royal Commissions as well as television and radio programmes.

Kinsey and 'Little Kinsey' and the sex surveys that followed provided information about behaviour that had been previously only a matter of often ill-founded speculation. However, they shared a major shortcoming concerning the assumptions of the researchers about what constitutes 'sexual activity'. Indeed, rather than reveal the sexual 'libertarianism' that the sex researchers espoused, these surveys largely reproduced the very attitudes they purported to challenge. First and foremost, all of the surveys were indisputably heteronormative. 'Sex' referred to heterosexual, penetrative intercourse. The researchers largely subscribed to the view that sex is a primal male drive. In other words, 'normal' sex referred to a very limited set of behaviours.

In contrast to 'normal' sex, the term 'petting' was used to encapsulate all other forms – the majority – of sexual behaviour. Here we see again the major failure of these surveys to actually attend to what their respondents were saying. First of all, the term 'petting' renders invisible all lesbian and gay sexual activity. In *Exploring English Character*, for instance, Gorer (1955) notes that people whose main sexual activity was comprised of 'petting' were 'not interested in sex', failing to recognise that these people were actually engaged in lesbian and gay sexual activity.

'Petting' is also used to describe all heterosexual behaviour that is not 'sex' (penetration). This leads the researchers to note people's first 'sexual experience' as the first time they engaged in penetrational (hetero)sexual activity. Moreover, each of the surveys repeatedly found that women reported much higher levels of dissatisfaction with sexual activity than men. Given that what these women actually reported was that they preferred non-penetrative forms of sexual activity (or, in some cases, more time spent in non-penetrative forms of sexual activity), the interpretation of this finding as evidence of women's 'conservative attitudes towards sex' is a remarkable testament to the researcher's failure to understand female sexuality. As Liz Stanley (1995) notes, as much as these surveys attempted to increase our understanding of sexual activity, in the end they did not attend to what their respondents actually reported about their sexual activity. There is a common expectation that sex surveys will reveal ever-increased 'enlightenment', progress and permissiveness towards sexuality. At the same time, sexuality is considered to be very personal, and sexual attitudes and behaviours are subject to strong disciplinary and regulatory societal structures. Consequently, the types of questions asked on sex surveys particularly shape the forms of response. However, since each survey changes the questions asked, surveys may more accurately chart changes in the sense of change in society as reflected by the survey creators, telling us more about the cultural bias of the survey creators than providing an accurate account of the sexual mores of the respondents to the survey.

Suggested further reading

Nye, R. (ed.) (1999) *Sexuality*. Oxford: Oxford University Press.

Reference

See also **Queer research**.

Stanley, L. (1995) *Sex Surveyed 1949–1994. From Mass-Observation's 'Little Kinsey' to the National Survey and the Hite Reports*. London and Bristol, PA: Taylor and Francis.

MYRA J. HIRD

Social change

See **Historical methods**.

Social fact

'Social fact' is a term that was developed by the French sociologist, Emile Durkheim (1858–1917), in *The Rules of Sociological Method* (1982 [1895]), to denote a social reality that was external to the individual, but which influenced the behaviour of that individual. Durkheim's belief in the existence of social facts was predicated upon a number of assumptions.

The first and most obvious assumption was his acceptance of *realism*. Realism, as a general philosophical doctrine, asserts that things exist independently of the human mind. This position is in contrast to *idealism*, which has it that things are products of the mind. As a social ontology, realism asserts the existence of social structures, over and above the existence of individuals and their actions. Here the contrasting position is that of *constructionism*, which posits that, rather than having an independent existence to individuals, the social world is actively constructed and reconstructed by human action.

The second assumption relates to the nature of reality that Durkheim believed existed. Durkheim adopted what is known as the emergent theory of reality. This involves the argument that more complex forms of reality emerge from the interactions of simpler forms. Thus, for example, water is emergent from the interaction of oxygen and hydrogen, but has properties that are found in neither of these gases. Durkheim argued that a similar process occurs when human beings interact with one another. He stated that

> society is not the mere sum of individuals, but the system formed by their association represents a specific reality which has its own characteristics . . . By aggregating together, by interpenetrating, by fusing together, individuals give birth to a being . . . which constitutes a psychical individuality of a new kind. Thus it is in the nature of that individuality and not in that of its component elements that we must search for the proximate and determining causes of the facts produced in it. (Durkheim, 1982: 129)

It was the emergent properties of the social world that gave sociology its *raison d'être* as a separate discipline. While psychology was well suited to study the individual psyche, sociology had a different object-domain, the social world, and therefore was required to provide explanations of that world using its own distinct principles. Durkheim likened the distinction between psychology and sociology to that between chemistry and biology. While it is true that all living things have chemical properties, they are distinguished by the fact that life emerged from the interaction of organic chemicals. Thus, if the study of living things was restricted to the use of the principles of chemistry, it would be impossible to explain the very thing that makes living organisms unique. Hence the need for the discipline of biology. Just as the living world's emergence from the interactions of organic chemicals required the development of the discipline of biology, so the social world's emergence from the interactions of individuals required the development of the discipline of sociology.

The third of Durkheim's assumptions related to the criteria for ascribing reality. He argued that social facts should be regarded as things. This is a very strong and, indeed, at first sight, nonsensical claim. After all, social structures are not things that we can see, feel or touch. Durkheim was prepared to accept that social facts were characterised by immateriality (1982: 162). Thus, he was not depending on what is now termed the perceptual criterion of reality to ground his assertion that social facts were real. Instead, he adopted a causal criterion of reality – under this criterion, things are regarded as real if they are capable of making events occur. As Durkheim succinctly put it, 'A thing is a force' (1982: 161). Once again, this may initially strike the reader as odd. However, within the realm of physics such 'things' are commonplace. One might think, for example, of magnetism or gravity. While these are not the objects of direct perception, we can perceive their effects, such as the patterning of iron filings or the falling of objects, and from observation of those effects extrapolate their reality. For Durkheim, society could cause the same kind of effects on individuals' thoughts and behaviour. The job of social research was to investigate these forces.

Given that social facts cannot be directly observed, how is the social researcher to investigate them? Durkheim's answer is that they can be indirectly observed by means of the comparative examination of social indicators. He argued that by observing changes in indicators, one could identify the manner in which under-lying relationships between social facts were developing. Thus, the use of social indicators, formulated as operational definitions, enabled Durkheim to link his theories about the nature of society with empirical analysis. Throughout his work, Durkheim used three main types of comparative indicators. In *The Division of Labour in Society* (1984 [1893]), he used legal codes as historical indicators to demonstrate how the nature of social solidarity changes with modern develop-ment. In 'mechanical' societies, more emphasis is placed on similarity and uni-formity. This is indicated by the prevalence of repressive laws, which are used to punish those who break commonly held codes. In contrast, 'organic' societies are characterised by difference and individualism. This is indicated by the prevalence of restitutive laws, the aim of which is to restore the equilibrium of inter-dependence when it is threatened or violated.

In *Suicide* (1951 [1897]), Durkheim used rates of an individualistic behaviour, suicide, as statistical indicators of a reality that was external to the individual, social integration; arguing that, to a point, there will be an inverse relationship between the degree to which a group is socially integrated and the proportion of that group which will commit suicide. Once again, he uses his comparative data to demonstrate that modernity involves an attenuation of social integration. Finally, in *The Elementary Forms of Religious Life* (1995 [1912]), Durkheim used anthropological studies of the religious practices of pre-literate native Australians as ethnographic indicators of the level of collective consciousness. He argued that the simplicity of the totemism practised by these groups meant that the function of ideologies, which was to encourage the individual to adhere to the collective consciousness of the group, could be clearly seen. For Durkheim, religion was simply the worship of society.

From the great variety of research methods used by Durkheim himself, ranging from the qualitative to the quantitative, we can see that his model of the social world does not warrant, or even favour, any particular method of social research. What is unique and contentious about Durkheim's approach is its ontology. It is not the method that the researcher uses, but the purpose to which she uses it, the reality that the method is designed to uncover, that distinguishes Durkheim's prescriptions about social research.

Durkheim's assertion of the existence of social facts has had a seminal effect upon social research, most notably on those who adhere to *structuralism*. How-ever, probably more influential has been the opposing voice of Max Weber, who refuted the notion that things emerge from the interaction of individuals. Weber argued that

> for sociological purposes there is no such thing as a collective personality which 'acts'. When reference is made in a sociological context to a state, a nation, a corporation, a family, or an army corps, or to similar collectivities, what is meant is . . . *only* a certain kind of development of actual or possible social actions of individual persons' (Weber, 1978: 14, emphasis in original)

Thus, Weber, through his development of the *Verstehen* method of sociological investigation, took the position that social research should concentrate its efforts on the understandings and motivations of interacting individuals, rather than chasing illusionary social 'facts' that transcend those individuals.

This divide has haunted social research for most of its history – should researchers be investigating the interactions of people in order to uncover the structures that govern those interactions, or should those interactions be examined by investigating the understandings, motivations and feelings of volitional agents? Fortunately, in recent decades, sustained efforts have been made to overcome this rather sterile and dichotomous debate, and to encourage social researchers to accept that adequate understanding of the social world requires that both structure and action be taken into account. Two main approaches have been taken. One, pioneered by Anthony Giddens (1984) in his structuration theory, argues that structure and action are essentially two sides of the same coin. While structures regulate the possibilities of social action, they are only brought into existence by instances of that action. In contrast to Giddens' model, critical realists (see the entry on *Realism*) such as Archer (1995) argue that structure and action exist as separate, but closely interacting entities. While it is possible to alter the nature of structures by means of social action, there are considerable differences in time-scale. Thus, we are born into a world in which social relations have been structured by the actions of our predecessors. Conversely, while our actions may alter these structures, this will rarely be an instantaneous process.

While adopting a different approach to the relationship between structure and action, in many other respects critical realism bears testament to the continuing influence of Durkheim's notion of the social fact. In common with Durkheim, critical realism asserts the reality of emergent social structures possessed of causal powers. Nor is it simply a matter of theory. Durkheim's empirical works still stand as exemplars of the relationship between theory and practice in research.

References

Archer, M. (1995) *Realist Social Theory: the Morphogenetic Approach.* Cambridge: Cambridge University Press.

Durkheim, E. (1951 [1897]) *Suicide.* New York: Free Press.

Durkheim, E. (1982 [1895]) *The Rules of Sociological Method.* London: Macmillan.

Durkheim, E. (1984 [1893]) *The Division of Labour in Society.* New York: Free Press.

Durkheim, E. (1995 [1912]) *The Elementary Forms of Religious Life.* New York: Free Press.

Giddens, A. (1984) *The Constitution of Society.* Cambridge: Polity.

SAM PORTER

Social indicators

Social indicators are scales developed from publicly available social statistics. A true social indicator has features that make it more than just a composite measure.

(1) A social indicator is a set of *normative statistics*. That is, the values that the social indicator statistics take on can range over an idea from 'good' to 'bad'.

What is 'good' and 'bad' is, of course, a value judgement. For example, a rising proportion of pupils attending grammar schools as opposed to comprehensive or secondary schools in the United Kingdom can be considered to be either 'good' or 'bad'. Grammar schools are comparatively 'elite' institutions, only taking students that have been assessed as having better academic potential.[1] Hence, a rising proportion of grammar schools in an educational system would imply that the system is becoming more highly selective and elitist. An arch-conservative would see this as 'a good thing', an egalitarian who believes in open access to education would see exactly the same statistic in the opposite manner.

(2) Social indicators should relate to *outputs* of social programmes rather than *inputs*. For example, the quality of health care being provided in a society would be more validly indicated by *genuine improvements in the health of the population* (an output of a health system) rather than gross *expenditure on the health services* (an input).[2]

(3) Social indicators should be *composite numbers* rather than being based on just a single fact (for example, the housing conditions of an area being based on what proportion of houses have basic amenities like hot water, indoor toilet, good wiring, central heating, etc. rather than any single fact).

(4) Social indicators should be *comprehensive*; that is, they should relate to broad concepts like educational level or juvenile delinquency rather than just to specific details of these broad concepts.

(5) Most importantly, the social indicator should be genuinely *indicative* of something. That is, you should be able to see an explicit link between the social indicator and a broader concept of 'goodness' *and* see why the particular measure being employed is a good shorthand for this concept. That is, the social indicator should have *face validity*.

Notes

1 Though some cynics have noted that 'having better academic potential' sometimes can be defined as having the right connections or the wherewithal needed to pay high fees or make a generous donation.
2 Note that governments tend to emphasise *inputs* when they are defending their record. Opposition political parties tend to emphasise (poor) *outputs* when they are making their criticisms.

See also Social statistics.

ROBERT MILLER

Social statistics

Social statistics are *official, descriptive* statistics.

(1) *Official* in that they are statistics produced by government or other recognised bodies as part of their routine operations. It is important to remember

that they are primarily collated and designed for the body's own, internal use, but, since they often are published or made available to others, outside researchers can also find them useful. Government is the single biggest producer but private enterprise and other bodies (for example, trade unions or non-profit-making institutions like charities) also produce social statistics.

(2) *Descriptive* in that these statistics are basically routine tabulations and organisations of quantitative information on the areas with which the body is concerned. This is in contrast to *analytic or inferential statistics*[1] which are the results of numerical manipulations of data.

The production of official statistics has accelerated enormously in recent times due to the increasing importance of bureaucratic organisation and to the vast increase in the technical ease of generating statistics through computers. Concomitantly, the amount and variety of official statistics available to academics and the general public for their own use has increased enormously. This is due in part to the above noted technological advances in computing. It is now much easier technically with wordprocessing technology to produce tabular information for publication. The protocols for transferring data between different computer systems are more standardised today so the procedures for passing the data themselves on to academics or others for secondary analysis[2] is easier and less expensive. In addition, the spread of 'sunshine' legislation in which government bodies are under legal obligation to make the information they hold available to the general public also has facilitated the growth of the secondary analysis of official statistics.

The main advantages of using social statistics are as follows.

(1) They are *much more extensive and comprehensive* than what researchers can hope to generate themselves. Governments especially have more resources (for instance, no individual researcher no matter how well-funded could afford to carry out a 100% census of the population). Furthermore, governments and official bodies can have more effective access through being in a position, in effect, to compel people to provide information or being in a position that requires people to give the information necessary for the statistics in order to receive a needed service. Note that this element of compulsion does not necessarily mean imposing a legal requirement to provide the information. Instead, by availing oneself of a service or benefit, the person automatically becomes part of the statistics. The only way to avoid this is to elect not to take up the service or benefit. For example, unemployment statistics are based on those who 'sign on' for unemployment benefit. The only way for an unemployed person to avoid becoming part of the statistics is for he or she not to register for unemployment support.[3]

(2) Social statistics *already exist*. Instead of collecting the data from scratch, all the researcher has to do is locate the relevant publication or data source (assuming they will receive permission to use it).

This feature also implies some disadvantages for researchers in that they are limited to using only what already exists. If the researchers are limited to using published statistics, they may be frustrated by discovering the information has not been presented in exactly the form needed. For example, an agency may collect and publish information on two key topics which a researcher strongly suspects are related. If the information on the two topics is published in the form of separate tables, however, the researcher cannot examine the suspected relation directly unless they are given direct access to the original or can persuade the agency to generate custom tables for them especially.[4]

Even if direct access to the data is possible, there still can be problems. The researcher cannot make the government collect exactly the data needed; important points of information may not be contained in the data or may be recorded or asked in a manner that does not correspond precisely with the researcher's needs. The researcher may be forced to make do with information that only approximates what he or she would like ideally.

Finally, there may have been a considerable gap in time since the information was collected. For instance, the census in most nations takes place only once in a decade. Hence, an analyst of official statistics data can be making use of information that is years out of date.

(3) They are *regular*. Many official statistics are generated periodically over a long period of time. For instance, government departments may produce statistics of their activities on a quarterly or even a monthly basis. Similarly, governments often support surveys in which the same questions are repeated on a regular basis, such as the General Household Survey and the Labour Force Survey which are carried out annually in the United Kingdom. Hence, the user of official statistics often can generate a picture of *trends* and change over time; that is, official statistics often have a *longitudinal* dimension.

Note that the same information must be collected and presented the same way each time. If it isn't, one doesn't have a truly consistent series and the longitudinal utility is damaged. For example, when the Conservative government of Margaret Thatcher was elected in Britain, the government made many changes in the definition of unemployment over the span of several years that made longitudinal analysis much more difficult.

(4) *Cross-national comparisons* are often possible (particularly within the European Community). Governments have made genuine attempts to harmonise their surveys and standardise the definitions of important variables.

(5) *Triangulation.* Even social statistics are not central to a researcher's needs, they still can use published social statistics to cross-check information that has been generated in other ways. In that manner, one can evaluate the reliability of these other sources of information.

Sociological criticisms of social statistics

From an official point of view, social statistics are impartial records of the facts, 'real' depictions of the 'true' situation in society. This official view is, however, open to two broad criticisms.

1. The interpretive or phenomenonological critique

From the 'official' point of view, social statistics are generated by a process of real-life events being placed reliably into categories, then totted up. However (i) different observers will have different commonsense ideas of what reality is, so they will see the same thing, but differently. The classic statement of this idea is J.M. Atkinson's critique of Emile Durkheim's study of *Suicide*. Durkheim's study of suicide rates carried out over a century ago is the seminal positivist statement and is based upon official statistics on suicide rates. Atkinson asserted that Durkheim ignored the social processes that take place when the cause of a person's death is recorded as suicide. Features such as the desire not to distress surviving relatives and commonsense notions about the kinds of people likely to commit suicide can affect the assigning of a cause of death. These effects are sufficient in themselves to cause the empirical regularities, such as suicide rates being lower in Catholic countries, that Durkheim attributed to the degree of social integration. From this point of view, apparent facts such as the recent rise in statistics on child sexual abuse and incest are not due to the modern world suddenly becoming more perverted in recent years, but rather are due to people – social workers/doctors/police/and the general public – becoming more aware that a problem exists and, therefore, more likely to recognise it. (ii) different recorders will understand the same categories differently so, even if the 'fact' is immune to commonsensical bias, different recorders will tabulate the same phenomenon in different ways anyway. For instance, excess drinking is defined as the consumption of units of alcohol over a set limit, with the amount set being lower for women. However, the number of units considered 'excessive' varies so wildly that one observer has commented that the real definition of 'excessive' appears to be more units than researchers themselves consume.

Note that these are problems of *reliablity*; that is, the social statistics are said to be not reliable because the same reality will not always be recorded in the same way.

At their most extreme, some interpretive sociologists would say that any form of social statistics, and any quantitative social science, is so unreliable and inaccurate that any quantitative analysis is not valid. This, however, is a grossly exaggerated position. Most quantitative social scientists are only too aware of the problems of reliability in their data that are described above and take steps to minimise them, both during the collection of the information and later in the discussion of empirical results.

2. The radical critique

While the interpretive critique of social statistics is one based on issues of reliability, the radical critique is based on issues of *validity*. Radical statisticians disagree that official statistics are what they claim to be – neutral representations of reality. Instead, all artefacts of a society, including its statistics, are expressions of the class/power relationships within the society. Social statistics serve the needs and reflect the conceptions of reality that are held by those who dominate the society – its ruling class. Hence, far from being neutral, official statistics are supportive of the status quo.

As we have noted already, the bodies that generate official statistics are doing so for their own purposes, not to benefit someone else. (For example, as noted previously, unemployment statistics are based only on those who 'sign on' – as far as the operations of government bureaucracy are concerned, these are the only people 'really' unemployed.) These generating bodies will use their own assumptions/ ideas about how the world is in order to determine categories, the form of presentation, to decide what information is important enough to be published, even what information is worth collecting in the first place. The result is that while official statistics sometimes may produce facts that are embarrassing to those in power, in a fundamental way they must reflect the viewpoint of those in power. An example of this type of phenomenon would be the lack of official statistics on the employment of women up until recent years through mechanisms such as housewives being classified as 'economically inactive' (that is, reflections of a general view that 'women aren't important').

It is important to note that the 'radical critique' is not just a crude conspiracy theory. The distortion in official statistics does not represent a deliberate attempt to misrepresent or deceive but rather comes from the official statistics unconsciously reflecting the dominant viewpoint. Nevertheless, from the point of view of the radical critique, it is an inevitable and pervasive bias in favour of those with power.

Notes

1 With inferential statistics, the analyst actively manipulates raw, or primary, data – using the statistics and the logic of hypothesis testing to generalise to a larger, unknown population or to a relationship which cannot be directly observed. See the entry on *Hypothesis testing* in this volume.
2 In *secondary data analysis*, the researcher adapts data or information for their own analysis that was originally collected for some other purpose. This can be contrasted with *primary data analysis* in which the researcher collects information directly.
3 There has been an ongoing controversy concerning the unemployment rate in the United Kingdom. The official rate always is lower than the proportion of people who will state they are unemployed for a survey or the census, leading to accusations of politically motivated manipulations designed to keep the rate low. This may be the case but, from the point of view of government, the rate is impartial, simply being generated as a by-product of the process of registering individuals as unemployed.
4 Asserting that prevalent features in two *separate* tabulations taken from the same set of cases are linked in a causal manner when in fact a direct link has not been shown is called the **ecological fallacy**.

Suggested further reading

Bulmer, Martin (1980) 'Why Don't Sociologists Make More Use of Official Statistics', *Sociology*, 14: 505–23.
Hakim, Catherine (1982) *Secondary Analysis in Social Research: a Guide to Data Sources and Methods with Examples*. London: George Allen & Unwin.

Irvine, John, Miles, Ian and Evan, Jeff (1979) *Demystifying Social Statistics*. London: Pluto Press.

> **See also**
> **Secondary**
> **analysis**.

ROBERT MILLER

Social surveys

The social survey is one of the best known and most widely used approaches to investigation in the social sciences. It is normally associated with the questionnaire, the most common technique for data collection used by surveys. However, the survey is more than a data collection technique. Rather it refers to a research design and can include a range of research goals.

A defining feature of the survey is that it is a structured method of data collection. Surveys collect information on the same characteristics or variables about each respondent or case. While surveys are used to collect information on individuals, groups and organisations (for example, schools), most often it is individuals who provide information about themselves. The term social survey usually implies interviewing a sample taken from the general population. Indeed the intention of a survey is usually to generalise from a sample to a population.

As a research design each survey should contain a statement of its purpose. The goals of survey research may be simply descriptive or may be explanatory. While the potential subject matter of surveys can be quite diverse, the survey is more appropriate to some topics of research than others. It lends itself to the collection of data on demographic characteristics and routine behaviour and to reporting opinions. A great variety of surveys are carried out by market researchers, government agencies and academics.

The focus of market research is typically on consumer behaviour. Market research companies also conduct opinion polls. Government agencies may conduct surveys to collect factual or administrative information. They may focus on particular policy areas, for example poverty or employment, and are often concerned with evaluating specific services. Governments may also conduct a national Census of Population that covers the entire population. In contrast to the Census, a nationwide sample survey may involve only a few thousand respondents.

Academic surveys are more likely to be in part driven by theoretical concerns and to aspire to an explanatory purpose. This may be seen in the type of analysis that is carried out once the data has been collected. If the goal is explanatory and not just descriptive the analysis may be quite complex, examining multiple relationships among variables. The researcher should think ahead to the type of analysis before carrying out the data collection in the survey.

The social survey offers many attractions to those who adopt it. This approach to data collection, especially the use of questionnaires, enables data to be collected about relatively large numbers of people. Because data are collected about the same characteristics from multiple respondents, it allows us to compare respondents. The data should be suitable for enumeration, facilitating quantitative analysis. The availability of computer software for data input and statistical analysis have greatly assisted this. When the respondents comprise a representative probability sample we can generalise from them to the entire population. Even the modest goal of the descriptive survey ensures the collection of relevant data on topics of interest and is a necessary stage in the progress of sociological investigation. Another commendable feature of the social survey is that the research process is relatively transparent. Each stage of the research design may be visible and can be replicated by other researchers as a check on the reliability of the data or results.

Despite the attractions of the social survey there are some problems and it has not been exempt from negative criticism. A main charge against the survey method is that it is liable to the criticisms directed at positivism generally. The survey method has been criticised for paying inadequate attention to the different meanings which respondents attribute to their actions. More directly, all respondents to a survey might not have the same understanding of the questions asked in the survey. These pose problems for the validity of survey research.

The survey approach also has been criticised for being superficial in its treatment of either complex or sensitive areas of research. When a questionnaire is used, the design must be such that it is easy to administer by the researcher and easily understood by the respondent. Therefore, the questions tend to be relatively simple and strive to quantify, which may be inadequate to capture complex situations or processes. The predetermined list of questions and fixed format of a questionnaire do not allow for probing the initial responses of respondents and make it inflexible for exploratory inquiry. Surveys assume that persons are comfortable in reporting their behaviour and opinions, as well as a certain level of communication skills and memory recall.

An important and growing methodological problem is that of non-response. Persons may decline to participate in the survey or they may refuse to answer some of the questions. Non-respondents tend to be different from respondents, for example older and less educated. This introduces a bias into the sample and consequently we can generalise to the population less confidently.

There are three main types of survey: the survey with personal interviews; the postal survey; and the telephone survey. The type of survey that the researcher proposes to use affects the ease with which a representative sample can be obtained, the type of questions which can be asked and the response rates.

In the survey with personal interviews, an interviewer is physically present in order to collect the data from the respondent. This has the effect of increasing the overall rate of participation in the survey and of reducing the number of individual questions that are left unanswered. The presence of an interviewer may allow more complex questions to be included in the questionnaire design, as the interviewer can advise on difficulties with completion. On the other hand, there is the possibility of an interviewer effect or bias if interviewers intervene in different ways. The main disadvantages of administering a survey face-to-face is that it is time-consuming to complete and expensive to conduct.

An interesting recent innovation in face-to-face personal interview surveys is *data collection at point of interview*. Instead of using a traditional interview schedule in which the questions are printed on paper, the interviewer uses a laptop computer in which questions are read off the screen as they come up. The interviewer types the answer directly into the laptop. The result is that the respondent's answers are immediately coded on the spot and stored on the laptop's hard disk for easy retrieval later.

In the postal survey a questionnaire is mailed to respondents, usually with an enclosed stamped addressed return envelope, and the participant completes it and returns it to the researcher. The main advantage of a postal survey is that it is much less expensive to conduct. Since there is no face-to-face contact with an interview, the postal survey also offers increased anonymity, which can be a major advantage if research is being carried out on sensitive topics. The main disadvantage of a postal survey is that it suffers from the problem of non-response. Typically, response rates in postal surveys can amount to no more than 50%; that is, less than half those contacted may reply.

The telephone survey has become increasingly popular in recent years. It is a favourite of market research companies. It has been aided by computer software similar to that used by data collection at point of interview which enables the interviewer to input the responses directly into a computer as they are provided by the respondent. It is faster and cheaper than personal interviewing. It has, for example, proved to be very useful in opinion polling of voting intentions. On the other hand, it must be stressed that telephone connection is still not universal, with lower possession among the poor and elderly and consequently the method suffers from problems of bias (exacerbated by the tendency for more affluent families to have multiple phone lines). Nor is it as suitable as the face-to-face situation for presenting questions with a complex structure.

Technological developments mean that the conduct of surveys is constantly changing. The decline in residential landline telephones poses a challenge to the telephone survey. More generally, problems such as that of non-response endure and are getting worse from a public increasingly weary of requests to co-operate with surveys. There is now also the issue in some countries of data protection legislation which places new responsibilities on researchers who use the survey method.

The survey should be an intellectual and not simply a technical exercise. Good practice when using social surveys should include a clear rationale for the choice of this particular research design, with clearly stated goals and precise research questions. Given the commitment of time and resources that a survey requires, the researcher should at the outset be sure that the information does not already exist in another survey or in some form, such as official statistics. The quality of a survey cannot be judged simply on the basis of a reading of the data collection instrument such as a questionnaire – it can only be judged on the basis of whether it is appropriate and meets its stated goals.

Suggested further reading

De Vaus, D.A. (1996) *Surveys in Social Research*, 4th edn. London: UCL Press.

Moser, C.A. and Kalton, G. (1971) *Survey Methods in Social Investigation*. London: Heinemann.

Oppenheim, A.N. (1992) *Questionnaire Design, Interviewing and Attitude Measurement*. London: Pinter.

RICHARD O'LEARY

Spatial statistical analysis

See **Geographic information systems**.

Standardisation

Standardisation is the process of converting a batch of data values into standardised units by removing the effects of the average size of the values in the batch (the *level*) and the size of the dispersion (or *spread*) of values around the average value. An analyst might wish to do this if he or she has to compare sets of figures in which both the average scale values of each set of figures and also the spread of values around the averages are quite different. For example, an analyst might want to compare the number of years of schooling of a group of people, where the mean number is quite small, say 12 years, and the dispersion of years of schooling around that mean is also small, say plus or minus 4 years, with the average annual incomes of the same group, where both the mean, say $65,000, and the dispersion, plus or minus $55,000, are relatively large. Standardisation usually is carried out on interval/ratio data.

To standardise interval/ratio data, we convert the distance between a particular data point and the mean from its original scale of measurement into a scale measured in standard deviation units. The distances measured on this scale are called *standardised* or *Z scores*. A data value is converted into standardised scores by subtracting it from the mean and dividing that by the standard deviation.

$$\text{Standardised score (Z)} = \frac{\text{Individual score minus Mean}}{\text{Standard deviation}}$$

This formula for interval/ration data can be generalised to apply to any measure of central tendency and any measure of dispersion.

$$\text{Standardised score} = \frac{\text{Individual score minus Central point}}{\text{Measure of dispersion}}$$

On the distribution of values on the *standardised scale* that results, the central point (the mean) is 0 and a unit of dispersion (standard deviation) equals 1.

In the case of interval or ratio data that falls into a normal distribution, the Z-scores can be used to derive very specific information about the data. For example, a Z-score of +2 is two standard deviations above the mean. Ninety-nine per cent of Z scores fall between -3 and + 3. The plus or minus sign refers to whether the data point is located above or below the mean. Once we convert a score into a Z-score we can consult published statistical tables for the normal distribution which report the percentage of cases in the distribution to be found between the mean and the particular Z-score. For example, for a Z-score of 1.25, 39.44% of the data values will lie between that point and the mean.

The use of Z scores to report how many standard deviations a particular case is above or below the mean is useful when we want to compare scores on different variables, which may originally have been measured on different scales. An illustrative example is provided by Agresti and Finlay (1997). How would we compare an individual's performance on two college tests, a score of 550 on an SAT exam and score of 30 on an ACT exam. We are told that the SAT exam mean score is 500 with a standard deviation of 100 and that the ACT exam mean score is 18 with a standard deviation of 6 and, most importantly, both test scores are normally distributed. On both tests the performances are above average but we cannot compare them because they are measured on different scales. However, we can compare them by standardising the scores. The calculated Z-score for the performance on the SAT is 0.5, i.e. it is 0.5 sd above the mean while the Z-score for the ACT is 2, i.e. it is 2 sd above the mean. Clearly the performance on the ACT test is relatively better. We can even calculate precisely the percentage placing achieved by the student on the two tests (that is, the percentage of cases below the particular Z-score) by referring to the published statistical tables for this.

Standardised scores are used widely in statistics. The advantage of using the standardised score is that it is independent of the scale on which the data were originally measured.

Suggested further reading

Clegg, F. (1982) *Simple Statistics*. Cambridge: Cambridge University Press.

Reference

Agresti, A. and Finlay, B. (1997) *Statistical Methods for the Social Sciences*. London: Prentice Hall.

RICHARD O'LEARY

See also **Central tendency** and **Dispersion and the normal distribution**.

Statistical interaction

In quantitative data analysis a statistical interaction can be defined as an expression of the linkage or association between two or more independent/causal variables. This linkage or association is beyond what would be expected by chance and means that one cannot just add together the effects of each independent variable upon a dependent variable; if an interaction is present the effect of each independent variable varies *depending upon* the other independent variable(s).

The concept of interaction

Understanding what interactions are and being able to distinguish them from the simple combined effects of two or more independent/causal variables is important for understanding multivariate analysis. First, let us examine a bad taste non-statistical example of an interaction. Suppose we have three Hollywood stars, all of whom go out for a wild night on the town. Star A drinks prodigious amounts of alcohol. Late the next day, she wakes up with a hangover. Star B does not drink but, when she arrives home, she takes several very potent sleeping pills. Late the next day, she wakes up with a hangover. Star C drinks prodigious amounts of alcohol and, when she arrives home, takes several very potent sleeping pills. Late the next day, instead of waking up with two hangovers, Star C wakes up dead. We can put this in a chart:

	Drug	Effect
Star A	Alcohol	HANGOVER
Star B	Sleeping pills	HANGOVER
Star C	Alcohol & Sleeping pills	DEAD

Safe dosages of the two drugs, alcohol and barbiturates, both of which have depressive effects upon the central nervous system, can *interact* in combination to depress neurological activity sufficiently to cause cessation of breathing and death. Doses of each drug that, singly, are not lethal, together can produce a combined effect that is fatal. The dangers of drug interactions are well known and often unpredictable.[1]

This phenomenon, that two independent causes (or variables) can have a different effect in combination than a simple addition together of their effects alone, is the essence of interaction.

Examples of types of statistical interaction

Let us assume that a university wishes to analyse the effects of Type of Subject (Science or Arts) and Gender (male or female) upon the final grade average of students. For the sake of argument, let us assume that Arts students on average receive higher grades than Science students and female students throughout the university as a whole get higher grades on average than male students. If the analysts are testing for a statistical interaction between Type of Subject and Gender, there are four possibilities.

(1) *No interaction between Type of Subject and Gender.* If the university finds that male students in Science subjects get the lowest grades, this may not be the result of an interaction; it can just be a result of their combined disadvantages of being male and taking a Science subject. To put it another way, the result can just be *additive*, due solely to the effects of Gender and Subject being added together. (Conversely, establishing that female students who took Arts subjects received the highest grades overall is just the same phenomenon looked at in the other way.)

(2) *Interaction, heightened effect of Subject and Gender.* It can be that the analysts find that the effects of the independent variables of Subject and Gender on the dependent variable of Grades are more than just adding together their separate effects. For instance, it may be that the higher grades received by the women who take Arts subjects are, on average, *even higher* than what one would expect if we just added together their advantages of being female and being in the Arts departments.

Note that it may be that only certain combinations of categories will show this heightened effect. For example, even though women in Arts do better than we would expect, it can also be the case at the same time that men in Science subjects do no worse than a simple addition of their disadvantages of being male and being in Science. This is similar to the 'hangover' example above. Something about being female *and* in Arts compounds the good effect on grades to be more than just the Gender and Subject added together.

(3) *Interaction, lessened effect of Subject and Gender.* On the other hand, the effects of the independent variables of Subject and Gender on the dependent variable of Grades could be *less* than adding together their separate effects. While less dramatic than a heightened effect, this is no less a statistical interaction.

As with heightened effects, it may be that only certain combinations of categories show this lessened effect. For example, we could find that the lower grades of the male Science students are not quite as low as we would expect if we just added the effects of Subject and Gender together.

(4) *Interaction, effects of Subject and Gender mutually cancelling each other out.* Finally, we could have a university where there appear to be no overall differences in the grade averages of either Arts and Science subjects or of female and male students. However, when the effects of the variables of Subject and Gender are looked at *in combination*, the analysts discover that there are in fact quite strong effects of Subject and Gender, only they cancel each other out. For instance, the analysts could discover that women in the Arts subjects receive much higher grades than men in Arts and that men in the Science subjects receive much higher grades than women in Science. The strong differences of Gender in each Subject, but running in opposite directions, mask each other.

This last example is particularly intriguing, because it means that it is possible to have an interaction between two or more independent variables that *is* significant while, at the same time, the direct effects of one or all of the independent variables are *not* significant.[2]

A great advantage of multivariate analyses, that means the models they generate go some way towards approximating social reality, is their ability to test for statistical interactions.

Notes

See also
Analysis of variance;
Correlation and Regression and **Loglinear analysis**.

1   Hence, the warnings with many drugs not to take them in concert with other drugs without medical advice.
2   Thankfully, this last example, where all independent variables examined singly do not have a significant effect on the dependent variable while, simultaneously, combinations of independent variables are exerting significant effects, is rare.

ROBERT MILLER

Statistical testing

See **Hypothesis testing**.

Structuralism/post-structuralism

In one sense structuralism describes any approach in the social sciences that accords primacy to social structures over human agency. Used in this way, it could cover work from that of the sociologist Talcott Parsons to the ideas of Karl Marx. In a more technical sense structuralism describes the movement of thought in French philosophy associated with Levi-Strauss, Althusser and Foucault that impacted the social sciences in the wake of the attack on positivism in the 1960s. The kernel idea is fairly simple. Reality is under-girded by deep-lying structures that give it a more fixed and determined character than how it appears to us at first sight given its superficial shifting and fluctuating features. Borrowing related terminology from Marx, there is a distinction between 'essence' and 'appearance', with essential structures underneath the way social reality appears. This idea was applied in social anthropology through the popularity of Levi-Strauss's semiotic analysis, in sociology through Foucault's work on knowledge, power and discourse, in psychoanalysis via Lacan and in Marxism through the writings of Althusser. In each, the central idea of structuralism was expressed in disciplinary terms but argued to the same point: the death, as Giddens put it in 1979, of the human subject and of their voluntary agency under the impact of deterministic structures. In psychoanalysis Lacan argued that Freud's work revealed that hidden unconscious desires structured human consciousness rather than reason and conscious thought; in Marxism Althusser showed that human beings are structured by sets of social relations determined by the nature of production; in social anthropology, Levi-Strauss pointed to the universal structures of the human mind that affected our understanding of things like kinship systems, totemism and mythologies; and in sociology Foucault alerted us to the underlying elements of discourse that structured language and knowledge and affected power relations.

This apparently simple idea within structuralism is more complex than it first appears. Behind the variety of languages, systems of signs, types of society or human behaviour (socially orderly or psychologically 'abnormal') lie fairly constant and unchanging structural factors. Societies appear to change much more than they actually do, since social change rarely involves a dramatic shift in the underlying structure. When it does, social change is often violent and radical rather than progressive and evolutionary. Moreover, what appear to us as normal parts of the natural or social world are actually artefacts of the structures that create them; 'the normal' and 'the natural' are social products created by the constellation of structural forces that underlie them. For example, what counts as 'truth' is socially constructed by the language games and discourse in which truth claims are made, gender is a social product and what is defined as psychologically 'normal' and 'natural' is likewise. Human beings therefore add little to the essential meaning of social reality: we are not authors of the world but products of it ourselves. Structuralism was, if you like, the social science equivalent of Darwinism. The theory of evolution had revealed that human beings were not the authors of creation and structuralism revealed that we are mere bearers of the social world, not its creators. We are subject to the structural forces that envelope us not free of them – prisoners of the unconscious mind, of discursive formations, of systems of signs or sets of social relations rooted in the system of production. In their turn, these ideas lost popularity when post-structuralism and postmodernism came to dominate the cultural sciences.

The philosophical and theoretical movement termed post-structuralism also originated in French philosophy, but quickly became popular in European social science generally. Post-structuralism is sometimes treated synonymously to postmodernism, although the former technically describes ideas within linguistics and literary analysis and the latter in social and cultural theory. The term post-structuralism is not used to suggest that the original ideas were wrong but to show the extent of continuity and change with the earlier work. Structuralism revealed the hidden structures that underlie reality, showing the limits to knowledge when these structures remain undisclosed. Post-structuralism changes the emphasis by focusing on the nature of surface knowledge and meaning, particularly as conveyed in texts. Saussure (in linguistics), Derrida and Baudrillard (both in literary criticism) placed emphasis on the rhetorical devices by which language and texts are constructed. They encouraged the development of *deconstruction* as a method of interpretation, through which the claims made in texts and discourse (religious claims in Scripture, truth claims in the natural sciences and so on) are analysed in terms of the devices used to make them. Foucault's writings on discourse are thus seen as a bridge between structuralism and post-structuralism. Derrida also reversed the structuralist dissolution of the individual by recognising that individual readers or listeners of texts are meaning-givers equal to the author-speaker. Moreover, he also argued that the 'true' meaning of a text can never be known and all interpretations are provisional (including those of the structuralist writers they superseded). Texts that make truth claims thus subvert themselves and should be deconstructed to identify the devices used to make and spuriously validate such claims. Derrida thereby challenged the assumption within both Western realism and in French structuralism that it is possible to represent the world objectively through language.

These post-structuralist writings in linguistics and literary criticism impacted on social science in two ways. They fed directly into critical discourse analysis, where the meanings of texts (written and oral) is seen as relative to the language games and discursive formation through which the claim is produced; post-structuralism adds to this also the rhetorical devices by which the claim is constructed. Secondly, they merged with postmodern ideas in cultural and social theory to form a thorough critique of the practice of social research. Most of the deconstruction of the practice of social research has been applied to qualitative research. However, social studies of scientific knowledge (for example, Gilbert and Mulkay's (1984) *Opening Pandora's Box*) deconstruct the language of natural scientists to focus on the rhetorical devices through which natural science research is written to give it its sense of authority. Qualitative post-structuralists, like Paul Atkinson, who address the rhetorical claims of social research, often disassociate themselves from postmodernism, with its stress on cultural fragmentation, scientific relativism and a denial of the idea of progress, but other writers recognise little distinction (for example, Travers, 2001).

The post-structuralist/postmodern critique of the practice of qualitative research is wide ranging and concerns the theories of knowledge (epistemology) used in social research, theories of the nature of social reality (ontology) underlying research practice, and the status of the claims made in research, such as the status of the written text and the rhetorical skills used to give the author's account validity (its representational claims). These concerns have particularly affected ethnography, with the development of post-structuralist deconstructions of ethnographic writings and text, particularly in cultural anthropology in the work of Clifford (1988) and sociology in the work of Atkinson (1990), as well as the emergence of various postmodern ethnographies that seek to capture the multiple realities that are said to exist in ways that do not privilege the ethnographer's account (Denzin, 1997). Postmodern and post-structuralist theories of knowledge deny the existence of absolute truth and with it the relevance of the scientific criteria by which truth claims are normally assessed, and deny the existence of objectivity and thus the very possibility of social science. Knowledge is relative, and so too is social reality. There are multiple versions – or voices as they often put it – in social reality that research must capture and in a way that does not give authority to the social researcher's account. This impacts on the way research should be written up and texts need to avoid the usual rhetorical devices by which the author's voice is privileged. Postmodernism and post-structuralism therefore refute the idea associated with various 'realist' epistemologies that we can represent the world in social research unproblematically. This has to do in part with the limits of social research, partly the opaque nature of the social world and also because of the problems around the language used.

Suggested further reading

Atkinson, Paul (1992) *Understanding Ethnographic Texts*. London: Sage.
Dickens, D. and Fontana, A. (eds) (1994) *Postmodernism and Social Inquiry*. London: UCLA Press.

Giddens, A. (1979) 'Structuralism and the Theory of the Subject', in his *Central Problems in Social Theory*. London: Macmillan.
Hammersley, M. (1993) 'The Rhetorical Turn in Ethnography', *Social Science Information*, 32: 23–37.

References

Atkinson, Paul (1990) *The Ethnographic Imagination*. London: Routledge.
Clifford, (1988) *The Predicament of Culture*. California: University of California Press.
Denzin, Norman (1997) *Interpretive Ethnography*. Thousand Oaks, CA: Sage.

Gilbert and Mulkay, (1984) *Opening Pandora's Box*. Cambridge: Cambridge University Press.
Travers, Max (2001) *Qualitative Research Through Case Studies*. London: Sage.

See also **Modernity**.

JOHN BREWER

Systematic review

A systematic review is a comprehensive review of literature which differs from a traditional literature review in that it is conducted in a methodical (or systematic) and unbiased manner, according to a pre-specified protocol, with the aim of synthesising the retrieved information through meta-analysis, often using statistical tests. A systematic review can be considered analogous as primary research where the cases are research publications. The reviewer must specify: how the publications (cases) will be selected; the type of instrument that will be used to obtain data from the publications; the methods to be used for this data collection; and the type of analysis that will be conducted on the data. Therefore, when undertaking a systematic review, the researcher must follow an explicit path. This will be outlined, with reference to an example of a systematic review conducted by Thomson, Petticrew and Morrison (2001).

Specify the question to be answered by the review

A systematic review aims to answer a specific question, which must be clarified at the outset. A general guideline for formulating the question is that a systematic review cannot answer questions that could not be answered using primary research. For example, the systematic review that we are using as an example aimed to answer the question: 'What is the effect on health of housing improvement interventions?'

Write a protocol (plan and design the review)

The *protocol* should begin with a background and rationale for the review and a statement of the review question. This should be followed by further details on the methodology of the review, with sufficient detail to allow replication. The main pieces of information usually contained in a systematic review protocol are as follows.

Eligibility criteria

The researcher must decide, on the basis of appropriateness and availability, what types of study design will be included in the review. For example, if the review aims to assess the effectiveness of an intervention, the researcher may decide that only studies following a randomised controlled trial (or true experimental) design will be acceptable. However, the researcher may believe that the review should be all-encompassing and include published material which has not been formally peer reviewed – the so-called 'grey literature'. In addition, the eligibility criteria should address issues such as the acceptable types of setting, participants, interventions and comparators (if appropriate), outcomes and any language or date restrictions. The eligibility criteria will help to narrow the amount of literature to be reviewed, and is analogous to specifying the population of interest in primary research.

The eligibility criteria helps to clarify any ambiguities contained in the review question. In effect, the eligibility criteria adds details to the review question. For example, the review question above was elaborated by stating that articles would be included in the review if they were primary studies, from any source, in any language, that used experimental or quasi-experimental approaches to examine the effects of housing improvements. Housing interventions were defined as rehousing or changes to infrastructure, such as installation of heating, insulation, double glazing or general refurbishment. The outcomes were based on the social model of health, including socio-economic changes and illness based outcomes. Articles were excluded from the review if they had a cross-sectional design, if the intervention was indoor improvements through the provision of furniture or equipment only, or if they were environmental studies of pollutants.

Search strategy

Articles for the review can be retrieved by searching electronic databases, by hand searching through appropriate journals and by contacting researchers in the area of interest. To avoid bias in the retrieval of articles (in much the same way as we wish to avoid bias in the selection of a sample for primary research) the search strategy specified in the protocol must include as much detail as possible. In most cases this amounts to a list of keywords and how they will be combined for use in electronic search engines. Some knowledge of the capability of each subject specific database is important at this point, as some databases operate a thesaurus search system and others operate on the basis of keywords only. For this reason, the assistance of an information specialist is invaluable during the early stages of a systematic review. For example, in our exemplar the reviewers searched 17 electronic databases, hand searched relevant articles for further references and contacted interested parties through interest groups and academic and government departments.

Validity criteria

Having decided on the type of studies to be included in the review, the researcher should now decide how the validity (or quality) of each study is to be assessed, because even published research can be poorly designed, analysed, interpreted or reported. Although quality checklists have been published for the assessment of many types of quantitative and qualitative research, the validity criteria will depend greatly on the types of studies to be included in the review. The reviewers in the housing intervention study decided to categorise each article into either: (1) a randomised controlled trial with objective assessment of the health outcomes; (2) a prospective study with a control group, limited control of confounding and appropriate assessment of health outcomes; or (3) prospective and retrospective studies that did not adjust for confounding factors. The reviewers decided that studies in the third category would produce biased/invalid results and therefore should be excluded from the review.

Data extraction, analysis and dissemination

The level of detail sought will depend very much on the type of review to be undertaken. For example, a data extraction form and plan of analysis can easily be designed and included in a protocol for reviews which are intended to include one type of study design only. Yet, with more complex reviews the data extraction form will begin broad and will be amended as the variety of information provided by the different types of studies becomes apparent. Whatever the case, the protocol should contain: some information about the type of data that will be sought during the review (based on a consideration of the users of the review); whether the synthesis of information will be narrative, statistical, or a combination of both; and how the results will be reported (usually in the form of a journal article but often a more detailed report will also be produced).

All the above components of the protocol should be piloted before embarking on the data collection phase of the review.

A protocol is a time-consuming but worthwhile part of the systematic review. It enables the researcher to consider the type of people that need to be included in the review team, it provides a focus for the team, it allows an assessment of the time required for the review (usually about 9-12 months) and it publicises the plans for the review. In health and social care research, protocols for reviews of interventions are published in the Cochrane Library [http://www.update-software.com/cochrane] and protocols for other reviews are published in the United Kingdom at the National Research Register of the Department of Health [http://www.update-software.com/national]. These outlets are a valuable method of obtaining peer feedback about protocols, thereby allowing amendments to be made at an early stage of the research.

Retrieve eligible literature

At this stage, a search for articles is conducted using the search strategy outlined in the protocol and articles are retrieved. Studies are then assessed to ensure that they meet the eligibility criteria. With some sophisticated search strategies, certain study designs can be included or excluded and this will reduce the time required for the assessment of eligibility. However when the topic of interest is not well indexed in the electronic databases, the search may result in a large number of articles. This was the case in our example review. The reviewers retrieved abstracts for 243 articles. A review of the abstracts narrowed this list to 185 potentially relevant articles. When the eligibility criteria was applied to the full text of the article, the total number of relevant articles for review reduced to eighteen. It is preferable that the eligibility assessment of articles is conducted independently by at least two reviewers and a statistical measure of inter-rater agreement, such as the *kappa* statistic, is calculated in order to alert the review team to any potential bias. Disagreements that cannot be resolved between the two reviewers should be referred to a third member of the review team. At this stage, it may be useful to remove the authors and journal name from the article to be assessed by the third reviewer, in case these have been the source of bias.

Collect data

After ineligible articles are excluded from the review (and a record of the reasons for exclusion has been completed), the remaining articles are assessed for quality. Again, this assessment should be conducted independently by at least two reviewers and their level of agreement assessed statistically. The review team needs to decide how to take the quality assessment into account. For example, the team could decide a priori on a quality cut-off score below which articles are excluded from the review (as was the case in our example review), they could decide to combine results sequentially based on the quality scores, or they could decide to incorporate the quality scores as a weighting factor in the analysis phase. (In practice, the latter option is chosen rarely.)

During this stage data is extracted from all articles included in the review. This is an attempt to reduce the information presented in each article to a manageable amount which will be included in the analysis. Reviewers must be wary of duplicate publications – the same study reported in different formats in different sources. Also, well-designed studies often may not report sufficient detail about the type of results the reviewers are seeking. These studies should not be discarded, but some attempt should be made to contact the study authors in order to retrieve the necessary detail. In the review on housing interventions the reviewers had to calculate probability (p) values in cases where such data was not provided for the group of interest.

Analyse data, draw conclusions and report findings

When the review includes quantitative information and the studies from which these data have been extracted are sufficiently similar, then statistical meta-analysis should be conducted. This is a procedure which will combine the data from the various studies and provide an overall effect size for the phenomenon under investigation. In other situations, a narrative synthesis of the data should be provided, which will summarise the findings from the different studies and present the reader with an answer to the original review question. The review used as an example here included a narrative synthesis. Readers should refer to other reviews (such as Simmonds et al., 2001), for an example of how to report statistical syntheses of data.

The results of the housing intervention review enabled the reviewers to state, unequivocally, that many studies show health gains after housing interventions, but small study populations and lack of controlling for confounders limit the generalisability of findings. Therefore, large-scale, well-designed studies are required before we have firm, rather than suggestive, evidence for the beneficial health effects of housing interventions.

The details and conclusions of other systematic reviews of interventions in health and social care are published in the Cochrane Library and reviews of the effectiveness of social and behavioural interventions in education, crime and justice and social welfare can be sourced through the Campbell Collaboration [http://campbell.gse.upenn.edu]. Published reviews are also found regularly in leading peer-reviewed academic journals.

Conclusion

As a postscript, it is worth noting that a major problem currently facing systematic reviewers is *publication bias*. Significant or 'favourable' results are more likely to be published than non-significant or 'unfavourable' results. Considering also that larger studies are more likely to achieve statistically significant results than studies with small samples and that larger studies are given more weight in the statistical meta-analysis, this is a dilemma that must be addressed in any systematic review and researchers are developing statistical procedures to compensate for this problem. However, as researchers can be sponsored by agencies that refuse to publicise 'unfavourable' results and can conduct studies that are never submitted for publication, it should be borne in mind that we will never know whether or not a review truly suffers from publication bias.

Nevertheless, the systematic review is a powerful research methodology which answers questions on the basis of good evidence and provides researchers with a valuable, impartial, comprehensive and up-to-date summary of the work conducted in a specific area.

Suggested further reading

Egger, M., Davey Smith, G. and Altman, D.G. (2001) *Systematic Reviews in Health Care: Meta-Analysis in Context*, 2nd edn. London: BMJ Books.

References

Simmonds, S., Coid, J., Joseph, P., Marriott, S. and Tyrer, P. (2001) 'Community Mental Health Team Management in Severe Mental Illness: a Systematic Review', *British Journal of Psychiatry*, 178: 497–502.

Thomson, H., Petticrew, M. and Morrison, D. (2001) 'Health Effects of Housing Improvement: Systematic Review of Intervention Studies', *British Medical Journal*, 323: 187–90.

See also
Literature searching.

MARTIN DEMPSTER

T

Telephone methods for social surveys

The main attraction of telephone interviewing is that it enables data to be collected from geographically scattered samples more cheaply and quickly than by field interviewing, but avoids the well-known limitations of postal surveys. Other advantages are that interviewing from a central telephone unit lends itself to careful supervision and control, and that it is possible to avoid cluster sampling, which incurs unfavourable statistical design effects but has to be used in field survey designs to control interviewer travel costs.

The problems, on the other hand, are to do with obtaining adequately representative samples of the general population and adequate response rates when persons or households are approached 'cold' by telephone. Doubts have also been raised about the quality of the data compared with face-to-face interviewing.

In this entry we consider to what extent – and in what circumstances – the potential advantages have been realised and to what extent technical problems and doubts about quality remain. It should be noted that strategies for dealing with technical problems will be country-specific to some degree. Wherever possible we will make general statements about the feasibility of telephone survey methods. However for the purpose of illustration we will draw on the United Kingdom's experience of telephone survey methods.

The main focus will be on using telephone methods to survey fresh samples of the general population rather than samples for which telephone numbers are known, such as businesses, persons contacted via their workplace, panels and customer lists. Clearly telephone surveys of the general population will only be feasible for countries with high telephone penetration.

Sampling

A critical problem raised by telephone-based surveys is that of obtaining representative probability samples. Not all households have a telephone in their home, and those that do may not be listed in telephone directories. The proportion of homes in developed countries that are without telephones is now very small, but the proportion of unlisted numbers is rising. Complete and accessible listings of all domestic telephone numbers do not exist.

In the face of these problems there is a division between the approaches adopted by quota and random samplers. Quota sampling assumes that a sample constructed by accepting persons who are immediately available for interview will be sufficiently unbiased, as long as it satisfies the quotas (and sometimes other constraints). But differences within quota cells between those who are reachable by telephone and ready and willing to respond (included) and those who are not (excluded), may nevertheless bias the results. The problem is exactly analogous to that which exists with field surveys based on quotas, where checks have shown that 60–70% of the individuals approached may fail to respond.

Random sampling, by contrast, requires a process for selecting members from a determinate population that enables each case to be assigned a probability of selection. No substitution of easy for hard-to-interview cases is allowed. Random samplers therefore worry about exclusions from the sampling frame, about uncontrolled variation in selection probabilities and about non-response that rises higher than (say) 20–30%.

Households with no telephone

There is, by definition, no direct way of covering in a 'telephone-only' survey persons who do not have a telephone in their home. In the UK such households tend to be small and to be headed by young adults and adults who are themselves unemployed, on low incomes, single parents, etc. Similar findings have been made in other countries. Persons and households without telephones are thus a deprived group which social researchers may be particularly keen to represent accurately.

On the other hand the proportion of households without a telephone is likely to be very small in most developed countries. For example, in the UK there has been a steady decline in the proportion of households without a fixed-line telephone from about 20% in the mid-eighties to about 4% in 1998 (Sykes and Collins, 1988; Bridgwood et al., 1999).

Meanwhile we have seen a proliferation in the use of mobile phones in most countries. Not only are mobile phones being used in conjunction with fixed lines, they are also being used instead of fixed lines. Additionally, in the UK there is some evidence to suggest that those who would not have had a telephone in the past are now using 'pay as you go' mobile phones. In August 2001, 93% of UK homes had a fixed line phone service, 6% of UK homes only used mobile phones, and only 1% of UK homes did not have any type of phone (OFTEL, 2001). Consequently, excluding households without any telephone in a survey of the general population is unlikely to introduce significant bias. However, this is only true if 'mobile only' households can be included in the sampling frame. Telephone surveys will remain problematic for populations and countries with low telephone coverage.

Households with ex-directory numbers

Persons who are members of households with ex-directory numbers tend to differ from the population mean. For example, in the UK they tend to be younger than average, to live in cities and, in particular, to be young women living alone. The part of the population which is ex-directory is much larger than the proportion of the population which does not have a telephone; more than one in three fixed lines are ex-directory (OFTEL, 1997). Additionally, 'mobile only' households tend not to be listed in published telephone directories. Consequently, the scope for bias is substantial and is in practice superimposed upon the 'non-owners' bias. Therefore telephone surveys based upon samples drawn from public directories are unlikely to be satisfactory, even when weighted.

In the USA, much work was done in the 1970s onwards to develop 'random digit dialling' (RDD) as a means of providing representative and unbiased probability samples of all telephone owners, including those who are ex-directory (Lepkowski, 1988). Only recently has this method been shown to be feasible in the UK (Nicolaas and Lynn, 2002). RDD starts from the population of all telephone numbers that have the standard numeric structure. In practice a high proportion of the possible range of numbers will be not in use, commercial, not for voice traffic, etc. so randomly dialling numbers within the whole of the possible numeric range produces very low hit-rates. What makes this crippling in practice is the fact that redialling numbers which appear to ring but do not answer uses up a large amount of time and effort, but is necessary in order to establish whether they are out of scope or belong to households which seldom answer. Therefore, successful application of RDD requires that the sampler has a detailed knowledge of how the telephone numbering system is structured (for example, which blocks of numbers are not in use, or reserved for special purposes). If such information can be obtained or inferred it enables the hit rate for RDD – that is, the proportion of selected numbers that will in fact yield private households – to be raised to economic levels.

In market research telephone surveys the 'directory plus 1' system is often used as a means of getting at households which are on the telephone, but have ex-directory numbers. A sample is first drawn from the public residential telephone directory and then 1 is added to each number drawn to provide the list of numbers actually dialled. This has the effect of drawing into the sample some households which have unlisted numbers. However, in areas where unlisted numbers are prevalent not enough numbers will be found in the first place, so the residents of such areas will still be under-represented in the 'directory plus 1' sample. In theory this might be corrected if we knew what proportion of domestic numbers in each exchange area were ex-directory, but this information is not readily available.

Mobile phones

As mentioned above, over the last few years we have seen a rapid increase in the use of mobile phones. For example, 73% of UK adults at present claim they own or use a mobile phone, and 6% of UK households have one or more mobile phones and no fixed line (OFTEL, 2001).

Owners of mobile phones who do not have a fixed line at their home address tend to differ from the population average; they are younger, more mobile people living in inner-city areas. Hence, the exclusion of 'mobile only' households is increasingly likely to introduce bias. At present it may still be possible to weight for the exclusion of 'mobile only' households but with the increasing numbers of 'mobile only' households there will come a point when this is no longer feasible. In most countries there is no publicly available full listing of mobile phone numbers but it is possible to include mobile phone numbers in RDD samples.

The inclusion of mobile phone numbers in telephone samples will have a number of consequences. It will be necessary to weight the data to take into account unequal selection probabilities, thus reducing the effective sample size. The allocation of mobile phone numbers is not done on a geographical basis, so it is not possible to include them easily in samples limited to regions or local authority areas. Because mobile phones are personal property rather than belonging to a household, the selection of mobile phones will complicate the enumeration of households and hinder access to other household members. Data quality could be compromised when interviews are conducted on mobile phones outside the home (the respondent may be on the road, at work, shopping and so forth). While this could be avoided by phoning back at a more convenient time, it may reduce response rates.

Obtaining response

As with face-to-face interviewing, the reasons for non-response to telephone surveys can be divided into non-contacts and refusals. Most centralised telephone interviewing installations now use automated call-scheduling systems. With these the making of multiple calls to catch the seldom-at-home is easier and cheaper. However, such systems are still bedevilled by the presence of out-of-scope numbers which appear to ring but never reply. Apart from the waste of time and effort, there are problems in deciding whether to classify these cases as non-response or as out of scope.

After contact has been established with someone at a number there are some additional sampling problems to be faced which increase the risk of telephone non-response.

In the first place, the interviewer has to determine whether the number is residential and deal consistently with special cases such as businesses run from the home and communal phones. Secondly, it is necessary to identify households possessing more than one telephone number, so as to establish their probability of selection. Thirdly, it is necessary to establish a unique association between each telephone number and the households or individuals at that number. This is analogous to identifying residents at an address in field interview surveys, but is harder to achieve where the interviewer cannot use observational cues and must rely on obtaining the required information orally.

When the interviewer has made contact with someone at the number dialled, certain field sampling procedures often need to be applied which can be more difficult to explain over the telephone than face-to-face and which incur risk of non-response. Often, the interviewer will need to enumerate all household members so that one can be selected at random. Even with field interviewing this is difficult, since detailed information has to be extracted before secure rapport can be established with a specific respondent and the risk of refusal to cooperate further is quite high. These problems are compounded when the procedure has to be administered by telephone.

As regards refusals, there is some truth in the intuitive impression that it is easier to put the phone down than it is to refuse a request from an interviewer calling in person. It is also true that broken-off interviews are commoner on the telephone than face-to-face, probably for similar reasons. These findings have made telephone survey designers cautious about interview length and there tends to be a rule of thumb that it is unwise to attempt interviews lasting longer than 20 minutes or so by telephone. However, much of the evidence comes from market research interviews which many respondents find rather boring and uninvolving. As in the case of face-to-face interviewing, a great deal depends upon the level of interest and involvement aroused by the subject matter.

To the extent that increased non-response tends to be associated with increased bias in survey estimates, lower response in telephone surveys is not a trivial problem. However, it need not be a crippling one. There is some evidence that with experience and effort rates of response will be perhaps 10 percentage points below those that would be expected if the survey were conducted face-to-face.

Quality of information obtained

Another important question to be asked about telephone surveys is whether they are a reliable way of collecting information from individuals. For example, will individuals answer sensitive questions related to their health and health-related behaviour truthfully over the phone? On the whole, research suggests that telephone surveys are at least as successful as face-to-face interviews in eliciting such information (Sykes and Collins, 1988; McQueen, 1989; de Leeuw and van der Zouwen, 1988).

Other research suggests that some questions are answered, on average, slightly differently over the telephone. In particular, item non-response rates tend to be higher, answers to open questions tend to be shorter, and the whole interview procedure tends to proceed more briskly than in the case of face-to-face interviews. For non-sensitive factual questions few differences have been reported in the distributions of responses obtained (though comparison is made more difficult where there is a difference in rate of response). Such differences as do occur may be due more to the fact that visual aids such as prompt cards cannot be used over the telephone, than to any difference in the way respondents react to being questioned by telephone. In some applications this inability to use multiple channels of communication, be it visual aids or body language, to build up rapport, can be a serious disadvantage.

There has been debate over whether questions of a sensitive or potentially embarrassing nature (for example, about intimate, dubiously legal or socially stigmatised forms of behaviour) are better or worse answered over the telephone. This is an inherently difficult topic to study and depends heavily on assumptions that higher rates of reporting certain behaviours (for example, alcohol consumption, drug taking) indicate higher validity. It is likely that factors such as perceived confidentiality and the relative impersonality of telephone interaction are involved here. At this stage we cannot confidently assert that telephone methods systematically improve or damage data quality compared with face-to-face methods. There may be an interaction with whether the prospective respondent agrees to be interviewed in the first place, with the result that non-response bias and reporting bias are confounded.

In the case of questions involving response scales (for example, where people express agreement with a statement on a scale ranging from 'strongly agree' to 'strongly disagree') respondents on the telephone have been found to be slightly more likely to choose one of the extreme categories. These differences can affect comparisons between results from face-to-face surveys and telephone surveys, but are not usually so pronounced as to lead to significantly different interpretations of the data.

Conclusions

Taking the survey scene as a whole, telephone interviewing has become commonplace as a data collection method in many developed countries. For surveys of businesses and other organisations it is now standard and indeed may be the preferred mode of data collection, often in combination with postal questionnaire methods. Market research companies also commonly use the telephone to identify and interview quota samples of consumers.

The adoption of telephone interviewing for social surveys of the general population has not been as straightforward in some countries. It is the main data collection mode for social surveys in the USA but not in the UK. Until recently it has not been possible in the UK to select a representative and unbiased probability sample of the general population but recent changes in the UK telephone numbering system have made strict probability sampling in the form of Random Digit Dialling possible.

Nevertheless, there are obstacles to further progress. The increasing use of mobile phones and, in particular, the growing number of 'mobile only' households present challenges to telephone sampling methods, interviewing procedures and data quality. The major challenge for telephone surveys is perhaps that of response rate maximisation. Response rates to telephone surveys have undergone a steep decline in most developed countries over the last two decades, mainly attributed to declining contact rates (Steeh et al., 2001).

As regards data quality, initial doubts about the reliability of factual information obtained over the telephone and its comparability with information obtained face-to-face have largely been discounted. There is evidence of some mode effects on telephone and face-to-face measures of attitudes, but these are not very large and there is no general reason to think that the measures obtained by telephone are less valid (it has been claimed that in some situations they are more valid). The most common cause of response differences between face-to-face and telephone surveys tends to be the difference in question construction.

Achieving cost reduction and speed without sacrificing other criteria of survey quality depends on careful selection of applications. The UK Labour Force Survey, for example, uses the telephone only in the case of households that have previously been interviewed face-to-face and have agreed to supply their telephone number. Telephone interviewing has not yet become a substitute for face-to-face interviewing across the board.

Note

This is a revised and updated version of an article first published in *Social Research Update*, 8 (Department of Sociology, University of Surrey).

Suggested further reading

Joint Centre for Survey Methods *Newsletter*, 11 (3) (1991) Telephone Surveys: the Current State of the Art. Papers by: J. Foreman 'Random Digit Dialling'; R. Thomas 'Characteristics of Households With and Without Telephones'; G. Pile 'Setting up and Managing a Large Scale Telephone Interviewing Facility'; E. Smith 'Telephone Surveys: the Business Research Angle'.

Groves. R.M., Biemer, P.P., Lyberg, L.E., Massey, J.T., Nicholls II, W.L., Waksberg, J. (eds) (1988) *Telephone Survey Methodology*. New York: John Wiley and Sons. Contains 32 substantial papers by authors from the USA, Great Britain and elsewhere on all aspects of telephone methodology.

References

Bridgwood, A., Lilly, R., Thomas, M., Bacon, J., Sykes, W. and Morris, S. (1999) *Living in Britain: Results from the 1998 General Household Survey*. London: The Stationery Office.

de Leeuw, E.D. and van der Zouwen, J. (1988) 'Data Quality in Telephone and Face to Face Surveys: a Comparative Meta-Analysis', in R.M. Groves, P.P. Biemer, L.E. Lyberg, J.T. Massey, W.L. Nicholls II and J. Waksberg (eds), *Telephone Survey Methodology*. John Wiley and Sons.

Lepkowski, J.M. (1988) 'Telephone Sampling Methods in the United States', in R.M. Groves et al. (eds), *Telephone Survey Methodology*. John Wiley and Sons.

McQueen, D.V. (1989) 'Comparison of Results of Personal Interview and Telephone Surveys of Behaviour Related to the Risk of AIDS: Advantages of Telephone Techniques', in *Proceedings of Healthy Survey Research Methods Conference*, National Centre for Health Services Research and Health Care Technology Assessment (DHSS publication no. (PHS) 89-3447).

OFTEL (1997) 'Provision of Directory Information Services and Products'. http://www.oftel.gov.uk/consumer/d-qchap.htm (December 1999).

OFTEL (2001) 'Consumers' use of Mobile Telephony – Summary of OFTEL Residential Survey', Q6 August 2001. http://www.oftel.gov.uk/publications/research/2001/q6mobr1101.htm (November 2001).

Nicolaas, G. and Lynn, P. (2002) 'Random Digit Dialling in the UK: Viability of the sampling method revisited', *Journal of the Royal Statistical Society Series A*.

Steeh, C., Kirgis, N., Cannon, B. and DeWitt, J. (2001) 'Are They Really as Bad as They Seem? Nonresponse Rates at the End of the Twentieth Century', *Journal of Official Statistics*, 17 (2): 227–47.

Sykes, W. and Collins, M. (1988) 'Effects of Mode of Interview: Experiments in the UK', in R.M. Groves, P.P. Biemer, L.E. Lyberg, J.T. Massey, W.L. Nicholls II and J. Waksberg (eds), *Telephone Survey Methodology*. John Wiley and Sons.

See also Probability sampling and **Social surveys**.

ROGER THOMAS, SUSAN PURDON AND GERRY NICOLAAS

Theory

The term 'theory' has technical and commonsense meanings; the problem is that these meanings overlap but have entirely opposite implications. In commonsense terms theory means ideas, propositions and explanations that get to the essential 'truth' behind something that is often hidden ('I have a theory about you'; 'I have a theory about that'). Theory and truth are equivalents in commonsense knowledge. In lay person's terms, theory is often understood normatively, as revealing a truth that lay people consider desirable or what normatively ought to be the case. Its technical meaning is the reverse. Theory is an inter-related set of ideas and propositions but in its technical meaning it proffers *conditional* knowledge and its explanations are not normative. Some theories – the theory of gravity – are not conditional in the sense of unproven but in the sense of being continually revised and refined as knowledge advances. Other theories however, are conditional in that they remain as yet unproven. This is particularly so with theories about social affairs and social life. Social theories are thus neither about establishing 'truth' in its normative sense ('what *ought* to be true'), because this is not legitimate as a goal of social science, nor in its realist sense ('this is what *is* true'), since all theories are conditional and related to the level of knowledge currently available.

Nevertheless, in the social sciences there are some theories that are clearly normative, in that they are sets of interrelated ideas and propositions that are embedded with an explicit value preference. Many others are tacitly normative in that they are biased toward particular values and political goals. This tacit value preference is sometimes deliberate, sometimes implicit and attributed by people with different values and goals.

'Grand' theory

Accusations of normative bias tend to be associated with what is called 'general theory'. These are interrelated sets of ideas and propositions on a grand scale that seek to encompass very general and abstract explanations of the social world as a whole. They go beyond what can be seen, observed and measured to embrace an explanation of society in the past, present and, occasionally, the future. In social science, Marx's theory of historical materialism is a general theory that seeks to understand the underlying dynamics of social life, which he saw rooted in the forces and relations of production, and projected both backwards to explain the unfolding of history and forwards to account for the emergence of a new form of social life, communism. There are many other general theories seeking to explain how society is structured (for example, Talcott Parsons' theory of the social system), general theories of social action (for example, Alfred Schutz's account of social phenomenology) and there are some general theories that encompass the link between social structure and social action (for example Giddens' theory of structuration). What is characteristic about general theories is that they are couched in highly abstract terms to parallel their grand focus and often not capable of translation into empirical statements that can be measured and tested (or, at least, only parts of the general theory permit this).

'Middle range' theory

In contrast to general theories are those theories that in 1957 Robert Merton called 'theories of the middle range'. These are interrelated ideas and propositions that can be translated into empirical, measurable and observable propositions capable of being tested in social research. They are often on less general and grand topics; rather than society or social action as a whole, theories of the middle range refer to discrete domains of society or social action in more manageable proportions. Thus, it is what they seek to explain that distinguishes theories of the middle range. Rather than seeking to develop an interrelated set of ideas and propositions to explain all observed uniformities in social life in the one grand theory, middle range theories seek to explain only some of the regularities, so middle range theorists proffer theories of crime, organisational change, the labour process and the like. Merton suggested this type of theory as the one more suitable to the social sciences, which should be concerning themselves neither with normative and ontological questions about the nature of society or social action in general form, nor with what he called abstract empiricism, which are studies supposedly devoid of theory. Merton called this kind of theory 'middle range' partly because it was also a middle way between two popular approaches in the social sciences at the time – grand theorising isolated from research, and abstract empiricism separated from theory. This suggests that research and theory need to be related and it is this research–theory linkage that gives the term theory most relevance to practising social researchers.

The relevance of theory to social research

There are three ways in which theory is relevant to social research. First, theories open up research problems by identifying what has hitherto been hidden, misunderstood or misinterpreted. Not all research issues are necessarily opened up by means of social theory, but many are. Theories offer ways of looking at the social world and the different social theories often explicate new domains, revise understandings of existing domains and offer competing interpretations of them that infuses social research practice.

Second, theory can draw together unrelated fragments of empirical evidence and research. The ideas and propositions that comprise theory can provide imaginative leaps in understanding that make connections between situations not before related or research data not previously seen as fitting together. Theory can thus highlight and explain the empirical regularities appearing in the social world.

Third, research is theory dependent. As argued in the philosophy of social research and in the critique of abstract empiricism, all research involves some theory. However, just what form this takes varies. Sometimes, theory-dependence is not acknowledged but theoretical assumptions and propositions are contained in the choice of research methods used or the way in which the research problem is defined. On other occasions, theory is present in the ideas that the research is designed from the outset to test or operationalise. This is what is called *deduction*: research is conducted in the light of theory and used to verify the original theoretical ideas. Sometimes theory is intended as the outcome of research, either in the form of theoretical inferences or some fully-fledged grounded theory. This is called *induction* and describes an approach by which theories develop from research. Induction and deduction offer alternative conceptualisations of the theory–research relationship, but in both views research is theory dependent. This dependency is mostly intended and deliberate, but it exists implicitly even where theory is unacknowledged by the social researcher.

Theory dependency is a virtue rather than something to be denied. It is commonly acclaimed that good social research is that which goes beneath surface level understandings and appearances or helps to understand social life in a new way. From this standpoint, empirical investigations concerned with how things occur will not generate good research unless theoretical questions are also asked. Profound social questions require theory in order to interpret the empirical observations; those empirical observations that can be explained without reference to theory are not likely to be illuminating in the questions they pose. Therefore, research is theory dependent since questions of fact that can be empirically pursued without theory are not the sorts of questions worth answering in social research.

See also
Deduction;
Grounded
theory and
Induction.

Suggested further reading

Bauman, Z. (1990) *Thinking Sociologically*. Oxford: Blackwell.

Merton, R.K. (1957) *Social Theory and Social Structure*. Glencoe: Free Press.

JOHN BREWER

Transsexualism

See **Gender Identity Dysphoria Assessment**.

Triangulation

Triangulation in social research is the combination of different methods, methodolgical perspectives or theoretical viewpoints. Taking the metaphors of the stability of a tripod or the need for navigators to take bearings on at least three points in order to locate themselves accurately on a map reference, proponents of 'triangulated' approaches to research assert that the result of combining varied approaches is a net gain – the strengths of each contrasting approach more than cancel the weaknesses of their counterpart.[1]

The type of triangulation most commonly found is some combination of 'quantitative' and 'qualitative' approaches. Proponents of this type of triangulation point out that the advantages of the 'quantitative' approach correspond to the disadvantages of the 'qualitative' approach and vice versa. This can be diagrammed in the chart below.

Main Advantages of Research Method	
Qualitative	Quantitative
Holistic, detailed view	Representativeness
Reactivity	Possibility of impartial disproof
Naturalism	Control (rigour)
Main Disadvantages of Research Method	
Non-representative	Limited scope of data
Lack of bias control (interviewer effect)	Artificiality (instrument effect)

As the above implies, the combination of qualitative and quantitative methods together could mean that the weaknesses of one approach are cancelled out by the strengths of the other. Hence, the basic idea of 'triangulated' research is multi-method social research.

What is meant by 'multiple approaches', however, can have more than one meaning. Norman Denzin (1978) has identified four different ways that a social research project can be triangulated.

(1) *Methodological triangulation.* As has been discussed above, using multiple, different research techniques in order to maximise the strengths of each. This can take two forms.

(a) *Between method triangulation.* Two different research techniques, usually one 'quantitative' and another 'qualitative' are combined together to exploit the strengths of each. A typical example would be that of Miller, Wilford and Donoghue's (1996) study of gender and political participation. A large sample survey of the general population in Northern Ireland was carried out to establish the gross extent and range of a variety of types of activities that could broadly be considered some sort of participation in politics or public life. Each respondent to the quantitative survey was given a score based on the level of their public activity. Then, the 'highest scorers' (presumably the most politically active) and a sample of extremely 'low scorers' (presumably the most apathetic) were recontacted for an in-depth qualitative interview about aspects of their public activity that were beyond the scope of a mass interview survey (topics like, for example, their personal history of how they became (or did not become) politically active, major influences on their political behaviour, the motivations for joining in and so forth). In this way, the researchers could comment validly about both the extent of public participation in the general population *and* the motives and experiences that underlay the participation of individuals.

(b) *Within method triangulation*. Only a single basic technique may be employed, but different variations of the technique are employed; for example, a questionnaire researcher may use several different sets of attitude scales – each of which purports to measure the same thing (let's say, three different prejudice scales being used on the same questionnaire). The use of several different scales should be better than relying upon only one scale alone.

(2) *Investigator triangulation*. 'Two heads are better than one.' Several investigators working together on a single research project should produce more valid and reliable results than one person working alone. What one researcher misses may be obvious or important to another. Note that researchers *themselves* can be ethnocentric. Cross-disciplinary research is the best example of this kind of triangulation. Miller, Wilford and Donoghue in the above mentioned study are, respectively, an American sociologist, a Welsh political scientist and an Irish psychologist. This variety in the research team was a strength.

(3) *Data triangulation*. As well as different methods, one can have different 'blocks' of data (information) taken from different times, different spaces/locations, or different people. For example, researchers often *replicate* a study that was carried out before. This can be either:

- a replication in a different time, say, returning to an area after years have passed to repeat a study to see what has changed (different time, same location and mostly the same people, for example, the Lynds' two studies of *Middletown* in the USA were separated by 20 years); or
- replication in a different area, going to a different place and repeating a study that was done somewhere else before to see if the same results apply (for example, Leonard repeated in West Belfast Pahl's London work on 'hidden economic activity'. The results were quite different from Pahl's due to the West Belfast area being more akin to a developing world economy with few resources to fall back on);
- Denzin gives the example of different groups of people being studied within a single time and location (his setting is a hospital and the groups are doctors, nurses and orderlies).

(4) *Theoretical triangulation*. Denzin's final type of triangulation, in which researchers employ more than one theoretical perspective with a single research project (most likely by having individuals who hold different perspectives working together on the same project). Perhaps not insignificantly, Denzin does not give a concrete example of a theoretically triangulated research project.

(5) Building on Denzin, Catherine Hakim (1987) has broadened the idea of triangulation further. She speaks of *research programmes* as being examples of triangulation. This reflects developments in the style of social science research in recent times. Nowadays, interdisciplinary research by teams of researchers has become much more common. Similarly, this interdisciplinary research can take the form of research programmes – a series of projects all linked by a single broad subject topic but each carried out separately by different teams of researchers. The contact, and the triangulation, comes about more through administrative

mechanisms. Sometimes a single sponsoring body will either provide the funding for a research initiative made up of a number of different projects all funded by the same body or the administrative body will provide means of bringing the researchers working on the same topic together. Probably the clearest example of this would be the research programmes of the European Community, where the main grantholder is required to include partners from at least two other European nations.

Finally, a note of caution. While many researcher practitioners are quite pragmatic and tend to be supporters of the triangulated approach because it works, there are many social scientists who do *not* believe that true triangulation is really possible. Denzin himself notes that different methods often imply differing theoretical approaches. Some who cleave strongly to either an extreme qualitative or an extreme quantitative approach will *not* agree that qualitative and quantitative positions can, or should, be combined within a single research project.

Note

1 Even though this combination of approaches is referred to as *triangulation*, usually only two, rather than three or more, approaches are combined.

References

Denzin, Norman K. (1978) 'Strategies of Multiple Triangulation', in Norman K. Denzin (ed.), *The Research Act: a Theoretical Introduction to Sociological Methods*. Chicago: Aldine. Chapter 12.

Hakim, Catherine (1987) *Research Design: Strategies and Choices in the Design of Social Research*. London: Allen & Unwin. (esp. pp. 144–5).

Miller, Robert L., Wilford, Rick and Donoghue, Freda (1996) *Women and Political Participation in Northern Ireland*. Aldershot: Avebury.

ROBERT MILLER

Type I and Type II errors

See **Hypothesis testing**.

U

Unobtrusive measures

Unobtrusive measures are those data collection techniques that do not involve direct elicitation from respondents so that the information is obtained without the subject's prior knowledge. Most social research involves respondents knowing they are research subjects and it is virtually impossible to estimate the impact this knowledge has on the subsequent data. This is what is called the 'reactive effect' and is an inherent part of most of the popular research techniques in the social sciences, as much a problem in quantitative research designs as qualitative research. It affects all interviews irrespective of the degree of standardisation, questionnaires, overt observation, ethnography, vignettes and most forms of discourse analysis. With respect to interviews the reaction is known as the interviewer effect, although this term also involves reference to the reaction taken by respondents to the person of the interviewer not just to the knowledge that they are subjects of research. Some of these obtrusive measures can be designed so as to moderate the reactive effect but it can never be eliminated totally and the quality of the data is thus impugned by an unknown distortion. In ethnography and participant observation, for example, fieldworkers are advised to develop rapport and trust with respondents over a long period and to try to blend into the setting to minimise the obtrusiveness of their presence. Early ventures in the field until the researcher's presence is routine, produce poorer quality data because of this. Advice on recording data takes into account the reactive effect of obtrusive forms, such as note taking and tape recording, and a range of advice exists for making this as unobtrusive as possible, such as reducing the visibility of the recording instrument, not recording in certain locations, and reassuring informants about the contents of the information that is collected. Reassurances about confidentiality is another way to manage the reactive effect of obtrusive data collection, and there is a wealth of advice on management of the interviewer effect. It remains the case, nonetheless, that an unknown bias is introduced into the data because of the uncertainty about the success of these measures in moderating the reactive effect.

There are, however, other reasons why unobtrusive measures are important. Data are socially constructed by the form and quality of the interaction between researcher and respondents. It is well known, for example, that people often give answers they think the questioner wants to hear. They tend to give socially desirable answers that suggest informants are well balanced, adjusted and happy and disavow extreme opinions, such that consensual middle ground opinions tend to be exaggerated in social surveys. The infamous Hawthorne effect stands testimony to the fact that people's behaviour is affected by the knowledge that they are being studied. The powerful placebo effect of non-medicinal forms of medical intervention is another example. Let one particular respondent articulate this himself. The well-known character 'Doc', who William Foote Whyte used as a gatekeeper to access urban youth gangs in 'Cornerville', an Italian neighbourhood in an America city, is quoted as saying: 'You've slowed me up plenty since you've been down here. Now, when I am doing something, I have to think of what Bill Whyte would want to know about it and how I can explain it' (Whyte, 1955). To avoid this kind of impact, *covert observation* is recommended by some social researchers despite its severe ethical problems. For all sorts of reasons, data collected by obtrusive measures is situated by the process of its collection. Post-structuralist and postmodern researchers argue that this is true for all research methods and, while no technique is infallible, neither are they equal in their fallibility. Proponents of unobtrusive methods contend that their techniques have fewer problems than most.

Unobtrusive measures are of many kinds. Some are ad hoc. Webb and colleagues, for example, suggest as sources of data things such as the wear on floor tiles near pieces of art in galleries to measure cultural interests, the size of suits of armour as access to body types and sizes historically, and the study of headstones in graveyards as glimpses of class and power. Others have the appearance of more authority, such as the use of various unsolicited documents like diaries, suicide notes and letters, use of cultural artifacts like wall murals, graffiti and poetry, or unobtrusive forms of observation such as from behind two-way mirrors, net curtains or park shrubs and covert participant observation. Some of these are long standing, and considerable experience and expertise has been established in their use. Letters home from Polish émigrés formed a part of Thomas and Znaniecki's sociological study of the Polish peasant in 1918 (*The Polish Peasant in Europe and America*); in 1967 Jerry Jacobs used suicide notes left behind by victims to access social meanings not accessible to Durkheim's study (*Social Problems*, vol. 15). Others are more recent and connected to the explosion of cultural studies in social science. For example, Rolston uses wall murals as measures to research political culture and conflict management in working class communities in Belfast (*Politics and Paintings*, 1991; *Drawing Support*, 1992, 1995). Erving Goffman has analysed the phrase 'oops' (*Forms of Talk*, 1981) as a slip of the tongue that is evocative of social relationships, as Freud had done in 1901 as glimpses into people's mental state. The Internet has the potential for the extensive collection of unobtrusive data through access to chat lines, discussion lists and other dialogue.

Webb and colleagues (1981) categorised these data collected by unobtrusive observation techniques into types: traces, observations and records. *Traces* are measures that are left behind as imprints of social action, such as material objects like needle exchange schemes used as an avenue into the study of heroin addicts or using litter and other rubbish to glimpse the social lives of those who discard it. Another type is what Webb and colleagues call '*simple observation*', which is that kind of observation done in settings over which the researcher has no control and in which they are passive. Researchers here might use physical signs (such as facial expressions), human movement (gestures, behaviour), naturally occurring conversations or features of the physical setting (such as the impact of its space on interaction, as for example behaviour in lifts or on park benches) as data. In some forms of observational research recommended by Webb et al. there is manipulation of the setting to facilitate observations, such as rearranging features of the physical location in order to engineer types of behaviour (moving chairs for example) although the subjects remain unaware that they are being observed. There is a close connection between these particular observational measures and visual ethnography, where the use of still photography and video seem suitable so long as they remain secretive. The third type is *archival*, exploiting living records such as advertisements, personal documents like diaries and letters, and societal records kept about people (bank records, medical notes, death certificates and the like). Advertisements, for example, have been used in the past to access gender social stereotypes, youth culture, globalisation and more. Recently, work has been done on the advertisements carried in newspaper dating and personal columns as indices of new patterns of emotional behaviour in modern societies. More recently, Lee (2000) distinguishes between the kinds of data these unobtrusive measures collect rather than the measures themselves. There is what he calls 'found data' (that left behind lying as traces), 'captured data' (that gleaned by watching and listening to what is happening now) and 'retrieved data' (that contained in and retrieved from records of things that have already happened). There are obvious links to the formulation of Webb and colleagues.

It is clear from these typologies that unobtrusive measures are themselves fallible. They are limited to what naturally occurs or has taken place already. To avoid this constraint by any form of manipulation to improve the opportunity for research breaches the principle of non-reaction.

The ethical dimension of unobtrusive observation, where people are involved as subjects and not asked their informed consent, is important. People can appear on video, in still photographs or be watched from behind net curtains without giving their permission. This is an invasion of privacy and might in some cases fall foul of the law. Non-reactivity and informed consent are contradictory goals and to avoid this the researcher is either restricted to those unobtrusive measures that embody people's actions as past traces and involve no real people in the present or to gaining people's consent after the fact.

References

See also **Ethics** and **Observation**.

Lee, R. (2000) *Unobtrusive Measures in Social Research*. Buckingham: Open University Press.

Webb E.J. et al. (1981) *Nonreactive Measures in the Social Sciences*. Dallas: Houghton Mifflin.
Whyte, W.F. (1955) *Street Corner Society*. Chicago: University of Chicago Press.

JOHN BREWER

V

Verbal protocol analysis

Verbal protocol analysis (VPA) is a method for collecting and analysing verbal data about cognitive processing. The method involves making a detailed record of a person's verbal report while they are engaged in carrying out a task, for example, doing a mental calculation, solving a problem, making a decision, or interacting with a computer. Such verbal reports are produced under specific instructions to 'think aloud' and the person is normally given minimum prompting. They are sometimes known as 'thinking aloud protocols'. If the verbal reports are made while the person is completing the task, they are called *concurrent* protocols and, if they are collected after the task is completed, the term used is *retrospective* protocol. The verbal reports are then transcribed, segmented into individual units or statements and coded, to enable the researcher to draw inferences about underlying cognitive processes. VPAs differ from other methods for analysing verbal data, such as conversational analysis or discourse analysis which emphasise the linguistic content and form of what is said.

VPAs are now used in such of wide range of research and R&D studies with differing aims and goals, and so many variations have emerged, that it is probably more precise to think of a family of techniques rather than a single method. A full analysis of VPA can be found in Ericsson and Simon (1993) which is regarded as the primary text on the topic.

Irrespective of the variations, VPAs are not collected in a theoretical vacuum and they carry assumptions about cognitive architecture, the relationship between long term memory and working memory, and in particular, the demands which the thinking aloud method places on the limited capacity of working memory. When a person is completing a task and providing a running commentary on their thought processes – as in a concurrent protocol – they essentially are doing two tasks at once. We know that only a limited range of cognitive processes are available for verbal report – or are heeded – in a specific circumstance. Highly practised tasks or very simple tasks can be so automatic that very little is available from working memory for verbal report. At the other extreme, complex and novel tasks can demand so much attention that the person may be unable to engage in any additional mental processing such as providing a verbal report. In addition, the verbal skills of the research participants must be sufficiently developed to permit reasonably fluent verbal reports. Younger children, therefore, may not always be suitable for VPA studies. Even with adults, there are wide individual differences in the quantity and quality of the verbal data produced.

We will now set out the steps required to complete a VPA and go through a specific example to show how the method can be used to analyse cognitive processes in a planning task. Then, questions of reliability and validity will be discussed and finally a range of applications and supplementary uses will be explored.

What steps are involved?

Irrespective of the task, VPA involves a number of steps or phases in collecting and analysing the data. In addition, the practicalities of collecting the data and time constraints must be considered.

Specifying the task and deciding if it is suitable for the thinking aloud method. In general, tasks that require a chain of thinking or multi-steps are likely to be better than single step tasks. Also, decisions will need to be made at this stage if concurrent or retrospective protocols are to be collected and the researcher will need to consider the pitfalls associated with each.[1] Whether protocols will be collected for all the participants or a sample will depend on the overall design of the research but may also be influenced by time considerations. Protocol analysis is time consuming.

Instructing and prompting the participants. In order to maximise both the quantity and quality of the protocol it is important that instructions invite participants to think aloud and report all that they are thinking about during the task. However, instructions should not ask for reasons or explanations or give hints about possible processes.

Encouragement may need to be given if participants fall silent (for example, 'Is that all . . .?' 'Is there anything else . . .?' 'What are you thinking about now . . .?'). There may be occasions when more prompted verbalisation may be necessary (for example, 'What were you referring to just then . . .?').

Collecting the data. For VPA, verbatim data is required so the verbal reports need to be audiotaped or videotaped. Quality of the recording is clearly important at this stage. Other sources of data may also be collected. For example, the actions which a person is carrying out as they describe their thinking such as key presses if it is a computer-generated task or eye movements if the task involves close visual analysis.

Transcribing the data. The data is then fully transcribed. Decisions need to be made about whether the transcript is to be time marked or not. Time marking shows how long the person spent on parts of the task and allows comparisons to be made. Also if more than one source of data is collected (auditory and visual), how are these to be integrated?

Adapting and/or generating a coding framework. If you are working on a topic or within a theoretical framework which has already used VPA then a suitable coding framework may already be available to guide the analysis of the data. If your work is more exploratory then you will need to develop a coding frame related to a theoretical perspective. Either way some exploration with a small sample of protocols will be necessary. If an established coding frame is available, you may just need to check that your data is 'fitting' the frame or if it needs to be adapted. Developing a coding frame from the beginning is a much more substantial exercise and will require that you iterate through the protocols on several occasions while you also develop a segmentation strategy (see below).

Segmenting the protocol. To further the analysis, the verbal report will need to be divided or segmented into units or statements. This is not always straightforward and may not map directly onto the sentence structure in the protocol (see example Table 1).

Encoding and analysing the data. The segmented units are then encoded into the coding framework by at least two raters. Some judgement is usually required and inter-rater reliability will need to be computed on at least a sample of protocols. This stage is time consuming if conducted completely by hand. There are now several computer packages (of various qualities) which can automate some of the VPA steps.

When the data has been quantified then they can be analysed using conventional statistical techniques. Despite the help which is available with automation, considerable judgement is required to make inferences about the underlying cognitive processes, particularly when sequences of processes are being tracked and/or a model of macro-processes is being constructed.

An example of VPA

The example is taken from studies on housewives' planning and metaplanning processes conducted by one of the co-authors.[2] The planning task is about going shopping when a number of errands are completed within a set time. Certain constraints are set – some tasks are appointments and have to be done at a specific time and some errands (buying ice-cream) have to be completed towards the end. The task required prioritising (all tasks cannot be completed within the time limit), sequencing, estimating time, choosing the best route, as well as acknowledging real world constraints (ice-cream melts). The task is complex and requires a chain of reasoning yet is clearly within the experience of most housewives (defined as those who had primary responsibility for management of the household).

While viewing a scaled model of a fictional town centre, the housewives were asked to complete the task and to 'talk aloud as they did the errands . . . to describe all the thinking that they did while developing their plan . . .' The protocol was concurrent and the housewives were audiotaped. Minimal prompting was required. Housewives took between 5 and 23 minutes to complete the planning task. The shortest protocol was segmented into 70 units and the longest into 263 units.

A coding framework for analysing planning processes – the opportunistic planning model – was available in the research literature (Hayes-Roth and Hayes-Roth, 1979). Readers do not need to know the details to understand the extract from the protocol in Table 1. Suffice to say that each segment was coded along several dimensions in the framework, two of which are included in Table 1. For the sake of simplicity, *plan level* can be interpreted as indicating the level of abstraction of the planning being reported. For example, segments which are coded at the level of *plan* and *world knowledge* are at a lower level of abstraction than those indicated by the codes of *executive* and *metaplan*. The second column shows a

Table 1 *Extract from the beginning of a verbal protocol from a housewife planning a simulated shopping trip*

Segment	Content	Coding Framework	
		Plan level	Plan type
1.	OK . . . the first thing I would do is to make a list of the shops that are quite close to each other	Executive	Generate plan
2.	and highlight the dance class remembering that it is at a specific time	Metaplan	Satisfy time constraints
3.	I would try to get to it first and get it over with . . .	Executive	Order messages
4.	probably, in reality I would drop it . . .	Executive	Evaluate plan Eliminate
5.	with all that to do for a birthday – it's more important . . .	Metaplan	Evaluate plan Do important
6.	I'd probably park in the Maple Street car park and walk, only 5 minutes from the ice-cream shop	Plan	Generate plan Estimate routes Estimate time
7.	OK, to work on this . . .	Executive	Generate plan
8.	and then go to get the kettle exchanged	Plan	Generate plan
9.	in case that took up more time, it would let me know what time I have left	Metaplan	Monitor Use time well
10.	say about 5 mins in the ice-cream shop	World Knowledge	Estimate time
11.	'cos I would have pre-phoned them and asked them to have it ready on a tight schedule	Metaplan	Review plan Use time well
12.	right, if I go to Truc electrical goods you would need possibly to see the manager	Metaplan	Satisfy implicit constraints
13.	so you could spend up to 20 mins in there	World Knowledge	Estimate time

And so on . . .

dimension which categorises the *type* of planning decision being described rather than the level.

Several points should be noted about the extract in Table 1: (1) Even a fluent verbal report will contain hesitations and linguistic *non sequiturs*; (2) A single segment in the protocol can be categorised along many different dimensions depending on the complexity and theoretical richness of the coding framework; and (3) Drawing inferences about cognitive processes, even from a well-developed coding scheme, is not straightforward. Some theoretical understanding of the cognitive demands of the task is also required.

Validity and reliability

Green (1995) provides a succinct summary of the validity and reliability issues associated with verbal reports as data and a fuller analysis can be found in the revised edition of Ericsson and Simon (1993). Green points out that it is important to distinguish between the validity and reliability of the technique and the validity and reliability of the encoded data.

The validity of the technique depends on the extent to which the cognitive processes which are attended to, or heeded, during task engagement are those that are verbalised. Following certain principles and procedures can guard against threats to validity. For example, the instructions to participants should discourage them from explaining and rationalising their thoughts. Concurrent verbal reporting – though not always possible – minimises the delay between the task and reporting and thus is likely to reduce error. Validity of the coding frame reflects the extent to which the codes adequately capture the cognitive processes demanded by the task. Validity checks can be made by comparing the verbal reports with other sources of information.

As Green points out, the reliability of the technique can be complicated by individual differences and contextual and task variables. Small changes in task structure and/or in instructions can change the nature of the task demands and result in different information being heeded and/or verbally reported. Reliability of coding segments to the coding frame can be safeguarded by seeking high inter-coder reliability.

Applications

Verbal protocol analysis has established itself as a useful method for analysing cognitive processes from a wide range of disciplinary perspectives. In psychology (cognitive, educational, social, organisational), it has been used both to generate and test specific hypotheses about complex cognitive processes such as problem-solving, planning, compositional writing, managerial decision-making, and resource allocation. It is also used to examine individual differences, particularly between novice and expert performance on a task and between skilled and unskilled practitioners. In cognitive science applications, the method is one of several knowledge-elicitation techniques for designing computer simulations and expert systems. In usability studies of the kind conducted in the computer software design industry, thinking aloud protocols are increasingly used to troubleshoot problems in interface design. Verbal protocols can also be valuable in validity studies of other more quantitative assessment instruments and questionnaires. By asking participants to think aloud as they answer questionnaire items or complete items in cognitive ability tests, researchers can make initial checks that the items are measuring what they purport to measure.

In summary, verbal protocol analysis provides rich data about cognitive processes. It can be used as a single methodology or in conjunction with other methods in the ways described above. Like many other qualitative techniques that generate verbal streams, the data are rich but they are time consuming to analyse and interpret.

Notes

1 Nisbett and Wilson (1977) are very critical of retrospective verbal protocols arguing that they are merely post-hoc rationalisations for task performance.
2 Part of on-going programme of PhD studies conducted by Vilinda Ross at the School of Psychology, Queen's University, Belfast.

Suggested further reading

Green, A. (1995) 'Verbal Protocol Analysis', *The Psychologist*, March: 126–9.

Green, C. and Gilhooly, K. (1996) 'Protocol Analysis: Practical Implementation', in J.T.E. Richardson (ed.), *Handbook of Qualitative Research Methods for Psychology and the Social Sciences*. Leicester: British Psychological Society Books.

References

Ericsson, K.A. and Simon, H.A. (1993) *Protocol Analysis: Verbal Reports as Data*, revised edn. Cambridge, MA: MIT Press. (Originally published 1984.)

Gilhooly, K. and Green, C. (1996) 'Protocol Analysis: Theoretical Background', in J.T.E. Richardson (ed.), *Handbook of Qualitative Research Methods for Psychology and the Social Sciences*. Leicester: British Psychological Society Books.

Hayes-Roth, B. and Hayes-Roth, F. (1979) 'A Cognitive Model of Planning', *Cognitive Science*, 3: 275–310.

Nisbett, R.E. and Wilson, T. (1977) 'Telling More Than We Can Know: Verbal Reports and Mental Processes', *Psychological Review*, 84 (3): 231–59.

See also
Conversation analysis and **Discourse analysis**.

CAROL MCGUINNESS AND VILINDA ROSS

Verstehen

Verstehen is a term associated with the *Geisteswissenschaften* tradition (translated roughly as cultural and social sciences) in German social philosophy in the nineteenth century, particularly through the work of Dilthey. It gained wider use in the social sciences through the writings of the German sociologist Max Weber at the beginning of the twentieth century and describes the special features of Weber's approach, the focus on the meanings of social action. However the term has come to refer to any approach that focuses on qualitative issues like social meanings and has been effectively replaced by its Anglicised equivalent, 'meaning'. *Verstehen* is properly understood as 'understanding' and is now rarely used as a term in the social sciences outside Weber's sociological work and hardly at all in the social research literature. Weber, however, was influential in validating the focus on social action and meanings in contrast to the approach of the French sociologist Emile Durkheim, Weber's contemporary, who was an adherent of positivism addressing social wholes through the analysis of what he called social facts. Durkheim was influenced in this by the French positivist tradition of his forerunner, Auguste Comte, while Weber was moulded by German social philosophy and the *Geisteswissenschaften* tradition, in which attention to meanings and the explication of social action was more appropriate.

In the light of subsequent work in sociology on social action and meanings, in such schools as phenomenology and ethnomethodology, there is comparatively little social action and attention to meaning in Weber's sociology. His greatest contribution was to introduce these terms into sociological discourse and to make possible further developments by giving legitimacy to the exploration of such topics. Weber defined social action as any act that is oriented to another and has meaning attached to it; a person riding a bicycle does not engage in social action but the attempt to avoid a collision with another cyclist does. Weber then went on to chart four ideal types of meaningful social action, some of which he later explored in other work, such as rational action in relation to a goal (exemplified as bureaucratic action and explored in his work on rationalisation and the ideal type of bureaucracy), rational action in relation to a value (exemplified by his work on the Protestant Ethic thesis where action is oriented toward achieving social values, such as moral and religious norms) and affective action motivated by emotion (exemplified by his work on charisma). Weber did not extend this work on meaningful social action and thus left us with an understanding of meaningful social action in ideal typical terms rather than based on actual research amongst real people. Weber was heavily criticised by the social phenomenologist Alfred Schutz for this, although Schutz fell into much the same trap, as those 1960s sociologists who developed Schutz's work argued. It was not until ethnomethodology in the 1960s that Weber's focus on meaningful social action led to social research amongst real people in order to explore their social meanings.

Remarkably, Weber's sociological writings did not impact the Chicago School of sociology that developed its own contribution to ethnography independently. Weber entered American sociology through the early work of Talcott Parsons who developed his general theory of social action. The research traditions represented by the Chicago School and the work of Parsons hardly communicated and thus Weber's impact on social research is less than his impact on theory.

Suggested further reading

Weber, Max (1949) *The Methodology of the Social Sciences*. New York: Free Press. (Edited and translated by E.A. Shils and H.N. Finch.)

Weber, Max (1964) *The Theory of Social and Economic Organization*. New York: Free Press. (Edited and translated by A. Henderson and T. Parsons.)

JOHN BREWER

Vignette

There are two meanings to this term in social research. The first is a data collection technique, used primarily within qualitative research, in which subjects are given hypothetical or real scenarios and asked to comment on how they feel they would have acted or how they feel a third party should act. They have been used in this way in the context of social survey research, where they are used as short stories featuring social circumstances or scenarios to which interviewees are asked to respond. In qualitative research the vignettes offered for response invariably involve some moral or ethical dilemma. It is thus often used to explore sensitive topics, like drug injecting and HIV risk or sexual and physical abuse of the elderly, and with sensitive groups like children, when it has been used to explore the effects of divorce and sexual abuse. Vignettes can also be used as an ice-breaker at the beginning of an interview or as a closure at the end as part of a multi-method approach to enhance existing methods. The stories in the vignettes must appear plausible and real, should not depict eccentric or extraordinary events, refer in some way to the respondent's personal experience, and describe events and circumstances they can understand.

The term is also used in a second way to describe a feature of qualitative data analysis where special parts of the data are selected for more detailed qualitative description as an exemplar or case study within the data. Usually these vignettes are highlighted and separated from the narrative text by being boxed and surrounded by a lined border.

Suggested further reading

Barter, C. and Renold, E. (1999) 'The Use of Vignettes in Qualitative Research', *Social Research Update*, 25.
Brewer, J.D. (2000) *Ethnography*. Buckingham: Open University Press.

Finch, J. (1987) 'The Vignette Technique in Survey Research', *Sociology*, 21: 105–14.

JOHN BREWER

Visual Research Methods

Visual data have been of concern to the social sciences in two ways: visual records produced by the investigator, and visual documents produced by those under study. In recent years, however, this dichotomy between the observer and the observed has begun to collapse (as it has across the qualitative social sciences more generally) and a third kind of visual record or, more accurately, representation, has emerged: the collaborative representation.

Thus visual anthropology and visual sociology proceed methodologically by making visual representations (studying society by producing images), by examining pre-existing visual representations (studying images for information about society), and by collaborating with social actors in the production of visual representations.

Issues of documentation

Methodologically, the use of photography, film and video to document areas of social and cultural life would appear to be straightforward and unproblematic. In the late nineteenth century (and later) photography was used by anthropologists and para-anthropologists to record and document supposed 'racial types' as part of the discipline's project to provide a scientific study of humankind. Photography was also employed as a 'visual notebook' by anthropologists to document aspects of material culture produced by a particular society. After the invention in 1895 of the portable motion picture camera, film was employed to the same ends.

In recent years anthropologists and others have begun to re-examine the products of colonial photography, being as interested as much in the ideas that led to the production of such photographs as in the societies and cultural forms they supposedly document (see the essays in Edwards 1992, and Scherer 1990).

Following on from the Victorian taxonomic and classificatory uses of visual media, photography, film and video have been used more recently to gather data for various other kinds of formalist analysis: proxemics (the study of personal spatial behaviour, see the chapter by Prost in Hockings, 1995), choreometrics and kinesics (the study of body 'style' and communication, see the chapter by Lomax in Hockings, 1995) and conversation analysis (see Goodwin, 1981). What many of these recent projects have in common with their Victorian and Edwardian ante-cedents is an approach to mechanical visual recording media which tend to treat them as neutral technologies capable of objectively recording social behaviour or visible 'givens'. Images are no more 'transparent' than written accounts, however, and while film, video and photography do stand in an indexical relationship to that which they represent they are still representations of reality, not a direct encoding of it. As representations they are therefore subject to the influences of their social, cultural and historical contexts of production and consumption.

Issues of representation

Thus the visual sociologist or anthropologist adopts a dual perspective on visual media. On the one hand they are concerned with the content of any visual representation, what is the 'meaning' of this particular design motif on an art object? Who is the person in the photograph? On the other hand, they are concerned with the context of any visual representation, who produced the art object, and for whom? Why was this photograph taken of this particular person, and then kept by that particular person?

When studying visual representations that have been created by others the dual strands of content and context are fairly easy to investigate in tandem. Most studies in the anthropology or the sociology of art, for example, proceed along this twin path (see for example Coote and Shelton, 1992; Fyfe and Law, 1988).

When, however, the visual representations are produced by the investigator there is a danger of content taking priority over context. Within documentary film, the 'direct cinema' movement in the 1960s sought to correct this imbalance by ensuring that the conditions of filmmaking were revealed to the viewer (see Barnouw, 1974 for a general history of documentary film, the essays in Rosenthal, 1988 for critical perspectives on this history, and Loizos, 1993 for a critical perspective on modern ethnographic film). Typically this involved the deliberate inclusion of the filmmakers' kit in the image (lights, microphones and so forth) or even the filmmakers themselves. Such ideas were absorbed into ethnographic film practice, simultaneously with techniques that were thought to bring the human subjects of the film closer to the viewer (principally, the use of sub-titles to render speech in foreign languages more 'neutrally' than an inevitably inflected voice-over translation). (See also essays in Rollwagon, 1988.)

With still photography, more sensitive or reflexive representations are perhaps slightly harder to accomplish. In many cases, social investigators choose to create some marriage of text and image, where each provides a commentary on the other. Doug Harper, a visual sociologist, has accomplished this to particularly good effect in his work (Harper, 1987; see also Berger and Mohr, 1975).

It is important to remember, however, that all visual representations are not only produced but are consumed in a social context, one which invokes a family resemblance to similar representations, cinema and television in the case of film and video. Members of an audience will bring to the screening certain expectations of narrative form, 'plot' development, 'good' and 'bad' composition, and so forth, however unconscious or inchoate their understandings. Nor can a single 'reading' of a film necessarily be presumed. Sociologists such as Stuart Hall have advocated the notion of 'preferred readings' (Hall, 1977), while an anthropological study of ethnographic films shown to students refutes the liberal assumption that such films encourage the viewers empathetically to narrow the gap between self and a radically different other (Martinez, 1990).

Issues of collaboration

Perhaps the least collaborative project within visual anthropology and visual sociology is the semi-mythical project of setting up a (possibly concealed) film or video camera in a village or neighbourhood for no other reason than to document whatever passes before it. Similar are the projects that involve leaving a camera running, or using a stills camera, to record a specific aspect of social behaviour, the agents of which are either unaware of being recorded or are encouraged to ignore the camera's presence.

It is, however, a premise of the ethnographic method that the investigator is to some extent involved in the cultural and social projects of those under investigation, if only to the extent that asking questions often forces those questioned to formalise social knowledge or representations that may have only a semi-propositional status.

As a result, visual anthropologists and visual sociologists often directly collaborate with their informants or subjects in the production of visual texts of various kinds. This may be done for purely documentary purposes; for example, asking a craftsperson to pause in the process of production at various stages in order to photograph the process. It may be done for some project that is of more interest to the investigator than the subjects; for example, Worth and Adair's extension of the Whorf-Sapir hypothesis concerning language and cognition into the realm of the visual, which involved giving film cameras to cinematographically illiterate Navajo and telling them to film what they liked (Worth and Adair, 1972). Or, perhaps most humanistically as well as most interestingly, it may involve working together on a project that simultaneously provides information for the investigator while fulfilling a goal for the subjects. Here a wide range of projects have been accomplished, from encouraging the subjects to discuss their family photographs (photo elicitation) and learn more about themselves (Geffroy, 1990; see also Collier and Collier, 1986), through helping people to document problematic or contentious areas within their own lives (van Wezel, 1988), to full-blown attempts to empower people through visual media. A particularly striking example of the last is provided by the work of the anthropologist Terence Turner with the Kayapo of Brazil. With the video cameras and editing facilities that Turner initially provided, the Kayapo have been exchanging messages and political speeches between villages, documenting their own rituals and dances, and documenting their protests against the Brazilian state's planned hydro-electric dam at Altamira (Turner, 1992). Many of their productions have in turn provided material for Turner's more academic analysis. The term 'indigenous media' is generally employed to cover those aspects of visual representation over which 'indigenous' people and others have direct control (such as local television broadcasting), although some have questioned the 'empowerment' that is supposed to ensue (see Faris, 1992; also Ginsburg, 1991).

While willed and active collaboration is the goal of many visual projects it is probably inadvertently present in all projects. During the course of my own early fieldwork with an urban religious group in India I found myself taking the majority of my photographs at communal, ritual events. On one occasion I took a number of photographs at a feast, organised to celebrate the conclusion of a period of fasting. In their content, my images display certain features that are undoubtedly important to my later analysis, the overall context of the courtyard in which the feast took place, the segregation of men and women, the seated feasters and the standing feast givers, and a variety of other spatial features.

However, after I had taken a few such photographs, I began to take closer portrait shots of various friends, including those who had brought me to the feast. This they tolerated for a while, and then gently began to suggest other people I should photograph. They were particularly insistent that I took a pre-posed photograph of the woman who had paid for the feast, ladling a dollop of a rich yoghurt-based dessert onto the tray of one of the feasters. Looking at this image alongside my earlier, wide-angle and contextualising images, I saw how the 'directed' photograph is a collaborative image. It was composed and framed according to my own (largely unconscious) visual aesthetic and is part of my own corpus of documentary images of that feast. But it is also a legitimisation and concretisation of social facts as my friends saw them: the fact that the feast had a social origin in the agency of one person (the feast donor) as well as by virtue of the religiously and calendrically prescribed fasting period that preceded it; the fact that the donor was (unusually) a woman and that in the photograph she is giving to men; the fact that this was a good feast during which we ate the expensive and highly valued yoghurt dessert. I 'knew' these social facts, because I had been told them on this or other occasions, but by being directed to capture them on film I was made aware not only of their strength and value but also of the power of photography to legitimise them.

Note

This entry first appeared as *Social Research Update*, 11 (published by the Department of Sociology, University of Surrey).

Suggested further reading

The journals *Visual Sociology*, *Visual Anthropology* and *Visual Anthropology Review* all contain articles of methodological interest from time to time.

Some electronic resources

VISCOM a discussion list 'devoted to an exploration of all aspects of visual communication'. Subscriptions to: listserv@vm.temple.edu.

PHOTOHST a discussion list focusing more narrowly on photography and photographic history. Subscriptions to: listserv@asuvm.inre.asu.edu.

The International Visual Sociology Association: http://www.uwindsor.ca/faculty/socsci/geog/ mogy/ivsa/ivsa.html.

The HADDON Project to catalogue early archival ethnographic film footage: http://www.rsl.ox.ac.uk/isca/haddon/HADD_home.html.

References

Barnouw, Erik (1983) *Documentary: a History of the Non-Fiction Film*, revised edn. Oxford: Oxford University Press.

Berger, John and Mohr, Jean (1975) *A Seventh Man: a Book of Images and Words about the Experience of Migrant Workers in Europe*. Harmondsworth: Penguin.

Collier, John Jr. and Collier, Malcolm (1986) *Visual Anthropology: Photography as a Research Method*. Albuquerque: University of New Mexico Press.

Coote, Jeremy and Shelton, Anthony (eds) (1992) *Anthropology, Art and Aesthetics*. Oxford: Clarendon Press.

Edwards, Elizabeth (ed.) (1992) *Anthropology and Photography 1860–1920*. New Haven: Yale University Press in association with The Royal Anthropological Institute, London.

Faris, James C. (1992) 'Anthropological Transparency: Film, Representation and Politics', in Peter Crawford and David Turton (eds), *Film as Ethnography*. Manchester: Manchester University Press in association with the Granada Centre for Visual Anthropology.

Fyfe, Gordon and Law, John (eds) (1988) *Picturing Power: Visual Depiction and Social Relations*. London: Routledge.

Geffroy, Yannick (1990) 'Family Photographs: a Visual Heritage', *Visual Anthropology*, 3 (4): 367–410.

Ginsburg, Faye (1991) 'Indigenous Media: Faustian Contract or Global Village?', *Cultural Anthropology*, 6 (1): 92–112.

Goodwin, C. (1981) *Conversational Organisation: Interaction between Speakers and Hearers*. New York: Academic Press.

Hall, Stuart (1977) 'Culture, the Media and "the Ideological Effect"', in J. Curran, M. Gurevitch and J. Woollacott (eds), *Mass Communication and Society*. London: Edward Arnold.

Harper, Douglas A. (1987) *Working Knowledge: Skill and Community in a Small Shop*. Chicago: University of Chicago Press.

Hockings, Paul (ed.) (1995) *Principles of Visual Anthropology*, 2nd edn. The Hague: Mouton.

Loizos, Peter (1993) *Innovation in Ethnographic Film: from Innocence to Self-Consciousness, 1955–1985*. Manchester: Manchester University Press.

Martinez, Wilton (1990) 'Critical Studies and Visual Anthropology: Aberrant vs. Anticipated Readings of Ethnographic Film', *CVA Review*, Spring: 34–47.

Rollwagon, Jack (ed.) (1988) *Anthropological Filmmaking*. Chur: Harwood Academic Publishers.

Rosenthal, Alan (ed.) (1988) *New Challenges for Documentary*. Berkeley: University of California Press.

Scherer, Joanna Cohan (ed.) (1990) Special issue of *Visual Anthropology*, 3 (2–3): *Picturing Cultures: Historical Photographs in Anthropological Inquiry*. Chur: Harwood Academic Publishers.

Turner, Terence (1992) 'Defiant Images: The Kayapo Appropriation of Video', *Anthropology Today*, 8 (6): 5–16.

van Wezel, Ruud H.J. (1988) 'Reciprocity of Research Results in Portugal', *Critique of Anthropology*, 8 (2): 63–70.

Worth, Sol and Adair, John (1972) *Through Navajo Eyes: An Exploration in Film Communication and Anthropology*. Bloomington: Indiana University Press.

MARCUS BANKS

World Wide Web

See **Internet**.